Women, Work and Care in the Asia-Pacific

This book provides a comparative analysis of the social, economic, industrial and migration dynamics that structure women's paid work and unpaid care work experience in the Asia-Pacific region. Each country-focused chapter examines the formal and informal ways in which work and care are managed, the changing institutional landscape, gender relations and fertility concerns, employer and trade union responses and the challenges policy makers face and the consequences of their decisions for working women. By covering the entire region, including Australia and New Zealand, the book highlights the way different national work and care regimes are linked through migration, with wealthier countries looking to their poorer neighbours for alternative sources of labour. In addition, the book contributes to debates about the barriers to women's participation in the workforce, the valuation of unpaid care, the gender wage gap, social protection and labour regulation for migrant workers and gender relations in developing Asia.

Marian Baird is Professor of Gender and Employment Relations and Director of the Women and Work Research Group at the University of Sydney Business School, Australia.

Michele Ford is Professor of Southeast Asian Studies and Director of the Sydney Southeast Asia Centre at the University of Sydney, Australia.

Elizabeth Hill is a Senior Lecturer in the Department of Political Economy at the University of Sydney, Australia.

Asian Studies Association of Australia Women in Asia Series
Edited by Louise Edwards (University of New South Wales)

A full list of titles in this series is available at: www.routledge.com/ASAA-Women-in-Asia-Series/book-series/SE0594

Recently published titles:

42 Trafficking Women in Korea
Filipina Migrant Entertainers
Sallie Yea 2015

43 Women and Sharia Law in Northern Indonesia
Dina Afrianty 2015

44 China's Leftover Women
Late Marriage among Professional Women and its Consequences
Sandy To 2015

45 The Micro-politics of Microcredit
Women, Gender and Neoliberal Development in Bangladesh
Mohammad Jasim Uddin 2015

46 Young Muslim Women in India
Kabita Chakraborty 2016

47 Women's Empowerment in South Asia
NGO Interventions and Agency Building in Bangladesh
Pranab Panday 2016

48 Women and the Politics of Gender in Post-Conflict Timor-Leste
Between Heaven and Earth
Sara Niner 2016

49 Sex Trafficking in Southeast Asia
A History of Desire, Duty and Debt
Trude Jacobsen 2016

50 Women, Work and Care in the Asia-Pacific
Edited by Marian Baird, Michele Ford and Elizabeth Hill

Women, Work and Care in the Asia-Pacific

Edited by Marian Baird, Michele Ford and Elizabeth Hill

Routledge
Taylor & Francis Group
LONDON AND NEW YORK

First published 2017 by Routledge

2 Park Square, Milton Park, Abingdon, Oxfordshire OX14 4RN
52 Vanderbilt Avenue, New York, NY 10017

Routledge is an imprint of the Taylor & Francis Group, an informa business

First issued in paperback 2018

British Library Cataloguing in Publication Data
A catalogue record for this book is available from the British Library

Library of Congress Cataloging in Publication Data
Names: Baird, Marian, editor. | Ford, Michele, editor. | Hill, Elizabeth, 1967- editor.
Title: Women, work and care in the Asia-Pacific / edited by Marian Baird, Michele Ford and Elizabeth Hill.
Description: 1 Edition. | New York : Routledge, 2017. |
Series: Women in Asia ; 50 | Includes bibliographical references and index.
Identifiers: LCCN 2016034110| ISBN 9781138119048 (hardback) | ISBN 9781315652467 (ebook)
Subjects: LCSH: Women--East Asia--Social conditions. | Women--Pacific Area--Social conditions. | Older people--Home care--East Asia. | Older people--Home care--Pacific Area. | Caregivers--East Asia. | Caregivers--Pacific Area. | Women employees--East Asia. | Women employees--Pacific Area.
Classification: LCC HQ1760.5 .W66 2017 | DDC 305.4095--dc23
LC record available at https://lccn.loc.gov/2016034110

ISBN: 978-1-138-11904-8 (hbk)
ISBN: 978-0-367-18617-3 (pbk)

Typeset in Times New Roman
by HWA Text and Data Management, London

Contents

Figures

Tables

Contributors

James Arrowsmith is Professor in the School of Management and Co-Director of the Massey University People, Organisation, Work and Employment Research (MPOWER) Group at Massey University, New Zealand. In recent years he has also been employed as a consultant to the International Labour Organisation, advising on temporary and seasonal work, child labour, employment policy and regulation across the South Pacific.

Hasan Ashraf is an Anthropologist and a PhD candidate at Heidelberg University. His PhD project concentrates on how ill health is generated in transnational garment factories located in Bangladesh. His research interests beyond the garment sector are labour history, political party culture, gender and sexual rights, religions, and eating (meat) and drinking (water) practices in Bangladesh.

Marian Baird is Professor of Gender and Employment Relations, Director of the Women and Work Research Group at the University of Sydney Business School and co-editor-in-chief of the *Journal of Industrial Relations*. Marian is one of Australia's leading researchers in the fields of women, work and family. She is published widely and is highly engaged with policy making at organisational and government levels.

Alifa Bandali is undertaking a PhD in the Department of Gender and Cultural Studies at the University of Sydney. Her research focuses on women, emotional work and perspectives of feminism in the not-for-profit sector in Malaysia. Further research interests include: feminist ideologies and perspectives of gender, the not-for-profit/NGO sector and its resonances in Southeast Asia.

Anne Boyd is a Labour Standards Specialist at the International Labour Organisation based in the Pacific Islands region. She provides technical support to Pacific Island countries engaged in labour law reform processes. Her research interests focus on gender responsive labour law reform in the area of maternity protection and equal remuneration for work of equal value.

Minglu Chen is a Lecturer in the China Studies Centre and the Department of Government and International Relations at the University of Sydney. Her research concentrates on social and political change in China, especially the interaction between entrepreneurs and the state. She is the author of *Tiger Girls: Women and Enterprises in the People's Republic of China* (Routledge 2011).

Rae Cooper is Associate Professor in Work and Organisational Studies at the University of Sydney Business School. She has published widely on industrial relations policy, trade unionism and collective bargaining and gender and work in leading journals and in major collections. Her research has been cited in several parliamentary inquiries into industrial relations and she is regularly called as an expert witness in cases and consultations relating to women and labour market issues.

Vicki Crinis is an Associate Researcher with the Law, Humanities and Creative Arts Faculty at the University of Wollongong, where she previously held a Postdoctoral Fellowship as part of an Australian Research Council Discovery Project on the garment industry in the Asia-Pacific. Her research focuses on the global clothing industry, trade unions and migrant workers in Malaysia, and she has published a number of book chapters and journal articles on these topics.

Michele Ford is Professor of Southeast Asian Studies, Australian Research Council Future Fellow and Director of the Sydney Southeast Asia Centre at the University of Sydney. Her research focuses on labour movements, labour migration, and women and work in Southeast Asia. Michele is the author of *Workers and Intellectuals: NGOs, Unions and the Indonesian Labour Movement* (NUS/Hawaii/KITLV 2009). She has also co-edited a number of volumes including *Women and Work in Indonesia* (Routledge 2008).

Jie Hao is a Lecturer at the School of Economics and Management, in the Department of Innovation, Entrepreneurship and Strategy at Tsinghua University. Her current research areas include: employability and entrepreneurship, women in the professional workplace, and forms of intellectual capital. Jie received her PhD from the University of Sydney, having previously completed her undergraduate BA double major in Psychology and in Media and Communications at Monash University.

Alexandra Heron is a Doctoral Student in the University of Sydney Business School. She has worked in policy and research roles relating to women and work. Her publications include *Migrant Women into Work: What is Working* (2005). Academic publications include a co-authored chapter entitled 'Women, Work and Elder Care: New Policies Required for Inclusive Growth' (2013) and 'Working Time and Managing Care under Labor: Whose Flexibility?' (2012).

Elizabeth Hill is a Senior Lecturer in the Department of Political Economy at the University of Sydney. Elizabeth is the author of *Worker Identity, Agency and Economic Development: Women's Empowerment in the Indian Informal Economy* (Routledge 2010). Elizabeth also co-convenes the Australian Work and Family Policy Roundtable, which promotes the development and dissemination of relevant Australian and international research on work and family policy in the public policy debate.

Joohee Lee is Professor of Sociology at EWHA Woman's University in South Korea. Her major research interests are changing industrial relations in a global economy, industrial democracy at the workplace, and strategies for political labour movements. Her books include the co-authored *The New Structure of Labor Relations: Tripartism and Decentralization* (2004) and *The Korean Trade Union Movement in the 21st Century* (2002, in Korean).

Ligaya Lindio-McGovern is Professor of Sociology at Indiana University Kokomo, specialising in gender and development, globalisation and international migration. She is the author of *Globalization, Labor Export and Resistance: A Study of Filipino Migrant Domestic Workers in Global Cities* (Routledge 2012) and *Filipino Peasant Women: Exploitation and Resistance* (1997); and co-editor of *Globalization and Third World Women: Exploitation, Coping and Resistance* (2009) and *Gender and Globalization: Patterns of Women's Resistance* (2011).

Lenore Lyons is Honorary Professor in the Sydney Southeast Asia Centre at the University of Sydney. She is internationally recognised as the leading scholar on the feminist movement in Singapore. She is the author of *A State of Ambivalence: The Feminist Movement in Singapore* (Brill 2004) and co-editor of *Men and Masculinities in Southeast Asia* (Routledge 2012) and *Labour Migration and Trafficking in Southeast Asia: Critical Perspectives* (Routledge 2012).

Gabrielle Meagher is Professor of Sociology at Macquarie University, and Visiting Professor in the Department of Social Work at Stockholm University. Her research focuses on paid care work and the impact of marketisation and privatisation on social services. Gabrielle is co-convener of the Australian Paid Care Research Network and of the Nordic Network for Research on Marketization in Eldercare.

Nurchayati is a PhD Candidate at the Department of Indonesian Studies at the University of Sydney and a recipient of a 2013 Prime Minister's Australia Asia Endeavour Award. In her doctoral thesis, she employs an interdisciplinary approach to analyse the interplay between gender and transnational labour migration. Her publications include 'Bringing Agency Back In: Indonesian Migrant Workers in Saudi Arabia', Asian and Pacific Migration Journal 20, no. 3–4 (2011): 479–502.

Reiko Ogawa is an Associate Professor in the Department of Cultural Studies at Kyushu University, where she works within the disciplines of sociology and anthropology. Her research interests include the globalisation of care work, gender and migration. Her publications include papers on 'Globalization and Transformation of Care in Japan', 'The Configuration of Migration and Long-Term Care in East Asia' and 'Conceptualizing Transnational Migration of Care Workers: Between "Skilled" and "Unskilled"'.

Rajni Palriwala is Professor in the Department of Sociology at the University of Delhi. Her research falls within the broad area of gender relations, covering care, citizenship, and the state, kinship and marriage, women and work, women's movements and feminist politics. Her publications include the co-authored *Care, Culture and Citizenship: Revisiting the Politics of Welfare in the Netherlands* (2005), and *Changing Kinship, Family, and Gender Relations in South Asia: Processes, Trends and Issues* (1994).

Jane Parker is Professor of Employment Relations and Human Resource Management and Co-Director of the Massey University People, Organisation, Work and Employment Research (MPOWER) Group at Massey University, New Zealand. Her research focuses on gender equality and diversity in the workplace, employment regulation and social movement unionism. Jane is the general editor of *The Big Issues in Employment: HRM and Employment Relations in New Zealand* (2013) and co-editor in chief of *Labour & Industry*.

Katherine Ravenswood is a Senior Lecturer in the Department of Management at Auckland University of Technology. Katherine's research interests focus on women and diversity at work, the aged care workforce, work-life balance and family-friendly policy. Katherine has published on paid parental leave in New Zealand (in the *New Zealand Journal of Employment Relations and Labour History*) and unions' role in family-friendly policy (*Journal of Industrial Relations*).

Dina Siddiqi, an Anthropologist by training, divides her time between the US and Bangladesh where she teaches in the Department of Economics and Social Sciences at BRAC University, Dhaka. She is currently working on a book-length manuscript tentatively titled 'Elusive Solidarities: Islam and Transnational Feminism at Work'. Her most recent publication is 'Scandals of Seduction and the Seductions of Scandal', which appeared in *Comparative Studies of South Asia, Africa and the Middle East.*

Belinda Smith is an Associate Professor at Sydney Law School at the University of Sydney. Her main field of research is anti-discrimination laws, with a focus on gender equality and workers with family responsibilities. She has worked extensively on promoting reform of Australian anti-discrimination laws, served on the board of the Disability Discrimination Legal Centre NSW and is a member of the *Australian Journal of Labour Law* editorial board.

Kristy Ward is a Research Associate and Lecturer in the Faculty of Arts and Social Sciences at the University of New South Wales. Her research interests include gender and urbanisation, migration and development ethnography. She has published on the gendered dynamics of rural–urban migration in Cambodia, forced migration and protracted urban asylum in South Asia, and community-led development. Kristy is a scholar-practitioner who has worked in numerous roles with non-government organisations.

Matt Withers is a PhD Candidate within the Department of Political Economy at the University of Sydney. His research focuses on the experiences of temporary labour migration in Sri Lanka, their relationship with structures of underdevelopment and their intersectionality with economies of ethnicity, gender and class. His publications include (with Janaka Biyanwila), 'Patriarchy, Labour Markets and Development: Contesting the Sexual Division of Labour in Sri Lanka' (*IIM Kozhikode Society and Management Review*).

Series editor's foreword

The contributions of women to the social, political and economic transformations occurring in the Asian region are legion. Women have served as leaders of nations, communities, workplaces, activist groups and families. Asian women have joined with others to participate in fomenting change at micro and macro levels. They have been both agents and targets of national and international interventions in social policy. In the performance of these myriad roles women have forged new and modern gendered identities that are recognisably global and local. Their experiences are rich, diverse and instructive. The books in this series testify to the central role women play in creating the new Asia and re-creating Asian womanhood. Moreover, these books reveal the resilience and inventiveness of women around the Asian region in the face of entrenched and evolving patriarchal social norms.

Scholars publishing in this series demonstrate a commitment to promoting the productive conversation between Gender Studies and Asian Studies. The need to understand the diversity of experiences of femininity and womanhood around the world increases inexorably as globalisation proceeds apace. Lessons from the experiences of Asian women present us with fresh opportunities for building new possibilities for women's progress the world over.

The Asian Studies Association of Australia (ASAA) sponsors this publication series as part of its on-going commitment to promoting knowledge about women in Asia. In particular, the ASAA Women's Forum provides the intellectual vigour and enthusiasm that maintains the Women in Asia Series (WIAS). The aim of the series, since its inception in 1990, is to promote knowledge about women in Asia to both academic and general audiences. To this end, WIAS books draw on a wide range of disciplines including anthropology, sociology, political science, cultural studies, media studies, literature, and history. The series prides itself on being an outlet for cutting edge research conducted by recent PhD graduates and postdoctoral fellows from throughout the region.

The series could not function without the generous professional advice provided by many anonymous readers. Moreover, the wise counsel provided by Peter Sowden at Routledge is invaluable. WIAS, its authors and the ASAA are very grateful to these people for their expert work.

Louise Edwards (University of New South Wales)
Series Editor

Preface

> Women stand at the crossroads between production and reproduction, between economic activity and the care of human beings, and therefore between economic growth and human development. They are workers in both spheres – those most responsible and therefore with most at stake, those who suffer most when the two spheres meet at cross-purposes, and those most sensitive to the need for better integration between the two.
>
> (Sen 1995)

The Asia-Pacific is marked by sharp contrasts – of wealth and poverty, of population growth and population decline and of the exportation and importation of care workers. In this context, Gita Sen's observation is pivotal to thinking about women, work and care and accurately reflects our thinking in the development of this volume. There are almost two billion women in the region. These are the women who work and provide care for infants, the elderly, their families and communities. These women are in paid and unpaid jobs, in high-skill and low-skill jobs, and in the formal and informal sectors. They and their contributions are sometimes supported by government policies, but often they are not. This volume has these women as its central concern.

In 2013, the University of Sydney funded a network of feminist scholars interested in policy making and the regulation and improvement of women's work. In 2014, we focused our thinking and planning around a single project: the production of a book, which we believed was sorely needed, on women, work and care in the Asia-Pacific. In 2015, our plans came to fruition and we held a workshop at The Women's College, in the grounds of the University. At the workshop scholars with particular country expertise gathered to discuss and debate the substance of their contributions. Those present came from a range of disciplinary backgrounds including sociology, industrial relations, political economy, political science, gender studies and Asian studies. Their papers focused on a range of countries: Indonesia, Singapore, Malaysia, Cambodia, the Philippines, Papua New Guinea, Bangladesh, Sri Lanka, India, Japan, China, New Zealand and Australia. Later we were fortunate to add contributions on South Korea and Timor-Leste to our collection. These were two very stimulating and full days of workshopping the chapters, with presenters and discussants, experienced and early-career researchers, all contributing equally, frankly and constructively.

We are grateful to the University of Sydney's Research Office for its financial support, which enabled us to bring the majority of the contributing authors and discussants together in Sydney. The Women and Work Research Group took responsibility for the coordination of the workshop, with PhD candidate Matthew Withers assisting with the logistical tasks. Our undergraduate student Georg Tamm kindly and carefully shepherded visitors from their hotel to our dinners and to The Women's College, and we greatly appreciated his help. Dr Andreea Constantin and Ms Carmela Chivers later assisted with data sourcing, collating and validating, and the Sydney Southeast Asia Centre provided additional administrative assistance as we finalised the manuscript.

The workshop was enhanced by the contributions from our discussants, Professors Barbara Pocock, Elspeth Probyn, Joellen Riley and Sarah Charlesworth and Associate Professors Susan McGrath-Champ and Beth Goldblatt, who each provided valuable feedback which was then incorporated into the chapter revisions. The book has also benefited greatly from comments provided by Professor Louise Edwards and Emeritus Professor Chilla Bulbeck, who both read the entire manuscript. The beautiful artwork for the cover is by Jennifer Keeler-Milne. Jennifer is a practising artist and drawing teacher whose work is held in two of Australia's largest drawing collections. Her artistic practice extends into painting fragments of textiles, mainly from Asia and made by women, and it is this work that fits so well with the scholarship presented in this book. Finally, our thanks must go to the authors of each of the chapters. Their work is presented in this volume and is testament to their sensitivity to the issues, their responsiveness to the workshop discussions and to our editorial guidance and direction. As editors it has been a pleasure to work with them.

The book was born out of cross-disciplinary collaboration and a common interest in advancing our understanding of the region in which we reside, work and care. Our objective was to highlight the important and essential links between women's labour market involvement, care work and policy frameworks. Each of the chapters highlights women's contributions to the economic growth and to social sustainability of their own country and thereby to the region. The chapters expose pressures associated with production and reproduction, and the links between them. To date, these issues have received attention in some, though not all, of the countries examined. But the interconnections between them have been under-examined and under-theorised. Our own introductory chapter offers a framework for analysing the relationship between care regimes and work regimes, and we look forward to its application in countries beyond those represented here.

With the growing focus around the world on women's labour market contributions, the book is a timely and valuable foundation for expanding our studies and for bringing a unique focus to the Asia-Pacific region. Above all, we hope that by bringing this volume to you, we move women in this diverse range of countries from Sen's crossroads, where they carry a double burden with little recognition of their work and care roles, to the front and centre of academic evaluation and policy making, where women's productive and reproductive contributions are recognised and properly compensated.

Marian Baird, Michele Ford and Elizabeth Hill
May 2016

1 Work/care regimes in the Asia-Pacific

A feminist framework

Elizabeth Hill, Michele Ford and Marian Baird

Gender equality is on the global agenda. International institutions such as the International Monetary Fund, the World Economic Forum, the OECD and the G20, the World Bank, the International Labour Organisation and numerous global consulting firms are producing glossy reports and new data sets that measure global gender gaps and advocate gender equality.[1] In all these reports, boosting women's labour force participation is presented as the key to long-term global economic growth and human development. On one calculation, if women participated in paid work 'identically to men' annual global Gross Domestic Product (GDP) would increase by 26 per cent, or USD 28 trillion, by 2025 (McKinsey 2015). But if women did take up paid work in a pattern similar to men, who would do the unpaid care and reproductive work women currently perform? Global estimates suggest women are responsible for around three-quarters of all unpaid labour, a category that includes care for children, the elderly, ill and disabled as well as household tasks.

Care work is critical to the gender equality equation but it is rarely included in standard prescriptions for maximising women's economic productivity, which assume women's time is infinitely elastic. Nor is women's unpaid labour factored into calculations of GDP. This leaves care invisible to policy makers. Yet, in reality, gender equality in the paid workforce cannot be achieved unless new and equitable ways of organising care and reproductive work are found. In many wealthy economies, there has been growing public debate and policy development around supportive work and care infrastructure. Paid parental leave, flexible work arrangements, affordable childcare and a range of tax policies form part of the policy framework aimed at supporting women in paid employment (Baird and O'Brien 2015; Gornick and Meyers 2003). Poorer nations struggle to prioritise these policy concerns, and yet the dynamics of women's work and care have a significant impact on the economic growth and wellbeing trajectories of emerging economies, large and small.

Tensions between women's economic participation and care work, between economic growth and social reproduction, are exemplified in the Asia-Pacific. Home to around 54 per cent of the world's population, the Asia-Pacific is a highly diverse and rapidly changing region of almost four billion people (UN ESCAP 2014). It brings together the advanced western-style economies of Australasia and the developing island states of the Pacific with the complex economic and cultural mosaic of Asia – defined here as stretching from Pakistan in the west to Japan in the east. The economic transformation of Asia since the mid-late twentieth century has lifted hundreds of millions out of extreme poverty, produced new patterns of production and international trade, opened up vast new consumer markets, propelled the emergence of a new middle class, and created new domestic and international labour markets, which together have created new patterns of regional and national inequality. The impact of this wholesale change on women has been profound. Educated, English-speaking women work the phones in Asia's burgeoning call-centres and back office processing units. Hundreds of millions of young rural women have been drawn to work in the new factories and export processing zones. Many leave their homes to take up these new employment opportunities, or seek employment in other countries, attracted by promises of improved standards of living. The changing employment landscape in these countries and the region has had significant implications for households and for the reproductive care work that is traditionally performed by women.

In this volume we map women's contemporary experience of work and care in fifteen countries across the Asia-Pacific. We are interested in women's employment patterns, how they manage childcare and eldercare, and how employment policy and practice (the work regime) and social policy and practice (the care regime) intersect to produce a national work/care regime (cf. Pocock 2005). This leads to a discussion on the extent to which employers, trade unions and the state are engaging with work/care dynamics, their stated priorities, policy interventions and the gaps that are left for households to manage through their own private arrangements. Consideration of the policy framework and how it structures work and care in the Asia-Pacific highlights the impact that inequality – both within and between countries – can have on women's agency. It also demonstrates how differences in national wealth and approaches to social policy have a significant impact on the quality and distribution of care. Patriarchal nation-states seeking improved economic growth and productivity, often with the expectation of women's increased participation in the labour force, tend to overlook the essential sphere of social reproduction and care. The chapters in this book show that this lack of public investment in care infrastructure curbs the wellbeing and freedom of women and those for whom they care.[2]

Work/care regimes

Gender inequality is a feature of all countries in the region, but how this shapes and is shaped by the prevailing work/care regime in specific countries varies considerably. Accounting for these variations requires an analytical framework that considers the sum of the labour used to produce new goods and services and the labour expended to reproduce human community and society, which together form the 'total social organization of labour' (Glucksmann 1995). Across the globe, the distribution of total labour has historically been highly gendered, with women under-represented in paid work and over-represented in unpaid care and subsistence labour.

Pocock (2005) argues that the practice of gender inequality in the distribution of total labour is determined by the contours of the prevailing work/care regime. National work/care regimes are in large part a reflection of dominant values, social norms and the institutions to which they give rise. Values and norms set the standard for how we think about work and care and how it is interpreted in the broader social context, defining what constitutes a 'good' or 'proper' mother, a 'good' or 'proper' father and a 'good worker' (Pocock 2005, 44–45). As Pocock argues, work/care regimes also reflect a much broader 'gender order' (cf. Connell 1987), which is likely to vary according to class, ethnicity, locality and religion. Institutions including regulatory frameworks, labour markets, childcare and school systems, workplaces, welfare arrangements and family structures articulate, legitimate and in turn reproduce the gender order as they define how, where and when men and women work and care. In short, 'At any point in time or place, work/care outcomes are the consequence of the gender order and its specific embodiment in a work/care regime' (Pocock 2005, 38).

Evaluating the work/care regime is a multifaceted exercise that must pay attention to the gender order, its expression in the dominant values, norms and culture that frame the practice of work and care, and the types of institutions that evolve to legitimate and reproduce these ideas. Any assessment of the constituent parts of a particular country's work/care requires answers to some basic questions: Who performs care? Who pays for care? And where is the care provided? Razavi's (2007) 'care diamond' provides a simple analytical tool for identifying the primary institutions responsible for delivering care: the state, the market, the family and the community or not-for-profit sector. The shape of the care diamond is determined by the specific structure of a country's economy, regulatory environment, social policy design and gender norms, and may change over time. The proportion of care labour delivered by each point of the diamond also varies for individuals as a consequence of class, ethnicity, religion and the urban/rural divide.

An advantage of the care diamond as a heuristic device is that it highlights the interdependent relationship between institutions of care provisioning and the structural tensions that lie at the centre of any care regime. Care labour is a necessity. If the state fails to provide care services, or does so only at a price that puts them out of the reach of many people, then households must find a way to provide the required care themselves. Likewise, any decline in the availability of familial care must be compensated for by an increase in the services offered by the state, the market, or the not-for-profit sector. Changes in the design of social policy or levels of state funding for care also alter the incentive structures within which the market and not-for-profit sectors provide care, in turn changing the way households configure their care arrangements.

Women and work

Women engage in paid work for a variety of reasons. In low-income communities and countries, poverty is generally the main reason why women work. Economic crisis can also be a catalyst for women to move into paid work (Karamessini and

Rubery 2014). This was the case in Indonesia in the wake of the Asian Financial Crisis of 1997–98 and in India, where widespread rural crises in the early 2000s saw millions of women take up 'distress employment' (Himanshu 2011). At the other end of the economic spectrum, educated women often work because they choose to, sometimes in defiance of prevailing gender norms. In Australia, for example, the complex interplay from the 1960s onwards of increasing female education levels and increasing levels of labour force participation was a catalyst for the introduction of some new workplace regulatory arrangements, which were also regularly contested by conservative elements of society (Baird 2005).

Economists use a U-shaped curve to hypothesise the relationship between women's labour force participation and stages of economic development. The expectation is that labour force participation rates in poor countries where women are engaged in subsistence activities are very high but then fall in middle-income countries because of urbanisation and the shift into industrial jobs taken up mostly by men. Women's participation rises again once economies begin to grow, women's education improves, fertility rates fall, and women take up new jobs in the service sector. In the Asia-Pacific, however, patterns of women's workforce participation are not so predictable. India, for example, has a much lower level of female labour force participation than countries with similar levels of per capita income, and China a much higher (though declining) level. Even within countries, the correlation between economic development and women's increased labour force participation is not automatic, as the latter depends also on socio-economic, cultural and political factors including women's education; social norms around marriage, fertility, and women's role outside the household; household characteristics; and institutional settings such as labour laws and social protection frameworks (Table 1.1).

Globally, female labour force participation rates have been stable over the past two decades, declining slightly for the total female working-age population (aged 15 years and above) from 52.2 per cent in 1992 to 51.4 per cent in 2012 (ILO 2015). This decline is largely due to an increase in girls' school enrolment and retention. For women 25 years and older there has been a small rise from 53.1 per cent in 1992 to 54.2 per cent in 2012. But global trends hide some interesting differences in national participation patterns across the Asia-Pacific (Table 1.2). Women's workforce participation has steadily increased since 1990 in Australia, New Zealand, Singapore and South Korea. It has also improved over the past twenty years in the Philippines, a middle-income country. By contrast, the large emerging economies of China and India have registered declining aggregate labour force participation rates for women, suggesting that rapid and high rates of economic growth have not delivered the 'inclusive development' their governments talk about. Women's rate of paid work has, meanwhile, remained relatively steady in Japan and Malaysia, but also in the poor developing economies of Cambodia, Sri Lanka and Papua New Guinea. Within these national trends, labour force participation rates vary according to women's class, ethnic, location and religious profile, accentuating certain patterns of inequality in the region.

The generally flat trend in women's labour force participation across the Asia-Pacific and the low status of much of their paid work raises a number of

Table 1.1 Women and care

	GII (rank/152)	*Women's average age at marriage*	*% of population aged 5 years old and under*	*% of population aged 65 years old and above*	*Fertility rate*	*Mean years of schooling of women aged 25 and above*
Singapore	0.090 (15)	27.9	4.9	11.1	1.2	10.1
South Korea	0.101 (17)	28.8	4.6	12.7	1.2	11.2
Australia	0.113 (19)	29.7	6.5	14.7	1.9	11.8
Japan	0.138 (25)	29.7	4.2	25.7	1.4	11.3
New Zealand	0.185 (34)	25.6	6.9	14.4	2.0	11.7
China	0.202 (37)	24.7	6.0	9.2	1.7	6.6
Malaysia	0.210 (39)	25.7	8.1	5.6	2.0	9.4
Sri Lanka	0.383 (75)	23.6	8.1	8.9	2.3	9.6
Philippines	0.406 (78)	24.4	11.2	4.5	3.0	8.4
Indonesia	0.500 (103)	22.3	9.7	5.1	2.3	6.7
Cambodia	0.505 (105)	22.0	11.5	4.0	2.9	3.2
Bangladesh	0.529 (115)	18.6	9.7	5.0	2.2	4.5
India	0.563 (127)	20.2	9.6	5.5	2.5	3.6
PNG	0.617 (135)	21.4	13.3	3.0	3.8	3.2
Timor-Leste	n/a	23.1	16.7	5.5	5.2	3.6

Notes: GII (Gender Inequality Index) measures gender inequalities in three domains of human development: reproductive health measured by maternal mortality ratio and adolescent birth rates; empowerment, measured by proportion of parliamentary seats occupied by females and proportion of adult females and males aged 25 years and older with at least some secondary education; and economic status expressed as labour market participation and measured by labour force participation rate of female and male populations aged 15 years and older (UNDP 2014, 172).

Women's average age at marriage (UN DESA 2013).

Population aged 5 years old and under, populaiton aged 65 years old and above and fertility rate (World Bank 2015).

Mean years of schooling of women aged 25 and above, 2010 (for all other countries than Timor-Leste) (UN Women 2015); for Timor-Leste (UNDP 2014).

Table 1.2 Gender and employment

	Gross National Income per capita (2014 PPP $)	Labour force participation rate (1990 and 2013 for women and 2013 for men)			Employment rate		Urban population (% of total)	% of female employment in agriculture	% of male employment in agriculture	Vulnerable employment		Public social protection expenditure (exc. health care) as % of GDP
		Women		Men	Women	Men				Women	Men	
Singapore	80,270	51.0	58.8	77.2	55.6	73.2	100	0.6	1.5	7.1	11.1	1.8
Australia	42,880	52.0	58.8	71.8	55.0	66.7	89.2	2.2	4.2	6.6	10.4	8.6
Japan	37,920	50.0	48.8	70.4	47.6	67.7	92.5	3.7	3.8	9.6	9.5	17.8
South Korea	34,620	47.0	50.1	72.1	49.6	71.4	82.2	6.9	6.4	25.8	23.8	5.1
New Zealand	33,760	54.0	62.0	73.8	59.5	70.8	86.2	4.4	8.6	9.1	14.5	8.0
Malaysia	24,080	43.0	44.4	75.5	51.9	78.3	73.3	8.2	15.1	21.4	21.3	0.9
China	13,130	73.0	63.9	78.3	71.1	87.2	53.2	n/a	n/a	52.9	44	5.6
Sri Lanka	10,270	36.0	35.1	76.3	32.0	72.2	18.3	34.7	41.6	43.0	39.6	1.8
Indonesia	10,190	50.0	51.4	84.2	47.0	78.4	52.3	34.5	35.5	65.7	60.8	1.6
Philippines	8,380	48.0	51.1	79.7	46.7	72.8	44.6	20.1	38.1	44.7	41.1	1.0
Timor-Leste	5,680	42.0	24.7	52.0	25.7	54.4	31.5	50.2	51.0	77.0	64.1	n/a
India	5,640	35.0	27.0	79.9	23.8	71.4	32.0	59.8	43.0	81.5	77.0	1.5
Bangladesh	3,330	62.0	57.4	84.1	33.9	79.2	32.8	68.1	41.8	85.5	82.4	1.6
Cambodia	3,100	77.0	78.8	86.5	77.6	88.4	20.3	52.8	49.3	69.7	58.8	0.7
PNG	2,510	71.0	70.5	74.0	68.6	72.7	13.0	72.0		82.5	71.7	0.1

Gross National Income per capita (2014 PPP $) GNI per capita based on purchasing power parity (PPP). PPP GNI is gross national income (GNI) converted to international dollars using purchasing power parity rates. An international dollar has the same purchasing power over GNI as a U.S. dollar has in the United States. GNI is the sum of value added by all resident producers plus any product taxes (less subsidies) not included in the valuation of output plus net receipts of primary income (compensation of employees and property income) from abroad (World Bank 2015).

Labour force participation rate is the proportion of the population ages 15 and older that is economically active (World Bank 2015).

Employment rate, or the employment-to-population ratio, is the number of persons who are employed as a percent of the total of working age population (ILOSTAT Database see https://www.ilo.org/ilostat/; Data for Timor-Leste (LFS 2015); Data for China (NBSC 2012); Data for PNG (ILO 2012). Employment figures for PNG are high because most people in rural areas are engaged in subsistence agriculture and the most recent employment data collected through the PNG 2000 Population and Housing Census census considers such people as being employed (ADB 2012,54).

Urban population (% of total refers to people living in urban areas as defined by national statistical offices. Calculated using World Bank population estimates and urban ratios from the United Nations World Urbanization Prospects (World Bank 2015).

% of female/male employment in agriculture, those who work for a public or private employer and receive remuneration in wages, salary, commission, tips, piece rates, or pay in kind (World Bank 2015).

Vulnerable employment includes unpaid family workers and own-account workers as a percentage of total employment. Own-account workers and contributing family workers have a lower likelihood of having formal work arrangements, and are therefore more likely to lack elements associated with decent employment, such as adequate social security and a voice at work data available at Social Security Expenditure database, ILOSTAT https://www.ilo.org/ilostat/. Data for Cambodia, Sri Lanka, Malaysia, New Zealand, South Korea, Japan, Australia and Singapore are available in Asian Development Bank (SDBS) https://sdbs.adb.org/sdbs/index.jsp.

important questions about the structure of economic growth, poverty alleviation and barriers to women's expanded participation in paid economic activity. There are high levels of gender disparity among formal wage and salary workers, with men disproportionately employed in relatively secure full-time jobs and women in less secure, often part-time, forms of work. In advanced capitalist economies, formal employment contracts and conditions dominate, although there is a trend towards informalisation, with an increasing proportion of workers employed on short-term contracts or in other non-standard forms of employment that include reduced conditions of pay, leave and access to social security (Williams and Windeband 1998; Standing 1999; Piketty 2014). In developing economies, informal employment is pervasive and formal employment hard to come by.

Current international guidelines define informal jobs as those in which the employment relationship is 'in law or in practice, not subject to national labour legislation, income taxation, social protection or entitlement to certain employment benefits' (ILO 2003, 51). This definition is broad and typically includes daily labourers and seasonal workers; own-account workers engaged in informal enterprise; employers in their own informal sector enterprises; contributing family workers; members of informal producers' cooperatives; employees holding informal jobs; and own-account workers producing goods for household use. Informal work can be skilled or unskilled and return high or low wages but, in the main, informal employment is defined by insecurity, low productivity, low levels of skill and low wages. Own-account workers and contributing family workers are particularly vulnerable, as the absence of a direct employer exposes them to highly exploitative work conditions with little or no social security and often no access to representation by unions or protection from the state. Unorganised and isolated, these vulnerable workers – found in high numbers in the less developed countries of the Asia-Pacific – have very low incomes, exposing them to the constant risk of poverty.

In addition to measuring women's labour force participation, it is also important to evaluate the employment outcomes for women who enter the paid workforce. Labour markets are deeply gendered institutions (Elson 1999): labour market segmentation embeds gender hierarchies that limit women's economic opportunities and security across the development spectrum. Gendered notions of women's and men's work mean that women tend to be concentrated in feminised occupations and in jobs with less responsibility and lower wages. They are over-represented in unpaid family labour and in informal employment, leaving them more exposed than men to vulnerable forms of employment. While this is especially the case in developing economies, the gender pay gap is a global phenomenon. One international survey paper that compared males and females with the same characteristics (age, region, marital status, presence of children or elderly relatives, hours of work, industry and employment status) calculated that the gender earnings gap across 64 countries fell within a range of 8 to 48 per cent of average female earnings, and was more pronounced among part-time workers and those with low levels of education (Ñopo, Daza and Ramos 2011). Of significant interest is the finding that the correlation between economic development and declining wage disparities is weak.

Unpaid and paid care work

Women in the Asia-Pacific bear major responsibility for reproductive labour. This includes all types of unpaid care and domestic work. Time use surveys show that across the region women, on average, do more than twice the unpaid work of men, although there is significant variability, with the female to male ratio of unpaid care registering between an average of 1.71 in New Zealand and 9.8 in India (OECD 2014). Men do not increase their unpaid care when women do more paid labour (Sayer et al. 2009) making women's total hours of work (paid and unpaid) in many cases higher than men's (Budlender 2008; UN Women 2015). Moreover, since the sexual division of labour remains relatively fixed, women are left with more intensive total workloads as they work *and* care, inhibiting their capacity to engage in the labour market on equal terms (Razavi 2007).

The lack of redistribution in the sphere of unpaid labour means women are left to devise individual strategies to manage the work/care nexus that confronts them. Strategies include reducing hours of paid work or accepting jobs of low status or low levels of responsibility and limited career paths. These outcomes limit the economic and social rewards women are able to gain from paid work (Antonopoulos 2009). Across the Asia-Pacific, there is also little state support when it comes to the provision of caring labour. Publicly provided child and eldercare services are not available, accessible or affordable in much of the region. In countries where the state provides some social support for care, the extension of these services is often challenged. Public health and education systems are also under increasing pressure, with new market-based arrangements limiting universal access and pushing responsibility for welfare provisioning back into the household and, more specifically, onto women.

Women's strategies for managing these dynamics and their impact on paid work and unpaid care vary enormously across the region. However, some patterns can be observed. In some countries part-time employment is a common strategy that allows women to engage in some paid work while still taking primary responsibility for care and reproductive labour. Australian women, for example, have some of the highest rates of part-time work in the world (AIFS 2008). However, in most wealthy Asian economies, part-time work is much less common. Middle-class and wealthy women in these countries often manage their work and care responsibilities through the employment of foreign domestic workers who perform paid care labour in private homes. This work is most often informally arranged and unprotected by formal regulation. The employment of paid household help is also the dominant strategy for many women in the large emerging economies of China and India, where rapid economic growth and pervasive inequality has produced what Palriwala and Neetha (2009, 17) call a 'servant employing middle-class'.

This strategy is so pervasive that the rapid growth in Asia's middle class (ADB 2010) has delivered a parallel growth in the number of paid domestic workers employed in the region. Between 1995 and 2010 the number of domestic workers employed in Asia and the Pacific increased from 13.8 million to 21.5 million, accounting for 41 per cent of the global total (ILO 2013, 24). The paid domestic labour sector is highly feminised, with women accounting for 81 per cent of domestic workers in the region (ILO 2013, 20). Inadequate regulation and the hidden nature of the work in private homes leave many domestic workers vulnerable to extreme forms of economic and physical exploitation. Domestic work nevertheless provides women with a pathway into paid labour, and potentially to economic independence. Some of the women who assume these roles are internal migrants who move from their villages to urban centres seeking work. This is a common and growing trend in China and India. Others migrate to work in the more prosperous countries in the region. Indonesia, the Philippines and Sri Lanka are major sending countries for female labour migrants, with most finding employment as domestic workers in the Middle East, but also in Malaysia, Hong Kong, Taiwan and Singapore. These countries also have sizable internal domestic worker markets. In Indonesia, for example, domestic work is one of the largest sources of wage employment for rural women with low levels of education (ILO 2013, 29).

The growing demand for domestic workers in the Asia-Pacific alerts us to the ways in which emerging labour markets are displacing old boundaries of national and rural/urban location. Households with different levels of wealth articulate with national economic development strategies to produce new and expanded feminised labour markets. Where households are rich enough to outsource reproductive labour, supply mirrors the traditional sexual division of labour in an uncontested fashion, highlighting the undervalued nature of reproductive labour, especially paid care labour, in the everyday running of the economy. The increasing reliance on this form of paid but informal, non-familial care produces care chains in which the reproductive and care labour that ceases to be performed by one woman is taken up in a commodified form by another woman of lesser economic and social means (Hochschild 2000). While transnational care chains have gained considerable attention in the literature (Parrenas 2000, 2001), intra-national care chains are also very significant in the region.

Demand for paid, informal, non-familial care is less well catered for in some of the wealthy economies, especially Australia, New Zealand, Japan and South Korea. In Japan and South Korea, deeply entrenched patriarchal social norms mean that there remain strongly equivocal attitudes to what role the state and employers should play in helping women to meet work and family responsibilities. In Japan, patriarchal attitudes to gender roles and antipathy to migrants have resulted in a policy stalemate as well as the paradoxical co-existence of low female workforce participation and a very low fertility rate. State policies are also deeply conservative in South Korea, reinforcing gender differences and roles in ways that position women as secondary workers and second class citizens.

In the case of Australia and New Zealand, the absence of affordable domestic labour has seen an increase in public pressure on government to develop policy measures that help women reconcile their paid and unpaid work responsibilities. The union movement has also come to play an increased role in the promotion of appropriate valuation of paid and unpaid care labour in these countries. Unions have advocated for state provision of paid parental leave and legislated provisions that allow employees with care responsibilities to request flexible working hours. Where government support is limited, sections of the private sector incorporate supportive work and family policies into their human resource strategies as part of their efforts to attract and retain skilled female staff (de Cieri et al. 2005). Unions have also advocated for, and in some cases won, wage increases for formal workers engaged in paid care labour as childcare or aged care workers – the majority of whom are women (Briggs, Meagher and Healy 2007).

Evidence of proactive government policy on work and care in the region's developing economies, meanwhile, is piecemeal. Organised labour movements have also largely failed to prioritise these issues, with only a few examples of women's unions developing innovative childcare and health insurance programmes to facilitate members' capacity to engage in more productive and secure forms of work (Hill 2008). In some cases, the absence of the state has seen the corporate sector in developing economies implementing their own internal policies to support workers with caring responsibilities (Chang 2015; Hill 2013). In other cases, the not-for-profit sector has developed programmes to support women's empowerment and improve their capacity to combine work and care in a more economically viable way. However, these iniatives remain small and coverage is patchy. Overall, policy vacuums in both the work and care regimes in the region's developing economies are significant.

Increasing care demands and emerging pressures

The young and the elderly are the largest dependent population groups in need of care, and hence are the focus of this volume. In the wealthy Asian economies of Japan, South Korea and Singapore, demographic trends point to a rapidly ageing population as a result of tightly managed migration policies and fertility rates that rank among the lowest in the world. China has also recently entered a period of rapid ageing as a consequence of its one-child policy. In these countries eldercare (and health) services are underdeveloped and in need of significant reform if they are to meet growing demand. Population size is less of an urgent issue in Australia and New Zealand, but other demographic pressures, such as the ageing of the workforce, are a concern for both countries. The least developed economies, particularly Timor-Leste and Papua New Guinea, have the highest fertility rates in the region and very young populations.

The pressures of an ageing population loom large, but the most pressing issue in the region as a whole is childcare. Across the economic spectrum, most families prefer familial care and, where the mother is not available, grandparents are considered the next best choice. In Singapore, the state has embedded expectations of familial care within its social policy, which makes grandparent care very common. In China, the *hukou* system of citizen registration means grandparent care is the only option for migrant workers who need to find work in other parts of the country. Full-time grandparent care is also commonplace in Sri Lanka, Bangladesh, Indonesia and the Philippines, where the absence of state support and labour migration turn grandparents into primary carers.

State support for childcare varies markedly across the region, driven by competing rationales. In India, childcare is linked to child welfare rather than women's employment. In China, young children's services are positioned as a precondition for inclusive economic development, as outlined in the 12th Five Year plan. This human capital approach to pre-school education is also prevalent in wealthy Asian economies like Singapore, where declining fertility rates and ageing population profiles support an 'investment' approach to children. But it is not always the state that supplies the care services: there is also strong demand for private pre-schools for young children and tutoring colleges for older children. In Australia, the debate about the purpose of childcare is yet to be settled: practitioners focus on a professionalised notion of Early Childhood Education and Care that is centred on child development, while the state emphasises the role that care services play in facilitating women's workforce participation (Productivity Commission 2014). Policy settings currently reflect state preferences. In New Zealand state investment in early childhood education is aimed at facilitating both improved educational and social outcomes for children and female workforce participation.

A feminist typology of work/care regimes

The majority of the literature on work/care regimes, particularly in a comparative perspective, is based on OECD economies. Scholarship on developing economies is nascent but gathering momentum (see Razavi 2007, 2012; Kabeer 2007, 2010). In this volume we map the contours of the contemporary work/care regimes in fifteen countries of the Asia-Pacific according to a feminist typology.[3] This exercise allows us to highlight how inequalities of wealth, different systems of employment regulation and variable provision of formal care services underwrite divergent work/care regimes and the unequal socio-economic prospects of women in the Asia-Pacific (Figure 1.1).

The care regime is located on the vertical axis of our typology. National care regimes are differentiated along a continuum in which the family is the dominant site of care, sometimes supplemented by varying amounts of informal paid care and/or formal paid care. The typology acknowledges the relevance and centrality of familial care in all the countries, regardless of their development status. Familial care may then be supplemented, depending on the level of women's participation in paid work, by forms of non-familial care – the vast majority of which is provided by women. Whether this care is provided informally or formally depends on the orientation of the state and its level of support of formal paid care services. Where these are not available, households pursue informal forms of additional care, often through the employment of domestic workers.

The dominance of the family as the locus of care reflects the ideology of gendered familialism that prevails in all countries of the Asia-Pacific. Gendered familialism reflects the belief that care is primarily a private familial (and female) responsibility, based on two assumptions: that families are altruistic and that care work is a natural function of women and girls. As a result, the primary responsibility of women and girls is to undertake unpaid reproductive labour,

		Work regime	
		More regulated	*Less regulated*
Care regime	Familial	Japan South Korea	Papua New Guinea Timor-Leste
	Familial/informal	China Malaysia Singapore	Bangladesh Cambodia India Indonesia Sri Lanka The Philippines
	Familial/formal	Australia New Zealand	

Figure 1.1 A feminist work/care typology for the Asia-Pacific

even at the expense of opportunities to engage in paid work. This construction of the dependent woman engaged in the private sphere of the household relies on the complementary ideal of a male breadwinner who is responsible for paid employment in the public sphere in all but the least developed economies in the region. Indeed, one cannot exist without the other.

The expectation that women should be the primary carers of dependent children and adults is deeply entrenched in every country represented in this volume. This is true even in post-communist Cambodia and China and the largely pre-capitalist economies of Papua New Guinea and Timor-Leste. However, the extent to which familial care is supplemented, and in what way, varies significantly. Leitner (2003) talks about 'varieties of familialism' when comparing care regimes across Europe. This is a helpful way of thinking about the way in which familial care is positioned across the Asia-Pacific. In the wealthy economies of Japan and South Korea and the poor economies of Timor-Leste and Papua New Guinea, there is little support for a non-familial care workforce, formal or informal. In Malaysia and Singapore, the state has explicitly privileged the development of an informal, non-familial care workforce over provision of formal care infrastructure. This is also true to some extent in China. Informal domestic workers also provide the dominant form of non-familial care in Bangladesh, Cambodia, India, Indonesia, Sri Lanka, and the

Philippines. By contrast, the state has been reluctant to support the development of informal, non-familial care in Australia and New Zealand, preferring instead to develop a formal (albeit inadequate) care infrastructure to support households.

These three types of care regime (familial, familial/informal, familial/formal) signal official expectations of women as carers, and determine the alternative care solutions available to households when women move into the paid economy. It is significant that non-familial care is in highest demand (and supply) in the most highly stratified societies and that this type of care in the Asia-Pacific is generally engaged as informal, home-based paid care rather than through formally organised services provided by the state or private sector. This speaks to issues of inequality that are widespread across the region and are deployed by states in the construction of national work/care regimes.

The horizontal axis of our typology represents the work regime, which may be 'more' or 'less' regulated. Wealthy, developed economies – Singapore, Japan, South Korea, Australia and New Zealand – have the most regulated work regimes in the region. The lower-middle and low income developing countries – Bangladesh, Cambodia, India, Indonesia, Papua New Guinea, Sri Lanka, the Philippines, and Timor-Leste – have less regulated work regimes, in which women are most likely to be employed informally without workplace entitlements that support care and few alternatives in the form of state-supported services. Elite women in these countries often have access to good employment opportunities, and the entitlements attached to them, in addition to household help that is typically low paid and poorly regulated. However, the majority of women in these developing countries are engaged in informal employment with no access to supportive care entitlements and prone to high levels of socio-economic insecurity. It is this insecurity that leads many women to seek employment as care workers in the homes of their wealthier compatriots or abroad. In developing Asia, including China and India, informal paid care workers are likely to be internal labour migrants. However, as noted earlier, many women from India, Sri Lanka, the Philippines, Indonesia, Bangladesh and Cambodia work abroad in informal care-related occupations, many of them in Hong Kong, Malaysia, Singapore and Taiwan.

The interaction between work and care regimes produces highly stratified outcomes for women from different countries and across class, ethnic, locational, religious and educational divides. This is further influenced by the prevailing national and transnational context. Both familial and paid care labour are in abundance for wealthy households in countries like Singapore, Malaysia, Indonesia, India, Bangladesh and the Philippines. But for the poorest households in these countries there is an acute deficit in both domains. Poor women and men who must engage in income-generating activities to earn even a meagre livelihood are often circumscribed in their capacity to provide adequate care, cannot afford alternative forms of care, and typically live where there is no social care provided by the state. In these households, dependent children, the ill or elderly are often left to care for themselves, or else receive minimal and very poor quality care from a young family member or neighbour. The differential care practices generated by economic inequality within countries and across the region reinforce the stratified nature of households in each of the societies addressed in this volume. But financial resources provide no guarantee of quality care. In Japan, and to a lesser extent South Korea, for example, policy approaches to care and migration mean that even wealthy households have little access to formal care services or informal paid domestic labour.

In more regulated work regimes there is a capacity for states to implement policies that support workers to combine paid work and family care responsibilities. Regulated work regimes also have the capacity to provide protection and better conditions for paid care workers. However the work/care regimes of Japan and South Korea on the one hand, and Australia and New Zealand on the other, demonstrate very clearly that there is no intrinsic relationship between a regulated work regime and state support of a robust care regime. The evolution of the work/care regime in these four countries demonstrates that whether more-regulated work regimes facilitate the development of robust national work/care regimes or not is determined not only by economics, but also by tradition, culture, and politics. As Razavi and Staab remind us: '... how care is organised and who bears the costs of its provision are inherently political decisions' (2012, 18). As our typology of work/care regimes shows, patterns of women's work and care are indeed politically determined and not solely the result of individual choice, preference or agency.

The politics of national work/care regimes

The state is never neutral, and its impact on the work/care regime fundamentally shapes gender relations and patterns of social equity. The state plays a central role in the development of national work/care regimes by prescribing the funding, delivery and design of care policies, and the structure and scope of the employment system. Some states locate women at the centre of their approach to economic growth – either as highly skilled contributors to the economy (Singapore, Malaysia) or as low-skilled labour in Export Processing Zones (Sri Lanka, Bangladesh). However, when the demands of the economy clash with a gender order that frames women as primary carers, the state tends to resist and truncate the development of a supportive work/care regime. For this and other reasons, the overall lack of commitment across the Asia-Pacific to the public provision of care means that the responsibility for care is primarily devolved back to families. This is clearly the case in the wealthy developed economies of Japan and South Korea, and more predictably in the very poor economies of Timor-Leste and Papua New Guinea. Where states allow, families are able to mitigate the impact of state inaction by engaging informal, paid care workers (sometimes local, sometimes foreign) to meet care deficits. This is a common strategy promoted by a range of Asian countries across the development spectrum. By contrast, widespread access to informal paid care has been restricted in Australia, New Zealand and Japan by immigration policies that limit the entry of low-skilled workers. Instead, limited public resources have been directed to the development of a formal care sector and have encouraged the marketisation of such care and the development of private-for-profit or not-for-profit services.

The state also plays a very important role in shaping a country's work regime. States can set and enforce the terms and working conditions for care workers. They can also legislate for workplace policies that facilitate, if not fully enable, women (and men) to meet their work and care responsibilities. This includes policies such as paid parental leave, public childcare and workplace flexibility provisions. Less regulated employment systems – a characteristic of many countries in the region – make it very difficult for states to build strong work/care regimes. But there is no clear correlation between formal, well-regulated work regimes and guarantees of decent workplace conditions for workers with caring responsibilities. Where the work regime has most impact on care work is in its regulation of the formal paid care workforce. In countries where employment is more regulated (for example, New Zealand and Singapore), the formal paid care workforce tends to experience better conditions of employment than in countries where employment is less regulated (for example, Sri Lanka and Cambodia). However, this cross-country comparison does not translate when we evaluate the conditions of paid care workers with those of other workers within a well-regulated country. In contexts with highly regulated work regimes, childcare, eldercare and disability care workers are among the lowest paid workers in the country. While they do receive the statutory employment provisions that are a defining feature of well-regulated employment systems, such as paid parental leave, sick pay, and the aged pension, their general conditions of work are poorer than those of the vast majority of workers. This is a pattern replicated in all countries with regulated work regimes and reflects the undervaluation of both care work and women's labour. Provisions for formal-sector care workers are, however, largely irrelevant in countries like Japan, Singapore and South Korea, which have highly developed formal work regimes but consider care a family and private matter. Employment law in Japan and South Korea, while robust, has not delivered working women (or men) access to adequate paid parental leave, carers leave or flexible working hours. Instead, a culture of long working hours prevails, and women, it would seem, are choosing to respond by not having children. In Australia and New Zealand the state has somewhat reluctantly attended more closely to work and family policies, as the pressures on working families have increased over the past two decades and the changing demographic and labour market patterns have made the issue a national concern.

With weak or non-existent state policies, it may be expected that unions and non-government organisations will intercede and advocate for change. But the experience of the region suggests that this is not a foregone conclusion. The post-colonial, communist and authoritarian political histories of much of the Asia-Pacific have meant that unions have had limited capacity to engage in advocacy or bargaining for more regulated working conditions, or to argue for better work and care polices of the state. Furthermore, in those countries with an independent labour movement, attention has rarely been focused on women's interests or care issues, but rather on minimum wages and conditions for (male) workers (Broadbent and Ford 2008). The ability of unions and labour movements to influence work and care policies is also constrained by the fact that the majority of female workers in the region are located in the informal economy, where they have been less exposed to organising by unions or to regulation and enforcement of standards. As unions have had less traction in care work and 'women's issues', the political space has opened for non-government and international organisations to attempt to have some influence (Ford and Gillan 2016). In countries such as the Philippines, Sri Lanka, India and Indonesia, women's organisations (sometimes aligned with the unions) have tried to improve conditions for women through campaigns on issues related to health, childcare, maternity leave and breastfeeding. In Cambodia and Timor-Leste, external organisations such as the ILO have influenced the policy frameworks for work and care.

The inadequacy of current work/care regimes and their contribution to pervasive gender inequality speaks directly to the global focus on gender equity and women's increased participation in the economy. It is clear that change is needed. This study of work/care regimes in the Asia-Pacific offers us an opportunity to think afresh about how work and care are constituted and the role that work/care regimes play in the push toward gender equality. The regional perspective also highlights the vast inequalities – within and between countries – that fundamentally shape women's prospects. Short of a radical restructuring of gender roles, women's engagement in paid work is most likely to remain lacklustre unless governments commit to funding well designed care infrastructure. In the absence of such commitment, many households across the region will continue to rely on the informal paid care workforce – where national migration and work regimes allow. Inequalities in wealth and education between households in and across the nations of the Asia-Pacific make this strategy possible, as they generate incentives for poorer women to seek out opportunities to engage in informal paid care work. But while these jobs do provide some women with an entrée into employment, and possibly some degree of class mobility, care work is unlikely to be the driver of gender equity and economic security unless the working conditions of paid care workers – informal and formal – are firmly on the policy agenda.

This volume

In the chapters that follow we have assembled surveys of the contemporary work/care regimes of fifteen countries in the Asia-Pacific. These countries represent the enormous diversity of the Asia-Pacific region. China, India and Indonesia are very large economies experiencing rapid economic and social change, expanding middle classes and increasing internal inequality. Japan, South Korea, Malaysia and Singapore are wealthy mature Asian economies. Australia and New Zealand are wealthy settler states with strong trade relations within the region. Bangladesh, Cambodia, Sri Lanka and the Philippines are very poor economies that depend on the region for economic opportunities. Papua New Guinea and Timor-Leste represent the many small underdeveloped states scattered across the Pacific.

Each country chapter provides an assessment of the status of women in the labour market; the dimensions and dynamics of the national work/care regime; the politics of work and care; and, finally, the pressures and challenges facing the prevailing work/care regime. Demographic pressures are a critical feature of the region. In some countries population ageing is pronounced, in others low fertility rates are most evident and in others there is evidence of a growing young population. This regional survey provides the empirical data that has allowed us to examine these cross-cutting themes in countries with very different levels of economic development, and provide a comparative analysis of the employment and care regimes that structure women's experience of paid work and unpaid care work. Collectively, these studies speak to broad debates about barriers to women's labour force participation, transnational care formations, the valuation of unpaid care, social protection and labour regulation for migrant and other care workers, and gender relations in developing Asia.

The chapters highlight beyond doubt the role and importance of women in providing care for children and the elderly, whether it be in their place of origin or in the places to which they migrate. This means that international goals of gender equality and women's increased participation in the labour force will not be achieved until care work, unpaid and paid, is valued and prioritised. Essentially, if there is to be progress in this regard, the state needs to intervene with new and specifically targeted policies. There are a suite of policies that can be utilised to address equality at work and in society. At their most basic, these include childcare, leave for parents and family carers, and minimum pay for all workers. Other policies address inequities in the workplace, such as gender gaps in leadership and pay. But state investment in adequate care infrastructure and intervention in the labour market is contentious because it directly challenges the prevailing gender order. For this reason, the development of decent care and work systems is not guaranteed. Such systems are, however, necessary if the wellbeing of women, children – and the aged, ill and disabled – is to be secured and if these societies are to be sustainable and flourish.

Notes

1 For example, Goal Five of the United Nations' new Sustainable Development Goals is gender equality https://sustainabledevelopment.un.org/topics.

2 Ford's contribution to this chapter was funded as part of an Australian Research Council Future Fellowship project entitled *'Trade Unionism and Trade Union Aid in Indonesia, Malaysia and Timor-Leste'* (FT120100778).

3 See Simonazzi (2009) for an analysis of several European nations along comparable, though different, lines.

References

AIFS. 2008. "Work and Family Responsibilities through Life." https://aifs.gov.au/sites/default/files/publication-documents/ssbrochure08.pdf.

ADB. 2010. *Key Indicators for Asia and the Pacific 2010.* Manila: Asian Development Bank.

ADB. 2012. *The Statistical Database System (SDBS).* Accessed 28 April 20. https://sdbs.adb.org/sdbs/index.jsp.

Antonopoulos, R. 2009. *The Unpaid Care Work – Paid Work Connection.* International Labour Organization Working Paper No. 86. Geneva: ILO.

Baird, M. 2005. "Parental Leave in Australia: The Role of the Industrial Relations System." *Law in Context: Work, Family and the Law* 23 (1): 45–64.

Baird, M. and M. O'Brien. 2015. "Dynamics of Parental Leave in Anglophone Countries: The Paradox of State Expansion in Liberal Welfare Regimes." *Community, Work and Family* 18 (2): 198–217.

Briggs, C., G. Meagher and K. Healy. 2007. "Becoming an Industry: The Struggle of Social and Community Workers for Award Coverage, 1976—2001." *Journal of Industrial Relations* 49 (4): 497–521.

Broadbent, K. and M. Ford. 2008. "Women and Labour Organizing in Asia." In *Women and Labour Organizing in Asia: Diversity, Autonomy and Activism,* edited by K. Broadbent and M. Ford, 1–14. London and New York: Routledge.

Budlender, D. 2008. *The Statistical Evidence on Care and Non-care Work across Six Countries*. Geneva: UNRISD.

Chang, C. 2015. "Comparative Analysis of Work–Life Balance Policies and Work Practices in Taiwan and Japan." In *Handbook of Research on Work–life Balance in Asia*, edited by L. Lu and C. Cooper, 251–270. Northampton: Edward Elgar.

Connell, R. 1987. *Gender and Power: Society, the Person and Sexual Politics*. Cambridge: Polity Press.

De Cieri, H., B. Holmes, J. Abbott and T. Pettit. 2005. "Achievements and Challenges for Work/life Balance Strategies in Australian Organizations." *International Journal of Human Resource Management* 16 (1): 90–103.

Elson, D. 1999. "Labour Markets as Gendered Institutions: Equality, Efficiency and Empowerment Issues." *World Development* 27 (3): 611–627.

Ford, M. and M. Gillan. 2016. "Employment Relations and the State in Southeast Asia." *Journal of Industrial Relations* 58 (2): 167–182.

Glucksmann, M. 1995. "Why 'Work'? Gender and the 'Total Social Organization of Labour'." *Gender, Work and Organisation* 2 (2): 63–75.

Gornick, J. and M.K. Meyers. 2003. *Families that Work: Policies for Reconciling Parenthood and Employment*, New York: Russell Sage Foundation.

Hill, E. 2008. "India: The Self Employed Women's Association and Autonomous Organizing." In *Women and Labour Organizing in Asia: Diversity, Autonomy and Activism,* edited by K. Broadbent and M. Ford, 115–135. London and New York: Routledge.

Hill, E. 2013. "Extreme Jobs and the Household: Work and Care in the New India." In *The Global Political Economy of the Household in Asia,* edited by J. Elias and S. Gunawardana, 194–210. Basingstoke: Palgrave Macmillan.

Himanshu. 2011. "Employment Trends in India: A Re-examination." *Economic & Political Weekly* 46 (37): 43–59.

Hochschild, A. 2000. "Global Care Chains and Emotional Surplus Value." In *On the Edge: Living with Global Capitalism*, edited by W. Hutton and A. Giddens, 130–146. London: Jonathan Cape.

ILO. 2003. *Report 1, General Report, Seventeenth Conference of Labour Statisticians*. Geneva: ILO.

ILO. 2012. *The ILO in Papua New Guinea.* http://www.ilo.org/wcmsp5/groups/public/-asia/-ro-bangkok/-ilo-suva/documents/publication/wcms_366539.pdf.

ILO. 2013. *Domestic Workers across the World: Global and Regional Statistics and the Extent of Legal Protection*. Geneva: ILO.

ILO. 2015. *Key Indicators of the Labour Market 2015*, 9th Edition. http://www.ilo.org/kilm.

Kabeer, N. 2007. *Marriage, Motherhood and Masculinity in the Global Economy: Reconfigurations of Personal and Economic Life.* IDS Working Paper 290. Brighton: IDS.

Kabeer, N. 2010. *Gender & Social Protection Strategies in the Informal Economy*. London: Routledge.

Karamessini, M. and J. Rubery, eds. 2014. *Women and Austerity: The Economic Crisis and the Future for Gender Equality.* London: Routledge.

Leitner, S. 2003. "Varieties of Familialism. The Caring Function of the Family in Comparative Perspective." *European Societies* 5 (4): 353–375.

LFS. 2015. "Timor-Leste Labour Force Survey 2013". Dili: Ministry of Finance and SEPFOPE (Sekretaria Estadu Política Formasaun Profisionál no Empregu (Secretariat of State for Vocational Training and Employment)).

McKinsey Global Institute. 2015. *The Power of Parity: How Advancing Women's Equality can add $12 Trillion to Global Growth.* McKinsey & Company.

NBSC. 2012. Women and Men in China, Fact and Figures 2012, Beijing: NBSC.

Ñopo, H., N. Daza, and J. Ramos. 2011. *Gender Earnings Gaps in the World.* IZA Discussion Paper No. 5736. http://ftp.iza.org/dp5736.pdf.

OECD. 2014. *Gender, Institutions and Development Database.* https://stats.oecd.org/Index.aspx?DataSetCode=GIDDB2014#.

Palriwala, R. and N. Neetha. 2009. *Paid Care Workers in India: Domestic Workers and Anganwadi Workers.* Geneva: UNRISD.

Parrenas, R.S. 2000. "Migrant Filipina Domestic Workers and the International Division of Reproductive Labor." *Gender and Society* 14 (4): 560–580.

Parrenas, R.S. 2001. *Servants of Globalization: Women, Migration and Domestic Work.* Stanford: Stanford University Press.

Piketty, T. 2014. *Capital in the Twenty-First Century*. Cambridge: Harvard University Press.

Pocock, B. 2005. "Work/care Regimes: Institutions, Culture and Behaviour and the Australian Case." *Gender, Work and Organization* 12 (1): 32–49.

Productivity Commission. 2014. *Childcare and Early Childhood Learning: Overview*. Inquiry Report No. 73, Canberra: Productivity Commission.

Razavi, S. 2007. *The Political and Social Economy of Care in a Development Context.* Geneva: UNRISD.

Razavi, S. ed. 2012. *Seen, Heard and Counted: Rethinking Care in a Development Context.* Chichester: Wiley-Blackwell.

Razavi, S. and S. Staab. 2012. *Global Variations in the Political and Social Economy of Care – Worlds Apart*. London: Routledge.

Sayer, L., P. England, M. Bittman and S.M. Bianchi. 2009. "How Long is the Second (Plus First) Shift? Gender Differences in Paid, Unpaid, and Total Work Time in Australia and the United States." *Journal of Comparative Family Studies* 40 (4): 523–545.

Simonazzi, A. 2009. "Care Regimes and National Employment Models." *Cambridge Journal of Economics* 33 (2): 211–232.

Standing, G. 1999. *Global Labour Flexibility. Seeking Distributive Justice*. Basingstoke: Macmillan.

UN DESA. 2013. *World Marriage Data 2012* (POP/DB/Marr/Rev2012). http://www.un.org/esa/population/publications/WMD2012/MainFrame.html

UNDP. 2014. *Human Development Report 2014, Sustaining Human Progress: Reducing Vulnerabilities and Building Resilience*. United Nations Development Programme, New York.

UN ESCAP. 2014. *Statistical Yearbook for Asia and the Pacific 2014*. http://www.unescap.org/sites/default/files/ESCAP-SYB2014_0.pdf.

UN Women. 2015. *Progress of the World's Women 2015–2016: Transforming Economies, Realizing Rights*. http://progress.unwomen.org.

Williams, C. and J. Windeband. 1998. *Informal Employment in the Advanced Economies: Implications for Work and Welfare.* London: Routledge.

World Bank. 2015. *World Development Indicators Database 2015*, http://databank.worldbank.org/data/home.aspx.

Part I
Familial/informal care regimes

2 China

The reconfiguring of women, work and care

Minglu Chen, Jie Hao and Marian Baird

The People's Republic of China (PRC) is the world's largest economy and the largest exporter of manufactured goods. China is also the world's most populous country, with an estimated 1.35 billion people and has the world's largest workforce. From the formation of the PRC in 1949 to the market-oriented economic reforms initiated in 1978 and continuing today, China has undergone profound economic growth and social transformation, and much of this change has directly affected women.

The undoing of the centrally coordinated socialist system of employment over the last few decades and the introduction of market-oriented approaches to work and care have impacted significantly on women and their roles in the labour market and in the home and family. Yet paradoxically, and in contrast to other countries in the region, women's participation rates in paid work are declining, despite the country's outstanding economic growth and the population's rising education levels. At the same time, the provision of care for the young and the elderly has been increasingly moved to the home or the market, as the central government and employers have retreated from providing such services. Furthermore, there is increasing use of internal female migrant labour to provide domestic help and care for the growing middle class in the rapidly expanding urban areas.

The recent history of women, work and care in China is thus both complex and at times, contradictory. To explain this situation, this chapter begins by outlining China's changing demographic, social and economic context. This is followed by a discussion of women and work in China today, and the provision of childcare and eldercare. The chapter concludes by identifying particular pressure points around women, work and care in China.

The changing context for women

Women's changing roles in China are set in the context of China's distinctive demographic, social and economic conditions. Compared with most other countries, China has an unusual demographic profile. In 2015, approximately 70 per cent of the population was of working age, with relatively lower proportions of young and old people (Figure 2.1). Demand for childcare, while increasing, differs between rural and urban areas. Demand for eldercare services has not yet reached

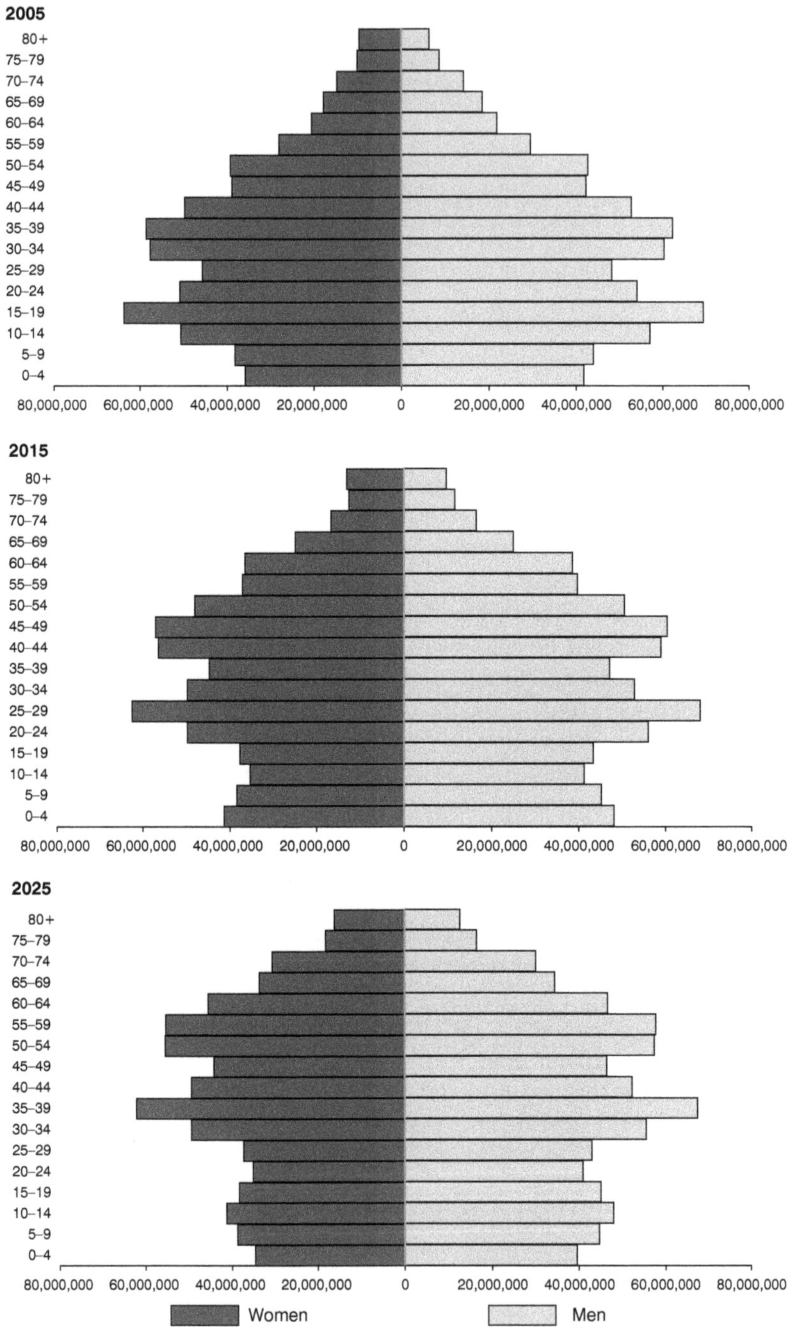

Figure 2.1 Population 2005, 2015 and 2025

Source: World Bank (2015).

the intensity experienced in some other countries, but the pressures for eldercare are set to increase, as China's population is projected to age rapidly after 2015. By 2025, it is estimated that 13 per cent of the Chinese population will be 65 or older. Furthermore, the gender imbalance of 51 per cent men to 49 per cent women is also likely to increase pressure on female caring roles.

A related feature of China's population profile is small family size, a consequence of the one-child policy introduced in 1979. This policy, together with the nine-year compulsory education policy introduced in 1986, has contributed to women's improving education and employment prospects. Having just one child in each household has reduced women's domestic burden, while nine years of compulsory education has equipped women with the basic skills to seek employment outside the home. Female participation in higher education has also increased. In 2013, the female enrolment rate in higher education was over 51 per cent, compared with 20 per cent in 1949 (Li, Tian and Wang 2013; Tan 2006). The Chinese government aims to further increase the female minimum higher education completion rate to 95 per cent by 2020 (State Council 2011).

The stark divide between rural and urban populations in China creates a number of gender, demographic and social pressures. The urban population has increased at a rapid rate, from approximately 11 per cent in 1949 to 18 per cent in 1978 and 53 per cent in 2012 (National Bureau of Statistics 2013). The rural–urban divide shapes housing, education and social security policy and fundamentally structures patterns of employment across China. The household registration or *hukou* system has implications for rural workers who migrate to urban areas seeking work, as they are restricted from accessing housing, education and welfare in areas outside their birthplace.[1] The rural–urban divide is also gendered, with rural female migrant workers typically filling jobs in low-paid domestic work in the urban areas and on the assembly lines of the southeast coast, while rural male migrant workers are employed in construction and heavier manufacturing (Shi 2008), patterns which are borne out in the labour market statistics discussed below.

Religion and social attitudes have also changed markedly. Historically, China was a Confucian nation with highly gendered norms, but following the Communist Revolution more egalitarian approaches were introduced in the policy framework and in some aspects of day-to-day home and work life. New laws were passed to address gender inequality, beginning with the Marriage Law passed in 1950. Since the 1990s, equality between men and women has been established as fundamental state policy (Yan and Quan 2015). A range of laws stipulates women's rights and interests in areas such as political participation, education, work, property and mothers' and infants' health and wellbeing. Specific labour laws also provide for protection of female workers, for maternity leave and also for the prevention of discrimination and harassment at work. While these policy structures are in place, implementation varies and there is considerable evidence of discrimination against women in the labour market.

The original attitude of the Chinese communist state towards women was summarised in Mao Zedong's famous statement that 'women hold up half the sky'. In the early 1950s, as part of efforts to restore economic order after years of warfare and disruption, women were encouraged to leave their homes and join the labour force (Gao 2005) and in the enthusiasm for the Great Leap Forward (1958–62), thousands of women were organised to work in state-owned units or collective enterprises. To liberate women from their domestic burdens, dining halls, nurseries, kindergartens and nursing homes were set up by collectives such as communes and brigades. However, within a few years, the political campaign had become an economic disaster, and women were forced out of the labour force (Wolf 1985).

During the Cultural Revolution (1966–76) a shortage of workers in China's cities meant that women were again called upon (Jiang 2003). Passionate claims such as 'whatever men can do, women can do too' were ubiquitous in this period, and the scale of female employment increased significantly. However, when the Cultural Revolution was brought to an end, young people who had been sent to work in the countryside returned to their home cities, generating a vast surplus of labour. Again, women were encouraged to stay at home. At that time, among the 'returned' unemployed youths, two-thirds were women (Honig and Hershatter 1988).

Under the 'reform and opening up' phase of economic transformation begun in the 1980s, the private sector re-emerged, foreign investment was welcomed and less profitable state-owned enterprises (SOEs) were declared bankrupt or sold to private owners. These changes led to considerable economic dislocation and labour market change. The private sector now accounts for over 60 per cent of the country's GDP (Pan 2013) and has replaced the state-owned sector as the major contributor of exports, taxation and employment. In urban areas many thousands of workers, disproportionally women, were laid off during the period of economic restructuring, and there were significant changes in the provision of welfare. Previously, SOEs were largely responsible for providing employees and their families with a 'cradle to grave' welfare package, which included childcare, education, housing, healthcare and an aged pension. With the closure of many SOEs, employees lost the benefits associated with state employment, and those employed in the newly emergent non-state sector experienced reduced job security and welfare benefits (Cooke 2005). In the rural areas, the reforms led to the erosion of the collective safety net for residents. The safety net, or 'Five Guarantees' programme, which included food, clothing, medical care, housing and burial expenses, only provided for the elderly, disabled, and minors who had no social support and coverage was marginal (Besharov and Baehler 2013). Economic restructuring also created a vast 'floating population' of migrant workers seeking jobs in urban areas. Much of this labour force consists of women providing domestic and care services to the rising middle classes in urban China.

Furthermore, since the late 1980s, responsibility for welfare provision has been devolved to local governments. In cities, local governments have taken the responsibility for providing mandatory social insurance (financed by employers and employees), as well as financing public education and health services. In some sectors (such as housing, education, child and aged care), private providers are allowed to enter the market, offering profit-based goods and services that were formerly provided by the state. As a consequence, the involvement of civil society organisations in welfare provision, while limited, has been growing. The central state is playing a 'shrinking role' in welfare provision because the delivery of 'social services has exceeded the state's capacity and willingness to provide' (Schwartz and Shieh 2009, 178). Families and households now play the most significant role in the care of children, the sick and elderly, the disabled and unemployed (Zhao 1998). The capacity of families to provide these care services is highly differentiated according to socio-economic class and location. In short, China's social welfare system is now a mix of state, market (private sector), family and non-government organisations (Carrillo and Duckett 2011).

Women and work today

The enormous changes in China's political economy have largely undone the system of work and care constructed during the Maoist era and the position of women has been heavily influenced by government policies and economic cycles. Data from the 2010 Chinese Census (National Bureau of Statistics 2012a) shows that women account for 44.7 per cent of China's workforce. For women aged between 16 and 59, the employment rate is 70 per cent, compared with 83.7 per cent for their male counterparts. However, despite the overall growth in the Chinese economy, the most recent decade has seen a decline in the labour force participation of both males and females. Male participation rates have fallen from 82.6 per cent in 1990 to 78.1 per cent in 2012, whereas female participation rates have dropped from 71.1 per cent in 2000 to 63.8 per cent in 2012. While participation rates for women are higher than in other countries, the decline is against the trend of other countries and marks the latest manifestation of women's somewhat conflicted and changeable position in the Chinese labour force.

There has been considerable commentary on reasons for the decline in women's labour force participation following the transition to a market-oriented economy in China. Some have attributed the decline to the removal of the protections offered by the previous system of life-time employment and employer-provided childcare (Yu 2002), while others suggest that discrimination against women has also played a part (Li 2010). Despite legislation banning discrimination against women, women lost jobs at higher rates than men following the economic restructuring of SOEs; they also experienced greater difficulty in finding re-employment (Appleton et al. 2002; Giles, Park and Cai 2006; Du and Dong 2013). For example, according to a 2002 analysis conducted in Beijing (Ma, Kiroko and Zhao 2004), 8.9 per cent of females, compared with 4.5 per cent of males, lost their jobs as a result of the restructuring. Women also withdrew from the labour market in greater numbers than men (Dong, Feng and Yu 2014; Maurer-Fazio, Hughes and Zhang 2007). Explanations for this discrepancy vary, but they include women's disadvantage in education and work experiences, protection for women in employment making them less desirable to employers, and the reluctance of women to take up temporary positions, often the only employment available to them.

Table 2.1 shows the gender distribution by industry. The data highlights the Chinese economy's focus on manufacturing, with one-quarter of men and almost one-third of

Table 2.1 Working population 15 years of age and over by industry and sex, 2011

Industry	*Female (%)*	*Male (%)*
Agriculture, forestry, husbandry, fishery	2.5	2.5
Mining	2.2	5.4
Manufacturing	30.9	26.9
Production and distribution of electricity, gas and water	1.8	2.6
Construction	4	16.5
Transport, storage and post service	3.4	5.3
Information transmission, computer service and software	1.6	1.4
Wholesale and retail	5.9	3.7
Hotels and catering services	2.5	1.2
Financial intermediation	4.9	2.7
Real estate	1.6	1.8
Leasing and business services	1.8	2.1
Scientific research, technical service and geologic prospecting	1.7	2.3
Management of water conservancy, environment and public facilities	1.8	1.5
Household service and other services	0.5	0.4
Education	15.7	8.7
Health, social securities and social welfare	7.9	2.9
Culture, sports and entertainment	1.1	0.8
Public management and social organisation	8.2	11.3
Total	100	100
Number of people (10,000)	5227.7	9185.6

Source: Table reproduced from Department of Social, Science and Technology, and Cultural Statistics (2012, 46).

women engaged in some form of manufacturing. While the proportions of males and females in manufacturing are similar (26.9 per cent and 30.9 per cent respectively), women work in lighter assembly roles and men in heavier manufacturing jobs. The industry mix also shows higher proportions of women in education and health, social security and social welfare, while men dominate construction.

The occupational mix, shown in Table 2.2 further demonstrates the gender segmentation of the labour force and the emergence of more traditional conservative attitudes towards women and their roles in Chinese society. Most pronounced is the preponderance of men in positions of authority and leadership, with men holding three-quarters of positions in head of government institutions, parties, civil societies, enterprises and public institutions.

Table 2.2 Working population by occupational category and sex, 2010

Occupation	*Female (%)*	*Male (%)*
Heads of government institutions, parties, civil societies, enterprises, public institutions	25.1	74.9
Professionals	51.1	48.9
Clerks and related personnel	33.0	67.0
Employees in commerce and service sectors	51.7	48.3
Employees in farming, forestry, husbandry and fishery sectors	49.2	50.8
Operators of production and transportation equipment and related personnel	31.6	68.4
Unclassified	37.5	62.5
Total	44.7	55.3

Source: Table reprinted from Department of Social, Science and Technology, and Cultural Statistics (2012, 43).

The gender disparities in labour force participation are also reflected in rates of pay. Research shows that in 1988, Chinese female workers' average salary was 84 per cent of that of their male counterparts. In 1995, the figure dropped to 80 per cent, and in 2002, it reduced further to 79 per cent (Li and Li 2008). Official statistics reveal that women's average annual earnings are 60 per cent of men's (National Bureau of Statistics 2012b, 57). As elsewhere, there are multiple causes of the gender pay gap. It is uncommon for an employer to pay a woman less than a man for substantially equal work, but as the labour force data illustrates, women tend to be employed in lower status industries; they also tend to be allocated work in lower-income positions and are poorly represented in the senior ranks of their occupations and employing organisations. Further differentiation occurs as women age. State policy encourages working women in China to retire at an earlier age than is the case for men. While men are allowed to retire at 60, women are required to retire at 55, or 50 if in manual work. As a result, women's opportunities for promotion and salary increases are more limited compared with their male colleagues and their income over the life course is considerably lower.

Despite the loss of jobs for women in the reform era, rising education levels and the new economic regime have created some new opportunities for women in professional areas and in self-employment, as discussed below. However these opportunities have also led to problems more commonly associated with advanced economies. In addition to their jobs outside the home, working women are delegated household tasks and their domestic roles are viewed as just as important as their careers, if not more so. In China it is commonly assumed by both sexes that housework is primarily women's responsibility (Honig and Hershatter 1988). Not surprisingly then, according to a study of professionals and managers, work intensification has become a major source of work–life conflict in China, especially for women (Xiao and Cooke 2012). The second national survey on the social status of Chinese women, conducted jointly by the Women's Federation and the State Statistical Bureau in 2001, reported that wives shouldered 85 per cent of daily domestic work and that women spent 4.0 hours each day on housework, 2.7 more hours than the time spent by men (cited in Yan 2008, 66).

In summary, although the process of China's reform has created new opportunities for some women, it has also functioned to further disadvantage other women (Edwards 2000). The successive waves of economic reform and expansion of the Chinese economy, coupled with small family size and increased education levels, have led to somewhat contradictory outcomes for women. On the one hand, women are more educated and more available for work than ever before, but on the other, labour market patterns are very highly gendered and the marketisation of the economy has left more women than men without employment. Furthermore, income and opportunity gaps between men and women, and rural and urban workers, seem to be widening rather than lessening. Symbolising these conflicting outcomes of reform and progress in China are two groups of female workers: female entrepreneurs and professionals, and female manufacturing workers.

Entrepreneurs and professionals

At first sight, women who work as entrepreneurs and professionals appear to have benefited from the opening up of the Chinese economy. The relatively sudden emergence of cooperative enterprises, joint ownership enterprises, share-holding enterprises, private enterprises and foreign-funded enterprises has provided these women with more employment opportunities than ever before. Yet studies also suggest that economic restructuring and the patterns of discrimination discussed above drove some women to start up their own businesses, or to turn to the newly emerging industries to seek employment. Chen's (2011) work showed that the more risk-taking and entrepreneurial women chose to start their own businesses. As of 2005, 84.2 per cent of China's female labour force was employed outside the state-owned sector (National Bureau of Statistics 2006). According to *The People's Daily* website, approximately 20 million female workers in China are enterprise owners or legally responsible individuals (*People's Daily* 2004). *The Third Survey on the Social Status of Women in China* (All-China Women's Federation and National Bureau of Statistics 2011) found that 9 per cent of women had received loans for production and business. Among the beneficiaries of loans, the proportion of women and men is similar, at 37.3 per cent and 36.9 per cent respectively. This group of entrepreneurial women is therefore a potential indicator of women's changing and mixed employment status in China.

However Chen's research has also revealed a more nuanced and gendered picture for Chinese businesswomen (Chen 2011), with traditional gender roles being maintained and reinforced through the distribution of tasks. These female entrepreneurs often rely on family members (often male) for network building, an obvious reflection of gender disparity. In these women's eyes, management, production, personnel and basic administrative duties are regarded as 'inside' work, to be taken care of by these women themselves. Activities such as entertaining clients, establishing business connections, dealing with government administrative units, demanding payments for debts and purchasing are 'outside' work assigned to their husbands. One reason that these female entrepreneurs keep away from the 'outside' sphere is social pressure: entertaining clients, for instance, is often regarded as inappropriate as a woman's activity and might turn them into targets of gossip and slander.

At home, these same entrepreneurial women still have to play the traditional family role of being 'a virtuous wife and good mother'. Many regard their family roles as a major hindrance to their career development. Housework still remains a major responsibility for them, but at the same time there are indications that husbands and other family members are sharing some of the household burden (Chen 2011). These women also more readily employ domestic workers (often migrants) to help with housework. Indeed, as in many other societies, the presence of maids in a household has become an important indicator of middle-class or new rich status (Sun 2008).

This pattern of outsourcing domestic work to lower-class women is replicated in the behaviour of female employed professional women. As Xiao and Cooke (2012, 17) observe in their research on female professionals and managers: 'for those who have childcare and/or elderly care commitments, outsourcing their housework and drawing on family networks for support seem to be the most commonly used personal coping mechanisms to reduce WLC [work–life conflict]'. Xiao and Cooke also note that employers tend not to implement organisational work–life policies but prefer to deal with one-on-one cases, thus leaving individuals, particularly women, to carry the burden. Similarly, a 2007 study of female IT managers in China by Aaltio and Huang found that 'women sought support from parents or parents-in-law, hired tutors for assisting with their children's homework, employed domestic helpers for child-minding, cleaning, cooking, shopping, and shared family responsibilities with their husband' (cited in Xiao and Cooke 2012, 17). The decline in state-supported care services and shifting approaches to women's formal employment has meant that professional women's employment and care patterns in China are reflecting similar patterns to those in more developed nations, with clear and ongoing gender unevenness in the labour market and family support or outsourced assistance needed to maintain the home and provide care.

Manufacturing workers

The experience of China's huge female manufacturing workforce, the majority of whom are located in China's rapidly expanding cities, is somewhat different from that of entrepreneurial and professional women. Much of China's economic growth has occurred as a result of the establishment of special economic zones (SEZs) in the southeast of the country. The development of export-oriented manufacturing industries in these zones has taken advantage of rural–urban disparities and gender inequalities (Ngai 1999). Knox (1997) estimated that 80 per cent of SEZ assembly line workers were female, mostly young and less educated than their urban counterparts. These women are 'not only migrant peasant workers, but also females, considered to be cheaper and easier to regulate. They were imagined to be more obedient, tolerant and conforming to the factory regime' (Ngai 1999, 18), and thus suitable for the repetitive and tedious nature of much of the assembly line work. The lives of these women have been studied closely by Davin (2004), who describes a complex interplay of gender, domestic and personal politics existing among these young female workers from rural origins. Living in the dormitories and working in the factories of the SEZs potentially provides them with more personal autonomy and opportunities for advancement through education, income and partnering than if they stayed with their families in their home villages. On the other hand, the pay rates are relatively low, hours of work are long and demanding and the living conditions and welfare are not as good as they are for non-migrants. Again, the experiences of these female manufacturing women demonstrate the contradictory nature of work for many women in China, with simultaneous opportunity and cost being the hallmarks of the transitions in China's social and economic environments.

Childcare and eldercare

The transition from a centrally-planned to a market economy was accompanied by a dramatic decline in publicly-funded childcare programmes. As a result, the responsibilities for care have shifted predominantly to the family, where women overwhelmingly are the primary caregivers (Cook and Dong 2011). According to Du and Dong (2013) the decline has adverse implications for women and children, particularly those in low-income families, and has become a major factor feeding into these women's weaker labour market position. Since publicly-funded nurseries do not accept children under three years old, many urban families must rely on private service or commercialised kindergartens to meet their childcare needs (Du and Dong 2013), which also raises concerns about availability, affordability and quality of service.

The changes in childcare provision have impacted on women in different ways. For wealthier families in urban areas, private childcare and preschools are becoming more common. However for women in less privileged labour market positions, the situation is different. Rather than private childcare, or employer-provided childcare, it is not uncommon for the extended family (typically grandparents) to take responsibility for childcare. In the rural areas of China the picture is somewhat different again, with both mothers and fathers migrating to fast-growing regions (Fan 2011) and often leaving their children behind, to be cared for by grandparents and other village members.

China's changing demographic profile, outlined earlier, also shows the looming problem of caring for the aged, many of whom are parents of a single child. It is predicted that in 2029 China's elderly population will for the first time exceed the child population (Wei and Liu 2009), a statistic that foreshadows major eldercare challenges in the next few decades. In 1997, the Chinese government introduced a unified old-age insurance system in urban areas, which requires a percentage contribution from both employers and employees. At first the system only covered those employed in SOEs and collectively-owned enterprises. It was expanded to include foreign-invested and private enterprises in 1999, and further expanded to cover urban employees in 2002 (State Council 2004). Since 2009, the central state has been promoting a trial cooperative rural pension system, which involves contributions from individuals, rural collectives and local governments. This system, 'together with family, land, and social endowment, will insure rural older people's basic livelihood' (State Council 2009). Although the Chinese central government is working to unify the urban and rural pension schemes, retiree public servants and employees of government departments and institutions usually enjoy more privileged access to aged care because of their employment histories (National People's Congress 2008).

The 'Law of the People's Republic of China on Protection of the Rights and Interests of the Elderly' places a legal obligation on children and other family members to provide for and look after the elderly by paying their medical expenses, arranging housing and help to farm the land (in rural areas). If family members do not live with their elderly relatives, they are legally obliged to visit them regularly and employers are required to provide them with aged care leave (National People's Congress 2012). Most recently, in 2013, the state suggested that older people might use their home equity to fund their caring needs, an initiative that has generated considerable debate (Xinhua News Agency 2014).

The state's retreat from welfare provision has added to the burdens on women, who have to balance their professional and domestic roles (Cook and Dong 2011). In conjunction with Confucian values and family responsibilities, population ageing has exacerbated the dilemma for middle-aged, married women attempting to fulfil multiple responsibilities. Most of these middle-income women play the role of caregivers for family members at different stages. This not only undermines the quality of care available to children and the elderly, but also limits women's employment participation and options.

Female domestic workers – providing childcare and eldercare

Estimates suggest that there are up to 20 million domestic workers in China (Dong, Feng and Yu 2014). From the perspective of female rural migrant workers, domestic work is perceived as a pathway into the labour market of China's expanding urban areas. Furthermore, in contrast to manufacturing work, domestic work is familiar terrain requiring minimal educational qualifications, and is therefore regarded as a realistic option for rural migrant females. As with attitudes to women's capacity to undertake assembly tasks, stereotyped views on women's ability to care prevail, with research demonstrating the common belief that 'being women, they are naturally talented at housework' (Zhou and Zhou 2007, 10). A series of case studies by Zhou and Zhou indicates that most domestic workers are either young single females in their late teens or early 20s, or married workers of 30 and above. The 30–45 age group is especially popular, as married women are considered to be more patient and experienced with children, and to be more stable, mature and focused on their work.

Not only is the provision of childcare services an issue; so too is the need to provide eldercare. A survey conducted by China's National Communication on Population Ageing indicated that over 80 per cent of the families in need of eldercare are unable to find quality domestic workers to provide those services (Dong, Feng and Yu 2014). The market for child and elder services in China is still developing, and information matching, specifying service details, setting standard pricing and on-going customer service, remain major problems.

Pressure points

The last three decades of economic and social change have reconfigured women's roles in China and have had substantial and specific consequences for female employment and care provision. As the economy has grown, women's overall participation in the labour market, while still high relative to other countries, has declined. In terms of meeting care needs, the decentralisation of governance and welfare provision, coupled with demographic shifts and the rapidly changing economy, are straining the ability of both local governments and national policies to meet the demands for child and eldercare.

There are specific population pressures in China. The ageing of the population is set to intensify demand for eldercare. At the same time, with the proportion of the working age population in decline, there will also be pressures on women to increase their labour market engagement. While the government is conscious of these pressures and is responding with some new policies, the current policy context does not seem adequate to meet the dual burden of work and eldercare for Chinese women. One area of policy change that may impact on the age-mix of the Chinese population has been in the one-child policy. The Chinese government has acknowledged potential labour shortages as a pressure point, and to address this, changed the one-child policy in 2013 to allow couples to have two children if either parent is an only child (Xinhua News Agency 2013). In 2015, a further proposal allowing each couple to have two children unconditionally was presented to the Chinese People's Political Consultative Conference (Li 2015). The results of these policy changes will, however, take some time to emerge.

The continuation of traditional attitudes to women at work and to gender equity in the labour market are also likely to be major pressure points. As China has become increasingly market oriented there has been, and continues to be, a significant reconfiguring of women's roles and attitudes to work and care. Chinese women have been a buffer for the shifting economic fortunes of the country, providing a reserve army of workers when needed and made redundant when not. Throughout the reform period, the thread of Confucian traditional attitudes to women at work has been present, manifested in discriminatory practices against women and preferential treatment of men. Stereotyped views of women's capacity to work and their place in the labour market appear to be widespread, reflected in strong sex segregation in occupations and industries and large gender pay gaps and leadership gaps. As the female population becomes more educated and mobile, these discriminatory practices and inequalities are likely to meet with increased resistance from women, where they have power to do so. Independent organisations such as trade unions or non-government women's advocacy groups have very limited voices in China, and are unlikely to be drivers of change. Greater responsiveness from the state and employers will be needed to improve gender relations and work–care tensions. Indeed, the Managing Director of the International Monetary Fund, Christine Lagarde (2015), has stated that gender inequality, along with rising income inequality and environmental concerns, are three of the most pressing challenges facing China's future growth and prosperity.

Note

1 The *hukou* system was instituted in the late 1950s. It identified a person as a resident of an area and determined his or her access to a food quota, housing and social welfare benefits. Under this system, individuals were broadly categorised as 'urban' or 'rural' residents and migration from rural to urban areas was strictly controlled by the state. This system was implemented to order to ease economic planning, reduce the need for flexible welfare services, and strengthen state control over the population. Although the *hukou* policy has been somewhat relaxed in the post-reform area, the rural–urban dichotomy still exists to a large extent.

References

All-China Women's Federation and National Bureau of Statistics of China. 2011. *Report on Major Results of The Third Survey on the Social Status of Women in China.* https://s3.amazonaws.com/landesa_production/resource/245/China_WomensFed_Third-Wave-Survey-Social-Status-Women_2011.pdf?AWSAccessKeyId=AKIAICR3ICC22CMP7DPA&Expires=1425215855&Signature=xLIL4UQmPViNZ3lm2JZPuzZlQtg%3D.

Appleton, S., J. Knight, L. Song and Q. Xia. 2002. "Labour Retrenchment in China: Determinants and Consequences", *China Economic Review*, 13 (2–3): 252–275.

Besharov, D. and K. Baehler. 2013. *Chinese Social Policy in a Time of Transition.* Oxford: Oxford University Press.

Carrillo, B. and J. Duckett. 2011. *China's Changing Welfare Mix: Local Perspectives.* London: Routledge.

Chen, M. 2011. *Tiger Girls: Women and Enterprise in the People's Republic of China.* London: Routledge.

Cook, S. and X.-Y. Dong. 2011. "Harsh Choices: Chinese Women's Paid Work and Unpaid Care Responsibilities under Economic Reform." *Development and Change* 42 (4): 947–965.

Cooke, F.L. 2005. *HRM, Work, and Employment in China.* London: Routledge.

Davin, D. 2004. "The impact of Export-Oriented Manufacturing on the Welfare entitlements of Chinese Women Workers." In Shahra Razavi, Ruth Pearson and Caroline Danloy (eds), pp. 67–90. *Globalisation, Export-oriented Employment and Social Policy: Gendered Connections.* UNISD/London: Palgrave.

Department of Social, Science, and Technology, and Cultural Statistics. 2012. *Women and Men in China – Fact and Figures.* http://www.unicef.cn/en/uploadfile/2014/0109/20140109030938887.pdf.

Dong, X., J. Feng and Y. Yu. 2014. "Relative Pay and its Underlying Determinants for Domestic and Eldercare Workers in Urban China." Department of Economics Working Paper 2014-01. University of Winnipeg.

Du, F. and X. Dong. 2013. "Women's Employment and Child Care Choices in Urban China during the Economic Transition." *Economic Development and Cultural Change* 62 (1): 131–155.

Edwards, L. 2000. "Women in the People's Republic of China: New Challenges to the Grand Gender Narrative." In *Women in Asia: Tradition, Modernity and Globalisation*, edited by L. Edwards and M. Roces, 59–84. St Leonards: Allen and Unwin.

Fan, C.C. 2011. "Settlement Intention and Split Households: Findings from a Migrant Survey in Beijing, China." *The China Review* 11 (2): 11–42.

Gao X. 2005. "'The Silver Blossom Competition': Gender Labour Divisions of Rural Women in the 1950s." [In Chinese] *Shehuixue Yanjiu* 4.

Giles, J., A. Park, and F. Cai. 2006. "How has Economic Restructuring affected China's urban workers?" *Journal of Comparative Economics* 34 (3): 582–607.

Honig, E. and G. Hershatter. 1988. *Personal Voices: Chinese Women in the 1980s*. Stanford: Stanford University Press.

Jiang, Y. 2003. "Chinese Urban Women's Employment under the Two Systems" [in Chinese] in *Funü Yanjiu Luncong* 1.

Knox, A. 1997. *Southern China: Migrant Workers and Economic Transformation.* London: International Relations.

Lagarde, C. 2015. 'China and the Global Economy: Creating New Ingredients for Growth'. http://www.imf.org/external/np/speeches/2015/032015.htm.

Li, C. and S. Li. 2008. "Rising Gender Income Gap and its Dynamics in China: Market Competition or Sex Discrimination." *Sociological Studies* 2: 94–117.

Li, L., G. Tian and Z. Wang. 2013. "Female Students Coming, Universities have more Women than Men". [in Chinese] http://www.jyb.cn/high/gjsd/201310/t20131017_555945.html.

Li, W. 2015. "Chinese People's Political Consultative Conference Member Proposes: Relaxing the One Child Policy to Allow Birth of the Second Child." [in Chinese] http://news.163.com/15/0307/15/AK46IBRF00014SEH.html.

Li, Y. ed. 2010. *A Study of Gender Discrimination in the Workplace in China.* [in Chinese] Beijing: Zhongguo Shehui Kexue Chubanshe.

Ma, J., I. Kiroko, and G. Zhao. 2004. "Analysis of Re-employment of Laid-off Workers in Beijing." *China Economic Quarterly* 3 (3): 657–678.

Maurer-Fazio, M., J. Hughes, D. Zhang. 2007. "An Ocean Formed from One Hundred Rivers: The Effects of Ethnicity, Gender, Marriage, and Location on labour force participation in urban China." *Feminist Economics* 13 (3–4): 159–187.

National Bureau of Statistics of the People's Republic of China. 2006. "2005 China 1% Population Sample Survey." [in Chinese] http://www.stats.gov.cn/tjsj/ndsj/renkou/2005/renkou.htm.

National Bureau of Statistics of the People's Republic of China. 2012a. *The 6th National Demographic Report (1st) 2011*. Beijing: China Statistics Press.

National Bureau of Statistics of the People's Republic of China. 2012b. *Women and Men in China: Facts and Figures 2012.* http://www.unicef.cn/en/uploadfile/2014/0109/20140109030938887.pdf

National Bureau of Statistics of the People's Republic of China. 2013. "China Statistical Yearbook 2013." China Statistics Press. http://www.stats.gov.cn/tjsj/ndsj/2013/indexeh.htm.

National People's Congress. 2008. *General Situation and Major Problems of China's Pension Insurance Scheme.* [in Chinese] http://www.npc.gov.cn/npc/zt/2008-12/22/content_1463515.htm.

National People's Congress. 2012. *The Law of the People's Republic of China on the Protection of Rights and Interests of the Elderly.* [in Chinese] http://www.gov.cn/flfg/2012-12/28/content_2305570.htm.

Ngai, P. 1999. "Becoming *dagongmei* (Working Girls): The Politics of Identity and Difference in Reform China." *The China Journal* 42: 1–18.

OECD. 2014. *Labour Force Participation Rate by Sex, 15+, 15–64 and 15–24 Years Old.* OECD. http://www.oecd.org/gender/data/labourforceparticipationbysex15and15-24years old.htm.

Pan. Y. 2013. "Private Economy Counts for over 60% of China's GDP. There are over 10 Million Private Enterprises Registered." [in Chinese] *People's Daily*, 3 February. http://finance.people.com.cn/n/2013/0203/c1004-20414645.html.

People's Daily. 2004. "A Series of Interviews on the Issue of Women: Successful Women." [in Chinese] 2 January. http://www.people.com.cn/GB/14641/14643/29161/.

Schwartz, J. and S. Shieh. 2009. "Serving the People? The Changed Roles of the State and Social Organizations in Social Service Provision." In *State and Society Responses to Social Welfare Needs in China: Serving the People*, edited by J. Schwartz and S. Shieh, 3–21. London: Routledge.

Shi, L. 2008. *Rural Migrant Workers in China: Scenario, Challenges and Public Policy.* Working Paper 89. Geneva: ILO. http://www.oit.org/wcmsp5/groups/public/-dgreports/-integration/documents/publication/wcms_097744.pdf.

State Council. 2004. "China's Social Security and its Policy." http://www.gov.cn/english/official/2005-07/28/content_18024.htm.

State Council. 2009. "The State Council's Guiding Opinions on Establishing a Trial New Rural Cooperative Pension Insurance System." [in Chinese] http://www.chinadaily.com.cn/opinion/2014-05/27/content_17542627_4.htm.

State Council. 2011. "China's Women Development Outline (2011–2020)." http://www.gov.cn/zwgk/2011-08/08/content_1920457.htm.

Sun, W. 2008. "Men, Women and the Maid: At Home with the New Rich." In *The New Rich in China: Future Rulers*, edited by D. Goodman, 89–102. London: Routledge.

Tan, L. ed. 2006. Report on Gender Equality and Women Development in China (1995–2005). Beijing: Social Science Literature Publisher.

Wei, C. and J. Liu. 2009. *Future Population Trends in China: 2005–2050.* The Centre of Policy Studies, General Paper G-191. Clayton: Monash University.

Wolf, M. 1985. *Revolution Postponed: Women in Contemporary China.* Stanford: Stanford University Press.

World Bank. 2015. *Health Nutrition and Population Statistics: Population Estimates and Projections.* http://databank.worldbank.org/Data/Views/VariableSelection/SelectVariables.aspx?source=Health Nutrition and Population Statistics: Population estimates and projections.

Xiao, Y. and F.L. Cooke. 2012. "Work–Life Balance in China? Social Policy, Employer Strategy and Individual Coping Mechanisms." *Asia Pacific Journal of Human Resources* 50: 6–22.

Xinhua News Agency. 2013. "The Decision on Major Issues Concerning Comprehensively Deepening Reforms." http://news.xinhuanet.com/politics/2013-11/15/c_118164235.htm.

Xinhua News Agency. 2014. "Focusing on 'Caring for the Aged through Home Ownership'." http://www.xinhuanet.com/house/sh/zt/140408_yfyl/140408_yfyl.html.

Yan, H. 2008. *New Masters, New Servants: Migration, Development, and Women Workers in China.* Durham: Duke University Press.

Yan, Y. and J. Quan. 2015. "Further Implement the Fundamental State Policy and Realise Equality between Men and Women in All Aspects." [in Chinese] *People's Daily*, 9 March. http://acwf.people.com.cn/n/2015/0309/c99060-26660429.html.

Yu, Y. 2002. "Research on the Current Situation of Chinese Women's Labour Participation and Solutions." [in Chinese] *Shanghai Lady*. http://shcdf.eastday.com/eastday/shnx/node3814/node3873/node4323/userobject1ai26873.html

Zhao, Z. 1998. "Demographic Conditions, Microsimulation and Family Support for the Elderly: Past, Present and Future in China." In *The Locus of Care: Families, Communities, Institutions and the Provision of Welfare since Antiquity*, edited by P. Horden and R. Smith, 259–279. London: Routledge.

Zhou, J. and D. Zhou. 2007. "Research on the Collective Characteristics of Domestic Workers: A Case Study of Casual Workers in China's Southeast Coastal Area." [in Chinese] *Journal of Southwest University for Nationalities (Humanities and Social Science)* 187: 10–16.

3 Malaysia

Balancing paid and unpaid work

Vicki Crinis and Alifa Bandali

In Malaysia, the challenges faced by working women differ according to social class and ethnicity. Social class strongly regulates women's access to professional employment, and ethnic background often determines women's employment prospects, in both the private and public sector. However, all Malaysian women are affected by deep-seated political and cultural beliefs regarding the respective contributions of men and women to the social and economic order. For Muslim Malays, the belief is that men and women are equal but different and as such they are encouraged to play complementary gender roles in society (Karim 1995). Within this division of labour, women are first and foremost responsible for reproductive labour. In Chinese and Indian Malaysian cultures, although different, patriarchy, hierarchy and age are important; men are usually heads of the family and women enjoy a relatively high status as mothers and grandmothers. Underpinned by a relationship of kinship, both young and elderly women reciprocate in childcare and aged care in the home (Karim 1995, 39–40).

Women who have entered the workforce thus find themselves in challenging situations when it comes to familial care needs, paid work, and finding a balance between the two. As Razavi (2007) warns in her mapping of ideas in relation to gender and care, reinforcing the belief that care work is something that only women can or should do leads to adverse consequences for women, including financial precarity and exclusion from the public domain. Significantly, the majority of women who drop out of the Malaysian labour market do so not only because of the difficulties of balancing work and family, but also because care work is considered to be primarily the responsibility of women (Sander et al. 2012). While the Malaysian government is moving towards thinking about care and care work in more formalised ways, such as incorporating care needs into employment policy, it also reproduces discourses of women's responsibility to the family as a good mother and wife informed by Islamic doctrine. The conundrum faced by the state is how to increase women's participation in the paid workforce without disrupting this normative framework.

This chapter explores these issues through a detailed discussion of work and care in Malaysia. It begins by placing questions of work and care in the context of Malaysia's demographic and labour market profile before outlining government policies designed to address women's struggle to remain in the workforce after childbirth and the increasing demand for women to care for children, the aged and people with disabilities. It then moves to a discussion of the ways in which the provision of care is managed, before concluding with an examination of pressure points in the work/care system.[1]

Work and care in context

Malaysia is a relatively small country of 30 million people. Men account for 50.7 per cent of the population and women for 49.3 per cent (Department of Statistics 2015). As a post-colonial state formed from former British territories in Southeast Asia, Malaysia consists of two distinct parts: Peninsular Malaysia to the west, and the states of Sabah and Sarawak on the island of Borneo. This geographic distinction is one of two important vectors of ethnic difference, the other being a colonial-era history of labour migration from India and China. The geographic and ethnic divisions created in the colonial period had significant outcomes in terms of politics and economic policy (Jomo 1988).

During the colonial period, the British government ruled the country by proxy through Malay traditional leaders. Chinese middlemen served the interests of the colonial economy, and the immigration of Chinese labour to work in the tin mining sector and Indian labour to work in the plantation sector enabled the development of export-oriented extractive industries. The Malay population remained in the subsistence sector. Prior to colonialism, the indigenous polities of the region were based on an agricultural economy characterised by shared work between men and women of different generations as well as children. Colonial rule promoted a shift from this assumption of shared responsibility for production towards institutionalised gender divisions and roles (Kaur and Metcalfe 1999). This gender division of labour relied on an ideology that placed women in the private sphere and men in the public sphere. Women's confinement in the home meant that women did not become strongly involved in the waged economy, with the exception of some Chinese and Indian women who participated in menial waged labour (Kaur and Metcalfe 1999).

As a consequence of colonial policy, at the time of independence, the Chinese inhabitants of the former colonies owned most of the private sector assets. The uneven division of economic resources fuelled tensions between the Malay and the non-Malay populations, which culminated in racial violence in 1969. In response, the Malaysian government introduced the New Economic Policy (NEP), which was designed to bring Malays into the economy and provide employment for the large numbers of Malay unemployed. The policy guaranteed Malays special rights, and aimed to increase Malay education, employment and entrepreneurship. The level of engagement of Malaysian women in paid work increased dramatically as a consequence of these changes and the economic transformations they delivered. In the 1970s the government called on young women to enter the labour market in the new export manufacturing sectors, where their 'nimble fingers' and 'docile disposition' were used to attract foreign investment (Heyzer 1988, 98). From the 1990s onward there was a shift from the manufacturing industry towards jobs in wholesale and retail trade, hotels and restaurants, and the financial services sector (UNDP 2013). By this time, many of the first generation of working-class Malay factory women had had children and moved out of factory jobs in order to balance work and care. Some of these women shifted to home-based work, the piece rates for which paid better than factory wages, which had been driven down by poorly paid migrant workers (Crinis 2013).

As a consequence of the government's proactive stance on women's engagement in paid work, women's participation in the labour force between 1975 and 1990 almost doubled, to around 50 per cent, where it has remained more or less stable for the last three decades (Government of Malaysia 2013). However, the number of working-age women in Malaysia who are employed or looking for employment is lower in comparison to countries with similar income levels (TalentCorp and ACCA 2012). Malaysian women aged 15 to 64 made up 46.8 per cent of employed workers in 2008, 49.5 per cent in 2012, and up to 52.4 per cent in 2013, although many drop out of the paid workforce during their childbearing years (Government of Malaysia 2013). As Table 3.2 indicates, women are most likely to be found in trade or manufacturing, though they are also represented in accommodation and food services and education.

Initially focused on getting women into labour-intensive manufacturing and typically feminised professions, the government has since encouraged women to engage as professional workers in the knowledge economy. This strategy has been only partially successful. In terms of their occupational spread, women dominate in the professional, clerical, service and sales occupations (see Table 3.1). However, they are less well represented in managerial positions, although they fare better in the public sector than the private sector (UNDP 2013). In 2010, there were over 600,000 men in positions as senior officers and managers compared with 200,000 women.[2] The number of women owners of small business also lags behind that of other countries in Southeast Asia (Teoh and Chong 2014). These disparities exist despite the fact that women are increasingly well educated. Since the beginning of the 1990s, enrolment ratios of females have been equal to or have exceeded those of males at all levels of educational attainment (Nagaraj 2014).

Women's participation in the labour market varies over the life cycle. According to the government-sanctioned employment service TalentCorp, women work in

Table 3.1 Working population by occupational category and sex, 2013

Occupation	*Male (%)*	*Female (%)*
Managers, professionals, and technicians	24.06	25.85
Clerical, service and sales workers	21.85	45.36
Skilled agricultural and trades workers	25.21	10.84
Plant and machine operators, and assemblers	15.44	6.76
Elementary occupations	13.43	11.20
Armed forces	0.00	0.00
Not elsewhere classified	0.00	0.00
Total	100.00	100.00

Source: ILO (2013).

Table 3.2 Working population 15 years of age and over by industry and sex, 2013

Economic activity	*Male (%)*	*Female (%)*
Agriculture, forestry and fishing	15.41	8.31
Mining and quarrying	0.85	0.35
Manufacturing	16.78	16.74
Electricity, gas, steam and air conditioning supply	0.59	0.25
Water supply; sewerage, waste management and remediation activities	0.83	0.30
Construction	13.77	2.20
Wholesale and retail trade; repair of motor vehicles and motorcycles	16.45	17.40
Transportation and storage	6.55	1.64
Accommodation and food service activities	5.97	10.54
Information and communication	1.43	1.48
Financial and insurance activities	1.80	3.44
Real estate activities	0.51	0.60
Professional, scientific and technical activities	1.91	3.00
Administrative and support service activities	4.47	3.84
Public administration and defence; compulsory social security	6.45	4.68
Education	3.31	10.96
Human health and social work activities	1.16	7.93
Arts, entertainment and recreation	0.61	0.58
Other service activities	1.06	2.09
Activities of households as employers; undifferentiated goods- and services-producing activities of households for own use	0.07	3.66
Activities of extraterritorial organisations and bodies	0.02	0.01
Total	100.00	100.00

Source: ILO (2013).

large numbers after graduating but leave the workforce midway through their careers (TalentCorp and ACCA 2013). Many women have difficulty negotiating a work–life balance that is acceptable to themselves and their families (Thambiah 2010). Women are also penalised in the workforce by employers, who regard them as less committed than their male counterparts (UNDP 2013). As a consequence, there is a certain amount of employer resistance to promoting married women in the workforce, especially those who have care responsibilities (Omar and Ahmad 2009).

Gender segmentation is also evident in the informal economy. As indicated in Table 3.3, women are over-represented in the category of contributing family workers. They are also over-represented in paid work in the informal sector.

Table 3.3 Employment status by sex, 2013

Status in employment	*Male (%)*	*Female (%)*
Employees	73.44	74.62
Employers	5.32	1.71
Own-account workers	18.76	15.26
Members of producers' cooperatives	0.00	0.00
Contributing family workers	2.48	8.42
Total	100.00	100.00

Source: ILO (2013).

According to one local women's non-governmental organisation (NGO), many women end up in low-paid contract work or home-based work because they have been laid off from their jobs in the agricultural and the electronic sector as a result of a decline in production or because of their age (UNDP 2013, 204). Consequently, these women end up in low-paid cleaning jobs or home-based piece rate work, producing a range of products and services including traditional handicrafts, labour-intensive work subcontracted from factories as well as knowledge-based work (Loh-Ludher 2007). Some home-based workers are categorised as own-account workers, but many are simply not recorded in official statistics. Malaysia is also a significant importer of labour, not only in the domestic services sector but also in manufacturing and agriculture. Almost three million unskilled migrant workers are working in Malaysia at any one time, including a considerable number of women employed in the low-paid factory jobs that Malaysian women have left behind.

At the same time as the government is increasing pressure on women to enter the paid workforce, women's care responsibilities are set to increase in response to an ageing population. In the early years of industrialisation, there was a policy push to reduce fertility rates. This approach was abandoned in the 1980s in favour of a policy that encouraged Malay women to have more children, in order to maintain Malay numerical dominance over other ethnic groups (Stivens 1987).[3] However, in the decades since this time, declining fertility rates have been evident among all ethnic groups. Women across all ethnicities marry later and have fewer children, or are choosing not to marry at all. Poorer women tend to have more children than women in higher socio-economic groups, although a woman's level of education is the measure most closely related to her fertility (Thambiah 2010).

As Figure 3.1 shows, in 2005 the majority of Malaysians were in the 15 to 64 age bracket, with only 6.6 per cent of the population above 65 years old. By 2025, people aged between 60 and 80 are expected to account for 13.4 per cent of the population. These changing demographic trends pose a number of challenges for Malaysian families in regard to childcare and aged care, especially as the prevalence of extended families has also declined. Many women have responded to the conflicting demands of paid work and care work by returning to or remaining in the home, while women engaged in the paid workforce rely predominantly on family and informal childcare.

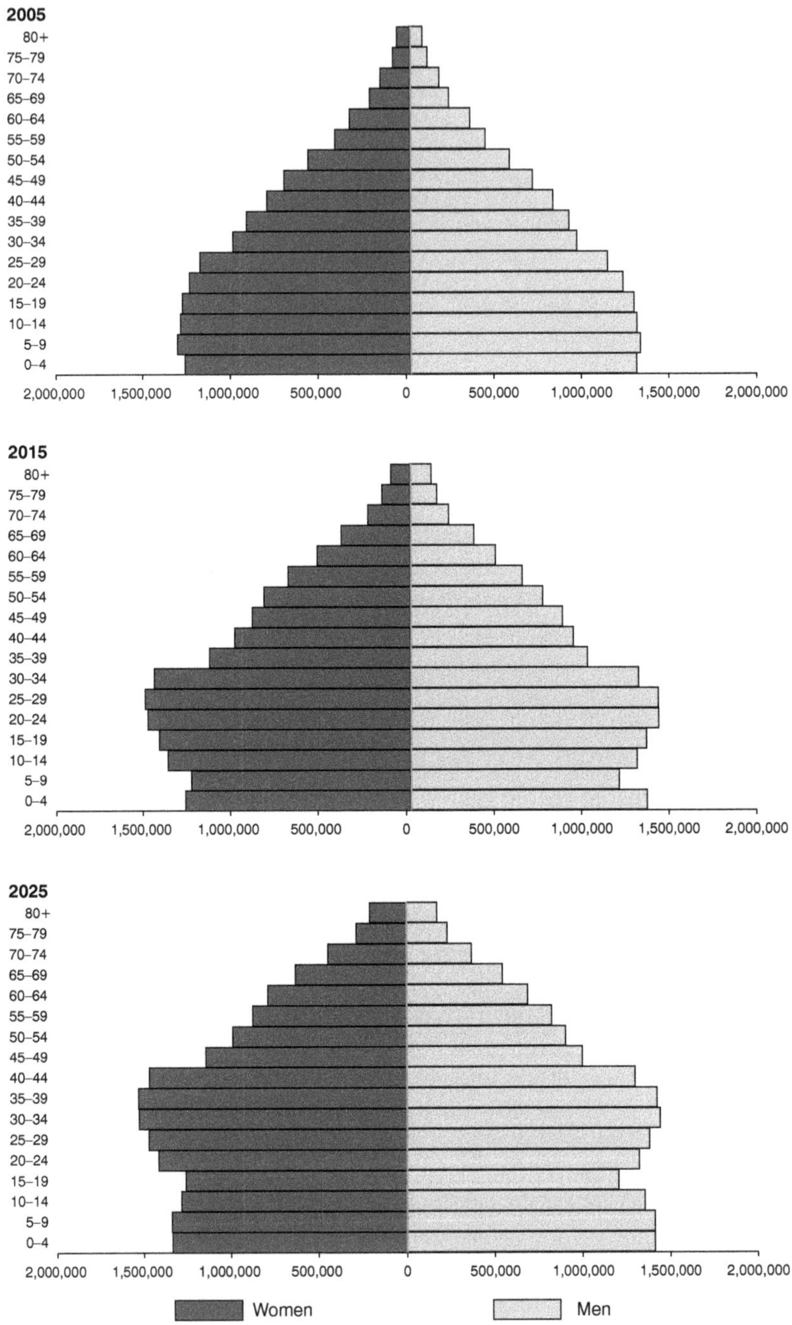

Figure 3.1 Population 2005, 2015, and 2025

Source: World Bank (2015a).

Regulating the provision of care

Since ratifying the United Nations Convention on the Elimination of All Forms of Discrimination Against Women (CEDAW) in 1995, Malaysia has made significant progress in terms of achieving more equal treatment of women in various areas, including employment (Sander et al. 2012). However, the focus has remained firmly on women's primary role within the family. This emphasis has been reflected in successive Malaysia Plans, starting with the NEP in 1971 and continuing with the Vision 2020 Plan in 1991 and successive five-year plans, which set out five-year goals designed to make Malaysia a fully developed state by 2020.

The first major initiative, which preceded the signing of CEDAW, involved setting up the Ministry of Women, Family and Development (MWFD), later known as the Ministry of Women, Family and Community Development (MWFCD). The MWFD was established in 1991 to deal with gender inequalities and to ensure that the problems families faced in the developing economy were adequately addressed. In the Seventh, Eighth and Ninth Malaysia Plans, the government started to focus more on women and employment. The Seventh Malaysia Plan (1995–2000) introduced flexible work into the Employment Act to bring more married women into the workforce. The Eighth Malaysia Plan (2000–2005) worked towards gender equality and the elimination of discrimination and sexual harassment in the workforce. The Ninth Malaysia Plan (2005–2010) focused on developing a national target plan of 30 per cent of women in decision-making positions and explicitly considered care options as part of this strategy. The Tenth Malaysia Plan (2011–2015) continued this strong emphasis on women's participation in the labour market. In addition, in 2011 the government directed extra funding to the MWFCD to support the establishment of formal childcare facilities, to make it easier for women to enter the workforce. While the Plans sustained attention to measures designed to increase gender equality, at the same time childcare was perceived as the primary responsibility of women.

The '1 Malaysia: People First, Performance Now' concept embedded in the Tenth Malaysia Plan is based on an inclusive society development approach, whereby all ethnic groups are guaranteed equitable access to economic participation. Since the 1 Malaysia Family First Programme continues to position the family as the key to the country's success, initiatives are mostly related to improving access to family-friendly services. Under the National Family Policy (2011), the government focused heavily on the bottom 40 per cent of households, flagging an intention to extend assistance to marginalised women, including widows, single mothers and those with lower incomes (UNDP 2013). More accessible institutional childcare is an important part of this strategy. In Malaysia, children start primary school at the age of six. Four- to five-year-olds may attend preschool although it is not compulsory. Children under four either remain at home with parents/grandparents, aunts and neighbours, or are cared for by domestic workers or placed in childcare centres.

Childcare centres are still in the early stages of development. The Education Act 1996 required certain standards at the pre-school level regarding teacher training, curriculum and facilities. A study of childcare programmes for the under-fives conducted around the same time resulted in the establishment of 600 training centres for childcare providers based on an English model. Rather than simply child-minding centres, the aim was to establish childcare centres with an educational curriculum (Heng Keng Chiam 2008). However, early childcare centres were not part of the government agenda until 2011, when the Ministry of Finance allocated RM 10 million to train home-based childcare providers. A further RM 3 million was allocated to the MWFCD and the Department of Social Welfare to subsidise childcare providers' participation in a Basic Childcare Course (KAAK). Grants of RM 55,000 were also offered to interested parties for the establishment of community childcare centres.

As a consequence of these initiatives, the number of registered childcare centres jumped from 245 in 2008 to 1,962 in 2012 (Department of Statistics 2015). However, the cost of formal childcare remains very high. As a consequence, most women tend to use the cheaper unlicensed childcare widely considered to be of a lower standard, with mostly untrained staff. Failing this, they rely on the assistance of neighbours and relatives – or, in its absence, keep children close by.[4] This is one of the reasons that many working-class women and especially single, divorced or widowed women, engage in home-based work, which allows them to care for children and the elderly (Loh-Ludher 2007).

In the public sector, the government has also initiated workplace practices that allow women to balance their work and care roles, including provisions that allow for career breaks so that women can concentrate on family issues. In 2006, the government sought to increase the number of childcare centres in public sector workplaces. To achieve this, the MWFCD allocated grants of RM 80,000 for the renovation and furnishing of childcare centres in government offices. Civil servants with a minimum household income of RM 3,000 per month are eligible for subsidies of RM 180 per child per month for kindergarten fees. The government also provides a subsidy for poorer families. Another public sector programme, called Parenting@Work, which was introduced in 2007, supports the provision of rooms for feeding mothers to express breast milk and soft-option work and parking facilities for pregnant women. Women who have left the paid workforce to concentrate on family issues are able to continue to practise their work skills through the programme, even though they are not formally working. The government has also changed the working day to three working periods instead of a one-size-fits-all nine-to-five schedule and has recommended that the concept of flexible working hours be introduced across the labour market. In addition, women have been increasingly allowed the option of teleworking (Mahari 2011). Paid maternity leave was increased to 90 days in 2012, along with seven days paternity leave for new fathers.

In terms of initiatives for private sector employment, the Women's Ministry and TalentCorp set up a database and internet site to identify suitable employment for professional women wanting to return to work after having children. Companies were also given the incentive of double tax deductions for training women for designated jobs. In addition, the government encouraged companies to adopt flexible workplace practices such as a compressed working week, flexible hours and weekend work (Karim 2014). However, aside from the limited maternity allowance offered by most of the private sector there is very little evidence of targeted support for women workers such as flexible work hours and childcare available in the private sector.[5] To address childcare needs, companies were offered a 10 per cent tax deduction for a period of 10 years and a capital grant of RM 10,000 to set up childcare centres in or near the workplace (Government of Malaysia 2010). However, according to a survey of publicly listed companies in Malaysia, only 6 per cent provided a childcare centre, 27 per cent provided a designated car park for pregnant women and 18 per cent had a nursing room for mothers to express breast milk. On the subject of flexible work policies, another survey across 11 industries (Boo 2014) found that only 12 per cent allowed telecommuting, 16 per cent offered flexible hours, 12 per cent had implemented job sharing and 33 per cent had shift-swapping policies. As of 2013, there were just 27 childcare centres at private workplaces registered with the MWFCD's Department of Social Welfare, compared with 82 childcare centres at workplaces in the public sector (Government of Malaysia 2010).

While the government has been addressing the need for formal childcare, eldercare has not received the same attention. In 2012, the government extended the age of retirement from 55 to 60, allowing workers, especially those in the public sector, to continue earning a living and saving for their retirement (Tung and Comeau 2012). The government also has in place a pension scheme that provides a small sum of money for people over 60 who have nowhere to live, no income and are in need of state protection. But aside from this safety net there is no government funding available for retirement. Institutional facilities are also rare. The government funds just 22 Activity Centres for the elderly and nine homes for the ageing poor. NGOs and church groups provide home visits to the elderly and the sick, and there are 96 homes run by NGOs for elderly patients requiring constant care. Aside from these charitable organisations little else is available (Ambigga et al. 2011). One exception is a number of aged care housing complexes modelled on aged-care facilities in Australia, targeted primarily at retired Chinese Malaysians, who buy units in these complexes and are moved on to full-time care facilities with trained staff, with the cost of care taken out of the unit price, when they become ill or frail (*New Straits Times* 2012). These aged care complexes are costly to buy into and beyond the reach of most families. Moreover, even if they were affordable, the majority of Malaysians of all ethnic backgrounds continue to believe that ageing parents are the responsibility of the family.

The story of Param, a woman in her 40s who cares for both her children and ageing parents, illustrates the problem of aged care in Malaysia (Interview, September 2014). Her parents would call her with problems on a regular basis, and she would drive to their home an hour away to make sure they were in good health and help them solve their problems. The phone calls and driving after a long day at work caused her great stress and anxiety, and eventually she decided that the best solution was to move her parents into her own home. As Param's experience suggests, care is still very much an individualised responsibility, and in her case a gendered one. The solution Param decided upon meets the obligations of filial piety as encapsulated in the Malaysian government's conception of 'Asian

Values' (Mahathir 1999).[6] It is also not unusual. A study conducted by Yusoff and Buja (2013) found that in 2008 a large percentage of the aged population were supported by their working children. Another study looking at the intergenerational relationships among the rural aged in Malaysia found that the family is regarded as a source of support for the care of the elderly (Aziz and Yusoff 2012).

While families prefer to care for their loved ones in need, balancing the demands of earning a living in the paid workforce and caring for family members is becoming more difficult. As a consequence, many middle-class Malaysian families depend on overseas domestic workers to meet their care needs. The increasing autonomy of middle-class women engaged in education, business and professional work, rests heavily on the availability of low-paid domestic help and childcare. Indeed, in the absence of satisfactory institutional arrangements, support for the employment of foreign domestic workers has been a key government strategy for encouraging middle-class women's sustained engagement in paid work (Chin 1998).

The number of registered foreign domestic workers has increased from around 70,000 in the 1990s to 300,000 in 2015 (World Bank 2015b). Since the 1980s, there have also been significant flows of irregular domestic workers recruited by families through contacts with other domestic workers. Anecdotal evidence suggests that large numbers of domestic workers without proper documentation are employed in the homes of lower-paid families as well as higher-paid households across Malaysia. Government regulations regarding the employment of foreign domestic workers allow only families with a certain level of income to employ domestic workers. However, many families that do not meet these requirements employ domestic workers without going through government channels.[7] Wealthier Malays employ migrant domestic workers from Indonesia, who share the same religion and language. Indonesian domestic workers are often incorporated into the patriarchal family alongside other female family members, albeit with fewer freedoms. It is not uncommon for domestic workers to stay with the same family for many years, especially if they are treated well, or to bring other family members to work for the relatives of their employers in Malaysia. Chinese and Indian Malaysians tend to employ more educated Filipino women if they can afford them, or rely on domestic workers from Indonesia or Cambodia to care for family and aged parents (Chin 1998).

These foreign domestic workers release Malaysian women from child and eldercare, as well as from household chores, leaving them more time to pursue their careers. Women's position as both producers and consumers of care work has thus been integral to the economic development of Malaysia.

Pressure points

While the Malaysian government has clearly made significant attempts to better address the care needs of pre-school-age children, its partial approach to care needs as a whole leaves many issues unaddressed. One of the main challenges is the declining fertility rate, which means that there will be fewer Malaysian citizens to provide the care and support necessary for an ageing population in the future. Policies to help improve the work–care balance for poor families and allow middle-class families access to low-paid foreign domestic workers go some way to shoring up women's increased labour force participation, but they are insufficient to deal with the magnitude of the looming demographic problem. To respond effectively, the government must address the social and cultural gender norms pertaining to responsibility for the provision of care. Directing policies at women, rather than parents in need of care, and to daughters, rather than male and female children equally, reinforces the assumption that childcare and eldercare are women's problems, not family problems. Shifting the focus of state and employer policies to include both male and female parents would at the very least encourage a more equal sharing of household, childcare and eldercare responsibilities.

Malaysia's reliance on foreign domestic workers as a way of meeting care needs also raises issues that have not been adequately addressed by the Malaysian government. The market for domestic workers rests on the government's recognition that domestic work is waged employment and domestic workers must be paid a minimum wage. Yet, as Elias (2013) has argued, the government in Malaysia has institutionalised a system that relies on foreign labour because it is so poorly paid. Moreover, the fact that the sector is dominated by migrant workers who live in their employers' homes raises the added issue of vulnerability to abuse. Employers control their domestic workers by holding their passports, limiting their time away from the family, and insisting they work long days. In 2009, the Indonesian government stopped the deployment of Indonesian women to Malaysia due to the high number of reported cases of domestic worker abuse.[8] Indonesia ended its embargo on domestic workers in 2011, after the Malaysian government guaranteed workers would be entitled to keep their passports and allowed one day off per week (Elias 2013). However, little has been done to enforce these provisions, as the government continues to assume that Indonesian or Cambodian women can be replaced with workers from poor countries elsewhere in the region if the embargoes are re-imposed. But basic rights remain a serious problem (Devadason and Chan 2014), which may eventually lead to a collapse of the system.

Civil society responses have been similarly inadequate. While trade unions have strategies in place to increase their female membership, they do not concentrate on how members manage work and care. Female unionists have claimed that there are programmes to address work–life balance in some union-friendly companies in the banking sector, but in many cases work and care is still considered a 'women's issue' that does not need to be dealt with by the union (Crinis 2008). Responses from women's groups have been more focused. The feminist Muslim NGO Sisters in Islam (2011) stresses that gender equality remains an important issue for a government that continues to discriminate against women by failing to introduce policies and incentives to make marriage and family compatible with the economic and political participation of women. However, most NGOs do not address the moral interpretations embedded in official positions on the role of women in the family.

Writing about feminism and the women's movement in Malaysia, Ng, Mohamad and Tan (2006) recommended that the government play a more interventionist role, putting policies in place to enable families to balance family and work and making them transparent and enforceable. Such a transition is likely to prove impossible without serious disruption of the gender roles entrenched in Malaysian society. Without such a disruption, women's participation in the workforce will not increase. Although the government has recognised the need to develop infrastructure to support women's attempts to balance the demands of work and care and has established a substantial policy agenda, these policies build on the status quo rather than disrupting it. As a consequence, difficult questions regarding gendered responsibility for care work and Malaysia's reliance on foreign domestic labour remain unanswered, leaving Malaysian society vulnerable to labour force deficits, the policies of foreign governments and women's changing expectations with regard to work.

Notes

1 The chapter is based on qualitative research conducted in Malaysia between 2013 and 2014, secondary sources and government documents, and on Crinis' earlier research on the history of Malaysian women and work. The interview sample consists of women and families of different classes and ethnicities in Peninsular Malaysia.

2 Statistics suggesting a dearth of women in the higher paying managerial positions in the private sector also obscure the fact that as women move up the scale their male counterparts continue to receive higher wages. While some women earn higher wages than male workers in unskilled work, they 'are more likely to receive less than male workers as they reach the higher-paying positions' (UNDP 2013, 195).

3 In a complementary strategy, the government stopped the entry of Indian and Chinese labour and allowed a number of Muslim Filipino refugees from the southern Philippines into Sabah as well as large numbers of Indonesian workers to enter the plantation sector (Pillai 1992).

4 Field observations suggest that women working in food-stalls and restaurants keep their children at the back of the premises. Female taxi drivers also often care for their school-aged children while they work. The children sit quietly in the front of the taxi until their mothers finish work.

5 Women employed in the private sector are entitled to 60 days leave or, in some companies, less time and no income or, in others, a partial income.

6 The Asian Values debate began in the 1990s, when the leaders of Malaysia and Singapore argued against universal human rights on the Western model in favour of an emphasis on economic development and communal values. The then Malaysian Prime Minister Mahathir (1999), who was critical of the rights of the individual over the rights of the community, argued that the family would take care of its members.

7 These migrant workers are utilised in the informal economy as well as the care economy. It is not unusual to find migrant workers helping their employers in street stalls and home-based work.

8 Similar embargoes were imposed by the Philippine government in the 1990s and the Cambodian government in 2011.

References

Ambigga, K.S., A.S. Ramli, A. Suthahar, N. Tauhid, L. Clearihan and C. Browning. 2011. "Bridging the Gap in Ageing: Translating Policies into Practice in Malaysian Primary Care." *Asia Pacific Family Medicine 10 (2).* http://www.apfmj.com/content/10/1/2.

Aziz, R.A. and F. Yusoff. 2012. "Intergenerational Relations and Communication among the Rural Aged in Malaysia." *Asian Social Science* 8 (6): 184–185.

Boo, S.-L. 2014. "Malaysia's Missing Women Workers." Malaymailonline, 1 July http://www.themalaymailonline.com/malaysia/article/malaysias-missing-women-workers.

Chin, C. 1998. *In Service and Servitude: Foreign Female Domestic Workers and the Malaysian 'Modernity' Project.* New York: Columbia University Press.

Crinis, V. 2008. "Malaysia: Women, Labour Activism and Unions." In *Women and Labour Organizing in Asia: Diversity, Autonomy and Activism*, edited by K. Broadbent and M. Ford, 50–65. London: Routledge.

Crinis, V. 2013. "Vietnamese Migrant Clothing Workers in Malaysia: Global Production Transnational Labour Migration and Social Reproduction." In *The Global Political Economy of the Household in Asia*, edited by J. Elias and S. Gunawardana, 162–177. Hampshire: Palgrave Macmillan.

Department of Statistics Malaysia, Official Portal https://www.statistics.gov.my/index.php?r=column/cthemeByCat&cat=155&bul_id=OWlxdEVoYlJCS0hUZzJyRUcvZEYxZz09&menu_id=L0pheU43NWJwRWVSZklWdzQ4TlhUUT09 (accessed March 2015)

Devadason, E.S., and W.M. Chan. 2014. "Policies and Laws Regulating Migrant Workers in Malaysia." *Journal of Contemporary Asia* 44 (1): 19–35.

Elias, J. 2013. "Foreign Policy and the Domestic Worker." *International Feminist Journal of Politics* 15 (3): 391–410.

Government of Malaysia. 2010. "Moving towards Inclusive Socio-Economic Development" Chapter 4 *Tenth Malaysia Plan.* https://www.pmo.gov.my/dokumenattached/RMK/RMK10_Eds.pdf.

Government of Malaysia. 2013. *Labour Force Survey Report.* Kuala Lumpur: Department of Statistics Malaysia. http://www.statistics.gov.my/portal/index.php?option=com_content&id=1864%-force-survey-report-malaysia&lang=en.

Heng Keng Chiam. 2008. "Childcare in Malaysia: Then and Now." *International Journal of Childcare and Education Policy* 2 (2): 31–41.

Heyzer, N., ed. 1988. *Daughters in Industry.* Kuala Lumpur: Asia Pacific Development Centre.

ILO. 2013. *ILOSTAT Database, Annual Indicators*. https://www.ilo.org/ilostat.

Karim, Wazir Jahan (ed). 1995. *Male and Female in Developing Southeast Asia* Oxford: Berg Publishers.

Karim, Dato' Sri R.A. 2014. "Statement of the Honourable Dato' Sri Rohani Abdul Karim, Minister of Women, Family and Community Development, Malaysia." Press Release, 11 March. http://niew.gov.my/…/press%20release%20YBM%20New%20York%201.

Kaur, A. and I. Metcalfe. 1999. "Economy and Society." In *The Shaping of Malaysia,* edited by A. Kaur and I, Metcalfe, 121–173. Basingstoke: Macmillan.

Loh-Ludher, L.L. 2007. "Homeworkers Online: Utilization of ICT for Home-Based Work in Malaysia." *The Electronic Journal on Information Systems in Developing Countries* 32 (5): 1–14.

Mahari, Z. 2011. "Demographic Transition in Malaysia: The Changing Roles of Women." Paper presented at the 15th Conference of Commonwealth Statisticians, New Delhi, India, 7–10 February.

Mahathir, M. 1999. *A New Deal for Asia.* Pelanduk Publications: Kuala Lumpur.

New Straits Times, 2012. "First Jeta Aged Care Opens in Malaysia." 28 June. http://www2.nst.com.my/nation/general/first-jeta-care-aged-centre-opens-in-jb-1.98996.

Ng, C., M. Mohamad and T.B. Hui. 2006. *Feminism and the Women's Movement in Malaysia.* Routledge: New York.

Omar, Z. and A. Ahmad. 2009. "Why Organisations Adopt Family Friendly Policy: A Case of Corporate Childcare Centre in a Manufacturing Company". *UNITAR E Journal* 5 (1): 1–19.

Pillai, P. 1992. *People on the Move: An Overview of Recent Immigration and Emigration in Malaysia.* Kuala Lumpur: Institute of Strategic and International Studies.

Razavi, S. 2007. *The Political and Social Economy of Care in a Development Context.* Geneva: UNRISD.

Sander, F., G. Intan, N. Jalil, X. Carpio, and K. Patrick. 2012. "Unlocking Women's Potential." *Malaysia Economic Monitor.* http://documents.worldbank.org/curated/en/2012/11/17017962/malaysia-economic-monitor-unlocking-womens-potential.

Sisters in Islam. 2011. "Closing the Gender Gap" *The Star*, 13 March. http://www.sistersinislam.org.my/news.php?item.775.6.

Stivens, M. 1987. "Family and the State in Malaysian Industrialisation: The Case of Rembau, Negeri Sembilan, Malaysia." In *Women, State and Ideology: Studies in Africa and Asia*, edited by H. Afshar, 89–110. London: MacMillan.

Sundaram, J.K. 1988. *A Question of Class: Capital, the State and Uneven Development in Malaya.* Singapore: Oxford University Press.

TalentCorp and ACCA. 2013. "Retaining Women in the Workforce." https://www.talentcorp.com.my/2013/03/06/talentcorp-acca-malaysia-report-on-retaining-women-in-the-workforce/.

Teoh, W.M.Y. and S.C. Chong. 2014. "Towards Strengthening the Development of Women Entrepreneurship in Malaysia" *Gender in Management: An International Journal* 29 (7): 432–453.

Thambiah, S. 2010. "The Productive and Non-(Re)productive Women: Sites of Economic Growth in Malaysia." *Asian Women* 26 (2): 49–76.

Tung, L.C. and J.D. Comeau. 2012. "Perceived Benefits and Drawbacks of the Retirement Age Policy in Malaysia: HR Perspective." *International Journal of Business and Management* 7 (19): 1–15.

UNDP. 2013. *Malaysian Human Development Report: Chapter 9: Women and Inclusive Growth in Malaysia*. Geneva: United Nations.

World Bank. 2015a. *Health Nutrition and Population Statistics: Population Estimates and Projections.* http://databank.worldbank.org/Data/Views/VariableSelection/SelectVariables.aspx?source=Health%20Nutrition%20and%20Population%20Statistics:%20Population%20estimates%20and%20projections.

World Bank. 2015b. *Malaysia Economic Monitor: Immigrant Labour*. http://documents.worldbank.org/curated/en/2015/12/25693867/malaysia-economic-monitor-immigrant-labor.

Yusoff, S.N., and G.A. Buja. 2013. "Aged Society: The Way Forward." *International Journal of Trade, Economics and Finance* 4 (4): 226–291.

4 Singapore

Contradictions in the work/care regime

Lenore Lyons

A highly industrialised city-state with a total population of 5.47 million, Singapore provides an instructive case study of the role of the state in managing the work of caregiving in ways that maintain strongly gendered roles within families and within society as a whole. Government policies actively entrench gender roles that see women as reproducers of the nation, while at the same time recognising that rapid social change has necessitated government intervention in family life (Graham et al. 2002; Lyons 2004). As the rate of women's participation in the labour force has increased, an endless array of social policies aimed at supporting 'family life' has emerged. Paradoxically, much of the policy effort in relation to care work is focused on limiting the government's role in relation to the care needs of the population. Implicit in these policies is the view that the burden of caring for the young and the aged is the responsibility of households and not the public or private sectors. As a result, paid care services occupy a very small sector of the economy; in the case of eldercare, in particular, state-operated care services are designed as an option of last resort. The government argues that these interventions are necessary to avoid the otherwise inevitable excesses of the welfare state and the harmful effects of 'westernisation' on traditional Asian family values.

While caregiving is regarded as a natural expression and outcome of women's reproductive and nurturing roles and capacities, not all women are targeted in policies directed at 'women' and 'the family' and not all play an equal role in producing the nation's young and caring for its elderly. For large numbers of women engaged in low- and semi-skilled low-income jobs, redeployment in caregiving roles within the family is seen as both strengthening 'family values' and opening up a space for unskilled male labour. By contrast, the caregiving responsibilities of those in skilled middle- and high-income occupations are outsourced to other women in order to ensure that the nation's economic prosperity is not compromised as a result of their exit from the paid workforce. For increasing numbers of middle-class households, these other women are foreign nationals who form part of a large migrant labour force. In these families, the physical work of care giving is performed by migrant workers and the emotional and intellectual labour of caring by their female employers.

This chapter explores a range of state policies which regulate women's labour and family formation in order to understand how ethnicity, class and nationality are embedded in the practices and politics of work and caregiving. It concludes that the Singapore state has been successful in its goal of limiting state responsibility for providing institutionalised care by drawing on the interconnected discourses of Asian family values and individual responsibility. The inevitable pressure points produced by the lived realities of managing the work/care nexus have been relieved by a reliance on cheap, unskilled migrant labour. The greatest challenge to this status quo will emerge as the full effects of a looming aged care crisis are felt.

Women and work

As a consequence of Singapore's rapid industrialisation since its separation from Malaysia in 1965, most Singaporeans are employed in formal sector occupations, with 85 per cent of employed persons designated as employees, and just 0.5 per cent as contributing family workers in 2014 (Ministry of Manpower 2014a). Singapore's industrialisation policies also prompted a significant increase in women's labour force participation. Through the 1970s and 1980s, the growth of export-oriented manufacturing saw large numbers of women enter into waged labour in factories. The subsequent shift from a manufacturing-based economy to one dominated by banking, finance and telecommunications in the 1990s opened

Table 4.1 Working resident population 15 years of age and over by industry and sex, 2014

Industry	*No. Workers ('000s)*	*Male (%)*	*Female (%)*
Manufacturing	249.3	65.3	34.7
Construction	98.2	74.3	25.7
Services	1,731.2	52.4	47.6
Wholesale and retail trade	346.3	50.9	49.1
Public administration and education	285.2	54.7	45.3
Transportation and storage	188.9	75.7	24.3
Financial and insurance services	165.6	48.9	51.1
Professional Services	153.0	52.5	47.4
Accommodation and food services	137.1	44.3	55.7
Health and social services	107.7	23.0	77.0
Administrative and support services	102.7	58.1	41.8
Information and communications	87.8	61.2	38.8
Other community, social and personal services	66.3	41.5	58.5
Real estate services	55.6	50.0	50.2
Arts, entertainment and recreation	35.1	47.9	52.1
Total	2,103.5	55.2	44.8

Source: June figures adapted from Singapore Department of Statistics (2015a).

up new employment opportunities for women, with this sector now employing almost equal numbers of women and men (Table 4.1).

These changes led to a doubling of the women's labour force participation rate in the space of 45 years, from 28.2 per cent in 1970 to 58.6 per cent in 2014. During this same period, male labour force participation declined, from 81.2 per cent in 1970 to 75.9 per cent in 2014 (Singapore Department of Statistics 2014c). When the data is limited to those of prime working age (25–54 years), the rate for men has been broadly stable at 92 per cent since the mid-1980s, whereas the employment rate for women rose to a record high of 76 per cent in 2014 (see Table 4.2). There are, however, some important differences in occupational spread. In the service sector, for example, women dominate low-paying health occupations, while men dominate the higher-paying information technology and communication sectors. When occupational category is considered, men comprise a larger proportion of senior officials and managers (66 per cent) and women dominate in the clerical and support sector (75.6 per cent) (Singapore Department of Statistics 2015a). These differences are reflected in average monthly earnings for employees: in 2013, men earned an average of $5,291 per month whereas women earned $3,909 (Ministry of Manpower 2014b).

Importantly also, the rate of economic inactivity among women (42 per cent) remains almost double that for men (24 per cent). This gap cannot be explained by differences in educational opportunities: the literacy rate for residents over the age of 15 years is 96.7 per cent, and 72.3 per cent of men and 67.1 per cent of women over 25 years of age have secondary or higher educational qualifications (Singapore Department of Statistics 2014a). Rather, the gap in economic activity

Table 4.2 Labour force participation rates (citizens and permanent residents), 2014

Age Group	*Overall*	*Male (%)*	*Female (%)*
15 – 19	12.3	14.9	9.6
20 – 24	61.8	63.6	59.8
25 – 29	89.0	89.4	88.6
30 – 34	89.9	97.5	83.3
35 – 39	88.8	97.2	80.9
40 – 44	87.1	96.8	78.1
45 – 49	84.7	96.4	73.7
50 – 54	81.8	93.8	70.4
55 – 59	74.3	87.5	61.4
60 – 64	61.2	77.0	45.5
65 – 69	41.2	54.1	29.5
70 – 74	25.7	37.3	15.6
75 & over	8.4	13.6	4.7
Total	67.0	75.9	58.6

Source: June adapted from Singapore Department of Statistics (2015c).

reflects differences in social expectations about men's and women's caring roles and responsibilities and a lack of flexibility in employment practices. As Table 4.2 indicates, participation rates for men and women are closest in the years prior to marriage. The gap begins to widen as women enter their thirties and forties and thereafter remains static. Of those women not employed in 2014, 80 per cent cited 'family responsibilities' as the reason they were neither working nor looking for employment. By contrast, the main reasons that men aged 25 to 54 cited for remaining outside the labour force were poor health/disability or education and training (Ministry of Manpower 2014a). Ethnicity is another key determinant of participation rates for women. The resident population consists primarily of three main ethnic groups – Chinese (74 per cent), Malays (13 per cent) and Indians (9.1 per cent) (Singapore Department of Statistics 2014b). Data from the 1980s and 1990s shows that the participation rate has consistently been lower for Malay women than for Indians and Chinese, a disparity that is largest during women's primary childbearing years (Yeoh and Huang 1995).

In an economy that is increasingly reliant on the highly skilled communications and finance sectors, relegating Singaporean women to necessary but unskilled occupations such as care work is seen as detrimental to continued economic growth (Table 4.3). Yet, in contrast to many other industrialised countries, the aim of increasing women's labour force participation has not been achieved through the promotion of part-time work. Government policies have focused instead on the importation of female domestic workers as part of a deliberate strategy to address the combined challenge of an extremely low fertility rate and an ageing population that places the 'self-reliant family' at its centre (Teo and Piper 2009). As of 2014 there were some 222,500 foreign women employed as domestic workers in Singapore, or approximately one worker to every five households (Singapore Department of Statistics 2015b). Relatively large numbers of women are also employed as nurses or allied healthcare workers. One study of Filipino nurses revealed that in 2008 there were 8,710 Filipinos, including Singapore permanent residents, working in nursing-related occupations in Singapore (Choi and Lyons 2012). Workers in nursing homes, meanwhile, are predominantly recruited from the Philippines, China, India and Myanmar (Huang, Yeoh and Toyota 2012).

Migrant workers of different nationalities are normalised in different roles that manifest as national and racial stereotypes about which migrants are the best

Table 4.3 Labour force composition by resident status, 2014

Industry	*Resident ('000s)*	*Foreign ('000s)*	*Total ('000s)*
Manufacturing	259.6	276.4	536.0
Construction	122.7	368.7	491.4
Services (including domestic work)	1,863.7	706.0	2,569.7
Other (including utilities, agriculture)	22.2	4.6	26.8
Total	2,268.2	1,355.7	3,623.9

Source: Adapted from Table 2, Ministry of Manpower (2015a).

fit for different types of work (Huang, Yeoh and Toyota 2012). Filipinas, while considered more outspoken, are also believed to be smarter, and therefore better suited to childcare than Indonesians, who are often described as 'docile and stupid', and therefore better suited to eldercare. This hierarchy of migrant status is also reflected in female migrant workers' immigration status, wages and conditions of work. Under the Employment of Foreign Manpower Act (EFMA) and associated regulations, migrant workers are divided into three broad categories, namely professionals (Employment Pass holders), mid-level skilled workers (S Pass holders) and unskilled workers (Work Permit holders). While the visa category is meant to reflect different working conditions, the boundaries are often blurred. For example, skilled nurses may find themselves working as foreign domestic workers in homes or as cleaners in hospitals (Choi and Lyons 2012).

In addition to having the lowest status, foreign domestic workers' conditions of work are subject to the least amount of regulation. The state consistently argues that it cannot regulate the working conditions of foreign domestic workers because the needs and requirements of each family are different, and so each household requires a unique care solution that cannot be dictated by a standard labour contract. This reluctance to grant greater labour protections to foreign domestic workers can be understood as a reflection of the desire to keep wages low in order to keep skilled Singaporean women in the workforce while alleviating the need for the state to play a more active role in the provision of viable care options outside the household (Lyons 2007).

Caring for children and the elderly

From a policy perspective, childcare has attracted a far greater level of scrutiny than eldercare in Singapore. Yet, in demographic terms, an ageing population is arguably the more pressing social issue, with life expectancy having increased from 72 to 82 years in the two decades to 2010 (National Population and Talent Division 2012) and the number of people 65 years and older projected to almost triple from 193,605 in 2005 to 588,000 by 2025 (Figure 4.1). The combination of low mortality and low fertility rates has a significant impact on the old-age dependency ratio – the number of residents aged 20 to 64 per resident 65 years and older – which is projected to decline from 5.2 in 2014 to 2.1 in 2030 (National Population and Talent Division 2012).

Yet while Singapore may now be described as having ultra-low fertility (Jones, Straughan and Chan 2008), this was not always the case. Between 1965 and 1984 the government's emphasis was on population control. The main family planning policies, implemented via the Singapore Family Planning and Population Board (SFPPB), were aimed at encouraging people to marry later, to delay having their first child and to 'Stop at Two' (Quah 1988). In combination with women's increased labour force participation rate, increasing educational levels, and rising affluence, these policies had the effect of dramatically reducing the fertility rate, which dropped from 4.62 in 1965 to reach the replacement level of 2.1 in 1975 (Saw 1990) and thereafter continued to decrease to an all-time low of 1.15 children per resident female in 2010 (Singapore Department of Statistics 2014d).

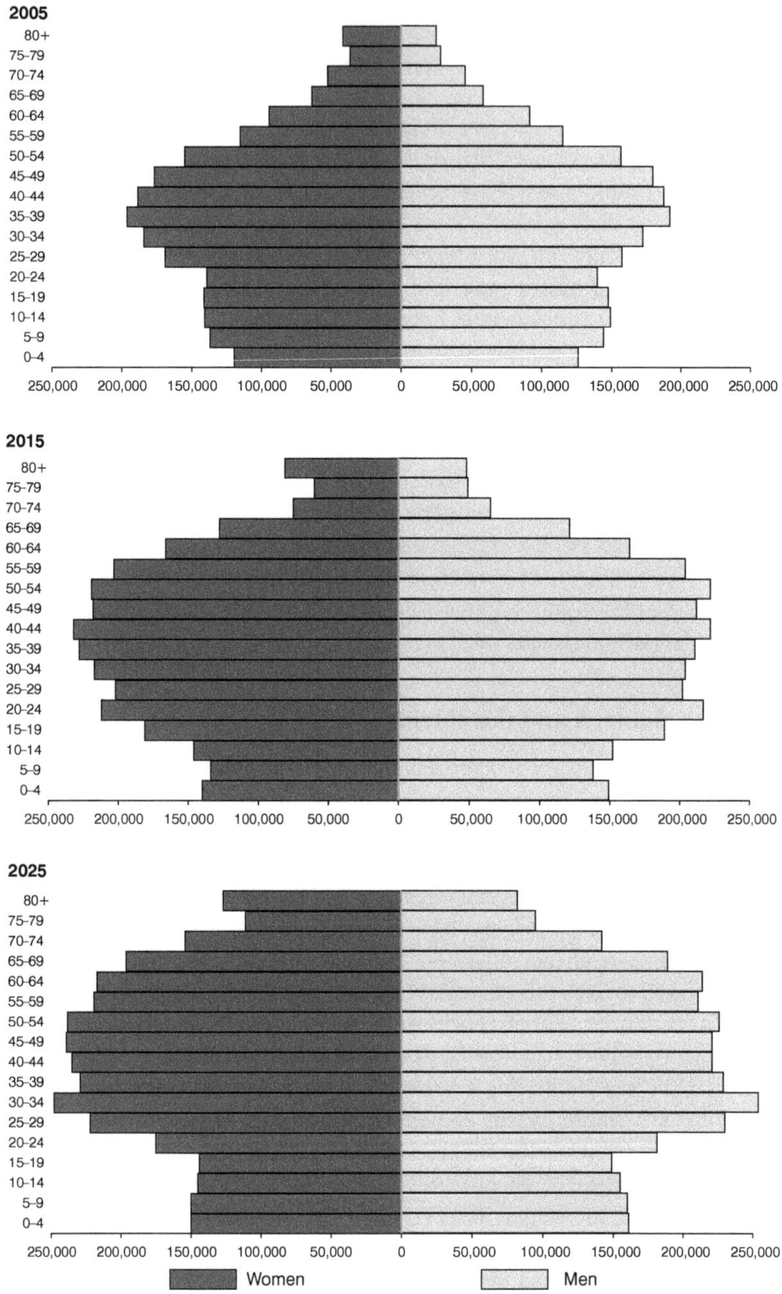

Figure 4.1 Population 2005, 2015, and 2025

Source: World Bank (2015).

An unintentional effect of these earlier policies has been a differential reduction in birth rates, whereby women with higher levels of education now have a significantly smaller number of children than less-educated women. This issue was first identified as a social problem in the mid-1980s when then Prime Minister Lee Kuan Yew called attention to a tendency for women with a tertiary education to delay or forgo marriage and children for their careers. Signalling his concern that a decline in the birth rate among the well-educated would result in a thinning of the gene pool, and subsequently to national economic disaster in a country whose only resource was its people, Lee asserted that well-educated women's roles as mothers was not only to pass on superior genes to their offspring, but also to instil superior Asian values through their roles as nurturers/educators (Lyons-Lee 1998). Lee's arguments also reflected a thinly veiled concern about the potential impact on economic growth and social stability if the proportion of Chinese (the largest ethnic group) were to decline (Heng and Devan 1995). In subsequent discussion of this issue, the two changes in demographic behaviour repeatedly referred to were the increasing number of unmarried women with tertiary education and the lower reproduction rate among Chinese.

Considered to be social problems because they contributed to a loss of talent, a loss of future labour power, and an imbalance in the proportion of aged dependants (Quah 1994), these trends prompted a dramatic change in government policy. A new form of pro-natalism, focused on more highly educated (Chinese) women, encouraged women to have two or more children, using a combination of carrot-and-stick strategies that included subsidies, tax relief, and differential access to childcare for women of different educational and class backgrounds (Lyons-Lee 1998). Combined with a selective migration policy, these strategies have succeeded in maintaining the balance in Singapore's ethnic composition. However, as young, professional women continue to delay marriage until their thirties and fertility rates are not rising, state incentives have failed to address the mismatch between Chinese Singaporean women's career aspirations and prevailing attitudes towards marriage and childrearing.

Childcare

In Singapore, most childcare takes place within the child's home or in the home of a family member, and is performed by a family member (usually by the mother or a grandparent) supplemented, where circumstances permit, by a foreign domestic worker. Where institutional childcare is provided, it takes three forms – infant care centres for children aged six to 18 months, childcare centres for children between 18 months and six years, and kindergartens for children aged four to six years, which they typically attend for three to four hours per day. The institutional care environment includes state-sponsored childcare organisations, subsidised state-licensed forms of care provided by religious and voluntary organisations including trade unions, and private sector organisations. In 1982 there were only 33 centres offering 2,023 places, but this grew to 319 centres offering 23,235 places by 1993 (Yeoh and Huang 1995), and 1,160 centres offering 111,535 childcare centre places as of January 2015 (Early Childhood Development Agency 2015). Despite the increasing number of places, however, these facilities remain undersubscribed. For example, in 2014, only 83,928 out of the 109,694 childcare centre places were taken up, and of these, just 75,518 were full-time enrolments (Early Childhood Development Agency 2015).

The relatively minor role performed by childcare centres is explained by a number of factors, including cost, convenience and the perceived quality of care. There are significant differences in preferences for the type of childcare among different ethnic groups. A study of childcare practices conducted in the 1990s found that 40 per cent of Chinese and Indian women employed a live-in domestic worker, whereas only 7.4 per cent of Malay women used this form of care. Chinese and Indian families were also more likely to use childcare centres than Malay families (Yeoh and Huang 1995). Among those who used childcare centres as their primary form of care, Indian women preferred half-day or shorter centre-based care, while Chinese women preferred full-day care. By contrast, Malay women working outside the home preferred informal arrangements where children were left in the care of grandparents or other relatives.

The choices made by women of different ethnic backgrounds reflect prevailing attitudes about the 'best' form of care, concerns about language and religious practices (particularly among the Malay community), and the strong correlation between ethnicity and income levels. Malay families make up the bulk of low-income households and are the least likely to be able to afford paid childcare. Birth rates are also highest among this group, reflecting the tendency for Malay women to marry earlier than their Chinese and Indian counterparts and cultural attitudes regarding preferred family size (Yeoh and Huang 1995). As noted earlier, in comparison to Malay women, Chinese and Indian women have higher education levels, marry later, and have higher incomes, giving them the financial means to subcontract childcare responsibilities using a combination of formal childcare, unpaid family care and/or foreign domestic workers. In addition, like many public institutions, childcare centres reflect the cultural and language practices of the majority Chinese population, despite the fact that they are open to all citizens, which reinforces the preference of minority groups for other forms of care.

Eldercare

As with childcare, the family is the primary site of eldercare in Singapore (Ansah et al. 2013). The vast majority of older Singaporeans remain in their own home or the home of a relative as they age. Unlike childcare, however, there is strong, unmet demand for institutionalised eldercare. In many cases, the elderly are cared for within the family because there are no alternative care options. As of 2013, there were just 10,410 residents – 2 per cent of the elderly population – in aged care homes (Singapore Department of Statistics 2014d). Already, consumer demand for eldercare is quite different from that for childcare. Whereas childcare places are undersubscribed, there are long waiting lists for aged care facilities. It is unlikely that institutionalised care organisations will be able to address the demand for nursing home places, even at current investment rates. Although the state has proposed increasing the number of nursing home beds by as much as 50 per cent by 2020 (Østbye et al. 2013), this will do little to address the demand for aged care services as the age dependency rate increases. The labour market dynamics of the sector are also different. Institutional childcare workers are primarily Singaporean nationals, reflecting social concerns about the transmission of cultural values. By contrast, foreign workers constitute 80–90 per cent of the workforce of nursing homes that provide long-term eldercare (Huang, Yeoh and Toyota 2012).

As with institutionalised childcare, affordability and accessibility are critical issues in the uptake of aged care services. Although government subsidies are available to assist with the costs of eldercare, families report that these are insufficient to cover long-term acute care or situations where the family unit is comprised of an unmarried or single adult looking after two elderly parents (Teo, Chan and Straughan 2003). Families who look after the elderly at home also face difficulties accessing non-residential day care services. They may be unable to transport their elderly parents to community centres due to a lack of private vehicles, the high cost of taxi services and/or a lack of disabled taxi services, and the location of facilities a long distance from their homes (Ansah et al. 2013). As a consequence, many families rely on a foreign domestic worker for the provision of care. One national survey found that 55 per cent of those aged 60 and above had a family member as the primary caregiver, and the remainder relied on foreign domestic workers – largely Indonesians – for primary care. Of these, 79 per cent had hired them specifically to look after aged persons (Huang, Yeoh and Toyota 2012).

Even more so than in the case of childcare, the state positions eldercare as a familial responsibility, as reflected in the fact that community support services for the elderly can cost up to 50 per cent more than the cost of hiring a foreign domestic worker to assist with eldercare (Ansah et al. 2013). From the perspective of family members, employment of a foreign domestic worker has the added benefit of additional services such as cleaning, cooking, and aspects of childcare. However, while in-home care in the form of foreign domestic workers would appear to offer the most viable solution for those families who can afford it, it is also fraught. The majority of foreign domestic workers who perform eldercare lack specific skills or training in the physical and mental healthcare needs of the elderly. The work they perform is repetitive, tiring, and emotionally charged, and most are unable to communicate effectively with their elderly charges and are subject to multiple power dynamics involving employers, other family members and care recipients.

Government policies on work and care

A defining feature of Singapore's regulatory regimes is that they are more discursive than coercive. The electoral dominance of the ruling People's Action Party (PAP) and legislative measures to effectively stifle alternative political voices mean that the state has been able to deploy discourses of 'national good' and 'meritocracy' to produce and reinforce its vision of nation-building and citizenship with relatively little dissent. The state's capacity to deliver prosperity and its demonstrated commitment to clean government means most citizens feel confident in their interactions with state and quasi-state organisations which, when combined with complex messages about benevolence and authoritarianism, encourages self-regulation by Singapore's citizens. These characteristics are evident in the cluster of policy arenas related to reproduction, including housing, superannuation, healthcare, childcare, aged care and migration, which together produce a generally coherent, if sometimes inconsistent, response to the work/care nexus in Singapore.

Avowedly anti-welfarist and pro-business, the government acts as both a defender of 'traditional Asian family values' and a supporter of women's access to employment based on the principles of meritocracy and national good. Although employers' associations and trade unions have been involved in tripartite discussions on ways to promote 'work–life harmony' – including discussion of flexible work practices and employee support schemes (Ministry of Manpower 2015c) – employers may choose to provide targeted benefits to attract and retain employees, but have no formal responsibility to do so. Instead, the Singapore state promotes the view that the provision of care for the young and the elderly is a private matter to be worked out between family members. The government's goal is thus to assist families (a euphemism for married women) to manage the competing demands of care work and paid employment by subsidising the care that takes place within the family through the provision of paid maternity leave, paid and unpaid childcare leave, a baby bonus, and increased tax relief, tax rebates and childcare subsidies (Sun 2012).

The application of these schemes reflects the state's differential approach to different social classes. For example, a key element of the Foreign Domestic Maid Scheme is the 'maid levy', which the state requires employers to pay monthly. Households are eligible for a concessional levy if they hire domestic workers to take care of children below 16 years old (Ministry of Manpower 2015b).[1] In addition, working mothers who are married, divorced or widowed are eligible for tax relief equal to twice the amount of the levy paid regardless of the number of hours worked. This relief is not available for unmarried women and men or divorced/widowed women without children even if they are the ones in a given household who pay the levy that this rebate is designed to offset (Teo 2007). Similar privileging of married mothers occurs in relation to the provision of childcare services, with working married women receiving SGD 300 and non-employed mothers SGD 150 in subsidies. Additional subsidies are available for children from households that earn less than SGD 7,500 (or SGD 1,875 per capita in households with at least five people, including at least two dependants), but to qualify for them a mother (or where no mother is present, a single father) must work at least 56 hours per month (Early Childhood Development Agency 2013). This system of tax relief and subsidies for married women reinforces the state's view that well-educated, *married* women should be mothers (the eugenics argument) and full-time workers (the nation needs indigenous talent to drive the economy). Importantly, while women are accorded primary responsibility for childcare, as full-time workers they can successfully perform this role via direct supervision of others (foreign domestic workers, relatives or care workers) who undertake the repetitive, mundane chores associated with the physical labour of caregiving.

State housing policies also support family-based care. The Housing and Development Board, which supplies over 80 per cent of housing in Singapore, stipulates eligibility criteria that reinforce the formation of heterosexual married families (Quah 1988). The Board prioritises applications for apartments that enable married persons and their families to live in close proximity to one another, through prioritisation of applications for flats in the same or adjoining blocks or under the same roof (Multi-Tier Family Housing), in order to make it possible for grandparents to care for young children and adult children to care for their elderly parents. These regulations also make it difficult for non-married persons to obtain access to public housing, with the result that many remain in the same household with their parents, which has the effect of reinforcing unmarried women's roles as carers for the elderly.

As suggested above, regulations governing the employment of migrant domestic workers are another policy tool used to decrease reliance on institutionalised eldercare. Families employing a foreign domestic worker may also apply to pay the concessional levy if their households include elderly persons aged 65 years or above. The reduction in the levy is seen by some commentators as one of the main factors determining the preference for and dependence on foreign domestic workers as eldercarers within the home (Østbye et al. 2013). By manipulating the cost of the levy, and making subsidies available for middle-class women in full-time employment, the state makes eldercare within the home a seemingly natural outcome of filial responsibility for *all* households. These strategies are supported by a legal framework, the Maintenance of Parents Act 1995, that makes it possible for older people to bring their children to court if they neglect to support them financially (Rozario and Hong 2011). While rarely employed, the Act nonetheless reinforces the state's message that adult children are obliged to provide eldercare.

Assuming that women will shoulder the primary burden in regard to eldercare through their roles as family caregivers, the state provides a 'last-resort safety net' (Teo, Chan and Straughan 2003, 405) through a state-regulated healthcare insurance scheme (Medisave). This scheme forms a subset of the mandatory government superannuation scheme to which employees contribute a portion of their wages to fund retirement and healthcare needs. It includes policies for severe disability (Medishield) and aged care (Eldershield) as well as a means-tested safety net for those in financial hardship (Ansah et al. 2013). The Eldershield programme covers out-of-pocket expenses for individuals who are unable to carry out at least three of six activities associated with daily living (e.g. washing, dressing, feeding) to a maximum of SGD 400 for a maximum period of six years. Importantly, reflecting the state's view that eldercare is primarily the responsibility of families, adult children can pay for their parents' out-of-pocket expenses or hospitalisation expenses using their own Medisave accounts (Wu and Chan 2011). However, health insurance schemes do not address the cost of medicines for long-term, treatable illnesses such as arthritis/rheumatism, hypertension, and cataract/glaucoma. In addition, pressure points have already emerged over the financial cost of delivering long-term, acute care. In some families, these costs have been addressed through several siblings paying the medical expenses of one parent (Teo, Chan and Straughan 2003), but with a birth rate below replacement level, this strategy is not sustainable, as married couples will increasingly find themselves responsible for two sets of parents.

As this discussion suggests, the Singapore state has effectively positioned care work as the responsibility of women. Which women undertake this care work is a matter of class, ethnicity and nationality. Singapore's lower-income and ethnic minority women are less valued for their roles in the economy and thus carry the primary burden for child and eldercare within their own homes. The care responsibilities of lower-class women effectively squeeze them out of the labour market, as there are limited opportunities for part-time work, and without work these women are not eligible for the rebates that would enable them to place their children in childcare centres. Similarly, the prohibitive cost of employing a migrant domestic worker ensures that lower-class women remain at home, where they perform eldercare services for a range of extended family members. By contrast, middle-class married women's caregiving responsibilities can be outsourced through their supervision of other women's labour. While many rely on their parents or parents-in-law for childcare, others take advantage of a range of government subsidies to employ migrant workers who perform the physically demanding work of childcare, housework and eldercare.

Pressure points

In the context of a state that has almost no tolerance for social or political opposition to its policies, it is unsurprising that the current care system has attracted little public dissent. The 'naturalness' of these arrangements is self-evident to both lower-class and middle-class women because it reinforces a gendered ideal that places married women at the centre of care-giving responsibilities. That does not mean, however, that it is an ideal to which they aspire. The consistently low fertility rate of the past four decades demonstrates that despite a range of incentives and a significant investment in public awareness campaigns, women continue to marry later and delay having children. This silent protest continues to confound government efforts to boost the birth rate. Recent research suggests, however, that although women are well aware of the problems posed by the low fertility rate and the impending age dependency crisis, they do not expect the government to take a greater role in providing childcare or eldercare (Teo 2014). Instead, they reiterate the government's own concerns about welfarism and hold the view that these problems are best dealt with by families themselves.

Yet while family-based care might be preferable from the perspective of both the state and individual families, it can be a source of stress for the married women who are responsible for the provision of that care. While the care of older people and young children can be meaningful and may help 'connect' family members, it can also be oppressive. Passing on the physical, emotional and financial costs of care to families places an enormous burden on the women who ultimately bear them (Hing

2004). Those with young children often struggle with feelings of guilt over leaving them in the care of others and worry about the influence of foreign domestic workers on their values and behaviours (Lam, Yeoh and Huang 2006). Grandmothers may also hold different values about childrearing from those of their daughters and daughters-in-law. Some research suggests that many grandparents express ambivalence about co-residence arrangements, and while they are prepared to help, would prefer to live apart and maintain their own homes (Teo et al. 2003). From the perspective of the women who are subject to the emotional and psychological tensions of family life, however, these are personal rather than social problems.

In the absence of a shift from family-focused models of care to a greater emphasis on institutional arrangements or more flexible modes of work, migrant labour appears to offer the only long-term solution to Singapore's care needs, especially in light of the looming demographic crisis. Recognising this, the state has projected that the demand for foreign domestic workers will increase to 300,000 by 2030, mostly due to their role in childcare and eldercare (Østbye et al. 2013). While many Singaporeans are perturbed by the presence of a growing migrant workforce, this strategy has been favourably received among the large middle class, who view the employment of one or more foreign domestic workers as an essential feature of their growing affluence. Foreign domestic workers thus provide a safety valve against the pressures that middle-class women face between their need and desire to work, and their childcare and eldercare responsibilities. At the same time, this strategy enables the state to address the problem of how it manages its unskilled and low-skilled labour force in the transition to a highly-skilled economy, as low-income, low-skilled women have little choice but to remain at home where they undertake childcare and eldercare for their own families, thus relieving the state of the challenge of addressing unemployment.

What remains unclear is how women and their families will respond to these challenges as the demands of an ageing population become more acute. As the elderly population grows and as older people live longer, the health and aged care sectors will struggle to keep up with the demand for their services. Family-based care might be preferable from the perspective of both the state and individual families, but in its current form it will not address the significant care burden associated with age-related disability and dementia. Moreover, as migrant-sending countries undergo rapid industrialisation and address their own demographic transformations, the economic costs of relying on an imported labour force may trigger a greater investment in institutionally-based care models. In the short term, however, unskilled migrant domestic workers will continue to relieve some of the pressures that are placed on families and the healthcare system, and married women will continue to bear the brunt of the responsibility for primary care.

Note

1 In 2015, the concessional levy was SGD 60 per month compared with the full levy of SGD 265 per month. In addition to the levy, employers pay a minimum of SGD 400–500 per month in wages.

References

Ansah, J.P., D.B. Matchar, S.R. Love, R. Malhotra, Y.K. Do, A. Chan, and R. Eberlein. 2013. "Simulating the Impact of Long-Term Care Policy on Family Eldercare Hours." *Health Services Research* 48 (2): 773–791.

Choi, S. and L. Lyons. 2012. "Gender, Citizenship, and Women's 'Unskilled' Labour: The Experience of Filipino Migrant Nurses in Singapore." *Canadian Journal of Women and the Law* 24 (1): 1–26.

Early Childhood Development Agency. 2013. *Childcare Link: Additional Infant and Childcare Subsidies.* http://www.childcarelink.gov.sg/.

Early Childhood Development Agency. 2015. *Statistics on Child & Infant Care Services,* Singapore: Early Childhood Development Agency.

Graham, E., P. Teo, B. Yeoh, and S. Levy. 2002. "Reproducing the Asian Family across the Generations: 'Tradition', Gender and Expectations in Singapore." *Asia-Pacific Population Journal* 17 (2): 61–86.

Heng, G. and J. Devan. 1995. "State Fatherhood: The Politics of Nationalism, Sexuality, and Race in Singapore." In *Bewitching Women and Pious Men: Gender and Body Politics in Southeast Asia*, edited by A. Ong and M. Peletz, 195–215. Berkeley: University of California Press.

Hing, A.Y. 2004. "Ideology and Changing Family Arrangements in Singapore." *Journal of Comparative Family Studies* 35 (3): 375–392.

Huang, S., B.S.A. Yeoh, and M. Toyota. 2012. "Caring for the Elderly: The Embodied Labour of Migrant Care Workers in Singapore." *Global Networks* 12 (2): 195–215.

Jones, G.W., P.T. Straughan, and A. Chan, eds. 2008. *Ultra-low Fertility in Pacific Asia: Trends, Causes and Policy Issues.* New York: Routledge.

Lam, T., B.S.A. Yeoh, and S. Huang. 2006. "Global Householding in a City-State: Emerging Trends in Singapore." *International Development Planning Review* 28 (4): 475–497.

Lyons, L. 2004. "Sexing the Nation: Normative Heterosexuality and the Construction of the 'Good' Singaporean Citizen." In *The Nation of the Other: Constructions of Nation in Contemporary Cultural and Literary Discourses*, edited by A. Branach-Kallas and K. Więckowska, 79–96. Torun: Wydawnictwo Uniwersytet Mikolaja Kopernika.

Lyons, L. 2007. "Dignity Overdue: Women's Rights Activism in Support of Foreign Domestic Workers in Singapore." *Women's Studies Quarterly* 35 (3/4): 106–122.

Lyons-Lee, L. 1998. "The 'Graduate Woman' Phenomenon: Changing Constructions of the Family in Singapore." *Sojourn: Journal of Social Issues in Southeast Asia* 13 (2): 1–19.

Ministry of Manpower. 2014a. *Labour Force in Singapore, 2014.* Singapore: Ministry of Manpower.

Ministry of Manpower. 2014b. *Singapore Yearbook of Manpower Statistics, 2014.* Singapore: Ministry of Manpower.

Ministry of Manpower. 2015a. *Labour Market, 2014,* Singapore: Ministry of Manpower.

Ministry of Manpower. 2015b. *Levy Concession for a Foreign Domestic Worker.* http://www.mom.gov.sg/passes-and-permits/work-permit-for-foreign-domestic-worker/foreign-domestic-worker-levy/levy-concession.

Ministry of Manpower. 2015c. *Tripartism in Singapore.* http://www.mom.gov.sg/employment-practices/tripartism-in-singapore/Pages/default.aspx#tcworklife.

National Population and Talent Division. 2012. *Citizen Population Scenarios.* Singapore: Prime Minister's Office.

Østbye, T., R. Malhotra, C. Malhotra, C. Arambepola, and A. Chan. 2013. "Does Support from Foreign Domestic Workers Decrease the Negative Impact of Informal Caregiving?

Results from Singapore Survey on Informal Caregiving." *Journals of Gerontology, Series B: Psychological Sciences and Social Sciences* 68 (4): 609–621.

Quah, S. 1988. *Between Two Worlds: Modern Wives in a Traditional Setting.* Singapore: Institute of Southeast Asian Studies.

Quah, S. 1994. *Family in Singapore: Sociological Perspective.* Singapore: Times Academic Press.

Rozario, P. and S.-L. Hong. 2011. "Doing it 'Right' by Your Parents in Singapore: A Political Economy Examination of the Maintenance of Parents Act of 1995." *Critical Social Policy* 31 (4): 607–627.

Saw, S.-H. 1990. *Changes in the Fertility Policy of Singapore,* Singapore: The Institute of Policy Studies.

Singapore Department of Statistics. 2014a. *Education and Literacy, 2014.* http://www.singstat.gov.sg/statistics/latest-data#18.

Singapore Department of Statistics. 2014b. *Population Trends, 2014.* Singapore: Ministry of Trade & Industry.

Singapore Department of Statistics. 2014c. *Time Series on Labour Force Participation Rate (as at June 2014).* http://www.singstat.gov.sg/statistics/browse-by-theme/labour-employment-wages-and-productivity.

Singapore Department of Statistics. 2014d. *Yearbook of Statistics, 2014.* Singapore: Ministry of Trade & Industry.

Singapore Department of Statistics. 2015a. *Employed Residents Aged 15 and Over by Occupation, Age Group and Sex, June 2014.* http://www.singstat.gov.sg/statistics/browse-by-theme/labour-employment-wages-and-productivity#sthash.tuxRFBiN.dpuf.

Singapore Department of Statistics. 2015b. *Foreign Workforce Numbers.* http://www.singstat.gov.sg/statistics/browse-by-theme/labour-employment-wages-and-productivity#sthash.tuxRFBiN.dpuf1.

Singapore Department of Statistics. 2015c. *Resident Labour Force Status by Age Group and Sex, June 2014.* http://www.singstat.gov.sg/statistics/browse-by-theme/labour-employment-wages-and-productivity#sthash.tuxRFBiN.dpuf.

Sun, S.H.-L. 2012. "Care Expectations, Mismatched: State and Family in Contemporary Singapore." *International Journal of Sociology and Social Policy* 32 (11/12): 650–663.

Teo, Y. 2007. "Inequality for the Greater Good: Gendered State Rule in Singapore." *Critical Asian Studies* 39 (3): 423–445.

Teo, Y. 2014. "Population Problems, Family Policies, and the Naturalization of Differentiated Deservedness." in *The Future of Singapore: Population, Society and the Nature of the State*, edited by K.M. Nasir and B.S. Turner, 64–82. London and New York: Routledge.

Teo, Y. and N. Piper. 2009. "Foreigners in our Homes: Linking Migration and Family Policies in Singapore." *Population, Space and Place* 15: 147–159.

Teo, P., A. Chan, and P. Straughan. 2003. "Providing Health Care for Older Persons in Singapore." *Health Policy* 64 (3): 399–413.

Teo, P., E. Graham, B.S.A. Yeoh, and S. Levy. 2003. "Values, Change and Inter-generational Ties between Two Generations of Women in Singapore." *Ageing and Society* 23 (3): 327–347.

World Bank. 2015. *Health Nutrition and Population Statistics: Population Estimates and Projections.* http://databank.worldbank.org/Data/Views/VariableSelection/SelectVariables.aspx?source=Health%20Nutrition%20and%20Population%20Statistics:%20Population%20estimates%20and593 %20projections.

Wu, T., and A. Chan. 2011. "Older Women, Health, and Social Care in Singapore." *Asia Europe Journal* 8 (4): 513–526.

Yeoh, B.S.A., and S. Huang. 1995. "Childcare in Singapore: Negotiating Choices and Constraints in a Multicultural Society." *Women's Studies International Forum* 18 (4): 445–461.

5 Indonesia

Middle-class complicity and state failure to provide care

Michele Ford and Nurchayati

Since the 1980s, a significant number of Indonesian women have made the shift from traditional forms of economic activity to waged work, finding employment in formerly male-dominated sectors of the economy and in new kinds of occupations. At a time when many of the agricultural tasks traditionally undertaken by rural women had been made redundant by the technological advances of the green revolution, foreign investors began establishing the factories that drew young women away from the villages to urban centres where a significant proportion of them found employment on light manufacturing production lines or in trade and other services. Changes in the economy as a result of industrialisation and the subsequent growth of tertiary industries also created new white-collar jobs that were open to women.

As women become increasingly engaged in more structured forms of employment, it is nevertheless widely accepted that they will continue to take responsibility for managing the home – a task that is understood to include the provision of care for children and the elderly. Although successive governments have encouraged women to assume both productive and reproductive roles, care work remains firmly in the domestic domain. Indonesia has almost no government-funded care infrastructure and provides no social security benefits for carers, no services or benefits in kind, and no incentives towards provisions in the market for the employment of service-providers (cf. Razavi 2007). As a consequence, most working-class women in paid employment rely upon extended family and neighbours for childcare and eldercare, or combine care and other family responsibilities with work in the informal sector – or, in the case of working-class women who migrate in the search of employment, leave their children with grandparents or other members of their extended family.[1]

Despite these obvious tensions, there is virtually no public debate about care work from the perspective of either gender politics or policy. An important reason for this is that middle- and upper-class women – even wealthier working class women – are almost never required to provide routine care for children or the elderly. Instead, they supervise the domestic workers, or less commonly nannies and nurses, who assume primary responsibility for these tasks. While this low-paid workforce remains available, there is little impetus for those who can afford to employ them to advocate for change, either in gender roles or in levels of state provision of care. In exploring this conundrum, this chapter begins with a discussion of the context in which Indonesia's work/care regime is situated before moving on to an overview of the ways in which care is provided. It concludes with a brief discussion of the politics of work and care, and the pressure points evident in the system.[2]

The work/care regime in context

Indonesia is the third-largest country in the Asia-Pacific region after India and China, with a population of 255.46 million in 2015 (BPPN, BPS and UNPF 2013). Its economy ranks sixth behind China, Japan, India, Australia and South Korea. Much of Indonesia's wealth is generated through its extractive industries. Manufacturing, which generates around a fifth of the country's Gross Domestic Product (GDP), is clustered around a few major urban centres and in dedicated export processing zones. Much of the sector is highly integrated into global production chains. Yet it employs just 13 per cent of Indonesia's labour force of a little over 118 million.

The majority of Indonesians work in agriculture; trade, restaurants and hotels; or community, social and personal services. One-third of Indonesia's labour force is employed in agriculture alone. At close to 85 per cent, men have a much higher labour force participation rate than women, whose participation rate is a little over 51 per cent – a figure that has remained relatively stable since the mid-1990s, having risen from 37 per cent in 1971 (ILO and ADB 2014).[3] Women account for just under 39 per cent of the workforce, and are most concentrated in trade and hospitality, where they constitute over half of all those employed in the sector, and almost half of all women working outside agriculture (Table 5.1). They are

Table 5.1 Working population 15 years of age and over by industry and sex, 2014

Sector	*Males*	*% Males Working*	*Females*	*% Females Working*
Wholesale and retail trade, restaurants, hotels	12,099,783	16.68	13,709,486	30.05
Community, social and personal services	9,895,073	13.64	8,581,214	18.81
Manufacturing	9,165,103	12.63	6,225,085	13.64
Agriculture, forestry, hunting and fisheries	25,377,461	34.98	15,455,591	33.87
Finance, insurance, real estate, business services	2,272,406	3.13	920,951	2.02
Mining and quarrying	1,451,236	2.00	171,873	0.38
Electricity, gas and water	280,384	0.39	28,204	0.06
Transportation, storage, and communications	4,953,821	6.83	370,284	0.81
Construction	7,044,914	9.71	167,053	0.37
Total	72,540,181	100.00	45,629,741	100.00

Source: Ministry of Manpower (2014b).

also over-represented both in community, social and personal services and in manufacturing, when compared with the labour force as a whole.

In terms of employment status, women are as likely as men to be own-account workers, and just a little less likely to be regular employees (Table 5.2). They are, however, less than half as likely to be employers and much more likely to be unpaid or family workers than men. The continuing dominance of agricultural employment and Indonesia's large number of self-employed and family workers contribute to its high level of informal employment. Informal sector jobs are most concentrated in agriculture, forestry, hunting and fisheries, as well as in trade, restaurants and hotels. In addition, more than half of all construction and transport, storage and communications jobs are located in the informal sector. Importantly, vulnerable forms of employment are common in both the formal and informal sectors, as private businesses, but also state-owned enterprises and even the core public service, employ workers on a daily basis or under some other temporary arrangement, which contributes to high levels of income insecurity.

Differences in labour force participation rates and occupational status cannot be attributed to educational opportunity. Although around 51.47 per cent of Indonesian women of working age have primary school education or less, the same is true for 44.68 per cent of men in the same age group (BPS 2014b). Moreover, women outnumber men among those with post-school qualifications (BPS 2014b) – a statistic reflected in occupational spread (Table 5.3). Almost 54 per cent of those employed in professional or technical occupations in 2014 were female, representing a little under 10 per cent of all employed women. By contrast, this category accounted for just 5 per cent of all employed men (BPS 2014b).

Indonesian women who make it into the senior ranks of management fare reasonably well. According to a comparative gender gap analysis prepared by the International Labour Organisation for the G20 Summit in 2014, Indonesia's

Table 5.2 Employment status by sex, 2014

Employment Status	*Male*	*% Males Working*	*Female*	*% Females Working*
Own account worker	12,469,143	17.19	7,851,528	17.21
Employer (temporary/ unpaid workers)	14,784,084	20.38	4,950,612	10.85
Employer (permanent employees)	3,374,974	4.65	768,538	1.68
Regular employee	28,193,986	38.87	15,154,975	33.21
Casual agricultural worker	3,040,955	4.19	1,698,355	3.72
Casual non-agricultural worker	5,748,254	7.92	1,002,141	2.20
Unpaid/family worker	4,928,785	6.79	14,203,592	31.13
Total	72,540,181	100.00	45,629,741	100.00

Source: Ministry of Manpower (2014c).

Table 5.3 Working population by occupational category and sex, 2014

Category	*Male*	*% Males Working*	*Female*	*% Females Working*
Sales	9,998,117	13.78	12,189,993	26.72
Professional and technical occupations	3,786,464	5.22	4,399,189	9.64
Community, social and personal services	3,614,528	4.98	3,204,004	7.02
Clerical and administrative occupations	3,730,769	5.14	2,801,068	6.14
Agricultural work	24,878,904	34.30	15,354,800	33.65
Machine operators and labourers	24,883,201	34.30	7,420,292	16.26
Managers	1,029,782	1.42	241,484	0.53
Other	618,416	0.85	18,911	0.04
Total	72,540,181	100.00	45,629,741	100.00

Source: Ministry of Manpower (2014a).

overall gender pay gap at 16.6 per cent is proportional to that of Australia and Germany, and among senior managers is relatively small (OECD et al. 2014). At the same time, however, the number of women in the ranks of senior management is low, with women accounting for just 19 per cent of managers and only 4 per cent of employers (Ministry of Manpower 2014a, c; OECD et al. 2014).

Caring for the young and the elderly

Care of the young and the elderly remains an overwhelmingly private, and female, concern. Traditionally, the extended family played an important role in care provision, but smaller family sizes and the increasing prevalence of nuclear families in recent decades have resulted in the reduced availability of family members to provide childcare and eldercare (Hoang, Yeoh and Wattie 2012). Indonesia has a relatively young population, although fertility rates have been curtailed in recent decades by a robust family planning programme.[4] Whereas families had an average of five to six children in the 1970s, in the 2000s the average had declined to only two or three (ILO 2011). The absolute number of children has, however, continued to increase, with the number of children under age 14 rising by 12 per cent to almost 69 million in the decade to 2010 (BKKBN 2014a, b).

Despite changes in patterns of employment and family structures, Indonesian children of pre-school age are relatively unlikely to spend time in any kind of institutional childcare. In 2001, the government released a plan to more than double the participation of children aged six or under in formal early childhood education by 2015 (UNESCO 2005). If children in the first year of primary school are excluded, the gross enrolment rate of children aged six or under in early childhood educational services in 2014 was just 8 per cent. Access to childcare is patchy, and mostly concentrated in urban areas (PUS 2013). Almost all facilities are privately run (UNESCO 2005).

Eldercare is also of increasing concern. The population pyramid (Figure 5.1) has shifted as a consequence of a significant increase in life expectancy, which rose from 52.39 in 1970 to 70.61 in 2012 (World Bank 2015b). It is projected that by 2050 Indonesia will be among the world's top ten countries in terms of the proportion of population aged 80 years and over (United Nations 2013).

These demographic changes are already making it more difficult for families to care for their elderly relatives (Arifianto 2006). Although an increasing number of elderly Indonesians are cared for in institutions, the majority of eldercare continues to take the form of informal care provided by the household without support or advice from professional caregivers (van Eeuwijk 2006). Expectations differ between different ethnic groups in Indonesia, but ageing parents are often cared for by a younger daughter in their own home. Daughters may take on this responsibility voluntarily, or may be pressured to do so by their parents or siblings. Among some ethnic groups, daughters who care for their parents can expect to inherit the family house (Kevane and Levine 2000).

According to the Indonesia Family Life Survey of 1993–2007, elderly people with higher household incomes are less likely to live with their children (Witoelar 2012). However, they are also unlikely to live in an institution, since they have the resources to pay carers or support poorer relatives looking after them in their own homes. Indeed, few Indonesians, regardless of economic circumstances, consider institutionalised care for the elderly appropriate. As Kadar et al. (2013) note, there is significant social stigma attached to sending one's parents to nursing homes. This assessment is confirmed by a survey of 240 family carers of older relatives in Depok, a satellite city in Greater Jakarta, which revealed that 51 per cent of carers (of whom 97 per cent were female) saw caring roles as a family obligation (Sahar, Courtney and Edwards 2003).

For those who require care, there is little choice in the way it is provided. The number of aged care facilities has increased, but remains tiny. One study suggests that the total number of aged care facilities in Indonesia rose from 141 to only 278 between 2000 and 2011 (Do-Le and Raharjo 2002; UNHCR 2011). Moreover, with the exception of institutions run by charities, residential care services for the elderly tend to be expensive, even for the middle class. For example, board and lodging for an elderly resident at Rukun Senior Living in Jakarta costs USD 1,000 per month (Vaswani 2013). Until recently, close to 90 per cent of Indonesian citizens were not covered by an old age benefit scheme (ILO 2013) so, in practice, most elderly Indonesians have no access to a pension. As a consequence, an individual's capacity to enter private institutional care is also limited by the capacity and willingness of family members to pay for the service.

The limited availability of affordable aged care facilities reflects the government's historic lack of interest in addressing this issue. Attitudes are changing; spending on social welfare for the elderly is more than 40 times that of a decade ago (Rachmaningtyas 2014). However, reform has been piecemeal

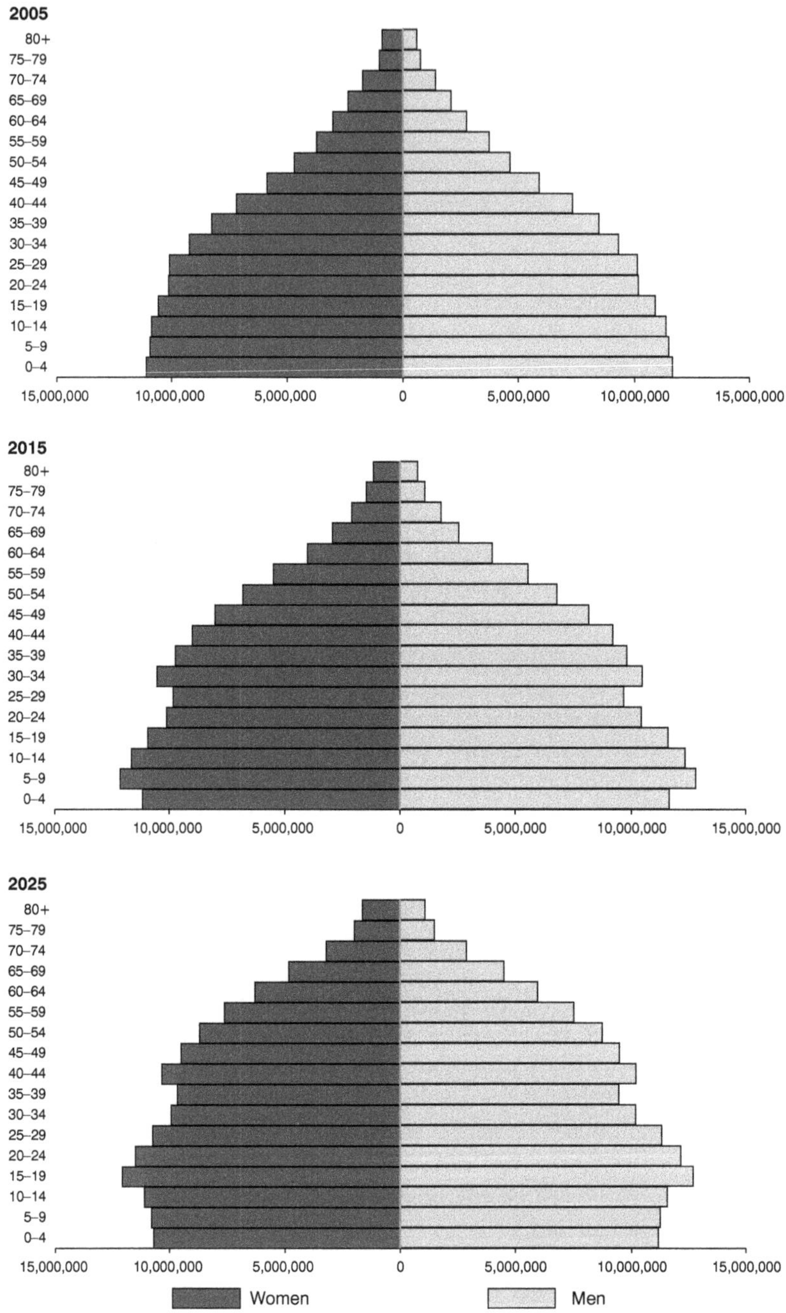

Figure 5.1 Population 2005, 2015, and 2025

Source: World Bank (2015).

and slow. Law No.13/1998 on Old Age Welfare stipulated that 'responsibility for the improvement of the elderly citizens' welfare should be shared by the government, the community and the family of elderly citizens themselves' (Arifianto 2006, 9–10). However, no particular programmes were put in place at that time. Further action was taken in 2003, with the announcement of Presidential Decree No.52/2004 on Creation of the National Commission on Ageing and the release of a five-year National Strategy to Improve the Welfare of the Elderly (Arifianto 2006). Since then, the government has implemented several programmes, including one that subsidises the basic needs of elderly persons living in nursing homes and another designed to provide training for families with elderly members of the household (UNHCR 2011). However the level of penetration of such services remains low.

On the related issue of aged pensions, these benefits were traditionally limited to civil servants, army personnel and a small proportion of formal private sector employees (Maliki 2011, 514). This narrow focus was formally redressed by Law No. 3/1992 on Workers' Social Security, which included provisions around retirement benefits for formal and informal sector workers. In practice, however, around 80 per cent of the workforce was not covered (Arifianto 2006). The issue was raised again with the passing of Law No. 40/2004 on the National Social Security System which, in addition to a limited form of universal healthcare, mandated an old age pension programme for formal and informal sector workers who had contributed to the programme for a minimum of 15 years (Arifianto 2006). The implementation of this law was a matter of considerable controversy, and it was not until 2014 that a universal social security system began to take shape (Cole and Ford 2014; Muliati 2013).

Workplaces and care

Women's increasing participation in paid work over the last several decades in Indonesia has exposed persistent assumptions about the division of labour within the home. Despite larger numbers of women entering the paid workforce, the deeply gendered division of labour means that even where a woman earns the larger share of household income she is likely to see herself – and be seen by others – as a secondary earner. The decision to work is not always obvious, even for women in female-headed households. With the exception of those living in Jakarta, male household heads are more than 90 per cent likely to be in some kind of employment. By contrast, the employment rate of female household heads varies from 52.5 per cent in Aceh to 87.0 per cent in Papua, with rates uniformly lower in Sumatra than elsewhere, and between 60.1 per cent and 63.2 per cent in Java, Indonesia's most industrialised island (BPS 2014a).

A woman's primary role as wife and mother (and by extension, carer for the elderly) is also institutionalised in Indonesia's employment relations framework. While men and women generally earn the same wages for the same jobs in large formal-sector workplaces, married men may receive extra allowances and pay less tax on the assumption that they are supporting a family (Tjandraningsih

2000).[5] Legally, there is no discrimination on the basis of gender with regard to who should receive the family allowance mandated under Law No. 13/2003 on Manpower; however, data from interviews with manufacturing workers suggests that it remains difficult for women in that sector to obtain benefits for their families, including health insurance coverage, as a consequence of legal recognition of men's position as head of the household in the 1974 Marriage Law.

Successive Indonesian governments have adopted a pro-family stance, which is reflected in employment law. Under the Manpower Law, female employees are entitled to 1.5 months of fully paid maternity leave before giving birth and 1.5 months after, and must be provided with facilities and time to breastfeed if needed during work time. It is also illegal to make women redundant on the grounds of pregnancy, birth, miscarriage or breastfeeding (APINDO and ILO 2013). In reality, however, few workplaces meet these requirements. To give substance to breastfeeding regulations, firms would either have to provide lactation rooms or allow mothers to go home during the day. The latter is generally not feasible since most people live a significant distance from their places of work.[6] A survey of female factory workers conducted in the late 1990s by Pangestu and Hendytio (cited in Kercheval et al. 2013) found that only 6 per cent of factories surveyed provided the required breastfeeding facilities. Another survey conducted by the Women's Committee of a major financial sector union in the mid-2000s concluded that there was unmet demand for breastfeeding and childcare facilities, as well as other forms of family-friendly practice such as flexibility to take time off to care for a sick child (Reerink 2006).

Given the high proportion of women who have responsibilities as carers – be it for children or elderly relatives – the issue of family-friendly workplaces is of great importance to working women. The absence of a supportive workplace culture has a measurable effect on women's decisions about whether or not to engage in paid work when their children are young. The difficulty of combining work and family responsibilities drives many working-class women to leave formal sector employment, as demonstrated by an analysis of data from the Indonesian Family Life Survey 1996–2007, which found that work interruption is common among women in Indonesia, most often as a consequence of marriage and motherhood (Setyonaluri 2014).

Having children has also been found to have a strong effect on the likelihood of women returning to work in the formal sector. A survey of close to 1,000 female trade unionists employed in garment factories confirms that many women leave their factory jobs before reaching their thirties as a consequence of childbirth and childrearing (Reerink 2006). In the mining industry, Lahiri-Dutt and Robinson (2008) found that women who were able to arrange satisfactory childcare remained in the job for 8 to 9 years, while those who could not tended to leave paid employment. Similarly, a study of the tourism industry in Bali found that women who remained in hotel work after having children most often relied on family networks for childcare, while others left formal sector employment in favour of informal sector work, which was easier to combine with childcare (Cukier, Norris and Wall 1996).

Of course, it is only in formal workplaces – and in practice, not always there – that women can have even the slightest expectation of access to any such provisions. The majority of Indonesian women work in the informal sector. These include the country's 11 million or so domestic workers, who staff the households of better-off Indonesians.[7] A large number of households can afford to employ household help because the wages of domestic workers are significantly below the minimum wage. In mid-2012 in Jakarta, the pay rate for skilled domestic workers was just Rp.750,000 (around USD 78.90) per month (Christie 2012), or a little under half the provincial minimum wage at that time. A report to the International Labour Organisation estimates the mean monthly wage of domestic workers in that year at Rp.704,000, with 30 per cent of domestic workers earning less than Rp.400,000 (Suhaimi, Farid and Ruslam 2013).[8] In addition to housework, cooking and errand-running, domestic workers are generally responsible for the routine care of their employers' children and ageing parents.[9] As they almost always live in the homes of their employers, their duties extend beyond standard working hours, often involving being on call during the night. Their live-in status, often hundreds of kilometres from their homes in a village – or thousands of kilometres, in the case of overseas domestic workers – also means that their mothers or husbands, or some member of their extended family, take responsibility for caring for their own children.[10]

Although some provincial and local laws protect domestic workers' rights, domestic workers are not covered by the national Manpower Law. Nor, as is the case in the Philippines (Lindio-McGovern, this volume), is there a national law on domestic work. There is significant resistance to extending legal coverage, in part because of cultural attitudes that frame domestic workers as 'helpers' (*pembantu*) rather than 'workers' (*pekerja*). Moreover, the relationship between employer and domestic worker is considered private, because it is conducted in the home, and therefore should be free of state intervention (ILO 2006). However, the absence of legal coverage also reflects a recognition by government of the pivotal role domestic workers play in providing reproductive labour in a context where families receive little state support. As a female representative of the Ministry of Manpower told a representative of Human Rights Watch, the regulation of domestic work would have implications for productivity, since 'factory workers couldn't go to work if they did not have domestic workers to look after their children' (Sheppard 2009, 28).

The politics of work and care

In understanding the politics of work and care in Indonesia, it is necessary to consider not only the material demands of living, but also cultural scripts of gender roles and norms concerning intra-household relations (Ford and Parker 2008b). The Indonesian state has long upheld the view that women can (and should) play both productive and reproductive roles. However, state discourse – which translates into policy frameworks – also continues to demand that women (as wives, mothers and daughters) remain first and foremost committed to caring for their husbands, children and parents. As Nilan and Utari (2008, 145) observe in their study of media workers, the women they interviewed were 'structurally located within the modernist work discourse of *wanita karier*' (career women), but also within cultural understandings of a woman's role being primary in the private domain, which they felt 'defined them as Indonesian women'. Thus 'in their accounts and discussions they moved between defence of themselves as good wives and mothers (either in the present or the future), and expressions of desire for personal fulfilment through their careers'.

As this observation suggests, the career aspirations of even middle-class women are tempered by their family responsibilities. Analysis of the 1996–2007 Indonesian Family Life Survey suggests that marriage has less of an effect on employment exit for women working in the public sector and those with a tertiary level education (Setyonaluri 2014). However, access to affordable domestic labour does not fully mitigate the effect of middle-class women's responsibility for the management of the household on their careers. As one mid-ranking civil servant explained, 'Women choose to stay at the non-managerial levels. The main thing is that we get our tasks done, receive our monthly salary, and that is that. That way, whenever one of our children gets sick, we can ask for leave and go home' (Interview, Kediri, August 2014). This understanding is, moreover, inter-generational. Bulbeck's (2005) multi-country survey of middle-class urban youth in the early 2000s found that the majority of young Indonesians believed that couples should share housework. However, they strongly disagreed with role reversal, and still understood men as being the breadwinners, using terms such as 'duty' and 'obligation' to explain their position. A 2004 survey of university students in Jakarta and Makassar revealed that they, too, overwhelmingly expected women to be secondary earners whose primary responsibility was to the household (Utomo 2012).

This is not to infer that such positions are uncontested. A survey of factory women returning to rural villages as a result of the 1998 economic crisis found that they were unhappy with expectations that they, but not returned males, should take responsibility for childcare, eldercare and domestic work (Silvey and Elmhirst 2003). In some cases, overseas domestic workers also reject dominant values around care work. For example, one Betawi widow explained that her primary reason for seeking work in Malaysia was to force her husband's family to take responsibility for her school-age daughter, whom she felt they had a duty to support (Interview, Tanjung Pinang, June 2001). Another, who had been deported from Singapore after being imprisoned for eight months for immigration infringements, had actively chosen not to resume responsibility for her first son, aged four, who lived with his grandparents in a village in Java. Pregnant with a second child, she planned to try her luck in Malaysia once she had given birth, rather than return to her family (Interview, Tanjung Pinang, November 2006). Some Indonesian women also of course continue to work for reasons of personal fulfilment. In such cases, however, women often feel compelled to spend their earnings on childcare. Rita, a 60-year-old university lecturer, reported that in 1981 she had spent her entire salary as a civil servant on a professional babysitter, who cared for her baby son (Interview, Surabaya, August 2014). Similarly, Yuli, a reporter interviewed by Nilan and Utari (2008), recalled spending almost her entire salary on the wages of two domestic workers to take care of her children.

This complex relationship between competing understandings (and desires) about work and care – along with the ease with which middle-class women can manage the demands of the 'double shift' – has resulted in a relative lack of social pressure for change, even from within the women's movement. Indeed, childcare and eldercare have been largely absent from policy debates.[11] In the recent past, the government worked with the Coalition Network for Pro-Women National Legislation to draft pro-gender equality legislation (UNCEDAW 2011). However, these efforts were focused primarily on domestic violence and trafficking in persons rather than on workplace issues or policies pertaining to care. Trade unions, too, have shown little interest in social policy concerned with childcare or eldercare, or more family-friendly forms of work, although they have played a pivotal role in revitalising debates around pensions and healthcare.[12] They have at times weighed in on the domestic worker issue, primarily at the behest of their international funders. In general, however, the unions have engaged very little, beyond pressing for implementation of legal provisions pertaining to women's access to family allowances, reproductive health and breastfeeding during enterprise level collective bargaining.

Pressure points

In the highly gendered context of Indonesian social relations, working women are caught between the state's desire to increase women's participation in the workforce while containing public spending, and their own (and others') desire to conform with social norms regarding management of the household. In the absence of a robust, publicly-funded care infrastructure, the burden of care is overwhelmingly carried by working women, the female members of their extended family, and – where circumstances permit – hired (female) help, who allow middle-class women to participate in the workforce without taking on the 'second shift'. Yet, even at their most successful, few working women occupy leadership positions in the workplace. From the point of view of business, women workers are incapable of giving their best because their primary focus is necessarily on caring for their family.

Indonesia's care regime is thus both familial and marketised (cf. Razavi 2007), but marketised in a very particular way. On the one hand, the vast majority of care work that takes place is unpaid. As the state provides very little in the way of institutional care, care facilities – be they for young children or the elderly – are primarily managed by the private sector on a user-pays or charitable basis. In between the family and institutional care sits the army of domestic workers who take up the care deficit. It is the informal 'market' service these women provide at low rates of pay that makes it possible for governments and employers to continue with 'business as usual' in the face of demographic and social change.

The balance is, however, a precarious one. As the population grows older and extended family structures attenuate, the burden of care on households will necessarily increase. The process of managing that burden is made more problematic by women's growing participation in the paid workforce and men's reluctance to accept their share of care responsibilities (Arifin, Braun and Hogervorst 2012). It is unclear, for now, whether stresses on working-class households will ultimately force the government or employers to reassess their approach to the provision of care, or whether increasing prosperity will lead to a shortage of domestic workers, leading to a mobilisation of the middle class. What is clear, however, is that as more women enter the paid workforce – as long-term trends suggest they will – households' capacity to manage that burden will become increasingly strained in the absence of a more proactive policy approach.

Notes

1 With the exception of domestic workers, who are generally required to live in their employers' homes, married women who migrate for work within Indonesia tend to migrate with their husbands but may leave their children with members of their extended family. In the case of women migrating for work internationally, one study has suggested that 71 per cent of fathers left behind were principal carers for their children, but shared care with the children's grandmother or another member of the extended family, who would look after the children during the day (Hoang, Yeoh and Wattie 2012).
2 The study on which this chapter is based was conducted as part of an Australian Research Council Future Fellowship project entitled *'Trade Unionism and Trade Union Aid in Indonesia, Malaysia and Timor-Leste'* (FT120100778). It draws on reviews of policy documents and interviews with trade unionists and working women conducted in 2014 and 2015 and on earlier research by Ford on women and work in Indonesia (see Ford and Parker 2008a).
3 These national figures mask important regional differences. Poor provinces with traditionally high rates of female labour force participation and wealthier regions with a history of lower rates of female labour force participation have tended to preserve these patterns even in the face of industrialisation (Manning and Pratomo 2013; Warouw 2008).
4 For a discussion of the history and current status of Indonesia's family planning programme, see Steedman (2013).
5 If both spouses are employed in the public service, family allowances are payable to the spouse who earns more.
6 A small-scale study conducted in the city of Solo suggests that only 11 per cent of women in paid work breastfeed exclusively compared with 22 per cent of women who are not in paid work. Indeed, employment status was found to be the only significant determinant of women's choices around breastfeeding during the first six months of a child's life (Rahmawati 2010).
7 Estimates of the number of domestic workers employed in Indonesia vary wildly. An International Labour Organisation study suggested that there were approximately 2.6 million domestic workers as of 2012, an estimate that seems extremely conservative. Jala PRT, the leading non-government organisation working in this area, estimates the total to be closer to 11 million (Interview with Lita Anggraini, Jakarta, 24 February 2015).
8 For a discussion of the issues surrounding foreign domestic work, see Ford and Lyons (2015). For a discussion of skilled Indonesian temporary labour migrants employed as care workers, see Ford and Kawashima (2013).
9 Less frequently, children are cared for by higher-paid nannies, who are referred to by Indonesians with the English term *babysitter*.
10 There is an extensive literature on global care chains. For an introduction to the issues, see Hoang, Yeoh and Wattie (2012).

11 Similarly, while scholars have conducted studies on the kinds of jobs women hold, the contributions they make to the maintenance of their families, and how they experience their professional and domestic lives, there is little discussion in the literature of the ways in which the care regime influences the strategies women employ to strike a balance between paid work and care.

12 For details of this ground-breaking campaign, which led to the passing of Law No. 24/2011 on Social Security Administrative Bodies, the implementing law required to give form to the 2004 Law on Social Security, see Cole and Ford (2014).

References

APINDO and ILO. 2013. *Code of Practice for Employers on Promoting Equality and Preventing Discrimination at Work in Indonesia.* Jakarta: International Labour Organisation.

Arifianto, A. 2006. *Public Policy towards the Elderly in Indonesia: Current Policy and Future Directions.* Jakarta: SMERU Research Institute.

Arifin, E.N., K. Braun and E. Hogervorst. 2012. "Three Pillars of Active Ageing in Indonesia." *Asian Population Studies* 8 (2): 207–230.

BKKBN. 2014a. *Jumlah Penduduk Tahun 2000 Nasional.* http://www.bkkbn.go.id/kependudukan/Pages/DataSensus/Sensus_Penduduk/Penduduk/Jumlah_Penduduk_2000/Nasional.aspx.

BKKBN. 2014b. *Jumlah Penduduk Tahun 2010 Nasional.* http://www.bkkbn.go.id/kependudukan/Pages/DataSensus/Sensus_Penduduk/Penduduk/Jumlah_Penduduk_2010/Nasional.aspx.

BPPN, BPS and UNPF. 2013. *Proyeksi Penduduk Indonesia 2010–2035.* Jakarta: BPS.

BPS. 2014a. *Percentage of Households by Province, Urban-Rural Classification and Sex.* http://www.bps.go.id/eng/tab_sub/view.php?kat=1&tabel=1&daftar=1&id_subyek=40&notab=4.

BPS. 2014b. *Population 15 Years of Age and Over by Sex and Educational Attainment, 2013.* http://www.bps.go.id/eng/tab_sub/view.php?kat=1&tabel=1&daftar=1&id_subyek=40&notab=10.

Bulbeck, C. 2005. "'The Mighty Pillar of the Family': Young People's Vocabularies on Household Gender Arrangements in the Asia-Pacific Region." *Gender, Work and Organization* 12 (1): 14–31.

Christie, S.A. 2012. "Mencari PRT yang Tepat? Baca Dulu Tipsnya." *Centro One*, 30 August. http://www.centroone.com/female/2012/08/4ac/mencari-prt-yang-tepat-baca-dulu-tipsnya/.

Cole, R. and M. Ford. 2014. *The KAJS Campaign for Social Security Reform in Indonesia.* Jakarta: Friedrich Ebert Stiftung.

Cukier, J., J. Norris, and G. Wall. 1996. "The Involvement of Women in the Tourism Industry of Bali, Indonesia." *The Journal of Development Studies* 33 (2): 248–270.

Do-Le, K.D. and Y. Raharjo. 2002. "Community-Based Support for the Elderly in Indonesia: The Case of PUSAKA." Paper presented at the IUSSP Regional Population Conference on Southeast Asia's Population in Changing Asian Context, Bangkok, June 11–14.

Ford, M. and K. Kawashima. 2013. "Temporary Labour Migration and Care Work: The Japanese Experience." *Journal of Industrial Relations* 55 (3): 430–444.

Ford, M. and L. Lyons. 2015. "Working for a Day Off: Advocating for the Rights of Migrant Women in Southeast Asia." In *Beyond Development and Globalization Projects: Critical Perspectives and Social Movements*, edited by D. Caouette and D. Kapoor, 145–164. Ottawa: University of Ottawa Press.

Ford, M. and L. Parker, eds. 2008a. *Women and Work in Indonesia*. Abingdon: Routledge.

Ford, M. and L. Parker. 2008b. "Introduction: Thinking About Indonesian Women and Work." In *Women and Work in Indonesia*, edited by M. Ford and L. Parker, 1–16. Abingdon: Routledge.

Hoang, L.A., B.S.A. Yeoh and A.M. Wattie. 2012. "Transnational Labour Migration and the Politics of Care in the Southeast Asian Family." *Geoforum* 43 (4): 733–740.

ILO. 2006. *The Regulation of Domestic Workers in Indonesia: Current Laws, International Standards and Best Practice*. Jakarta: ILO.

ILO. 2011. *Decent Work Country Profile: Indonesia*. Geneva: ILO.

ILO. 2013. *Labour and Social Trends in Indonesia 2013: Reinforcing the Role of Decent Work in Equitable Growth*. Jakarta: ILO.

ILO and ADB. 2014. "ASEAN Community 2015: Managing Integration for Better Jobs and Shared Prosperity." Bangkok: ILO.

Kadar, K., K. Francis and K. Sellick. 2013. "Ageing in Indonesia – Health Status and Challenges for the Future." *Ageing International* 38 (4): 261–270.

Kercheval, J., D. Markowitz, K. Monson and B. Read. 2013. *Women in Leadership: Research on Barriers to Employment and Decent Work for Women*. Jakarta: ILO.

Kevane, M. and D. Levine. 2000. *The Changing Status of Daughters in Indonesia*. Berkeley: Institute for Research on Labor and Employment.

Lahiri-Dutt, K. and K. Robinson. 2008. "Bodies in Contest: Gender Difference and Equity in a Coal Mine." In *Women and Work in Indonesia*, edited by M. Ford and L. Parker, 120–135. Abingdon: Routledge.

Maliki. 2011. "The Support System for Indonesian Elders: Moving toward the Sustainable National Pension System." In *Population Aging and the Generational Economy: A Global Perspective*, edited by Ronald Lee and Andrew Mason, 513–527. Cheltenham: Edward Elgar.

Manning, C. and D. Pratomo. 2013. "Do Migrants Get Stuck in the Informal Sector? Findings from a Household Survey in Four Indonesian Cities." *Bulletin of Indonesian Economic Studies* 49 (2): 167–192.

Ministry of Manpower. 2014a. *Penduduk yang Bekerja Menurut Jenis Pekerjaan/ Jabatan dan Jenis Kelamin*. http://pusdatinaker.balitfo.depnakertrans.go.id/kunasional/pyb/PENDUDUK_YANG_BEKERJA_MENURUT_JENIS_PEKERJAAN2FJABATAN_DAN_JENIS_KELAMINsmry.php?sv_tahun=2014&sv_bulan=Februari&Submit=Search.

Ministry of Manpower. 2014b. *Penduduk yang Bekerja Menurut Lapangan Usaha dan Jenis Kelamin*. http://pusdatinaker.balitfo.depnakertrans.go.id/kunasional/pyb/PENDUDUK_YANG_BEKERJA_MENURUT_LAPANGAN_USAHA_28929_DAN_JENIS_KELAMINsmry.php?sv_tahun=2014&sv_bulan=Februari&Submit=Search.

Ministry of Manpower. 2014c. *Penduduk yang Bekerja Menurut Status Pekerjaan dan Jenis Kelamin di Indonesia bulan Februari tahun 2014*. http://pusdatinaker.balitfo.depnakertrans.go.id/kunasional/pyb/PENDUDUK_YANG_BEKERJA_MENURUT_STATUS_PEKERJAAN_DAN_JENIS_KELAMINsmry.php.

Muliati, I. 2013. *Pension Reform Experience in Indonesia*. Tokyo: World Bank.

Nilan, P. and P. Utari. 2008. "Meanings of Work for Female Media and Communication Workers." In *Women and Work in Indonesia*, edited by M. Ford and L. Parker, 136–154. Abingdon: Routledge.

OECD, ILO, IMF and World Bank. 2014. Achieving Stronger Growth by Promoting a More Gender-Balanced Economy: Report Prepared for the G20 Labour and Employment Ministerial Meeting. Melbourne, Australia, 10–11 September 2014.

PUS. 2013. *Laporan Tahunan: Pendidikan Untuk Semua (PUS) Nasional Tahun 2012*. Jakarta: PAUD.

Rachmaningtyas, A. 2014. "Kemensos Sebut Anggaran untuk Lansia Alami Penurunan." *SindoNews*, June 8. http://nasional.sindonews.com/read/871347/15/kemensos-sebut-anggaran-untuk-lansia-alami-penurunan-1402214155.

Rahmawati, M. 2010. "Faktor-Faktor yang Mempengaruhi Pemberian ASI Eksklusif pada Ibu Menyusui di Kelurahan Pedalangan Kecamatan Banyumanik Kota Semarang." *Jurnal Kesmadaska* 1 (1): 8–17.

Razavi, S. 2007. *The Political and Social Economy of Care in a Development Context: Conceptual Issues, Research Questions and Policy Options*. Geneva: United Nations Research Institute for Social Development.

Reerink, A. 2006. *Report on a Survey of Women and Gender Issues in Trade Union Organisations in Indonesia*. Jakarta: ILO.

Sahar, J., M. Courtney and H. Edwards. 2003. "Improvement of Family Carers' Knowledge, Skills and Attitudes in Caring for Older People Following the Implementation of a Family Carers' Training Program in the Community in Indonesia." *International Journal of Nursing Practice* 9: 246–254.

Setyonaluri, D. 2014. "Women Interrupted: Determinants of Women's Employment Exit and Return in Indonesia." *Bulletin of Indonesian Economic Studies* 50 (3): 485–486.

Sheppard, B. 2009. *Workers in the Shadows: Abuse and Exploitation of Child Domestic Workers in Indonesia*. New York: Human Rights Watch.

Silvey, R. and R. Elmhirst. 2003. "Engendering Social Capital: Women Workers and Rural–urban Networks in Indonesia's Crisis." *World Development* 5: 865–879.

Steedman, K. 2013. "Decentralisation, Family Planning and Political Will." Honours Thesis. Sydney: University of Sydney.

Suhaimi, U., M.N. Farid and P. Ruslam. 2013. *Technical Report: The Estimation of Total Domestic Workers in Indonesia*. Jakarta: ILO.

Tjandraningsih, I. 2000. "Gendered Work and Labour Control: Women Factory Workers in Indonesia." *Asian Studies Review* 24 (2): 257–268.

UNCEDAW. 2011. "Consideration of Reports Submitted by State Parties under Article 18 of the Convention on the Elimination of All Forms of Discrimination Against Women." In *Combined Sixth and Seventh Periodic Reports of States Parties*. Geneva: United Nations.

UNESCO. 2005. *Policy Review Report: Early Childhood Care and Education in Indonesia*. Paris: UNESCO.

UNHCR. 2011. *Information on the Implementation of General Assembly Resolution 65/182 Entitle "Follow-Up to the Second World Assembly on Ageing" in Indonesia*. New York: UNHCR.

United Nations Department of Economic and Social Affairs, Population Division. 2013. *World Population Ageing, 2013*. New York: United Nations.

Utomo, A. 2012. "Women as Secondary Earners: Gendered Preferences on Marriage and Employment of University Students in Modern Indonesia." *Asian Population Studies* 8 (1): 65–85.

van Eeuwijk, P. 2006. "Old-Age Vulnerability, Ill-Health and Care Support in Urban Areas of Indonesia." *Ageing and Society* 26 (1): 61–80.

Vaswani, K. 2013. "Are Indonesia's Elderly Changing Course?" *BBC News*, 17 October. http://www.bbc.com/news/business-24530350.

Warouw, N. 2008. "Industrial Workers in Transition: Women's Experiences of Factory Work in Tangerang." In *Women and Work in Indonesia*, edited by M. Ford and L. Parker, 104–119. Abingdon: Routledge.

Witoelar, F. 2012. "Household Dynamics and Living Arrangements of the Elderly in Indonesia: Evidence from a Longitudinal Study." In *Aging in Asia: Findings from New and Emerging Data Initiatives*, edited by J. Smith and M. Majmundar, 229–260. Washington: National Academies Press.

World Bank. 2015a. *Health Nutrition and Population Statistics: Population Estimates and Projections.* http://databank.worldbank.org/Data/Views/VariableSelection/SelectVariables.aspx?source=Health%20Nutrition%20and%20Population%20Statistics:%20Population%20estimates%20and%20projections.

World Bank. 2015b. *Life Expectancy.* https://www.google.com.au/publicdata/explore?ds=d5bncppjof8f9_&met_y=sp_dyn_le00_in&idim=country:IDN:USA:IND&hl=en&dl=en.

6 The Philippines

Pressures for change in the work/care regime

Ligaya Lindio-McGovern

As a major supplier of global care labour, the Philippines is an important site for research into women's work and care in the Asia-Pacific. While on the national scale the country faces challenges in adequately meeting the care demands of its local population, the Philippines' role in the economies of other countries in the region and beyond, through its army of migrant domestic workers, places it at the centre of global networks of care labour supply and demand (Lindio-McGovern 2012; Lindio-McGovern and Wallimann 2013). This phenomenon is partly shaped by the global expansion of capitalism propelled by neoliberal policies such as privatisation and deregulation. As the global expansion of capitalism intensifies, the separation of reproductive and productive labour in order to reduce the cost of the latter is likely to become more prominent, with consequences for the social construction of women's work and care regimes.

Starting from the assumption that any consideration of care work regimes must be framed within the concept of human rights – which demands that society and its institutions begin to question the dominant ideology that positions care work as a function of the family and examine who bears most of the burden in that kind of social arrangement – this chapter examines the political economy of care in the Philippines. It discusses the social profile that provides the context of women's work and its implications for care work, the ideological nature and contradictory features of the Philippine political economy of care, the regulatory framework relevant to care work, and some initiatives that offer possibilities for more fundamental changes in the political economy of care in the Philippines.

A brief demographic profile

Although the Philippines has experienced a declining birth rate (World Bank 2015), its population has grown steadily from 85 million in 2006 (Bangko Central ng Pilipinas n.d.) to 103 million in 2015, with projected growth to 111.7 million in 2020 (PSA 2014a) and to 120.2 million in 2025 (NSO 2012). However, the Philippines is not experiencing the pressures of an ageing population, as are many other countries in the region (Figure 6.1).

As of October 2014, the overall labour force participation rate was 64.3 per cent, or 78.4 per cent for males and 50.3 per cent for females (PSA 2014a). Although

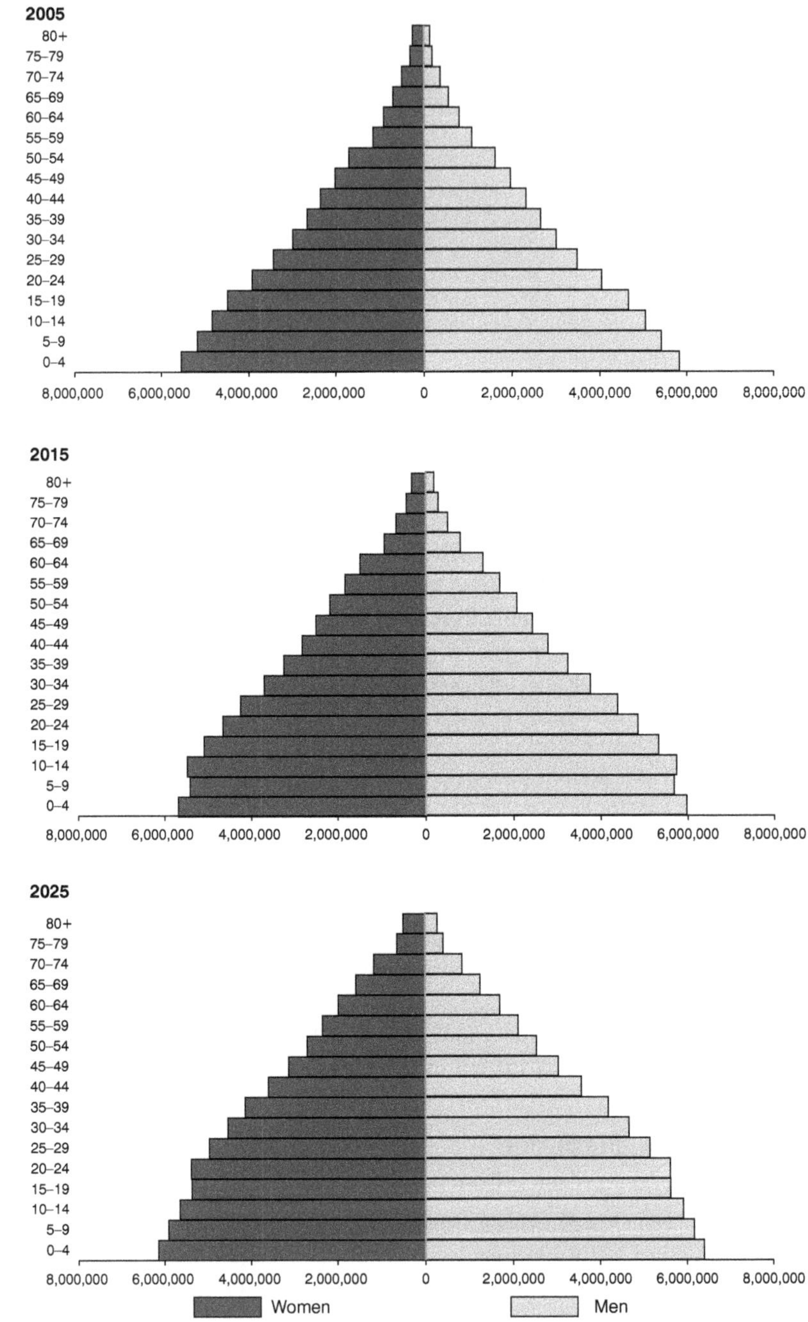

Figure 6.1 Population 2005, 2015, and 2025

Source: World Bank (2015).

female labour force participation remains lower than male, it has increased from 28.2 per cent since 2006 (NSCB 2013). Men and women have almost equal mean hours of work, although the figure for women, at 41.49 hours per week, is slightly higher than that for men, at 40.6 hours per week.

As Table 6.1 demonstrates, the major source of employment in the Philippines is agriculture and forestry. Women participate in all major industry groups; however, in comparison to men, they are more concentrated in wholesale and trade, while men are more concentrated in agriculture. There is also considerable participation of women in agriculture, and women outnumber men in manufacturing (the third largest source of employment), accommodation and food services, education,

Table 6.1 Working population 15 years of age and over by industry and sex, 2014

Occupational group	*Total (%)*	*Male (%)*	*Female (%)*
Number of employed persons (in thousands)	38,453	23,242	15,210
Agriculture, hunting and forestry	26.6	31.7	18.7
Wholesale and retail trades; repair of vehicles	18.8	12.5	28.2
Manufacturing	8.3	7.6	9.3
Transportation and storage	7.0	11.1	0.7
Construction	6.6	10.8	0.3
Other service activities	5.8	2.7	10.6
Public administration; defence; compulsory social security	5.1	4.9	5.6
Accommodation and food service	4.3	3.1	6.3
Fishing	3.5	5.2	0.9
Education	3.4	1.5	6.1
Administrative and support service activities	2.9	3.1	2.6
Activities of household as employers, etc.	1.5	0.3	3.4
Financial and insurance services	1.2	0.9	1.7
Human health and social work activities	1.2	0.7	2.1
Information and communication	1.0	1.0	0.9
Arts, entertainment and recreation	0.8	0.8	0.9
Mining and quarrying	0.6	0.9	0.2
Professional, scientific and technical activities	0.6	0.5	0.6
Real estate activities	0.5	0.4	0.6
Electricity, gas, steam and air conditioning supply	0.2	0.3	0.1
Water supply, sewerage, waste management	0.1	0.2	0.1

Source: July data, Philippine Statistics Authority (2014b).

health and social work, as well as domestic production by households for private consumption.

The distribution of employed persons by sex and occupation, as shown in Table 6.2, reveals that close to one-third of employed people in the Philippines work as labourers and unskilled workers. Since the majority of these are waged workers, they are most likely to be employed in factories, on the assembly lines of multinational corporations in export processing zones and in small and micro-enterprises. As in Indonesia (Ford and Nurchayati, this volume), women are over-represented in clerical, sales and service work, as well as in technical and para-professional occupations. Significantly, three times more women than men work as professionals. More women than men also work as government officials or for special interest organisations, as corporate executives, managers, managing proprietors and supervisors. This pattern can be partly explained by the tendency for women to see education as a means of upward mobility. Middle-class women may seek work outside the home for self-fulfilment (Munoz 2008), and are better able to access education and postpone marriage in order to develop a career. The proportion of women who work as professionals, however, is much smaller than the proportion of women who work as labourers or unskilled workers, as is also the case for men. These class disparities in income and working conditions have implications for women's access to resources for caring for parents and children and even for themselves. Even though reproductive labour is largely considered to be women's responsibility, the lack of resources and low income for working-

Table 6.2 Working population by occupational category and sex, 2014

Occupational group	*Total (%)*	*Male (%)*	*Female (%)*
Number of employed persons (in thousands)	38,453	23, 242	15,210
Labourers and unskilled workers	31.6	31.0	32.6
Government officials, special-interest organisations, corporate executives, managers/managing proprietors/ supervisors	16.1	13.9	19.4
Farmers, forestry workers and fishers	13.6	18.7	5.8
Service workers and shop and market sales workers	12.5	10.2	16.6
Trades and related workers	6.8	9.4	2.7
Clerks	6.3	3.9	9.9
Plant and machine operators and assemblers	5.3	7.6	1.8
Professionals	5.1	2.8	8.5
Technical and associated professionals	2.6	2.0	3.4
Special occupations	0.3	0.4	0.1

Source: July data, Philippine Statistics Authority (2014b).

Table 6.3 Employment status by sex, 2014

Class of worker	*Total (%)*	*Male (%)*	*Female (%)*
Number of employed persons (in thousands)	38, 453	23, 242	15, 210
Wage and salary workers	58.4	60.0	56.0
Private household	5.3	1.3	11.3
Private establishment	44.8	52.1	33.7
Government/government-controlled corporation	7.9	6.2	10.6
Worked with pay in own family farm or business	0.4	0.4	0.3
Self-employed without any paid employee	28.0	28.5	27.1
Employer in own family-operated farm or business	3.3	4.1	2.0
Worked without pay in own family farm or business	10.4	7.5	14.9
Total	100.0	100.0	100.0

Source: July data, Philippine Statistics Authority (2014b).

class men affect the well-being of their households, including women's capacity to balance work and care.

As shown in Table 6.3, the majority of the labour force consists of wage and salary workers, accounting for more than 58 per cent of employed persons, or 60 per cent of the male workforce and 56 per cent of the female workforce. Almost 77 per cent of wage and salary workers are employed by private establishments. A particularly salient feature of the figures relating to wage and salary workers is the fact that 11.3 per cent of women are employed in private households. This level of domestic work reflects the Philippines' very high rate of poverty, which was recorded at 24.9 per cent at the first quarter of 2013 (Bersales 2014). Between 1.9 million and 2.5 million women, predominantly from poor rural families from the Visayas, Bicol and Southern Tagalog, were employed as domestic workers in urban areas (ILO 2013; Sayres n.d.), and particularly in Metro Manila, where the largest concentration of domestic workers can be found. These women, who are generally between the ages of 15 and 24, have little prior work experience and low levels of educational attainment, often no more than elementary school.

Poverty also drives contract work abroad. Over 1 million overseas contract workers migrate annually, encouraged by the labour export programme, which is one of the contradictory features of globalisation in the Philippines (PSA 2014a). Based on the 2013 survey on overseas Filipino workers (PSA 2014b), 25 per cent of the male overseas contract workers were trades and related workers, with a further 21.5 per cent employed as machine operators and assemblers. By contrast, 51.4 per cent of the female overseas contract workers were employed in unskilled occupations as domestic workers, cleaners, launderers and related workers.

A further 18.8 per cent were employed in services or sales. Overseas domestic workers are generally older than local domestic workers, mostly aged between 25 and 34. Overseas domestic workers also have a much broader range of work experience and high school or college education, in contrast to local domestic workers who have mainly elementary education and little prior work experience.[1]

As these statistics suggest, women are very much part of the formal labour force, and as their place in it expands, care work for children and the elderly will become an increasingly pressing problem. Moreover, given that the majority of the workforce is employed in private establishments and the Philippine economy operates within the principles of capitalist relations, it follows that the social reproductive functions of the family benefit the maintenance of this system through the reproduction of labour power.

The political economy of care

The 'necessary labour' (cf. Gimenez 2012) of care work and other social reproductive functions is crucial to human survival, for attaining sustainability or quality of life, and for the maintenance of social institutions. Care work in the Philippines is still largely considered a private matter, a responsibility that belongs mainly to the family. Care for children is primarily the responsibility of mothers and domestic workers. Middle-class families may be able to place their preschool-age children in privately run childcare centres, but these are costly. According to a director of the Department of Social Welfare in the province of Albay, local government has made an effort to increase the level of institutional support available, opening preschool centres for 3- to 4-year-olds (Telephone conversation, March 2015). Priority is given to poor and working-class parents so that they can leave their children while they are at work. However, the centres run morning and afternoon sessions, meaning that children at best have access to a half-day of care. For working-class mothers who do not have access to such arrangements and cannot afford a paid domestic worker, unpaid relatives such as grandmothers and siblings generally provide care.

Elderly Filipinos, too, have been historically dependent on their families for economic and other forms of support. As Abejo (2004, 2–3) notes, citing Hollnsteiner:

> The children, in particular, are expected to provide care and economic security to their parents in old age. This is because the children are said to incur 'utang na loob' (a debt of gratitude) not only for all the sacrifices their parents have made in the process of raising them but for giving them life itself.

As Abejo goes on to observe, it is commonly believed that the traditional familial care remains the dominant mode of care for the elderly. Yet only 68 per cent of the elderly in the Philippines may actually be co-residing with at least one of their children. In both urban and rural areas the incidence of poverty is lower when the elderly live in extended families where there are some members who are gainfully employed. The poverty rate is particularly high among elderly men and women living alone, especially in rural areas (Abejo 2004), where the poverty rate among elderly women living alone is 79 per cent and among elderly men as high as 85 per cent. It is important to note also that the elderly may have particular healthcare needs and are at risk of developing disabilities. The majority of elderly Filipinos suffer from low vision and partial (or total) deafness, and a significant number from paralysis brought about by stroke and heart failure (Carlos 1999). The additional care burden associated with illness and disability has implications for the families caring for the elderly.

As this suggests, the political economy of care work is fraught with contradictions. The sources of these contradictions include the co-existence of a semi-feudal regime with global capitalism, structures of gender and class and the dominant ideology that defines reproductive labour. Despite the existence of a strong women's movement, care work is still considered to be women's work in the Philippines. In the face of women's increasing participation in the labour force, Filipino women's work not only maintains the family but also the reproduction of the country's semi-feudal and capitalist systems (Lindio-McGovern 1997, 2012). In many instances, the peasant woman who together with her husband tills land that belongs to a landlord also does chores for the landlord, often unpaid. Or in a crop-sharing system, women may help their husbands with farm work, but crop-sharing is only based on the male peasant's work. This semi-feudal system co-exists with a capitalist economy that has come to be defined by the neoliberalism that continues to aggressively shape Philippine development. In the capitalist economy, women in paid work are mainly concentrated in low-level formal sector employment and informal sector employment where wages are generally low.

While the current social structure provides a comfortable lifestyle for the classes that benefit most from it, these working-class women experience the double burden of production and social reproduction. As noted earlier, in working-class households, care for the young and the elderly is generally relegated to members of extended families or older siblings while parents are at work. However, social reproduction also involves maintaining a class, mostly made up of poor women, who can be paid extremely low wages, and for survival have no choice but to take on such work at such pay. The work of this under-class of women is a necessary component of the day-to-day maintenance of the household as well as the formal labour force where most middle-class women and professional women are employed.

Care work and other forms of social reproduction are something that wealthy and middle-class families relegate to other women, or even children, of a lower class status. The labour of domestic workers thus allows rich, middle-class and professional women to participate in the formal labour force without having to take on a double shift. Sometimes wealthy families hire nursemaids to undertake childcare along with domestic chores. In some cases, having a nursemaid, who may be a poor relative or distant kin, is simply a status symbol. But middle-class professional women hire nursemaids if they have young children and wish to continue to participate in the formal labour force. Middle-class households also hire domestic workers to attend to the daily needs of the elderly if they can no longer care for themselves. Generally, however, the extended family system means that the care of the elderly involves a mix of family care and paid care by domestic workers.

Another contradictory feature of the Philippine care work regime is the formation of two classes of domestic workers who do paid social reproductive labour as a consequence of overseas labour migration. As women in destination countries join the formal labour force, Filipino overseas domestic workers do the housework that they used to do. The cheap labour of Filipino overseas domestic workers allows destination countries to privatise care work while outsourcing the attendant social costs. The domestic labour of Filipino overseas domestic workers thus supports the national economies not only of the Philippines, but of the destination countries, albeit in contradictory ways. While their remittances contribute to the Philippine economy, the Philippines as a country and the families of overseas domestic workers subsidise the care regimes of destination countries through their investment in human capital. Importantly also, the overseas migration of married women with children opens a labour market for local domestic workers, who are paid lower wages. This creates a status inconsistency (cf. Lindio-McGovern 2012) for overseas domestic workers, whose occupations may be the lowest-paid in the foreign country but nevertheless attract a level of income that allows their families to hire a local domestic worker back in the Philippines. This status inconsistency supports a reproduction of poorly paid domestic workers that maintains the privatised care regime in the Philippines.[2] To resolve these contradictions different stakeholders – including the state, workplaces, various institutions and civil society, including social movements and non-government organisations – must give greater attention to the structures and ideologies that shape the care regime in the Philippines.

The state and the regulation of care

The struggle to change the gendered organisation of productive and reproductive labour necessarily requires challenging the ideology that delinks social reproduction and the maintenance of the economic system and therefore absolves states and workplaces of responsibility. By keeping the wages of domestic workers low, the state makes it possible for care work to be viewed neither as a public responsibility that must be subsidised nor as something that should be paid for or provided by employers. The perpetuation of an ideology that regards care as something to be managed within the household legitimises both this view and the delinking of social reproduction and the economic system. In the Philippine cultural context, this view intersects with cultural expectations that children will take care of their ageing parents, and assumptions that the system will be propped up by cheap domestic labour.

State subsidies for families caring for young children or the elderly, or those with disabilities, provide some safety net for poor families struggling for subsistence. However, the 1986 Philippine Constitution relegates care for the elderly mainly to the family, stating that '[t]he family has the duty to care for its elderly members although the State may also do so through just programs of social security' (Carlos 1999, 5). Social security is defined as a retirement benefit for those who are employed in the private sector and the employer contributes partially to the fund. Although those who work in the informal economy can also put a portion of their income into social security, they have no employer to contribute to their funds. With inadequate income even to meet their daily needs, there is a great likelihood that poor people will forego setting aside money to support themselves in old age. As a consequence, many working in the informal economy may not have been able to contribute to their social security due to low or inadequate levels of income, so in their old age they will be dependent on their children or other relatives.

There are some measures that provide senior citizens with benefits. For example, Filipinos aged 60 or above can avail themselves of the Senior Citizen's identity card that provides a 20 per cent discount on medicine. They are also now covered by PhilHealth, a government health insurance scheme, if they have no employed children who can claim them as dependants. The Department of Social Work and Development (DSWD) has also established a social pension for indigent senior citizens. This provides them with a small stipend of 500 pesos a month if they have no employed children (Telephone conversation with DSWD director, 19 March 2015). In terms of institutional care, Republic Act No.7876, An Act Establishing Senior Citizens Centers in all Cities and Municipalities of the Philippines and Appropriating Funds Therefor 'recognizes the Senior Citizens' right to have access to vital facilities to be able to achieve a more productive, healthful and satisfying life'. The centres mandated under the Act provide recreational, educational, health and social programmes for the elderly (Carlos 1999). In the case of the abandoned elderly, residential facilities are provided by the government and charitable institutions. As of 1999, there were 12 accredited homes known to cater only to the abandoned, needy, neglected or unattached elderly. Being small, these homes are generally overpopulated (Carlos 1999), indicating the need to expand this service.

Steps have also been taken by the government to better provide for pre-school childcare. On 5 December 2000, the government promulgated the Republic Act No. 8980 (Government of the Philippines 2000), An Act Promulgating a Comprehensive Policy and a National System for Early Childhood Care and Development (ECCD), Providing Funds Therefor and For Other Purposes. The Act provides for the establishment of childcare centres for children aged three and four in every local government unit (Arellano Law Foundation, n.d.). The Act also states that national and local governments, non-government organisations and private organisations have joint responsibility for its implementation, and provides an incentive for corporations to provide childcare centres:

> [...] workplace-based or related ECCD programs should be supported by corporations and employers in the form of physical facilities and recurrent operating costs. The operating cost incurred for employer or corporate-sponsored ECCD programs can be deducted from taxable income: provided the employer or corporation will not charge user fees (Section 9.b).

It is unclear, however, to what extent corporations are responding to those incentives.[3]

Finally, the Act contains provisions for the establishment of mechanisms to professionalise Early Childhood Care and Development service providers, including provisions for training and educational programmes. Some private colleges have already offered degree programmes for preschool education.

Regulation of domestic work

The government has also passed legislation to regulate domestic work. The Republic Act 10361, An Act Instituting Policies for the Protection and Welfare of Domestic Workers, was signed into law in 2013.[4] Also known as the 'Batas Kasambahay' or Domestic Workers Act, it defines domestic work as 'work performed in or for a household or households' and a domestic worker (*kasambahay*) as 'any person engaged in domestic work within an employment relationship such as, but not limited to, the following: general house help, nurse maid (*yaya*), cook, gardener, or laundry person, but shall exclude any person who performs domestic work only occasionally or sporadically and not on an occupational basis'.

A striking feature of domestic work in the Philippines is the presence of child domestic workers. The Domestic Workers Act allows for the hiring of child domestic workers aged 15–17 and entitles them to the minimum wage and all benefits provided for under the Act. Sayres (n.d.) suggests that domestic workers often begin working before they reach 15 years of age, in some cases working alongside their mothers. Some view domestic work as a stepping stone to upward social mobility for poor children, but this fails to take into account the fact that their work schedule does not allow them to pursue formal schooling and that what they earn may be spent entirely on support for their families (PSA 2014b). Thus, the presence of child domestic workers aids in the reproduction of future generations of domestic workers, necessary to maintain the privatisation of care work, and relegates it mainly to the family, with the social and economic costs borne by adult and child domestic workers – who are mostly poor women and girls migrating from barrios to towns, from rural areas to cities, separated from their immediate families.

More generally, while the Domestic Workers Act is a 'landmark piece of labor and social legislation', it does not contain any provision requiring the state to share the cost of social reproduction. Another issue is that the very low minimum wage – set at 2,500 pesos (USD 58.13) per month for those employed in the National Capital Region, 2,000 pesos per month for those employed in charter cities and first class municipalities, and 1,500 pesos for those employed in other municipalities – is insufficient to raise domestic workers' families out of poverty. In July 2014, the price of one sack of rice in the province of Albay was 1,600 pesos. Thus, while the Act indeed formalised the regulation of domestic work and recognised it as work, it has legitimised this form of labour as super-low wage work in the service of rich and middle-class households. The Act does extend benefits to domestic workers that are available to workers in the formal labour market, such as health insurance, thirteenth month pay, a written employment contract upon hiring, and official registration of employment. It also requires employers to make a part contribution to the social security benefits of domestic workers if they are paid at least 5,000 pesos per month or shoulder the premiums in full if they are paid less than that amount. There are no stipulated sanctions for non-compliance, although the Act suggests that labour disputes will be handled by the Department of Labor and Employment (DOLE) Regional Office, providing domestic workers with some recourse for grievance.

Pressures for change

The social construction of care work within the framework of a human rights regime requires involvement, advocacy and collective action on the part of social movements from civil society that can exert pressures for change. This is because social inequalities that result from the ideologies and policies that shape productive and reproductive work are embedded in power structures that enable some to accumulate wealth and power, while others are exploited and made powerless. Changing these power structures will require counter-collective power from below. Secondly, as capitalism constantly seeks ways to reduce the cost of labour, the delinking of productive and reproductive labour becomes a subtle mechanism to lower the cost of the productive work of women, subsidising it through women's reproductive work, whether as a double shift for working mothers or as super-cheaply paid work by poor women.

In contrast to other countries in developing Asia, the Philippines women's movement and non-government organisations have played a major role in raising awareness about women's work and care. As far back as 1988, peasant women organised under Amihan, the progressive peasant women's movement in the Philippines, raised the issue of childcare as a collective community concern and the government's responsibility for providing it.[5] Peasant women of a local chapter of Amihan in Mindoro, who saw the need to have their children cared for while they worked in the fields, established childcare centres in their villages, involving their husbands in their construction. In one village they convinced the local municipality to pay the staff member's honorarium. Other than establishing childcare centres, Amihan's long-term agenda is to transform the feudal and semi-feudal agrarian system in the Philippines within the development framework of land to the tiller, with provisions responsive to the needs and rights of peasant women (Lindio-McGovern 1997). Such a long-term goal, once achieved, will have a positive impact on the productive and reproductive roles of women who work in the agricultural sector since, as shown in the previous tables, a considerable number of women work in this largely male sector.

GABRIELA, the national alliance of women's organisations in the Philippines, of which Amihan is a member, also set up childcare centres in Metro Manila that play a big role in the socialisation of children. In opposition to the capitalist logic of delinking productive and reproductive work, GABRIELA advocated for its demands during the drafting of the new 1987 Philippine Constitution, calling on the government to ensure that 'women have the right to maternity benefits and the right not to lose jobs because of pregnancy', and that the welfare and rights of women, family, and children be fully promoted and protected, along with their workplace-related demands for equal pay, equality before the law, and gender equality in marriage (Freisen 1989, 682).

Another organisation in the Philippines that has raised the issues of women's work and care is the Kilusan ng Manggawang Kababaihan (Women Workers' Movement, KMK), which is part of the Kilusang Mayo Uno (May First Movement), a progressive trade union. The Kilusan ng Manggawang Kababaihan represents approximately 2 to 3 per cent of the total membership of the Kilusang Mayo Uno (West 1997); it is also the largest member organisation of GABRIELA. Working-class women generally experience the double burden of productive and reproductive labour more acutely. A KMK leader observed that women workers she had come into contact with frequently raised the implications of women's 'double burden', pointing out that responsibilities at home, such as domestic chores (cooking, cleaning, washing clothes) often make women late for work and expose them to the risk of dismissal (West 1997). In response, the KMK developed a legal and workplace reform programme, the Demands of Women Workers, as part of its focus on developing and influencing policy geared to women's issues and needs.

The Demands of Women Workers demonstrate an awareness that issues related to productive and reproductive work must be addressed simultaneously, thus linking instead of separating them. With regard to women's reproductive role, it advocated protection for pregnant women workers from the risks of heavy work that can harm the health of the unborn child, four months maternity leave, parental leave, social services such as childcare centres for working mothers, an assurance that pregnancy not be used as basis for retrenchment, and three-day menstruation leave (as women workers often complained of the difficulties associated with factory work during their menstrual cycle). With regard to productive work, the demands included full employment and equal pay for women, abolishment of the piece-rate system and forced overtime, and a guarantee of regular work for women (West 1997). The Kilusan ng Manggawang Kababaihan tries to promote these demands at the national level, for example, campaigning for their inclusion in the 1987 constitutional reform process, although in this case their demands went unheard. However, the organisation seems to be making inroads in targeting individual worksites and through collective bargaining, where it continues to struggle for equal pay for equal work (West 1997). It has also bargained for better facilities for working mothers. For instance, in one factory the workers succeeded in convincing the management to establish an on-site day care facility. Management paid the union to hire a childcare worker and provided the space for the facility (West 1997). Thus, while women workers' organisations maintain a separate identity, they are also part of the larger labour movement, providing a voice and platform for specific issues affecting women workers. Being part of the larger labour movement has been even more important when KMK has sought to mobilise support from activists elsewhere in the Asia-Pacific to strengthen their demands for reforms. This is particularly the case in the export processing zones, such as the Bataan Export Processing Zone, where transnational corporations have opposed the unionisation of workers, with support from the government as part of its neoliberal policies to attract transnational capital (Margold 1999).

In addition to movement organisations and unions, non-government organisations have also played an important role with regard to women's rights at work and the welfare of domestic workers. Non-government organisations provide assistance to women workers in the form of organising, leadership training, educational and consciousness-raising activities and other social service needs such as legal assistance with labour issues and complaints. Some provide shelters, counselling, legal and medical assistance for abused domestic workers, and conduct research on domestic workers, child domestic workers and try to draw attention to the reluctance of employers to acknowledge the presence of child domestic workers in their households (Sayres n.d.). Non-government organisations have also engaged at the national policy level in recent years, as evidenced by the passing of the Domestic Workers Act, which indicates a growing awareness of care work as a political issue. The Act came about as a result of pressures from activist groups through lobbying and joining mass demonstrations.[6] One organisation of domestic workers, called the Association of Domestic Workers in the Philippines (Samahan ng mga Mangagawang Pantahanan sa Pilipinas, SUMAPI) was established in 1995 with the assistance of non-government organisations and other advocates. SUMAPI has over 5,000 members nationwide, 20 per cent of whom are male. It engages in awareness-building, advocacy, empowerment, capacity-building and social activities, as well as in rescue operations of abused domestic workers in coordination with local governments, the police and Department of Labor officials. SUMAPI is in the process of assessing whether to register as a workers' union, weighing up the advantages and disadvantages of such a move (Sayres n.d.).

The struggle of Filipino migrant domestic workers abroad has played a role in introducing human rights concerns into the care regime in the Philippines. The formulation of the Domestic Workers Act was patterned after the International Labour Organisation Convention No.189 concerning Decent Work for Domestic Workers, which the Philippines was the second country to ratify.[7] Some local and overseas Filipino domestic workers' organisations participated in negotiations on this Convention. Internationally, Filipino migrant worker organisations, supported by non-government organisations, also play a significant role in organising migrant domestic workers to defend their rights and influence policies affecting them. For example, in Hong Kong, United Filipinos of Hong Kong (UNIFIL), an organisation comprising mostly domestic workers, targets both the Philippine government and the Special Administration Government of Hong Kong with regard to policies that affect them (Lindio-McGovern 2012). In another example, the militant transnational alliance Migrante International, which has chapters in different countries where there are overseas Filipino workers, including domestic workers, was instrumental in the formation of the International Migrants Alliance, comprising mostly domestic workers in Asia.

These initiatives indicate that there are possibilities to position change within women's work and the care regime in the Philippines in a human rights framework. As has been shown here, reproductive labour and productive work impact on each other and are intricately, though often invisibly, linked in women's lives. Their social construction within a human rights framework requires the involvement and cooperation of various stakeholders: civil society, social movements, the state and workplaces. But it is persistent pressures from below that will provide the engine for change. When people come together to claim their rights, they create communities of struggle that carry the vision and values necessary to build a sustainable future that includes developing a shared responsibility for the work of care.

Notes

1 Most overseas domestic workers originate from Metro Manila, Southern Tagalog, Ilocos, Cagayan Valley, Central Luzon, Soccsksargen and Western Visayas, whereas local domestic workers migrate to urban areas or towns mainly from the Visayas, Bicol and Southern Tagalog (Sayres n.d.).
2 For a more thorough discussion of the situation and experiences of Filipino migrant domestic workers in Hong Kong, Taiwan, Rome, Chicago and Vancouver, see Lindio-McGovern (2012).
3 One large semi-private corporation that once established a day care centre for its own employees is NAPOCOR (National Power Corporation) in Daraga, Albay province. The day care centre was located in the compound of the company so that workers could bring their children as they came to work. The parents contributed to the honorarium paid to staff. The company contribution consisted of the provision of the facility, facility-related expenses (electricity, etc.) and school supplies. However, the company was unable to sustain the initiative (Telephone conversations, March 2015, April 2015).
4 The Act can be accessed in full at http://www.gov.ph/2013/01/18/republic-act-no-10361.
5 An example is documented in Lindio-McGovern (1997, 109–112).
6 Before the Domestic Workers Act there was already legislation on local domestic workers but there was a low level of implementation and public awareness of the law.
7 Some Filipino migrant domestic workers were engaged in policy advocacy around the Convention. Following consultation meetings with other domestic workers, they wrote a position paper with the support of the Mission for Filipino Migrants in Hong Kong. Among the demands presented was the right to collective bargaining and unionisation. As only unions were allowed to participate in deliberations on the convention on 1 June 2011, and domestic workers are not unionised, a delegate from the May First Movement of the Philippines (KMU) represented domestic workers in the deliberations.

References

Abejo, S. 2004. "Living Arrangements of the Elderly in the Philippines." Paper presented at 9th National Convention on Statistics (NCS), EDSA Shangri-la Hotel, 4–5 October.

Arellano Law Foundation. n.d. Republic Act No. 8980 December 05, 2000. An Act Promulgating A Comprehensive Policy and National System for Early Childhood Care and Development (ECCD) Providing Funds Therefor and for Other Purposes. http://www.lawphil.net/statutes/repacts/ra2000/ra_8980_2000.html.

Bangko Sentral ng Pilipinas. n.d. "Philippines Population." Accessed 28 February 2015. http://www.tradingeconomics.com/charts/philippines-population.png?s=phl+sp.pop.totl.

Bersales, L. 2014. "One in Every Two Female OFW is an Unskilled Worker (Results from the 2013 Survey of Overseas Filipinos)." Philippine Statistics Authority, Republic of the Philippines. http://web0.psa.gov.ph/content/one-every-two-female-ofws-unskilled-worker-results-2013.

Carlos, C. 1999. "Concerns of the Elderly in the Philippines." *Philippine Social Review* 56 (1–4): 2–40.

Freisen, D. 1989. "The Women's Movement in the Philippines." *NWSA Journal* 1 (4): 676–688.

Gimenez, M. [2009] 2012. "Global Capitalism and Women: From Feminist Politics to Working Class Women's Politics." In *Globalization and Third World Women: Exploitation, Coping and Resistance,* edited by L. Lindio-McGovern and I. Wallimann, 35–48. Abingdon: Routledge.

Government of the Philippines. 2000. *Republic Act No. 8980, December 5, 2000, An Act Promulgating A Comprehensive Policy and National System for Early Childhood and Development (ECCD), Providing Funds Therefor and for Other Purposes.* http://www.lawphil.net/statutes/repacts/ra2000/ra_8980_2000.html.

ILO. 2013. Philippines Enact New Law Protecting Domestic Workers. http://www.ilo.org/wcmsp5/groups/public/---ed_protect/---protrav/---travail/documents/publication/wcms_211052.pdf

Lindio-McGovern, L. 1997. *Filipino Peasant Women: Exploitation and Resistance.* Philadelphia: University of Pennsylvania Press.

Lindio-McGovern, L. 2012. *Globalization, Labor Export and Resistance: A Study of Filipino Migrant Domestic Workers in Global Cities.* Abingdon: Routledge.

Lindio-McGovern, L. and I. Wallimann. 2013. *Globalization and Third World Women: Exploitation, Coping and Resistance.* New York: Syracuse University Press.

Margold, J. 1999. "Reformulating the Compliant Image: Filipina Activists in the Global Factory." *Urban Anthropology and Studies of Cultural Systems and World Economic Development* 26 (1): 1–35.

Munoz, G. 2008. "Seeking Self-Worth. Fighting Boredom: Why Women Choose to Work in Catbalogan, Samar, Philippines." *Sojourn: Journal of Social issues in Southeast Asia* 23 (2): 186–215.

NSCB. 2013. *Sexy Statistics – Gender Equality in the Philippines, What's the Real Score.* http://www.nscb.gov.ph/sexystats/2013/fig3.jpj.

NSO. 2012. *Demography: Philippine Yearbook 2012.* Manila: NSO.

PSA, Philippine Statistics Authority. 2014a. *Gender Quickstat.* http://web0.psa.gov.ph/statistics/quickstat.

PSA, Philippine Statistics Authority 2014b. *July 2014 Labor Force Survey.* Available at http://web0.psa.gov.ph/node/49445.

Sayres, N. n.d. "An Analysis of the Situation of Filipino Domestic Workers." ILO Special Action Program to Combat Force Labour: Mobilizing Action for the Protection of Domestic Workers From Forced Labour and Trafficking in Southeast Asia.

West, L. 1997. *Militant Labor in the Philippines.* Philadelphia: Temple University Press.

World Bank. 2015. Health Nutrition and Population Statistics: Population Estimates and Projections. http://databank.worldbank.org/Data/Views/VariableSelection/SelectVariables.aspx?source=Health%20Nutrition%20and%20Population%20Statistics:%20Population%20estimates%20and%20projections.

7 Cambodia

Managing work and care in a post-conflict context

Kristy Ward

The interaction between work and care in Cambodia is shaped by the intersecting dynamics of labour transitions, demographic shifts, entrenched societal norms regarding men's and women's roles in the family, the central role of families as care providers in state policy and social discourse, and state regime change. This complex web of factors affects women's engagement in the labour market, leading to a gender gap in decent work and compounding women's economic and care burden.

In Cambodia, the balance of care is distributed rather unevenly across the household, the community, the state and, to a lesser extent, the market. Childcare and eldercare is predominantly provided by extended families – and within this domain almost exclusively by women. Traditional family structures are changing as a consequence of migration and constrained labour markets, which have increased the need for non-familial care. Many households, however, are unable to afford private day care centres or domestic workers. This in turn influences women's decisions on whether or not to work and the types of work that women are able to perform.

Limited government policy and employer responses to women's increased labour force participation echo wider public discourses and stereotypes about men's and women's roles in society. A policy lacuna has constrained women's labour choices to forms of work that provide flexibility for care arrangements; it has also resulted in a dramatic increase in not-for-profit care provision for vulnerable families, which is problematic given the limited enforcement of child protection regulations. The market has been unable to fill the gap in public sector childcare services, as less affluent households – which make up a high percentage of the population – are unable to afford the cost of fee-paying care. In addition, state preschool availability in rural areas is extremely limited, resulting in community- and home-based responses that are dependent on women's voluntary and unpaid work. The situation is further complicated by a growing demand for eldercare. Cambodia's population profile is relatively young as a consequence of high rates of morbidity during the Khmer Rouge era (1975–79). However, the percentage of older persons is increasing. Due to the lack of comprehensive social protection policies and changing family structures, Cambodians often work well into their elder years or are cared for by adult children. As a consequence of high rates of internal and international migration, older people are themselves also important care providers for young children.

This chapter examines the provision of care across family, state, market and the not-for-profit sector. It shows how a gendered pattern of care distribution limits women's work and life choices, and that Cambodian government policies entrench rather than challenge this status quo. First, it discusses the demographic and historical trends that have shaped the work/care nexus, including women's increased labour force participation, the diversification of employment to manufacturing and the prevalence of informal sector employment. Accompanying these workforce transitions are changes in family composition arising from post-conflict legacies including a high proportion of female-headed households, older female widows, children under 15 years and persons with disabilities. The chapter then explores the various institutions that provide care, highlighting the gender norms that underpin the skewed distribution of care provision and the limitations of state and community early childhood care and education programmes. Policy interventions, where they exist, reinforce ideas about what care is and who it should be provided by. Also analysed here are civil society responses to issues of work and care, including the feminisation of voluntary work as an extension of women's care roles. The chapter concludes by exploring the challenges generated by the work/care regime for women, highlighting women's preference for low-paid and unsafe informal sector work because of the flexibility it offers in managing the disproportionate work/care balance.

Care and work in context

Cambodia has a population of 14.6 million with a sex ratio of 94.3 males for every 100 females (NIS 2013). Just over 29 per cent of the population is aged less than 15 years, including almost one-third under 6 years (Figure 7.1). A small but increasing percentage of the population (5 per cent) is over the age of 65. Fertility rates remain relatively high when compared with other countries in the region, at an average of 2.7 live births per woman, a rate that has reduced from 4.0 in 2000 (NIS 2013).

Extended familial arrangements, where several generations co-reside, are common in Cambodia. There is a growing tendency toward nuclear arrangements, where newly married couples initially live with the bride's parents before establishing independent households. The number of nuclear households grew at the end of the 1990s, but this trend then reversed marginally from 2000 as a consequence of social and work transitions including labour migration and chronic economic vulnerability (Demont and Heuveline 2008). Extended households are more prevalent in urban areas as a consequence of higher living costs. As of 2014, 22.3 per cent of Cambodian households were headed by women (NIS 2014).

The composition of households in Cambodia is also influenced by rural–urban and international labour migration. Patterns of labour migration are often circular, with migrants returning home to care for elderly relatives or when younger family members are old enough to migrate. While females have traditionally dominated labour migration flows, in 2011 there were 10,656 documented female and 15,563

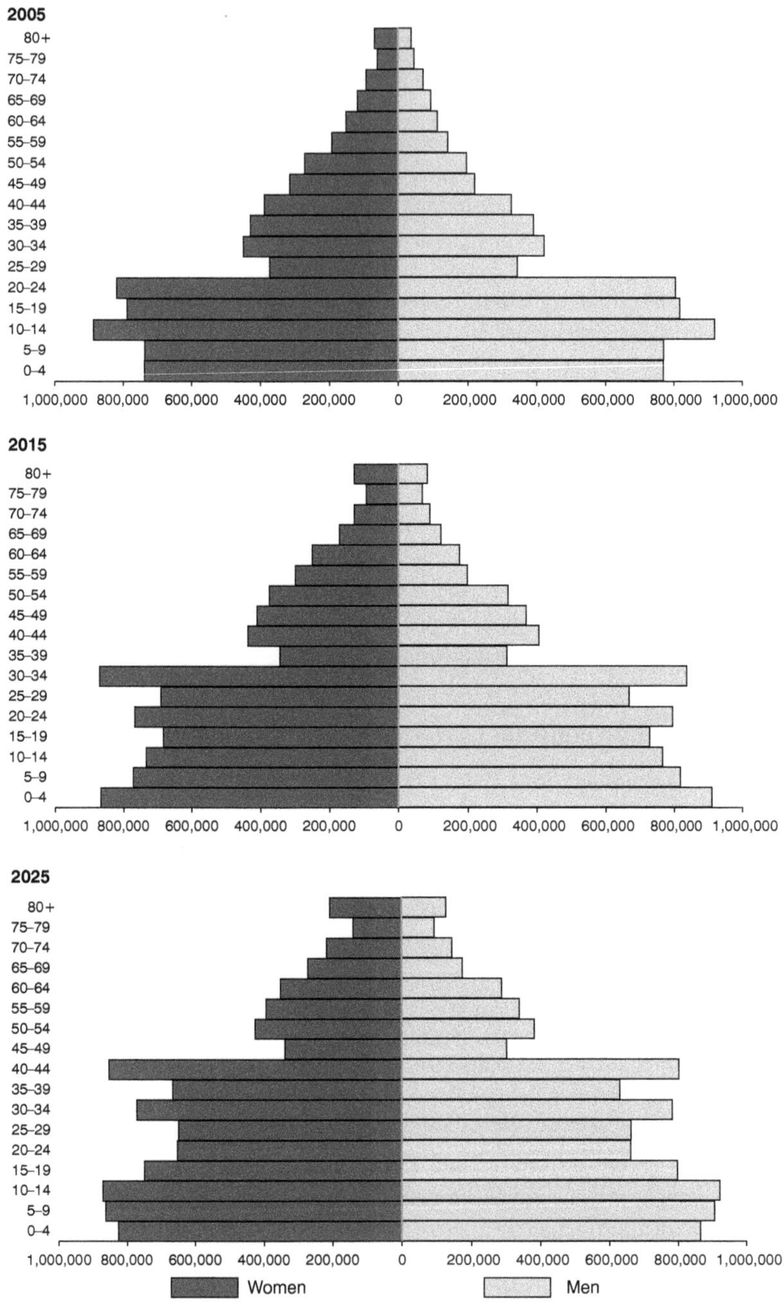

Figure 7.1 Population 2005, 2015, and 2025

Source: World Bank (2015).

male labour migrants abroad. Undocumented labour migration figures are believed to be considerably higher (around 250,000), with many crossing Cambodia's porous border with Thailand for work (Tunon and Rim 2013). Meanwhile, gender disaggregated data on rural–urban migration within Cambodia indicates that 33.7 per cent of all migrants are young single women. One in five migrants left children under 15 years in their village of origin and, of those, 84 per cent left children with a parent (Ministry of Planning 2012). For women with children, care responsibilities often shift to female members of extended families in their places of origin, including grandmothers, elder female siblings and aunts.

Disability compounds these care responsibilities. Cambodia has a high incidence of disability due to several decades of civil conflict, traffic accidents and the availability, cost and quality of healthcare (Connelly 2009). As of 2012, some 8.2 per cent of the population lived with at least one type of disability, many involving mobility and vision impairment (NIS and ILO 2013). Persons with a disability have little access to health and education services, which means that not only are families the only care provider, but the care required is more complex. Fewer than 10 per cent of children and young persons with a disability have access to education due to a lack of accessibility and discrimination. Persons with a disability of all ages face similar barriers in regard to healthcare, despite a 2004 Ministerial Proclamation guaranteeing free access (Connelly 2009).

Cambodia's economic transition has paralleled demographic change, further complicating familial arrangements for the provision of care. Since the 1980s, positive economic growth and export-oriented industrialisation have contributed to a marginal diversification of employment opportunities for both men and women. In 2013 the number of employed persons in Cambodia was 8.1 million, with almost equal numbers of men and women. Just over half of the labour force is employed in agriculture (NIS 2010). While Cambodia's economy remains highly informalised – 81.2 per cent of the workforce is engaged in the informal sector (NIS and ILO 2012) – there has nevertheless been some redistribution of employment from agriculture to services and manufacturing.

As Table 7.1 shows, women's labour is concentrated in skilled agriculture and fisheries, followed by wholesale and retail trade and manufacturing. Less than 1 per cent of women are employed in public administration. As in Bangladesh and Sri Lanka (Siddiqi and Ashraf, this volume; Withers, this volume), female garment workers make an important contribution to the economy. Although manufacturing accounts for just 13.73 per cent of female employment, 90 per cent of garment sector employees are women, usually single, who migrate to Phnom Penh for work as a rural household livelihood strategy. As Derks (2008) identifies, women also move in search of modernity and independence in the city. Secondary and tertiary sector employment for men, who find work in manufacturing (8 per cent), construction (7.40 per cent), transportation and storage (7.42 per cent) and public administration and defence (4.98 per cent), is marginally more dispersed.

The concentration of women in a narrow range of industries seems inconsistent with their high rate of labour force participation. At 78 per cent, women's labour force participation rates in Cambodia are among the highest in the region, and

Table 7.1 Working population 15 years of age and over by industry and sex, 2013

Economic activity	*Male (%)*	*Female (%)*
Agriculture, forestry and fishing	52.91	55.36
Mining and quarrying	0.35	0.07
Manufacturing	8.00	13.73
Electricity, gas, steam and air conditioning supply	0.64	0.03
Water supply; sewerage, waste management and remediation activities	0.58	1.25
Construction	7.40	0.43
Wholesale and retail trade; repair of motor vehicles and motorcycles	7.89	17.93
Transportation and storage	7.42	0.64
Accommodation and food service activities	1.88	3.81
Information and communication	0.28	0.20
Financial and insurance activities	0.37	0.23
Real estate activities	0.02	0.03
Professional, scientific and technical activities	0.40	0.13
Administrative and support service activities	2.19	1.73
Public administration and defence; compulsory social security	4.98	0.65
Education	2.34	1.33
Human health and social work activities	0.47	0.31
Arts, entertainment and recreation	0.57	0.50
Other service activities	0.68	1.31
Activities of households as employers; undifferentiated goods- and services-producing activities of households for own use	0.00	0.00
Activities of extraterritorial organisations and bodies	0.57	0.30
Not elsewhere classified	0.06	0.05
Total	100.00	100.00

Source: ILO (2013).

have increased considerably since 2004 (NIS 2014). Higher rates of workforce participation are found amongst women aged 35–44 years (87.7 per cent) when compared with other age groups. However, rates are lower for urban women (67 per cent) than for rural women (80.3 per cent), reflecting the number of women in agricultural production. Women's choices regarding work, and their ability to pay for care, are dependent on their access to resources. In less financially secure households men and women – and often children – work as a survival strategy. In more affluent urban households women may not work, and are more able to afford to pay for care through private preschools or by hiring domestic workers.

Table 7.2 Working population by occupational category and sex, 2013

Occupation	*Male (%)*	*Female (%)*
Managers, professionals, and technicians	5.58	2.67
Clerical, service and sales workers	14.11	23.96
Skilled agricultural and trades workers	55.32	58.37
Plant and machine operators, and assemblers	6.19	0.46
Elementary occupations	17.32	14.43
Armed forces	1.47	0.11
Total	100.00	100.00

Source: ILO (2013).

As Table 7.3 shows, over 60 per cent of working Cambodian women are engaged in either unpaid or irregular own-account employment. Women are twice as likely as men to perform unpaid family work and are less likely to be in an employment arrangement and thus covered by the labour law. In most cases, women in the informal sector find work as street vendors, market traders, waste-pickers or sex workers (Derks 2008). Women's disproportionate representation in the informal sector is a consequence of both structural limitations, for example, in relation to access to education, and women's responsibility for provision of care. There is a high degree of diversity among female informal sector workers engaged in trade, who are distributed across more diverse age and socio-economic groups when compared with primarily young unmarried women in garment factory and sex work. The diversity of women in trading also reflects women's carer responsibilities. Derks (2008) found that day-time market traders were older women aged 40 years and above, while younger women were involved in night stands and itinerant trade. By contrast, young unmarried women with fewer domestic responsibilities engage in work that is less accommodating of unpaid caregiver roles, such as garment factory work, where hours are long and highly regulated.

The spread of employment based on occupation (see Table 7.2) largely mirrors its sectoral spread. However, aggregate figures conceal the correlation between age, gender and occupation. Younger women aged 15–19 are concentrated in skilled manual labour (24.5 per cent), those aged 45–59 dominate agricultural employment (65.1 per cent), and sales and service employment is consistent across most age ranges (20–49 years) at 22 per cent (NIS 2010). By comparison, men are more likely to be employed in agriculture in their younger years (72.6 of 15- to 19-year-old males) and skilled manual labour between the ages of 20–29 years (26.95 per cent). Although men across all age groups are more likely to be located in managerial and professional roles, women in their 20s are better represented in professional and managerial positions than older women. Younger women occupy 6.5 per cent of these positions, compared with an aggregate figure for women of 2.67 per cent. This points, in part, to a growing number of girls and young women attending primary and secondary education (NIS 2014).

Table 7.3 Employment status by sex, 2013

Status in employment	*Male (%)*	*Female (%)*
Employees	51.52	39.89
Employers	0.47	0.31
Own-account workers	34.46	32.59
Contributing family workers	13.54	27.22
Workers not classifiable by status	0.00	0.00
Total	100.00	100.00

Source: ILO (2013).

To sum up, employment in Cambodia is centred on specific occupations and industries in which both men and women are found in large numbers. Although women are concentrated in a small number of industries, the main type of employment for women and men remains agriculture and the informal sector (much of it own-account trading and vending), which is generally unskilled/semi-skilled and low paid. This predominance of low-paid informal sector work means that lower-income families are unable to pay for care. A further complicating factor is entrenched social norms regarding productive and reproductive roles, which determine the highly gendered and familial provision of care.

The provision of care

Despite the complex interactions between Cambodia's history, patterns of labour and mobility and gender roles, social norms regarding women and their role in society have continued to pervade and dictate state responses to the work–care dynamic. Public value is ascribed to women's roles in unpaid care work. Women and men are both responsible for the (re)production of these social norms (Brickell 2011). For example in one survey, 81 per cent of female respondents stated that women should remain at home and care for their children and husbands, compared with 77 per cent of male respondents (Brickell, Prak and Poch 2014). It is these social and cultural norms regarding men's and women's roles that shape the gendered provision of care in Cambodia across various social institutions, including the household and workplace, and in public policy debates.

Prior to 1970, women's prominence in the household, including in relation to economic matters, and their role in agricultural production led to assertions that Cambodian women enjoyed a relatively equal position in society (Ebihara 1968). In practice, however, there were – and still are – deeply entrenched expectations that women preserve traditional values in order to maintain Khmer cultural identity, enforced through strict codes of moral behaviour (Jacobsen 2008; Derks 2008). Women's role as bearers of culture and tradition has become more pronounced in the aftermath of the Khmer Rouge, when social norms, institutions and social bonds were intentionally dismantled by the regime. In the post-conflict context, women who digress from socially prescribed roles, as dutiful daughters and mothers who care for families and obey husbands and fathers, may be seen as a threat to Cambodia's national identity (Brickell 2011; Derks 2008).

These deeply embedded beliefs have intersected with political regime transitions since the 1980s, with the latter substantially influencing the role of the state in the provision of care. During the period of the People's Republic of Kampuchea in the 1980s, the government established a centralised governance structure informed by socialist ideologies. Through this structure, social services were provided by various agencies including youth associations, women's associations, the National Salvage Front, trade unions and agricultural cooperatives (Nuon and Serrano 2010). Childcare was funded by the government with facilities provided in state-run factories, ministries in Phnom Penh, and cooperatives in rural areas.

The transition to a market economy in the early 1990s led to a focus on the privatisation of social services previously funded by the government. In addition, a state budget crisis between 1989 and 1992 prompted the closure of most state-sponsored childcare centres, as the state further reduced public expenditure in favour of neoliberal growth policies (Netra and Sovann 2007). Since that time, a number of other social policies have been put in place to indirectly support women in their care roles, but these have not been developed in response to the way women and families arrange paid work and care, or to the disproportionate care burden placed on women that entrenches inequitable patterns of workforce participation. As a consequence, and as argued in this chapter, institutional arrangements to balance care and paid work have remained largely absent or ineffective. Thus care remains highly informalised and familial.

Economic growth strategies have been supported by labour regulation considered necessary to build confidence in Cambodia as an ethical garment producer, and to facilitate bilateral trade agreements and export quotas favourable to sustained foreign investment (Oka 2015). Propelled by the International Labour Organisation (ILO), labour reforms from the late 1990s onwards have included consideration of care responsibilities through provision of maternity leave, return to work arrangements and other special leave provisions. The 1997 Labour Law contains detailed maternity leave provisions. All employed women are entitled to 90 days maternity leave at half salary for women with a year of uninterrupted service, and breastfeeding mothers are entitled to a one-hour break per day for up to 12 months after giving birth. In addition, enterprises employing more than 100 employees are required to either establish nursing rooms and day care centres or pay for the cost of childcare for employees. In the garment manufacturing sector, the majority of female employees are aware of these maternity leave provisions (ILO 2012). Compliance is, however, highly problematic. A third of factories monitored by Better Factories Cambodia were found to use fixed duration contracts to subvert legislative maternity leave provisions (ILO 2012). In addition, visibly pregnant workers are often not hired, childcare facilities in larger factories are non-existent, and subcontracting factories are largely non-compliant (Human Rights Watch 2015). Moreover, in practice, maternity leave provisions apply to only a marginal percentage of the female workforce. As most women are engaged in either own-account or informal sector work, legislative reform with regard to employment relations has had minimal impact on women's childcare responsibilities.

The promotion of gender equality, employment and economic growth in regard to women's paid work has focused for the most part on vocational training and skills development. The Ministry of Women's Affairs (MoWA) and the Asian Development Bank have attempted to increase women's participation in the formal labour sector through training and skills development (MoWA 2009). This approach – which has not been complemented by appropriate consideration of how women reconcile work/care responsibilities – suggests that informal sector work and inequitable pay are solely an issue of skills deficit, rather than one of care deficit. While skills capacity may assist women to access more work options, in practice women's ability to attend vocational training is limited by their disproportionate care responsibilities. MoWA's five-year strategic plan identifies the need to provide day care facilities and kindergartens to support women's skills development, however fails to propose any specific strategies to address this deficit (MoWA 2009). Such policy responses entrench the idea that only women provide care, rather than supporting women to challenge household inequality.

Razavi (2007) argues that social protection policies funded by the state enable families to better balance care and work needs. Support may take the form of direct care provision (preschool childcare centres), ancillary policies and programmes (elderly pensions, health funds, school feeding programmes), or cash transfers to pay for care. In Cambodia, social protection policies prior to 2011 and the complementary Social Protection Law provided disability, death and old age pension coverage for public sector employees, and a limited range of coverage for private enterprises (Kwon, Cook and Kim 2014). There was, however, no coverage for informal sector workers, small private enterprises or vulnerable groups. In an attempt to address this gap, a National Social Protection Strategy for the Poor and Vulnerable was released in 2011. The Cambodian policy has been identified as 'care friendly' (Chopra 2014) due to the inclusion of a public works component with a focus on women and the provision of crèche facilities. Other provisions include social security for the elderly and female-headed households. While beneficial, the intention is to prevent child labour – itself a positive focus – rather than to redistribute responsibility for care to the state. However there are no provisions for redirecting care provision to men. Further, coverage is limited and the policy is yet to be implemented due to coordination issues between the numerous development actors involved (Kwon, Cook and Kim 2014).

Education policies and programmes have also failed to sufficiently address the care requirements of many families. Early childcare and education for children up to six years of age has attracted attention from Cambodian policymakers in recent years. Although enrolment numbers have increased, only 34 per cent of children aged three to five were enrolled in preschool in 2014. State programmes dominate, and are largely located in urban areas, covering 18 per cent of the total three- to five-year-old population (Khieng et al. 2015). In terms of the distribution of enrolments across the four main types of preschool education, state enrolments account for 32.7 per cent of enrolments for the three to five age group and 56.5 per cent for five to six year olds. Considerably lower enrolment is found in community preschools, home-based programmes and private preschools, at 6.5 per cent, 5 per cent and 4 per cent respectively (Rao et al. 2012). Despite the renewed government interest in early childhood education, the Ministry of Education Youth and Sport's (MoEYS) National Action Plan of Early Childhood 2014–2018 explicitly states that primary responsibility for early childcare and education rests with families and the community (MoEYS 2014). As stated in the MOEYS Action Plan, it is expected that the costs of home- and community-based programmes will be met by communities.

Community-based preschool programmes are primarily located in peri-urban and rural areas where limited formal education and private care facilities exist. Although policy directives for community preschools were initiated by the Ministry, programmes are financed by non-government organisations through international donor funding and are implemented in partnership with elected local governments (Rao et al. 2012). Female participation and management is critical to these programmes which require the unpaid work of mothers' groups to run. Home-based programmes are also organised and staffed by volunteer local mothers' groups. This not only indicates that care work is highly gendered and under-valued, but also calls into question the quality of early childhood education. Similarly, urban and rural poverty reduction programmes funded by non-government organisations, and, to a lesser extent, the state, consistently establish management committees, user groups and savings groups with gender targets. While men often take leadership roles, women's participation is seen as essential in these projects as a means of 'empowerment' (Chant and Brickell 2014; Chant 2008). As the case of community preschools demonstrates, these initiatives can have a contradictory effect, as they require women to take on unpaid roles to promote participation and as a cost effective mechanism for project implementation. While this extends responsibility for care beyond the household, it entrenches care work as 'women's work' with no economic value.

Another development in the not-for-profit provision of childcare over the last decade is the substantial increase in residential care facilities. A 2014 study conducted by UNICEF and the Ministry of Social Affairs, Veterans and Youth Rehabilitation (MoSVY) identified 11,453 children in 228 residential care facilities throughout Cambodia, with the number of facilities increasing by as much as 75 per cent between 2005 and 2011. A 2016 mapping study by MoSVY shows this number to be much higher. In only five provinces[1] 11,788 children were being cared for across 267 residential care institutions (MoSVY 2016). Of these 84 had no agreement with any Ministry to operate,[2] 37 were completely unregistered, and only nine (3 per cent) were state run.

Labour migration and economic vulnerability have led to much higher rates of residential care for children, with only 23 per cent of children in residential care having no living parent (UNICEF 2011). In the absence of state social protection programmes residential care becomes the only option for many parents unable to afford the cost of food and education for their children. The majority of institutions (74 per cent) are found in Phnom Penh and Siem Reap. For the most part, this increase can be attributed to orphanage tourism, which is utilised as a strategy to raise funds for the operation of care facilities (UNICEF 2011). While poor families view residential care as a last resort, high numbers of children with parents in care can also be attributed to divorce and active advertising and recruitment by residential institution management (MoSVY 2016).

Although the MoSVY's Minimum Standards of Alternative Care require facilities to register with the Ministry to implement child protection measures, there remains no mechanism for background checks on facility staff and volunteers. A UNICEF report on residential care facilities in 2011 highlights that facilities are able to operate unregistered, or with registration through other ministries, thus raising concerns regarding child safety and well-being. In addition, monitoring and enforcement by provincial departments of education is irregular and has led to only a small number of facility closures through non-compliance with minimum standards. A sub-decree issued by the Ministry in September 2015 aiming to address the escalating numbers of children with parents in orphanages, and the safety of children in residential care, gives the MoSVY sole discretion to register and monitor residential centres and reports of abuse, and close unregistered or non-compliant centres (Royal Government of Cambodia 2015).

By contrast, the market has minimal involvement in childcare provision in Cambodia. Private and state preschools and kindergartens mainly operate in larger towns or city centres. The demand generated by higher household incomes in urban areas has prompted an increase in the number of private fee-paying kindergartens in Phnom Penh in particular (Khieng et al. 2015). As in neighbouring countries such as Singapore, Malaysia and Indonesia, wealthier women from middle-class families may also hire other Cambodian women to assist with childcare and household work, including cooking and cleaning. Domestic workers are specifically excluded from the 1997 Labour Law and the Government of Cambodia has not signed ILO Convention No.189 concerning Decent Work for Domestic Workers, despite pressure from civil society. Failure to ratify the convention appears inconsistent with the government's decision in 2011 to ban Cambodian women from migrating to Malaysia for domestic work in response to reports of exploitative working conditions and physical and sexual abuse.[3] Moreover, the reluctance of the Cambodian government to ratify the Domestic Worker Convention is perhaps in part due to the importance of transnational labour migration for remittances – a convenient fix for domestic poverty and formal employment gaps – and the low value of domestic work in Cambodia (Gartrell 2010).

Social protection gaps are also evident in relation to older persons. A 2004 study showed that older Cambodians are more likely to be women (59.8 per cent) who are widowed (64.3 per cent). Only 31 per cent of women aged over 60 years were married. In comparison, 81.5 per cent of men in the same age group were married and 16 per cent were widowed (Knodel et al. 2005). Aside from pensions for public sector employees and veterans, there is no state-funded pension scheme and aged care facilities are almost non-existent. In the absence of social protection policies, older persons rely on a combination of economic activity and support from children and neighbours. Inter-census data from 2013 indicates that 39.3

per cent of women aged 65 and above are economically active, with a higher rate of 61.3 per cent for men, a slight decrease from the 2008 figures (NIS 2013). Economic activity among older persons, primarily farming, gardening and small-scale trade, is more common in rural areas (Knodel et al. 2005). Support from children supplements economic activity and is crucial for older persons unable to work due to health or disability impairments. Some 80 per cent of older persons lived with at least one child, with older women more likely to be living with unmarried female children and one in ten living with widowed daughters (Zimmer and Kim 2001). Thus older women provide care to households, including the provision of childcare, while simultaneously receiving care.

Limited access to health facilities in rural areas, and for the urban poor, makes care for the aged more complex, as do the psychosocial impacts of the Khmer Rouge (Chhim 2013). A 2005 survey of elderly Cambodians (Knodel et al. 2005) found that 88 per cent of women and 71 per cent of men had a functional limitation that affected their capacity to live independently. Half of the respondents reported daughters as their main caregivers followed by grandchildren (25 per cent). The survey did not identify the gender of caregiving grandchildren, but social norms regarding care in Cambodia would suggest granddaughters rather than grandsons perform these care duties. By comparison, sons were reported as the primary caregivers by 8.1 per cent of respondents. Thus women and girls perform the bulk of eldercare.

The failure of the public sector and the market to keep pace with the care demands associated with changing labour and household dynamics forces responsibility for care back onto the household. In the absence of more accessible formal care options, these responsibilities are met primarily by extended co-habiting families. Familial support networks perform multiple functions, including care provision and the reduction of household expenditure. These arrangements continue to be critical in a context where social protection safety nets for vulnerable groups are not fully developed, or have not been implemented. But whereas households have traditionally managed care in extended (and gendered) arrangements, increases in women's engagement in paid work and in labour mobility as a part of a household's livelihood strategy mean that women are required to make choices between work, care and economic security. In some cases, families and women manage the consequences of these choices with the assistance of female family members. In others, however, women choose to leave formal sector employment and its limited regulatory protections for informal sector work, despite irregular and lower incomes, in order to access the flexibility required to meet care responsibilities.

Pressure points

Cambodian women's increased labour force participation in paid roles, and the moderate diversification of the types of work that women undertake, have failed to disrupt social expectations around women's unpaid care and work roles in the domestic sphere. It is partly as a consequence of entrenched gendered norms that women's complex work transitions have not been accompanied by a more sustainable distribution of the responsibility for care. Social expectations, compounded by inadequate state policies and unaffordable market-based childcare, continue to constrain both women's ability to engage in paid work and the type of work they are able to do. For example, many garment workers are forced to seek work in the informal sector to accommodate their caregiver roles. Women make this constrained choice in order to be able to determine their own hours, earn daily income and work from home. Informal work also allows women the flexibility to have children accompany them to work. But in the process, they relinquish regular wages and the formal labour rights protections afforded to them under the labour law.

There has been a marginal policy shift to better enable households to manage care, and shift responsibility for care from the household to the state or the market. However, it is necessary to make two important qualifications to this observation. First, policies and social attitudes are focused on supporting women in their care roles, rather than redistributing responsibilities to men. As Brickell (2011) argues, women see limited scope to challenge the status quo, and believe that failing to perform unpaid house and care work may result in divorce or abandonment. The sex ratio as a result of high rates of male morbidity during the Khmer Rouge era and the stigma surrounding divorced women compound this situation. As discussed above, these social values are reflected in state policies on education, gender equality and social protection.

Second, women's care responsibilities over the life cycle are shaped by the structure of the economy and work opportunities, the absence of state social protection and education policies to support accessible and affordable non-familial childcare and eldercare provision, as well as entrenched stereotypes about women's and men's roles in society. As 'dutiful daughters', young women are expected to perform unpaid family work, which includes care for elders. Those who migrate at a young age often maintain economic responsibility in their care roles through remittances. In this situation, it is often female relatives who provide care for young children. In adult years, women care for their own children, but may also be targeted by the state and non-government organisations in the delivery of community services, including unpaid caring for other people's children and community management. More affluent women hire other women as domestic workers, often in exploitative and low-paid work arrangements.

For the most vulnerable, the only option is to place their children into unregulated residential care where children's safety and educational development are at risk. In the absence of state initiatives, the level of chronic vulnerability in rural and some urban areas has led to an increase in residential care facilities and programmes supported by non-government organisations that operate as a social welfare safety net. These trends have resulted in disconnected families, institutionalised care arrangements with inadequate frameworks for child protection and monitoring, and a lasting impact on both parents and children. Should the state fail to address the nexus of work and care and its gendered dimensions, women will increasingly seek alternative care arrangements as a last resort, with implications for the social and developmental rights of children and their families.

Changes in the profile of Cambodia's population indicate a declining percentage of children, due to lower fertility rates and an ageing population. Although aged care is not yet a pressing policy issue, by 2050 one in four Cambodians will be aged over 60 years. Combined with a decrease in the number of adults in the labour force, aged care is thus likely to be an emerging pressure point. These shifts require comprehensive social protection policies to ensure that care of children, elders and those with a disability is more evenly distributed across the family, state and market. While attention is increasingly being paid to gender equality in the labour market (Asian Development Bank 2013; MoWA 2009), much less has been paid to the structural impediments to women's full participation in the labour market. If progress towards gender equality is to be achieved then it is necessary to establish policies that recognise women's inequality as a product of interconnected problems of care distribution, labour market structures and entrenched gender stereotypes.

Notes

1 There are 25 provinces in Cambodia.
2 Compulsory government registration was not required prior to September 2015.
3 In late 2015 the Cambodian and Malaysian Governments signed a Memorandum of Understanding to lift the ban and implement measures to ensure workers' rights (Chhay and Cuddy 2015). As of early 2016, however, both countries were yet to ratify the Domestic Workers Convention.

References

Asian Development Bank. 2013. *Gender Equality in the Labour Market*, Phnom Penh.

Brickell, K. 2011. "The 'Stubborn Stain' on Development: Gendered Meanings of Housework (Non-)Participation in Cambodia." *Journal of Development Studies* 47 (9): 1353–1370.

Brickell K., B. Prak and B. Poch. 2014. *Domestic Violence Law: The Gap between Legislation and Practice in Cambodia and What Can Be Done About It: Preliminary ESRC/DFID Research Report.* http://www.katherinebrickell.com/katherinebrickell/wp-content/uploads/2014/01/DV-Law-Prelim-Report-2014.pdf.

Chant, S. 2008. "The 'Feminisation of Poverty' and the 'Feminisation' of Anti-Poverty Programmes: Room for Revision?" *The Journal of Development Studies* 44 (2): 165–197.

Chant, S. and K. Brickell. 2014. "Domesticating (and De-patriarchalizing) the Development Agenda: A Need for Greater Household (and Family) Engagement in Gender-related Policy Interventions." In *New Frontiers in Feminist Political Economy*, edited by S. Rai and G. Waylen, 85–113. New York and Abingdon: Routledge.

Chhay, C. and A. Cuddy. 2015. "Maid Pipeline Resumes: MoU Reopens Door to Malaysia for Domestic Workers 4 Years after Ban." *Phnom Penh Post*. 11 December.

Chhim, S. 2013. "Baksbat (Broken Courage): A Trauma-based Cultural Syndrome in Cambodia." *Medical Anthropology* 32 (2): 160–173.

Chopra, D. 2014. *Towards Gender Equality with Care-Sensitive Social Protection.* IDS Policy Briefing No. 49, Brighton: Institute of Development Studies.

Connelly, U.B. 2009. "Disability Rights in Cambodia: Using the Convention on the Rights of People with Disabilities to Expose Human Rights Violations." *Pacific Rim Law & Policy Journal* 18: 123.

Demont, F. and P. Heuveline. 2008. "Diversity and Change in Cambodian Households. 1998–2006." *Journal of Population Research* 25 (3): 287–313.

Derks, A. 2008. *Khmer Women on the Move: Exploring Work and Life in Urban Cambodia.* Honolulu: University of Hawaii Press.

Ebihara, M. 1968. "Svay, A Khmer Village in Cambodia." PhD Thesis. Columbia University.

Gartrell, A. 2010 "'A Frog in a Well': The Exclusion of Disabled People from Work in Cambodia." *Disability & Society* 25 (3): 289–301.

Human Rights Watch (2015) *Work Harder or Get Out: Labour Rights Abuses in Cambodia's Garment Industry.* https://www.hrw.org/sites/default/files/reports/cambodia0315_ForUpload.pdf

ILO. 2012. *Practical Challenges for Maternity Protection in the Cambodian Garment Industry*. Phnom Penh: ILO Regional Office for Asia and the Pacific. http://www.ilo.org/wcmsp5/groups/public/-asia/-ro-bangkok/-sro-bangkok/documents/publication/wcms_203802.pdf.

ILO. 2013. ILOSTAT Database, Annual Indicators. https://www.ilo.org/ilostat.

Jacobsen, T. 2008. *Lost Goddesses: The Denial of Female Power in Cambodian History.* Copenhagen: NIAS Press.

Khieng, S., S. Madhur, and R. Chhem, eds. 2015. *Cambodia Education 2015: Employment and Empowerment.* Phnom Penh: Cambodia Development Resource Institute.

Knodel, J., S.K. Kim, Z. Zimmer, and S. Puch. 2005. *Older Persons in Cambodia: A Profile from the 2004 Survey of Elderly*. Population Studies Center, University of Michigan.

Kwon, H.J., S. Cook, and Y. Kim. 2014. "Shaping the National Social Protection Strategy in Cambodia: Global Influence and National Ownership." *Global Social Policy* 15 (2): 125–145.

Ministry of Planning. 2012. *Migration in Cambodia: Report of the Cambodian Rural Urban Migration Project.* Phnom Penh. http://cambodia.unfpa.org/sites/asiapacific/files/pub-pdf/Rural-urbanMigrationinCambodiaReport2012_EngVersion.pdf

MoEYS. 2014. *National Action Plan of Early Childhood 2014–2018*. Phnom Penh. http://www.moeys.gov.kh/en/policies-and-strategies/838.html#.VxWHVUZ3C7Q.

MoSVY. 2016. *Preliminary Data Compilation and Findings: Mapping of Residential Care Institutions.* http://www.unicef.org/cambodia/MAPPING_REPORT_5_provinces_ENG.pdf.

MOWA. 2009. *Neary Rattanak III Five Year Strategic Plan 2009–2013*. http://www.svri.org/Cambodianational.pdf.

Netra, E. and S. Sovann. 2007. *Where Did All the Day Cares Go? A Gender Analysis of Day Care Needs in Relation to Time Poverty and Employment Opportunities for Poor Women*. Phnom Penh: Ministry of Women's Affairs and World Bank.

NIS. 2010. *Cambodia Demographic and Health Survey 2010*. http://dhsprogram.com/pubs/pdf/FR249/FR249.pdf.

NIS. 2013. *Cambodia Inter-censal Population Survey 2013*. http://countryoffice.unfpa.org/cambodia/?publications=8711.

NIS. 2014. *Cambodia Socio-Economic Survey 2014*. Phnom Penh. http://www.nis.gov.kh/nis/CSES/CSES_2014_Report.pdf.

NIS and ILO. 2013. *Cambodia Labour Force and Child Labour Survey 2012*. Phonm Penh: ILO.

Nuon, V. and M. Serrano. 2010. *Building Unions in Cambodia*, Singapore: Friedrich-Ebert-Stiftung Office for Regional Cooperation in Asia.

Oka, C. 2015. "Improving Working Conditions in Garment Supply Chains: The Role of Unions in Cambodia." *British Journal of Industrial Relations*. doi: 10.1111/bjir.12118.

Rao, N., J. Sun, V. Pearson, E. Pearson, H. Liu, M.A. Constas, and P.L. Engle. 2012. "Is Something Better than Nothing? An Evaluation of Early Childhood Programs in Cambodia." *Child Development* 83 (3): 864–876.

Razavi, S. 2007. *The Political and Social Economy of Care in a Development Context.* Geneva: UNRISD.

Royal Government of Cambodia. *Sub-Decree No. 119 on the Management of Residential Care Centre.* Phnom Penh: September 2015.

Tunon, M. and K. Rim. 2013. *Cross-border Labour Migration in Cambodia: Considerations for the National Employment Policy.* Phnom Penh: ILO Regional Office for Asia and the Pacific.

UNICEF. 2011. *With the Best Intentions: A Study of Attitudes towards Residential Care in Cambodia.* Phnom Penh, UNICEF Cambodia.

World Bank. 2015. *Health Nutrition and Population Statistics: Population Estimates and Projections.* http://databank.worldbank.org/Data/Views/VariableSelection/SelectVariables.aspx?source=Health%20Nutrition%20and%20Population%20Statistics:%20Population%20estimates%20and%20projections.

Zimmer, Z. and S.K. Kim. 2001. "Living Arrangements and Socio-demographic Conditions of Older Adults in Cambodia." *Journal of Cross-Cultural Gerontology* 16 (4): 353–381.

8 Bangladesh

Class, precarity and the politics of care

Dina Siddiqi and Hasan Ashraf

Several interlocking and contradictory elements mediate the work and care nexus for women in contemporary Bangladesh. On the one hand, the imperatives of a postcolonial development agenda and nationalist anxieties over the country's place in the world converge to ensure sustained attention to the 'woman question' in the public sphere. Donor policies, neoliberal ideologies of female empowerment and the national economy's shift from aid to trade dependency similarly underscore the importance of women's labour to national aspirations for global recognition. On the other hand, the relationship between women as productive beings (in the public realm of the market) and as reproductive bodies (in the so-called private sphere) remains relatively unproblematised.

Women's labour force participation in Bangladesh has increased steadily since 1990. However, tensions between gendered expectations of care work and formal labour force participation have received little attention in policy or scholarly circles (Huq 2015). The scholarly literature on women's work focuses primarily on potential drivers, 'pathways' and obstacles to women's empowerment through participation in the formal labour market. Against this backdrop, care work appears only as a constraint to women's full participation in the labour market. Nevertheless, new spaces in the policy debate appear to be opening up, at least in the formal recognition of unpaid care work as a significant topic (Huq 2015). This chapter contributes to this emerging debate and fills some of the gaps in the scholarship on women and care work in Bangladesh. Moving beyond a conceptualisation of care work as an obstacle to individual economic empowerment, it situates questions of social reproduction and the sexual division of labour within a broadly structural analysis of economic policy and social transformation.

The chapter maps the work/care nexus in Bangladesh through an examination of the tensions that emerge when women are regarded primarily as productive bodies but no attempt is made to recast gender norms in regard to reproductive responsibilities. These tensions are reflected in public policy and in the responses of individual households to increased rates of female participation in the paid workforce. Socio-cultural norms continue to reify women as wives and mothers even as government commitment to export-oriented development policies encourages working-class women to engage in paid work. Contradictions between state/civil society rhetoric on gender equality and everyday gendered practices in the public and domestic spheres shape individual women's experience of work and care. The chapter concludes that, while such contradictions affect all Bangladeshi women, the experience of the work and care nexus is fundamentally differentiated by class. In recent years, the state has promoted the commercialisation of care services but these formal services are limited in number and out of the reach of all but the most affluent women, exacerbating existing pressures on non-elite women. Meanwhile, female domestic care workers – whose labour middle and upper class women depend upon to sustain their professional lives – are the group perhaps most affected by the combination of highly exploitative and precarious conditions of work and inadequate access to supportive care services.

The demographic landscape

Home to some 149 million people, Bangladesh is the most densely populated country in the world. It is overwhelmingly rural, although this situation is shifting rapidly. In 2011, just over 28 per cent of the population lived in towns and cities (Index Mundi 2014). However, rapid urbanisation is expected to see almost 100 million people – around half the country's population – domiciled in urban areas by 2030 (Rahman 2014). Rural dispossession, displacement due to natural disasters, demographic pressures and related landlessness are all drivers of rural–urban migration. Extreme weather and rising sea levels brought about by climate change, to which Bangladesh is inordinately vulnerable, are displacing many. This, in turn, intensifies the process of urbanisation.

When Bangladesh achieved independence in 1971, prevailing development theories associated entrenched poverty with rapid population growth. In response, the new government implemented robust population control policies. Carried out for the most part without coercion and with the help of a vast army of female recruits, these policies resulted in a dramatic decline in total fertility rates in Bangladesh, from 7.3 in 1974 to 2.2 in 2011 (Bangladesh Demographic and Health Survey 2011; National Institute of Population Research and Training 2013). As a consequence, the proportion of persons under 15 years declined from 43 per cent in 1989 to 35 per cent in 2011. During the same period, the proportion of people aged between 15 and 59 increased. Greater life expectancy means the proportion of people over 60 is also increasing (Figure 8.1). At 69, women's life expectancy is slightly higher than men's, reversing a long-standing South Asian trend of greater male longevity.

These demographic trends have influenced average household size, which has declined from 5.26 people per household in 1995 to 4.44 in 2012 (Huq 2015, 11). Urbanisation and increased 'nuclearisation' of the family has brought a shift away from traditional extended family structures, and thus has also had a significant impact on family formation. Marriage, however, remains almost universal; 94 per cent of women and 99 per cent of men are currently married. Both women and men have traditionally married young. According to a 2014 UNICEF report, 33 per cent of women between the ages of 15 and 49 had been married before the age of 15 (UNICEF 2014, 1). However, rates of early marriage are decreasing, with

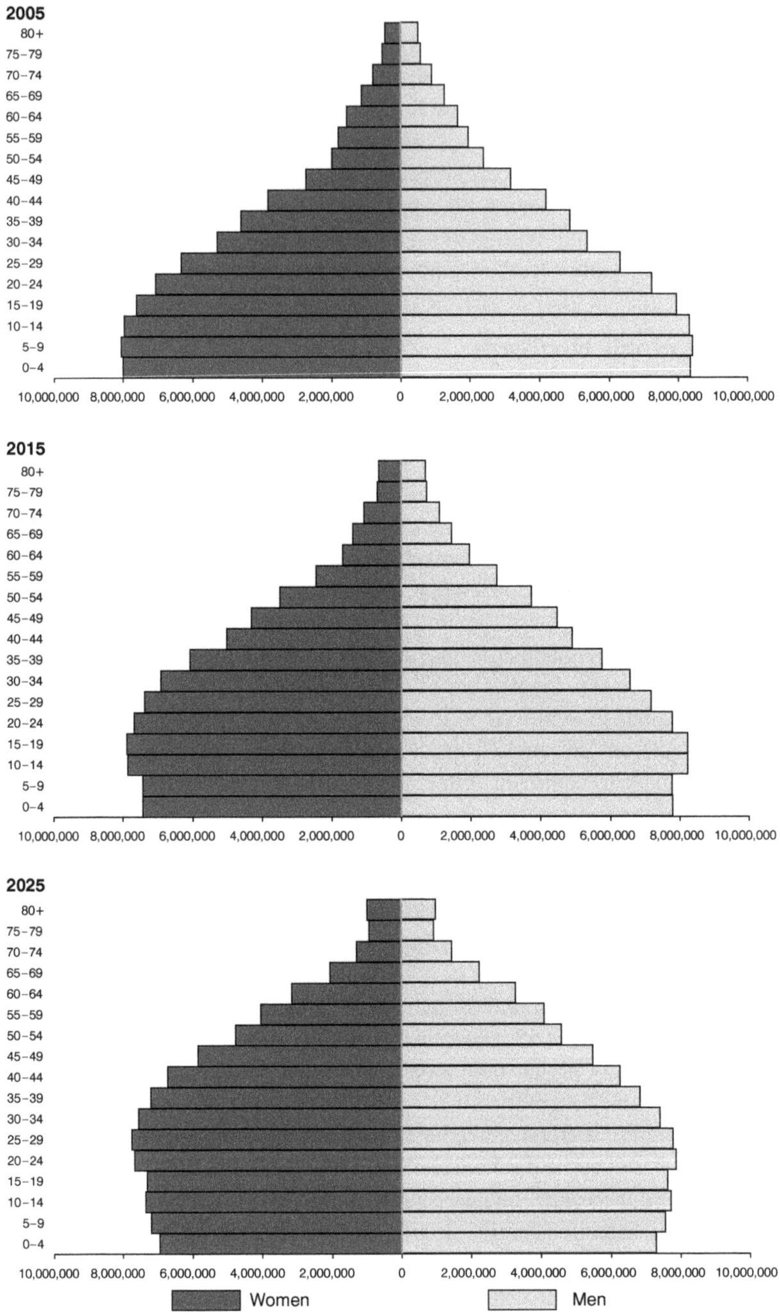

Figure 8.1 Population 2005, 2015, and 2025

Source: World Bank (2015).

the proportion of women aged 15–19 defined as never-married increasing from 30 to 54 per cent between 1975 and 2011 (National Institute of Population Research and Training 2013, 47).

Changes in household size and structure have implications for the distribution of the burden of child and aged care. Ultimately, smaller households are expected to provide care for a growing group of ageing relatives and children without the support of the extended family (Huq 2015, 11). Conventional moral norms and kinship obligations are increasingly tested in such circumstances. Traditional middle-class expectations that a daughter-in-law will provide emotional and other forms of support to her husband's ageing parents are no longer viable. Most middle-class households need two incomes, and married women are increasingly taking up full-time employment. These middle and lower-middle class women resolve tensions between work and care by employing domestic workers to assist with household chores and take care of ageing parents and/or children in their absence. If they are fit enough, mothers and mothers-in-law may also be called on to tend to young grandchildren. Working-class households, particularly those who have migrated from rural areas, face the same double burden of work and care within a different set of constraints. Poorly paid, precarious work in the vast informal economy means that domestic workers, factory workers, construction workers and others employed in informal sector occupations cannot afford to hire domestic help of their own. In many cases the final responsibility for care work falls on older children, especially daughters (Kabir 2014).

Labour force participation: trends and patterns

In terms of sectoral distribution (Table 8.1), women continue to be concentrated in the agricultural sector, a trend that is growing, contrary to expectations (Jaim and Hossain 2015). This is significant, given that traditionally women have been absent from agricultural field work in Bangladesh. Researchers attribute some of the sharp increase in women's labour in the agricultural sector to changes in definition and improved enumeration processes (Rahman and Islam 2013, 21). But Bangladesh is also experiencing what has been called the 'feminisation of agriculture' (Jaim and Hossain 2015). This has been generated in part by the migration of men from rural areas, but also by the rapid expansion of microcredit programmes run by the government or non-governmental organisations (NGOs) such as Grameen Bank and BRAC. This development has seen many Bangladeshi rural women drawn into small-scale forms of paid non-agricultural activities that have increased women's labour force participation and provided a new source of income for women (Rahman and Islam 2013).

Although just under 12 per cent of women are involved in the manufacturing sector, primarily in apparel production for export, it is their presence that represents the fundamental shift not only in the Bangladesh economy but in women's engagement in paid work. A sustained increase in women's labour force participation from 4 per cent in 1974 to 36 per cent in 2012 corresponds with the period of trade liberalisation and the open economy promoted by successive governments

Table 8.1 Working population 15 years of age and over by industry and sex, 2010

Economic activity	*Male (%)*	*Female (%)*
Agriculture, forestry and fishing	40.18	64.84
Mining and quarrying	0.25	0.10
Manufacturing	12.75	11.77
Electricity, gas, steam and air conditioning supply	0.24	0.03
Water supply; sewerage, waste management and remediation activities	0.06	0.02
Construction	6.31	1.40
Wholesale and retail trade; repair of motor vehicles and motorcycles	17.24	6.34
Transportation and storage	9.87	1.51
Accommodation and food service activities	2.05	0.35
Information and communication	0.14	0.02
Financial and insurance activities	0.83	0.32
Real estate activities	0.09	0.01
Professional, scientific and technical activities	0.25	0.14
Administrative and support service activities	1.17	0.27
Public administration and defence; compulsory social security	1.33	0.22
Education	2.54	2.01
Human health and social work activities	0.70	1.02
Arts, entertainment and recreation	0.16	0.04
Other service activities	4.33	4.43
Activities of households as employers; undifferentiated goods- and services-producing activities of households for own use	0.43	5.22
Activities of extraterritorial organisations and bodies	0.01	0.00
Total	100.00	100.00

Source: ILO (2013).

since 1981 (Huq 2015, 10). Some of the sharpest growth was registered between 1995 and 2003, a period in which export-oriented production, primarily in the garment sector, expanded exponentially (World Bank 2008, 55). Openness to the global economy and a national commitment to export-orientated growth reflects the shift from socialist planning to a model of privatisation, trade liberalisation, and the 'structural reforms' favoured by the Euro-American donor community. The restructuring of global trade agreements in the 1980s in particular underwrote the rapid expansion in the garment sector. During this period, labour force participation rates for women aged from 20 to 24 years increased by almost two and a half times, as women were drawn into the factories (World Bank 2008, 57).

While the proportion of women engaged in manufacturing remains relatively small, rapid expansion in ready-made garment exports has made this the sector in which there has been the most visible growth in female employment in recent decades (Hossain 2011, 13). Bangladesh is currently the second largest exporter of garments in the world, second only to China (WTO 2014). According to the Bangladesh Garment Manufacturers and Employers' Association, the 4,296 factories in operation around Dhaka and the port city of Chittagong employed 4 million workers in 2013–14 (BGMEA 2015). Women and girls flooded into Dhaka and Chittagong in unanticipated numbers, desperate for the presumed stability of factory work but also to escape multiple crises in the countryside caused by displacement through natural disasters and stagnation in the agricultural sector. Initially, it was very young women who found employment in these factories. This changed rapidly, however, in the decade from the mid-1990s, with the average age of garment workers rising from 19 to 25. There was a corresponding increase in the proportion of married women working in the industry, up from 38 per cent of women workers to 59 per cent in 2006 (Khatun et al. 2008). While there are serious concerns about the conditions of work for women in this sector, regular paid work has produced a positive 'empowerment' effect for women (Kabeer, Mahmud and Tasneem 2011).

Tensions between gender norms and the neoliberal imperative to increase women's rate of labour force participation are clearly evident in the manufacturing sector. However, they are even more apparent in policy toward women's international migration. Remittances from male migrants have long constituted the largest source of foreign exchange for the country, accounting for USD 145,543 million in 2015 (BMET 2015). Yet it was only in 2006 that the government recognised the equal rights of men and women to migrate for employment. Before then, successive governments placed partial or full bans on the overseas migration of unskilled and semi-skilled women. For example, in 2003, the government stipulated that only married women over 34 years who had obtained written permission from their husbands were eligible for overseas migration. Nevertheless, from less than 1 per cent in 1990, the number of women migrants as a proportion of total migrants rose to just over 7 per cent in 2010. As of October 2015, 19 per cent of Bangladeshis working overseas were women (BMET 2015).

These changes in women's labour force participation rates have been accompanied by a significant shift in the pattern of women's engagement in paid work over the life cycle (Figure 8.2). Younger women (15–19 years) are delaying their entry into the labour market but once they take up paid employment they remain engaged for longer. As a consequence, participation rates for women between the ages of 20 and 50 have more than doubled over the past decade. This shift may be a reflection of more years of schooling, delayed marriage and childbirth, and the need for a cash income. However, given that over a third of women are married and have their first child by the time they are in their early twenties, it appears that the number of married women with children who are employed has increased substantially. Women who are divorced, separated, or widowed are much more likely to be employed than currently married women (World Bank 2008).

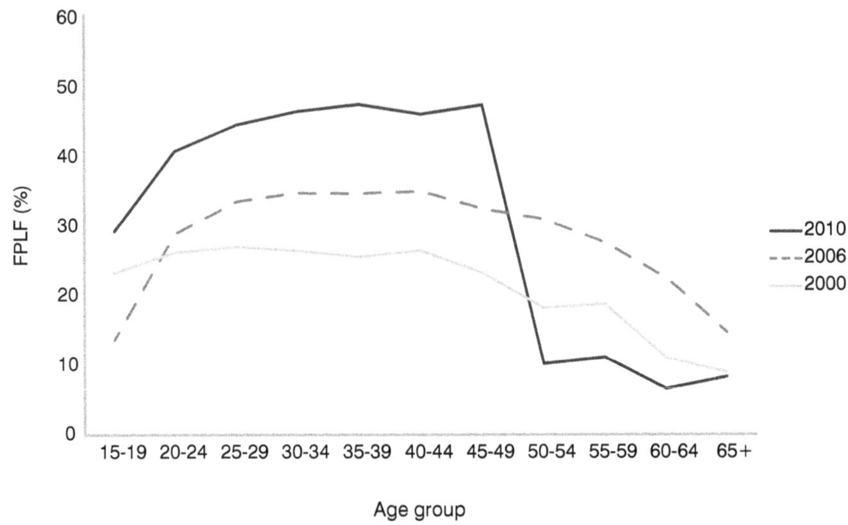

Figure 8.2 Female participation in the labour force

Source: Rahman and Islam (2013).

Increased rates of female labour force participation among older women have not been accompanied by a concomitant increase in their status at work. In aggregate terms, almost one fifth of women fall into the category of managers, professionals and technicians, a percentage roughly equal to that of men (Table 8.2). There are legislated reservations for women in public sector jobs in Bangladesh, but in practice these are only available to a minority of educated urban women. Other forms of 'respectable' employment for women who have completed at least secondary education have been made available through state family-planning programmes (Kabeer, Mahmud and Tasneem 2011). However, in spite of women's presence in formal sector employment the figures on occupational status are somewhat deceptive in their suggestion of a degree of gender equality

Table 8.2 Working population by occupational category and sex, 2011

Occupation	*Male (%)*	*Female (%)*
Managers, professionals, and technicians	20.12	19.31
Clerical, service and sales workers	10.48	19.52
Skilled agricultural and trades workers	43.99	37.38
Plant and machine operators, and assemblers	9.32	2.96
Elementary occupations	15.85	20.74
Not elsewhere classified	0.25	0.08
Total	100.00	100.00

Source: ILO (2013).

at the professional level because of the open-ended nature of the category. Middle- and upper-middle class women have joined the ranks of lawyers, doctors, workers from non-governmental organisations and corporate executives, but the top positions are still filled by men. The authoritarian and hierarchical nature of the private sector, in particular, encourages women to 'adapt and accommodate' rather than challenge gender dominant social norms (Andaleeb 2010).

Women's lack of occupational mobility is also clearly evident in the garment factories. The majority of female garment workers are employed at the lowest level, as helpers, or on the production lines as machine operators. Women are noticeably absent at the managerial level and lower supervisory levels. According to a recent study, women comprise 80 per cent of operators but only 10 per cent of line supervisors (Naeem and Woodruff 2014). Despite the presence of a small number of dynamic and socially prominent female factory owners, middle management remains a primarily male arena. The dynamic between primarily male managers and female assembly line workers invariably reproduces dominant social norms and practices. This is not to suggest that Bangladeshi factory workers are pliant and passive. But while there are many instances of individual and collective resistance, it is clear that paid work, even at this scale, brings no guarantee of 'empowerment' or of the transformation of social norms.

Balancing work and care

The increased number of married mothers in the labour force means the question of care work has become both more pressing and more significant in a relatively short period of time. Among other things, this can lead to a moral crisis for working women, who face the prospect of balancing cultural expectations as good mothers, daughters and daughters-in-law with their professional obligations. Married daughters must fulfil basic kinship obligations of care, not just for their own parents but, as indicated earlier, for their husband's ageing family members as well.

The expectation that women must be carers first, and only then workers, has a distinct class dimension. For their part, educated middle-class working women find themselves caught in a cultural double bind, facing tremendous pressure to prove that they are not shirking their reproductive duties in order to fulfil their personal ambitions. There are few privatised childcare services that would meet the standards of middle-class parents and are within reach financially. In any case, leaving an infant or a young child at a crèche is readily interpreted as the callous prioritising of career over motherhood. As a consequence, middle-class working mothers do not necessarily seek access to formal day-care centres, drawing instead on a combination of family and paid domestic help.

Highly successful professionals – lawyers, doctors and business executives – rely on a combination of household help and extended family connections. For individual women who belong to well-resourced families, this system works well. Reliable, well-trained domestic workers may even be employed across generations. But this privatised system of care is deeply flawed because it allows only those women with access to certain kinds of resources to succeed professionally. Such an exclusionary model is not scalable; it simply reproduces class privilege.

At the other end of the social spectrum, women engaged in urban informal work rely exclusively on support from their immediate families. Most migrants seek out new lives in one of two or three key urban centres. The capital Dhaka – one of the fastest growing megacities in the world – is a city of slums (World Bank 2007). Nearly two-thirds of Bangladesh's urban population are slum dwellers, many of them new migrants. They live in cramped spaces and pay inordinately high rents for housing that often lacks adequate infrastructure such as cooking and sanitation facilities (HDS 2014). Having left their parents and extended family at home in the village, migrant women have to rely on their immediate nuclear families or develop personal strategies to manage domestic and care labour.

Slum life requires the careful calibration of social ties in an essentially alien environment. Thus, provision of care for infants and young children constitutes a major burden for working mothers. Most women depend on older relatives, or more likely older female children, to supplement their own care obligations in their physical absence. Slum life takes a specific toll on children, especially girls. Slum children are two and a half times more likely to be excluded from schooling than the national average (UNICEF 2014, 6) and the pressure for girls to drop out of school is particularly intense. Girls of 10 or 11 are expected to leave school in order to carry out everyday chores, take up menial jobs to supplement household income, and tend to younger siblings or elderly relatives. Working mothers without this option and who have not been able to establish trusting relations with neighbours are compelled to send children to their village of origin to be cared for there, or leave paid work altogether.

In some ways, the demands of balancing work and care are even greater for the women employed in Bangladesh's garment factories than for women eking out a living in the informal sector. Owners' preference for female workers hinges on women's perceived docility and manageability. Women workers, it is assumed, are less likely than their male counterparts to protest against flexible terms of employment, and less likely to organise or be susceptible to 'anti-management propaganda' from outside (Khan 2001; Mahmud 2010). Consequently, managerial practices frequently blur the lines between the productive worker and the 'good' woman who is docile and manageable and prioritises her domestic responsibilities over disreputable activities such as labour organising (Siddiqi 2000).

At times, the state and capital have selectively deployed the discourse of poor women's liberation from the bonds of poverty or of Muslim women's escape from Islamic patriarchy to liberation through paid work in the export economy (Siddiqi 2009). Yet at the same time, women who work are not seen as *proper* breadwinners. The symbolic success of garment work stands in sharp contrast to, indeed is a reminder of, distressingly high levels of male under- and unemployment in the countryside. The image of a vast army of women walking to and from factories every day ruptures sexual and spatial codes of gendered conduct in the city. Indeed, the visibility of female factory workers has become symbolic of male failure – the failure of Bangladeshi men as breadwinners and as heads of households able to keep 'their' women from public male spaces (Siddiqi 2000). The ensuing crisis of masculinity provides one explanation for the very high levels of hostility and sexual harassment experienced by garment workers (Siddiqi 2004).

Decades after its emergence, this predominantly female workforce is by now a familiar feature of the social landscape, yet there has been no explicit shift in the sexual division of labour in the domestic sphere. As a consequence, expectations of women's care work have not dissipated with formal employment, as husbands and fathers seldom step willingly into the breach. Instead, women workers must squeeze the labour of social reproduction in and around the inflexible hours of formal work. This is accentuated for those in the slums, where unpredictable delays in access to basic services directly affect women's lives at work (Afsar 2002). Not only are electricity and water supplies irregular, but with the high population density, women cannot necessarily predict how long they will need to wait for access to drinking water, bathroom and cooking facilities. The time-sensitive nature of garment production strongly disinclines management from exercising flexibility in relation to working hours, so workers are frequently financially penalised for lateness. Employers' desire for capitalist 'time discipline' invariably clashes with reproductive responsibilities that cannot always be predicted or managed to fit a particular schedule.

State policies on work and care

As the discussion above reveals, the work of care – the social reproduction of everyday life and labour – falls not just on individual households, but primarily on women. It is women workers who must negotiate the tensions left by the gap between policy that casts them as productive bodies and the institutional and social norms and practices that envision them as carers and reproductive beings.

Like other postcolonial states, newly independent Bangladesh promised full citizenship through nationalising industries and public utilities and offering a range of subsidised or even free services, including healthcare and education. In the 1980s and 1990s, the imposition of structural adjustment policies fundamentally restructured the terms of this social contract. The major conditionality for international loans – reduced state expenditure – led to the withdrawal of subsidies for food, fuel, pharmaceuticals and fertilisers. The subsequent rise in the price of basic commodities and (newly privatised) essential services effectively redistributed the costs of care, including the opportunity cost, to individual family members, especially women (SAPRIN 2004).

In the post-structural adjustment period, the state's formal commitment to the provision of welfare and expressed desire to mainstream social safety nets as part of a sustainable anti-poverty strategy stand in tension with its overall policy emphasis on the marketisation of basic services. This is exemplified in recent national budgets, in which funding available for social safety nets has increased at the same time as public investment in healthcare subsidies has decreased. Some of this shortfall is met through the non-government sector, which is a significant provider of health and education in Bangladesh.

National budgets have always included safety net programmes that target 'vulnerable' populations. In recognition of the growth in the number of the elderly as a proportion of its population, the government instituted old age allowances in 1997 (N. Siddiqi 2015). This initiative was premised on an assumption that familial and community-based informal safety nets were unravelling. Although it is symbolically important, the amount – less than USD 4 every other month – is grossly inadequate. Maternal health voucher schemes and stipends for primary and secondary school students also form an important part of the Bangladesh social safety net, while other programmes target 'widowed, deserted and destitute' women.

Perhaps because the object of development policy remains the very poor, the state has put little thought into the needs of lower-middle or middle-class working women, especially in urban areas. This is in part because state exhortations regarding the benefits of women's economic empowerment tend to unfold separately from discussions on legal measures and the institutional provision of care. Bangladesh has no provisions for institutional aged care. The government and the private sector run a handful of old age residential facilities in key urban areas but for the most part, individual households are responsible for caring for the elderly.

There is also little in the way of institutional formal childcare available to women of any class. As noted above, middle-class and elite women have little interest in formal care facilities. Working-class women face a different set of circumstances and would certainly benefit from broader availability of institutional childcare. It is mandatory for all garment factories to provide crèches and/or day-care centres, although this is a rule more honoured in the breach than in its observance. The powerful trade organisation, the Bangladesh Garment Manufacturers and Employers Association (BGMEA), also runs a handful of schools for workers' children. Some NGOs also provide day-care facilities and schooling for children of poor working women, although their reach is limited by resource constraints. The National Women's Development Policy of 2011 recognised the need for 'supportive services' such as day care and crèches to facilitate women's participation in the labour force (Huq 2015, 22). As the policy is still under consideration by the government, no action has been forthcoming.

In terms of family-related workplace entitlements, legal measures are uneven, do not cover all women and for the most part are not enforced. On the whole, maternity benefits are seen as a privilege rather than a right (Ahmed 2014). The 2006 Bangladesh Labour Act guarantees women workers a total of 16 weeks fully paid maternity leave. In January 2011, this was extended to six months, but it remains unclear whether this will be implemented outside the civil service. The current provisions are limited in that they are applicable only for a woman's first two children and explicitly exclude women at the management level in the private sector, who have no legal entitlements. In the private sector, leave is granted to management-level women at the discretion of the employing organisation. Carer's leave or breastfeeding rights do not exist. And as labour laws in Bangladesh do not cover agricultural labour or those in the informal sector, such as domestic care workers, these groups have no access to such entitlements.

Often cast as a shadow state in Bangladesh, non-governmental organisations have assumed responsibility for many aspects of social welfare, especially education and healthcare.[1] The cultural logic that provides women with the moral imperative to take responsibility for their household is the same logic deployed by non-governmental organisations that target women as microcredit recipients whose success in the market, it is assumed, will enhance their ability to care for their families. In addition, much of their advocacy foregrounds gaps in the law and its implementation. It was their activism, for instance, that first highlighted the problematic aspects of state policy on women's overseas migration and lobbied for policy reform.

Apart from demands for day-care facilities for garment workers, questions of care work have rarely been a priority for a feminist movement preoccupied with combatting violence – public and private – and the need for more meaningful economic empowerment policies. One exception to this generalisation is the growing call for a revaluation of women's invisible or hidden economic activity, captured in a 2012 National Plan of Action that grew out of the 2011 National Women's Development Policy. These can be directly attributed to the involvement of leading feminist activists and researchers in a series of consultations with the Ministry of Women's Affairs (Huq 2015, 23).

But while some progressive policies for women workers in the formal sector do exist, such as the provision of paid maternity leave, there has been little room for rethinking broader institutional arrangements, for example state-subsidised day-care facilities, paternal leave or – most important – redressing the systemic nature of gendered inequalities and the precarity of available employment. The alternative report to the CEDAW Committee submitted in 2010 pointed to the need to question a dominant development paradigm that advocates 'growth above all else', discounting inequality, social dispossession and unsustainability as inimical to the rights of women who provide the cheap labour necessarily for this growth (CIC-BD 2010, 10). The majority of Bangladeshi women do not have the security of a permanent and safe job, nor can they escape the gendered expectations of care work. Clearly, any meaningful intervention must take into account the precarious conditions under which most women in Bangladesh labour, conditions that directly shape their ability to care and work. Serious change will come only if the structural issues of uneven development policies are addressed. As long as there is no space to engage and reconfigure dominant neoliberal paradigms, women, with the exception of the most privileged, will continue to be subordinated economically and socially.

The futures of care and work

The state and capital in Bangladesh successfully tap into the idea of the woman worker as an empowered productive body, while avoiding any consideration of women's responsibilities for household reproduction and childcare. This is to the benefit of both, as women's reproductive duties effectively subsidise the cost of their formal labour. But as Bangladesh faces increasing pressure to liberalise its economy further and enters the ranks of a middle-income country, the state will be forced to modify its view of care work as merely an obstacle to 'real' paid work.

In the meantime, the trade-off between work and care that women (except perhaps the very affluent) must negotiate on an everyday basis undermines both paid work and the work of care. Workers in the informal sector are not covered by protective labour laws. Formal sector workers who are protected under the law, and eligible for family-related workplace entitlements such as the Maternity Benefit Act do not have access to formal childcare or eldercare facilities. Many of these middle-class women may have the resources to employ other women to undertake care work, but they also confront ideologies of care that militate against their full participation in the labour market. Ultimately, this uneasy status quo does not serve anyone well, least of all women workers who remain trapped between contradictory social and economic expectations and inadequate care support.

In the absence of radical structural transformation, a careful unpacking of the highly classed and gendered work/care binary in Bangladesh makes it possible to work toward a more equitable political economy of care. At an abstract or theoretical level, this would require thinking of care and work as mutually supportive categories rather than in competition with each other. At the level of policy and decision making, a fundamental recasting is required for the state to move beyond its current instrumentalist approach to the provision of care services. A more expansive understanding of the relationship between care and work (one that is not centred on 'freeing' primarily poor women to sell their labour power in the market) opens up the possibility of seeing care work as an essential feature of the social reproduction of society and of citizen welfare. Collective state responsibility that takes into account uneven structural and global factors could shift some of the burden of care from individual women and their families to society as a whole. Lastly, at the level of everyday social life, it is critical to challenge gendered expectations and normative ideologies of care that associate women with care and stigmatise men for engaging in caring labour. This means, among other things, refusing to categorise and rank women as either productive bodies or primarily reproductive beings.

Note

1 This is also the case in Cambodia. See Ward (Chapter 7 this volume).

References

Afsar, R. 2002. "Internal Migration and the Development Nexus: the Case of Bangladesh", Paper prepared for DFID conference on Migration, Development and Pro-poor Choices in Asia, Dhaka, June 22–24.

Ahmed, S. 2014. "Maternity Benefits, Rights or Privilege?" *The Daily Star*. August 26. http://www.thedailystar.net/maternity-benefits-right-or-privilege-38659

Andaleeb, S.S. 2010. "Participation in the Workplace in Bangladesh: Gender Integration Issues for Organizational Leaders." in *Managing Gender Identity in Asia: A Research Companion*, edited by Mustafa Ozbilgin and Jawad Syed, 72–85. Northampton: Edward Elgar.

BGMEA. 2015. *Trade Information*. http://www.bgmea.com.bd/home/pages/TradeInformation #.VdGu_nGqqkp.

BMET. 2015. *Overseas Employment in 2015 (up to 11 April, 2016).* http://www.bmet.org.bd/BMET/stattisticalDataAction.

CIC-BD. 2010. *Combined Sixth and Seventh Alternative Report to the UN CEDAW Committee.* Dhaka: Steps Toward Development.

HDS (2014), *Urbanization: Challenges and Opportunities.* Lahore: Mahbubul Haque Human Development Centre.

Hossain, N. 2011. "Exports, Equity and Empowerment: The Effects of Readymade Garments Manufacturing Employment on Gender Equality in Bangladesh." Unpublished paper.

Huq, L. 2015. *Unpaid Care Work in Bangladesh: Policies, Practice and Evidence.* IDS Working Paper No 452. Dhaka: BRAC Institute of Governance and Development.

ILO. 2013. *ILOSTAT Database, Annual Indicators.* https://www.ilo.org/ilostat.

Index Mundi. 2014. *Bangladesh Urbanization.* http://www.indexmundi.com/bangladesh/urbanization.html.

Jaim, W. and M. Hossain. 2015. "Women in Agriculture." In *Leading Issues in Rural Development: Bangladesh Perspective*, edited by M. Hossain and A. Bayes, 73–90. Dhaka: AH Development Publishing House.

Kabeer, N., S. Mahmud, and S. Tasneem. 2011. *Does Paid Work Provide a Pathway to Women's Empowerment? Empirical Findings from Bangladesh*, IDS Working Paper No. 375, Brighton: Institute of Development Studies.

Kabir, M. 2014. "Urbanization and its Discontents: Educating Dhaka's Slum Children." http://blogs.worldbank.org/endpovertyinsouthasia/urbanization-and-its-discontents-educating-dhaka-s-slum-children.

Khan, S. 2001. "Gender Issues and the Ready Garment Industry of Bangladesh: The Trade Union Context." In *Globalization and Gender: Changing Patterns of Women's Employment in Bangladesh*, edited by Sobhan, Rehman and N. Khundker, 167–218. Dhaka: University Press.

Khatun, F., M. Rahman, D. Bhattacharya and K.G. Moazzem. 2008. *Gender and Trade Liberalization in Bangladesh: The Case of the Ready-Made Garments.* Dhaka: Centre for Policy Dialogue.

Mahmud, S. 2010. "Why Do Garment Workers in Bangladesh Fail to Mobilize?" In *Citizenship and Social Movements: Perspectives from the Global South,* edited by L. Thompson and C. Tapscott, 60–86. New York: Zed Press.

Naeem, F. and C. Woodruff. 2014. *Managerial Capital and Productivity: Evidence from a Training Program in the Bangladeshi Garment Sector.* London: International Growth Center.

National Institute of Population Research and Training. 2013. *Bangladesh Demographic and Health Survey 2011* Dhaka: NIPORT.

Rahman, H. 2014. *Urbanization in Bangladesh: Challenges and Prosp*ects. Dhaka: Bangladesh Economists' Forum.

Rahman, R. and R. Islam. 2013. *Female Labor Force Participation in Bangladesh: October 2013: Trends, Drivers and Barriers.* New Delhi: ILO.

SAPRIN. 2004. *The SAPRIN Report: The Policy Roots of Economic Crisis, Poverty and Inequality.* London: Zed Press.

Siddiqi, D. 2000. "Miracle Worker or Womanmachine? Tracking Transnational Realities in Bangladeshi Factories." *Economic and Political Weekly* 35 (21/22): L11–L17.

Siddiqi, D. 2004. *The Sexual Harassment of Industrial Workers: Strategies for Intervention in the Workplace and Beyond.* CPD-UNFPA Programme on Population and Sustainable Development. Dhaka: Centre for Policy Dialogue.

Siddiqi, D. 2009. "Do Bangladesh Sweatshop Workers Need Saving? Sisterhood in the Post-Sweatshop Era." *Feminist Review* 91: 154–174.

Siddiqi, N. 2015. *Changing Socio-economic and Psychological Status of Older Women*. Dhaka: Women for Women.

UNICEF. 2014. *Ending Child Marriage: Progress and Prospects*. New York: UNICEF.

World Bank. 2007. *Dhaka: Improving Living Conditions for the Urban Poor*. Bangladesh Development Series, Paper No. 17. Dhaka: World Bank.

World Bank. 2008. *Whispers to Voices: Gender and Social Transformation in Bangladesh*. Bangladesh Development Series Paper No. 22. Washington DC: World Bank.

World Bank. 2015. Health Nutrition and Population Statistics: Population Estimates and Projections. http://databank.worldbank.org/Data/Views/VariableSelection/SelectVariables.aspx?source=Health%20Nutrition%20and%20Population%20Statistics:%20Population%20estimates%20and612 %20projections.

WTO. 2014. *International Trade Statistics 2014*. Geneva: WTO.

9 India

Economic inequality and social reproduction

Elizabeth Hill and Rajni Palriwala

Indian women's lives are structured by a number of contradictions that affect them as citizens, as workers and as carers. At independence women were guaranteed constitutional equality with men. Almost 70 years on, however, this promise is not reflected in the everyday reality of pervasive gender inequality. Instead, national development planning, with its primary focus on economic growth and poverty alleviation, has tended to subsume women's issues and the expectation that women's rights would be attended to once the 'larger issues' of political decolonisation had been settled, has not been fulfilled (Bulbeck 2009, 90). Even where specific government policies have aimed to 'improve the position of women' or facilitate 'women's empowerment' they have often had little impact on the lives of most women because they have failed to destabilise or transform the prevailing construction of women as primary and primarily carers. In combination with widespread issues of inequality and poverty, mainstream policy approaches underwrite women's low rates of work participation and their concentration in insecure and degraded forms of informal employment.

The impact of the contradictions embedded in the state's approach to women, their work and care responsibilities, are highly differentiated according to inequalities of class, caste, religion, ethnicity and the rural/urban divide. Women from middle-class and wealthy households typically have some choice about how they mobilise state, employer and family resources to manage work and care responsibilities, even if the gendered divisions remain largely intact. Poor women do not. Instead they are most often left to manage with little or no support from the state and employers, and in response attenuate their work and their care in ways that produce stress and ill-being for themselves and those they care for. In this way, economic inequality drives inequality in the spheres of social reproduction and care. This chapter explores women's contemporary experiences of work and care and the pressures for change, through an evaluation of demographic, economic, political and historical trends. We conclude that for Indian women to win their constitutional right to equality the current work/care regime requires radical transformation.

Demography, work and care

India is the third largest economy in Asia. With a population of more than 1.2 billion, it is projected to become the world's most populous nation by 2030 (United

Nations 2013). Half the population is below the age of 25 and more than 65 per cent is under 35 years (see Figure 9.1). Around 300 million people are expected to reach working age between 2010 and 2040. It is hoped that this 'demographic dividend' will lead to enhanced economic growth and rising standards of living (Aiyar and Mody 2011). However, realisation of the latter will require, among many other things, the development of supportive childcare infrastructure. With so many young people entering the labour market, childcare is emerging as a critical issue that requires a coordinated solution.

In the longer term, demographic trends point to a rapidly increasing dependency ratio and ageing profile. In 2014 the number of elderly citizens (older than 60 years) crossed the 100 million mark (HelpAge India 2015). By 2050 it is estimated that India will have 324 million citizens (about 20 per cent of the population) above 60 years of age, including 48 million people over 80 (United Nations 2013). This trend suggests that public support for aged care services – including pensions and public healthcare – as well as workplace policies to support care of the elderly will soon be an urgent issue (Tripathi 2014). At present most of the elderly remain dependent on employment and almost three-quarters reside with family members (Barik, Agrawal and Desai 2015, 111). Government-provided pensions play only a small role in supporting the elderly, even as the proportion of households receiving some form of government assistance has increased over the decade (Barik, Agrawal and Desai 2015).

A second feature of India's demography is the very low sex ratio. Gender disparity has been a defining feature of independent India with men consistently outnumbering women. While the national sex ratio has improved slightly over the past 25 years, it remains alarmingly low. According to the 2011, there are just 944 women per 1000 men, while the child sex ratio has worsened. The sex ratio is a reflection of the extremely low social, economic and political status of women and girls in Indian society and the strong desire for male children, on whom parents have traditionally depended for security in old age. Pervasive gender inequality is manifest in basic socio-economic indicators such as women's education, health, employment and income, making the task of building an equitable work/care regime both challenging and urgent.

Labour force participation

Indian women make up only about a quarter of the total Indian labour force. Official rates of women's labour force participation are very low and vary significantly across the urban/rural divide. Over the past 25 years urban women's participation has ranged between 13.8 and 16.6 per cent, with participation rates for rural women double those of urban women, although the gap has narrowed over the past decade (see Figure 9.2). Both urban and rural men have had much higher participation rates than women – between 50 and 55 per cent. The largest difference is between urban men and urban women, with men almost four times as likely to be in the workforce (54.6 per cent) compared with their female counterparts (14.7 per cent) in 2011–12.

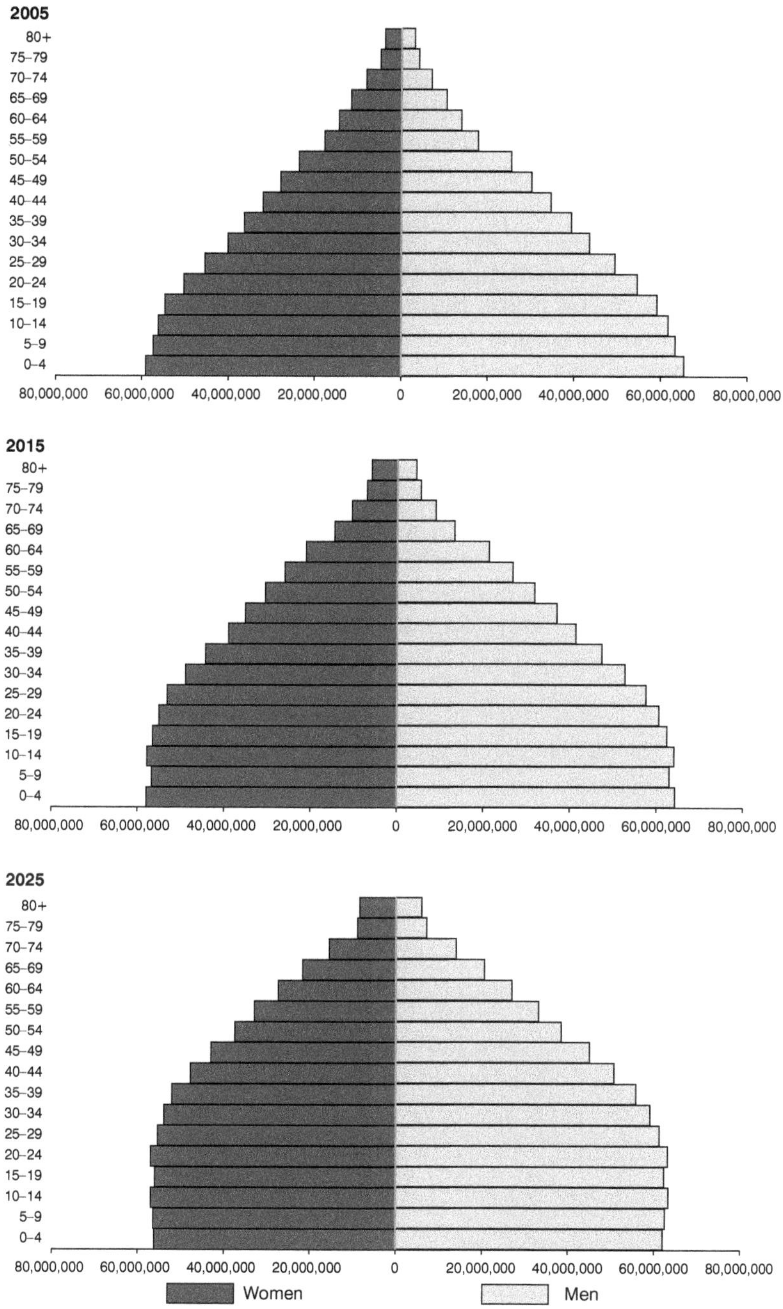

Figure 9.1 Population 2005, 2015, and 2025

Source: World Bank (2015).

Even the period of strong economic growth between the late 1980s and the Global Financial Crisis of 2007–08 did not lead to improved labour force participation for women. Instead, women's labour force participation has remained weak relative to men's and has worsened since 2007–08. During this period, the number of employed women declined from 148.6 million (2004–05) to 129.1 million (2012) even as the size of the total workforce increased to 472.9 million, up from 457.4 million in 2004–05. In this short period the female proportion of the workforce declined from 32.5 per cent to only 27 per cent.

Among women who do work, two-thirds are concentrated in agriculture (see Table 9.1) with manufacturing and other services the next most common employment sectors. Of greater significance, however, is women's employment status and the related rewards for work and access to support for care. Sixty per cent of rural women workers and 43 per cent of urban women workers are self-employed (GOI, NSSO, Ministry of Statistics and Program Implementation 2015). Self-employment can be further broken down into three sub-categories: employers, own-account workers and unpaid family workers. In both rural and urban settings the proportion of female employers is negligible, at less than 1 per cent (Mazumdar and Neetha 2011). The most common form of 'self-employment' is unpaid family labour performed in household enterprises and family businesses. In rural areas three-quarters of self-employed women are unpaid family workers. In urban areas the proportion is less, but still significant at 44 per cent (Mazumdar

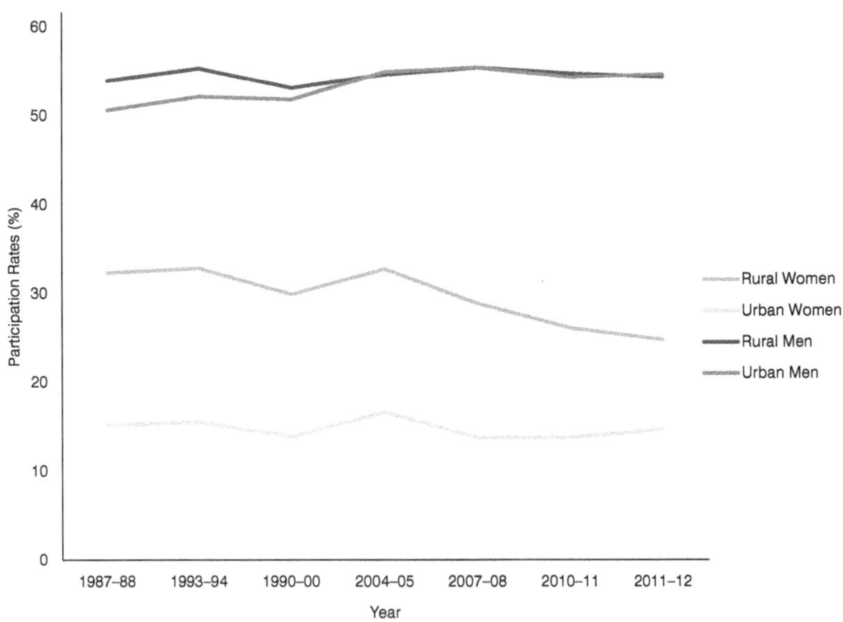

Figure 9.2 Workforce participation rates 1987–2012

Source: Data from GOI, NSSO, Ministry of Statistics and Program Implementation various rounds.

Table 9.1 Usual workers by industry and sex, 2009–10

Sector	*Males ('000s)*	*Females ('000s)*	*Female share*
Agriculture	156 224 (47.1 %)	87 566 (68.7 %)	35.9%
Mining and quarrying	2 653 (0.8 %)	382 (0.3 %)	12.5%
Manufacturing	36 817 (11.1 %)	13 766 (10.8 %)	27.2%
Electricity, gas and water	995 (0.3 %)	127 (0.1 %)	11.3%
Construction	37 481 (11.3 %)	6 501 (5.1 %)	14.8%
Trade, hotels and restaurants	44 446 (13.4 %)	5 481 (4.3 %)	10.9%
Transportation, storage and communications	19 569 (5.9 %)	510 (0.4 %)	2.5%
Other services	33 500 (10.1 %)	13 129 (10.3 %)	28%
Total	331 686 (100 %)	127 462 (100 %)	27%

Source: Calculated from Mazumdar & Neetha (2011), NSSO various rounds.

and Neetha 2011). As unpaid family workers, women are expected to maintain responsibility for care and household reproduction even while they contribute to the economic security of the family. In urban areas, more than half the women categorised as self-employed are own-account workers, where dependent relationships with contractors tend to structure the process of production, distribution and wage negotiation in ways that undermine their economic security and capacity to care (Hill 2010).

Formal categories of occupational sector and employment status provide important information for evaluating women's employment experience. However, it is the broader structure of the political economy within which employment is situated that has the most significant impact on women's daily experience of work and care. Informal employment dominates the labour market. Economic informality is common in most low-income economies, but in India it is the norm. Ninety-three per cent of all workers and 96 per cent of all women workers are employed under informal arrangements beyond the purview of protective labour legislation and basic social security provisions (GOI 2009). In the recent high-growth era informal employment has increased in number and proportion, as many regular/formal jobs in the public and private sectors have been informalised – mostly through contracting out (GOI 2009). Some of these workers earn reasonable wages, but the vast majority of informal workers – especially women workers – are engaged in work that is precarious and characterised by low productivity, poor working conditions and low wages. In the absence of a formal employment relationship and associated social security measures, informal employment curtails women's economic security and diminishes their personal well-being and the well-being of those they care for.

The new economic policy of the 1990s and its liberalisation, privatisation, globalisation agenda has encouraged widespread informalisation of the labour market, with ongoing negative consequences for the economic and social security of the majority of working women. However, for a minority of educated women, globalisation has delivered some desirable new employment opportunities. This is particularly the case in the burgeoning Information Technology Enabled Services and Business Processing Outsourcing (ITES-BPO) sector (Palit 2008). Firms looking to build their competitive advantage in the global marketplace have targeted educated, English-speaking women as new recruits. In 2008, the National Association of Software and Services Companies reported that 30 per cent of employees in the sector were women and that by 2020 women will make up 50 per cent of the total ITES-BPO workforce (NASSCOM 2009). The recruitment of women into this sector is an intentional and coordinated strategy that has had positive employment outcomes for a minority of women. Middle-class educated women also continue to dominate the feminised sectors of nursing and education. Forty-seven per cent of all elementary school teachers are women although this proportion varies enormously between states, with women making up around three-quarters of the elementary school teachers in Kerala but only one-third in Rajasthan (NUEPA 2016).

Analysis of the contemporary work/care regime highlights the dependent relationship between the majority of (poor) women who are employed informally and the new economic prosperity of the middle classes. As educated women have increased their participation in the labour market and households have accumulated additional wealth, the demand for paid domestic service work has grown. At the same time, widespread agrarian distress along with industrial restructuring and the loss of jobs in the organised industrial sector by male household heads has meant there has been a ready supply of women looking for employment as domestic workers (Neetha and Palriwala 2011; Palit and Singh 2011). As in many other countries in developing Asia, these dual trends have culminated in the burgeoning of a 'servant-employing middle class' (Palriwala and Neetha 2009, 17). Official data, which only began to be collected in 1999–2000, shows that domestic work is growing as a major source of women's employment, and is now the dominant form of urban women's employment, up from 447,100 to more than 2.5 million in 2004–05 (Neetha and Palriwala 2011).[1]

Under a work/care regime in which the family, state and capital are reluctant to support women in their role as workers and where contemporary care regimes continue to assume that women are primary carers, domestic workers provide middle-class and wealthy working women with an accessible and affordable form of non-familial care labour. Domestic work undertaken in private households is informal and therefore not covered by protective labour laws or mandated social security provisions. Instead the quality of the employment relationship is determined by the employer, exposing domestic workers to various forms of economic, physical and/or emotional exploitation and abuse. Increased hiring of female domestic labour (often from rural India) by urban households is producing care chains (Hochschild 2000) that reflect and embed inequalities of class, caste and gender (Palriwala and Neetha 2011).

The practice of work and care

The 4 per cent of working women employed in formal positions in the public and private sectors do receive some support in managing paid work with care – especially childcare. Employer-provided crèches are mandated in the Factory Act 1948, the Plantation Act 1951, and the Mines Act 1952, although in practice these obligations are easily avoided. Paid maternity leave has been a condition of public sector employment since the Maternity Benefit Act of 1961 and has been extended twice for central government employees by the Central Pay Commission – from 90 to 135 days in 1997, and then to 180 days in 2008 (GOI 2008).[2] Paternity leave of 15 days was also made available to central government employees in 1999. In 2008, the extended maternity provisions were supplemented with flexible childcare leave and flexible working hours schemes. The childcare leave provisions allow women employees with school-aged children two years of paid leave (in addition to maternity leave) to take care of (two) children under 18 years. Leave is intended to be used when a child is sick, undertaking school examinations, or for any other childcare related need as it arises (GOI 2008, 278). The flexible working hours scheme also supports working mothers, allowing them to begin work early or finish late provided they are at their place of work during the core hours of 11 am to 4 pm. Across the different state jurisdictions maternity and childcare leave provisions vary, with generous central government provisions extended in full to women employed in the West Bengal state government in 2012 and the Bihar government in 2015 (TNN 2012; PTI 2015).

In the formal private (corporate) sector, company policy determines the level of support available to women with care responsibilities. In the highly feminised ITES-BPO services sector and parts of the finance sector, companies have made an explicit effort over the past decade to develop human resource strategies that attract and retain female talent. These have included policies on maternity leave (paid and unpaid), childcare and family care. Many of the large domestic and global IT corporations offer female employees support in procuring childcare – either formal centre-based care or private ayah (nanny) care. Some companies have established their own childcare centres. Others have formal links to centres close to their offices that give priority to company employees. There are also companies that assist in procuring other domestic services including housekeepers and cooks, all of which help employees reconcile paid work duties with domestic responsibilities (Hill 2013). These types of company policies assist privileged women workers to reconcile demanding jobs with care and reproductive duties, albeit in a way that does not challenge the prevailing gendered notions of women as primary carers.

However, for the vast majority of working women, the absence of a formal employment contract and associated conditions means that workplace support for caring labour is completely absent. Even where minimal maternity or childcare provisions are mandated by law, women are often unaware of their entitlements and compliance is extremely poor. Pressure to weaken industrial laws can only make them more vulnerable. For most women the absence of reliable childcare means that work has to be fitted around care. Home-based work is a common employment strategy because it allows women to provide basic necessary care for small children while working in textiles, food preparation, or a myriad of small production line tasks. As convenient as home-based work might be, this type of work is defined by piece-rate wages that are very low. In addition, workers are isolated in their homes, trapped in dependent relationships with contractors who control the provision of work and the purchase price of finished goods, leaving women vulnerable to excessive exploitation (Hill 2010). Home-based work can also compromise the care a working mother is able to provide for her children, as tight deadlines, toxic chemicals, fibres and other dangerous goods and machines may expose children and other dependants to a range of health and safety risks.

Some women attempt to manage their work and care responsibilities by opting for very short hours of paid work – a strategy that undermines their capacity to earn a decent wage or find secure work. Other women leave small children at home to be cared for by grandparents, neighbours or older female children who are taken out of school to provide care. Migrant workers who travel to take up work in the cities often leave their children in their home village to be cared for by family networks. Many women find that in the absence of care support they must leave their children unattended or take them along to the work site. Both these options expose children to significant risks and cause stress for mothers. Non-government organisations (NGOs) and some trade unions provide formal childcare services for the children of women workers, but these are small efforts that are unable to meet the broader need. In general, the lack of appropriate and reliable childcare constrain women's employment 'choices', reduce their productive capacity and limit their attachment to the workforce (FORCES/CWDS 2013, 6).

In recent years the lack of social protection available to informal workers has made its way onto the political agenda. The Unorganised Sector Workers Social Security Act 2008 mandates life and disability cover, health and maternity benefits and old age protection delivered through the State Welfare Boards. However many states are yet to implement that law and coverage is patchy (Agarwala 2013). The 2015 Union Budget extended the provisions of the 2008 Act, signalling a raft of additional measures that could lead to a universal social security system (GOI 2015). Inadequate funding and problems with the implementation of the existing Social Security Act, however, suggest that the apparently extended social protection regime will face similar challenges.

In the absence of employer-based childcare and the limited availability of NGO and trade union services, there are some universal provisions available for women from low-income households employed in informal work. The Integrated Child Development Scheme (ICDS) is the lead government programme for children's welfare, with a focus on child nutrition, immunisation and health for children aged 0–6 years, as well as pregnant and lactating mothers. These services are provided through local Anganwadi centres. Childcare is also a formal part of the ICDS, but the centres are open for only a few hours each morning, limiting the usefulness of the ICDS to working women who require longer periods of sustained childcare. In recent years, attempts to extend the services provided at the Anganwadi centres, such as increasing the hours and including preschool education, have been somewhat successful in some states (Tamil Nadu, Pondicherry and Kerala) and better meet the needs of working women (Palriwala and Neetha 2009). For older children, the Right to Education Act 2009 makes school free, compulsory and a right for children aged 6–14, potentially alleviating some of the childcare pressure on working women. However, the history and practice of child welfare policy as part of state planning for poverty alleviation and development has meant that childcare has formally been separated from women's labour force participation, leaving the majority of low-income working women with inadequate childcare options.

In addition to caring for children, women are also expected to manage the care needs of the elderly and ill. The Maintenance and Welfare of Parents and Senior Citizens Act 2007 legally obliges adult children to care for elderly relatives. This expectation, combined with poor provision of public health facilities for the elderly, almost non-existent respite services and an inadequate aged pension system, concentrates the demands on women for work and care in support of aged relatives – often at the cost of their own well-being and economic security. The National Old Age Pension Scheme is a central government programme that pays Rs 75 per month to those over 65 with an income below the poverty line. This is supplemented by the states and the Indira Gandhi National Old Age Pension Scheme that pays Rs 200 per month to those below the poverty line aged between 60–79 years and Rs 500 per month to those 80 and above. These are clearly inadequate: according to the 2014 State of the Elderly Report more than 50 per cent of elderly Indian citizens currently live below the poverty line. Civil society organisations argue that at only 0.32 per cent of GDP, current expenditure on (and budgets for) the aged pension is too little and that coverage is insufficient, with only 25 per cent of the eligible population receiving the payment (Doval 2015).

The politics of work and care

To understand the work–care landscape discussed above, it is necessary to place the (non)recognition and construction of care in the context of the politics and history of national development policy and how this nexus has been articulated by the labour, women's and other social movements. The removal of poverty, the expansion of social justice through the reduction of caste, gender, and religious inequalities and discrimination, and the assertion of self-reliance along with economic growth emerged from the anti-colonial struggle as key concerns in public discourse. Until the late 1980s, government policy was developed within the structure of a mixed economy and a centralised planning process. The public sector was expected to provide the infrastructure necessary for industrial growth and the model for labour relations, with the state taking responsibility for the 'vulnerable'. Since then, the expansion of a neoliberal model of market-driven economic growth has seen universal state provision of basic goods replaced by targeted, often cash-based schemes and a push to deliver social programmes via the market. The shifting political culture is also reflected in the way in which sections of the elite and growing middle class increasingly emphasise formal equality as against substantive and growing inequalities.

In the early years of independence, women's right to the vote, education, and employment were core concerns. Many middle-class and elite women gained access to higher education and paid, formal employment, leading to a sense that the instrumentalities for gender equality had been put in place. Under pressure from the labour movement and socialist politics, laws covering factories, mines, plantations and some unorganised sectors such as construction were passed, mandating maternity benefits and crèches as rights for women workers, along with equal wages for equal work and, in some sectors, employment security, sickness benefits and pensions. A combination of factors, however, including the small number of women workers in the organised, formal, and public sectors, the poor monitoring of labour laws, the large informal sector and prevailing caste and class hierarchies, resulted in limited implementation and little public attention to the gendered nexus of paid work and unpaid care.

Dominant public discourses have assumed that women are secondary earners and, as family members, the primary carers for children, the elderly and the sick. In this context, childcare has received the most attention, initially through a framework that positioned children as the nation's future. In recent years the approach has shifted and childcare is now elaborated in terms of human capital. The state is expected to intervene in the case of family failure, whether the result of a lack of family (orphanages); the 'forced' absence of 'poor and destitute' women who have to work (day-care centres); or the ignorance of carers (moral education and training in nutrition and hygiene). Concerns over infant and child malnutrition and mortality and maternal mortality (in part a response to the politics of the international development discourse reflected in the Millennial Goals and various United Nations bodies and conventions) led to a limited but nation-wide crèche scheme and the ICDS as well as the 1975 National Policy on Children and the 2005 National Plan of Action for Children, in which child rights figure prominently. These and other similar policies are predominantly the responsibility of the Ministry for Women and Child Development, the financial allocation for which was drastically cut in the 2015 budget. Over the past decades, the language of 'women's empowerment' has become more visible in official discourse, but ideas of 'social evil' and 'ignorance', rather than the structural roots of inequality or the gendered divide in care, continue to form the foundation of gender-related policies. National campaigns around the right to food, the rights of children to education, health, and food, against child labour, along with research and lobbying on day care for children and the requirements of early childhood care and education have challenged moves toward state withdrawal from social programmes and schemes on the grounds of fiscal prudence.

Despite robust campaigns around women's rights, there has been limited change, ideologically, politically and in practice, in familial relations and responsibilities pertaining to care. A renewed women's movement since the late 1970s, and the 1975 report of the Committee on the Status of Women in India, along with the Shramshakti Report on self-employed women and women in the informal sector (GOI 1988), saw a shift in the official approach from charity and welfare to development and a focus on women's 'productive potential'. These remain important touchstones in political and policy framing. Yet, even as women's work has gained attention, policy initiatives continue to be premised on their compatibility with women's primary domestic roles. For example, the current emphases on education and economic empowerment through informal schooling and literacy programmes, nutrition programmes, micro-credit and self-help groups do not interfere with women's familial care responsibilities. At the same time, some women's groups have conducted campaigns demanding women's right to paid employment and decent work conditions, including maternity benefits and childcare facilities, as a path to economic independence (e.g. All India Democratic Women's Association, Self Employed Women's Association, Mobile Crèches, FORCES). As a result, crèches were mandated in the national flagship workfare programme, the Mahatma Gandhi National Rural Employment Guarantee scheme (MNREGA), but were rarely set up. Further, despite campaigns by health rights activists, the privatisation of healthcare continues, with little expansion of public medical facilities, leaving care for the ill and disabled primarily the responsibility of women in the home (see Langer et al. 2015).

Following wide-ranging and sustained pressure, the current Twelfth Five Year Plan (2012–2017) reiterates the expansion of crèches (though not for infants under the age of three) in various government programmes as part of the rights of the child *and* as an instrument of women's empowerment (Planning Commission 2013). The international discourse on the elderly and the disabled and pressure from domestic disability rights activists stimulated policy documents that specifically mention care needs. Advocacy for the provision of new care services cite the withering of the joint family and the need to support women as key reasons for policy development in the care sector. However a common feature of these initiatives is the reliance on NGOs as care service providers, rather than the state, and a low ratio of care workers to those who are to receive care in any one facility. Further, the wages and salaries of the associated care workers, as in other government-funded social schemes, are treated as an 'honorarium' and fixed at less than the official minimum wage – even lower than the wages of hired domestic workers and private nannies. Unionisation of workers in these schemes and campaigns around issues of wages, pensions, and job descriptions have attempted to counter this. These policy developments demonstrate that even when care labour is acknowledged, it is framed by an official ideology and political economy within which it remains devalued and poorly understood.

Over the last decade a growing public discussion on the link between gender equality and the paid work–unpaid care nexus has perhaps been pushed aside, with violence becoming the overarching concern in relation to women. Recognition of the care burden has been further constrained by the emergence of a right-wing political culture that emphasises women's embeddedness in extended families as natural, Indian, and proper. In this articulation, care needs are seen as not being met because people are forgetting their culture and women are no longer fulfilling their proper responsibilities. Rather than structures and systems that will facilitate women's paid work as well as the care of children, the sick and the elderly within both personal relations and in social facilities, there are calls for a strengthening of gendered familialism as a response to current needs. Another view often articulated is that the limited use of non-familial care facilities indicates that Indians have a preference for family-based care. The latter path dependency has been challenged by highlighting that women opt out of paid work and promising careers to devote themselves to family-based care due to the absence, expense, or poor quality of care facilities. Lack of viable alternatives for care constrains women's choice considerably.

Work and care at a crossroads?

Demographic trends and the neoliberal turn in economic and social policy-making highlight ongoing difficulties for women's economic security and well-being as they negotiate the competing needs of paid employment and unpaid care for children and the elderly in an unsympathetic policy environment. Demographic trends suggest that women's paid work and care work should be urgent political issues. As many celebrate the current 'youth bulge' and the associated 'demographic dividend' for economic growth, the care of the young continues to fall almost entirely on women, who find that the Indian state, employers and family do not provide a work/care regime that facilitates either decent work or support for the care of children. The health and well-being of children and their working parents and households depend on improved public support for childcare – especially amongst low caste and tribal women, as well as working and lower-middle class women. At the same time, a rapid escalation in the number and proportion of elderly citizens over the next two decades will require appropriate social and health policies to support the care and well-being of the aged. This must include increasing the amount paid as the aged pension and its accessibility.

Progress in the area of work and care policy has been curtailed by the policy directions of an increasingly neo-liberal state. For example, the fleeting rhetoric of universal early childhood care and education made in the Twelfth Five Year Plan (Planning Commission 2013, 192) is undercut by broader developments in social policy that emphasise market-led, targeted programmes and cash transfers in place of universal provision of services by the state. The right to unionisation, collective bargaining and security of employment have been systematically reduced through legislation and the expansion of de facto contractual employment in recent years. These trends began to gather momentum with proposed 'reforms' under the auspices of the National Democratic Alliance government, directly undercutting policy initiatives to improve protection for women and informal workers. Meanwhile women employed in the public sector and private corporate sector have access to generous formal care provisions and flexible work conditions, in addition to other employment protective measures. However, as with most policies in India, implementation remains problematic and accessibility and compliance require evaluation.

Funding a satisfactory work/care regime is also contested. In thinking about the future of work and care in India it is necessary to untangle the politics of rhetoric from the politics of funding. Attention to the work/care nexus or the economic, social and gender relations that may be central to the reorganisation and redistribution of care work rarely go beyond official statements. A 2001 document on the empowerment of women did state that the expansion of crèches, homes for the aged and the disabled are required as support services to women to enable their 'full cooperation in social, political and economic life' (GOI 2001). However, not only was this aspiration not realised in the design of new programmes or the accompanying financial estimates, but allocations in the recent 2015 budget suggest that these ideas have not gained support within the current government. Scholars maintain that governments are currently oblivious to the looming crisis in eldercare, while NGOs argue that 1 per cent of GDP must be allocated for the aged pension (Tripathi 2014, 221). The gap between rhetorical aspiration and the funding and design of appropriate programmes obscures the broader and systemic challenges that women face and policy makers and politicians refuse to confront. Narrow economistic thinking provides the framework in which the opportunity costs of work and care mean that women's unpaid care work is prioritised over gender equity, economic independence, and quality care for dependent children and the elderly.

In India, the necessity for state action to enhance women's access to livelihood opportunities and decent care services continues to be debated, even as the forces of market liberalisation and globalisation become increasingly powerful and entrench inequality. Within this debate the family is positioned as essential to the smooth running of the minimalist welfare state, and women's care labour as indispensable to the family. In the evolving policy regime even when women are recognised as workers, women's rights and gender equality are not seriously considered. Cutting across this mainstream approach is a vibrant community of advocates who organise and campaign around issues of improved regulation of employment, social protection for informal workers, the right of contract workers to organise, improved pay and conditions for domestic workers, decent wages for women working in government programmes as childcarers and healthcare workers, improved public health services for the elderly and more generous aged pensions, among many other concerns that directly affect the economic security and well-being of women and dependent family members. These campaigns and movements point to the urgent need to develop a more comprehensive and emancipatory Indian work/care regime that helps women, and particularly poor women, achieve social and economic well-being.

Notes

1 Given systemic problems with counting women's informal employment and the private location of domestic work, it is reasonable to assume the total number of

women employed in this sector is significantly greater than the figures captured in official data, with some economists estimating the number to be more than 3 million (Chandrasekhar and Ghosh 2007). All data points to a growing number of women employed in domestic work and its increasing feminisation.

2 The Central Pay Commission is intermittently constituted by the government of India to provide recommendations on the salary structure of government employees. Since independence, there have been seven Central Pay Commissions.

References

Agarwala, R. 2013. *Informal Labor, Formal Politics, and Dignified Discontent in India.* Cambridge: Cambridge University Press.

Aiyar, S. and N. Mody. 2011. *The Demographic Dividend: Evidence from the Indian States.* IMF Working paper no.38. http://www.imf.org/external/pubs/ft/wp/2011/wp1138.pdf.

Barik, D., T. Agrawal, and S. Desai. 2015 "After the Dividend: Caring for Greying India." *Economic and Political Weekly* 50 (24): 108–112.

Bulbeck, C. 2009. *Sex, Love and Feminism in the Asia Pacific: A Cross-cultural Study of Young People's Attitudes.* London: Routledge.

Chandrasekhar, C.P. and J. Ghosh. 2007. "Women Workers in Urban India." February 6. http://www.macroscan.net/fet/feb07/fet060207Women_Workers.htm.

Doval, N. 2015. "20% of Population to be Elderly by 2050: HelpAge India Report." *Live Mint.* http://www.livemint.com/Politics/z6BacVOwf5SvmpD9P1BcaK/20-of-population-to-be-elderly-by-2050-HelpAge-India-repor.html.

FORCES/CWDS. 2013. *Need Assessment for Crèches and Childcare Services.* http://www.cwds.ac.in/books.htm

GOI. 1988. *'Shramshakti': Report of the National Commission on Self-Employed Women and Women in the Informal Sector.* New Delhi: Jain Books.

GOI. 2001. *Ministry of Women and Child Development, National Policy for the Empowerment of Women.* http://www.wcd.nic.in/empwomen.htm.

GOI. 2008. *Report of the Sixth Central Pay Commission.* http://finmin.nic.in/6cpc/6cpcreport.pdf.

GOI. 2009. *The Challenge of Employment in India: Report of the National Commission for Enterprises in the Unorganised Sector.* New Delhi: Academic Foundation of India.

GOI. 2015. *Union Budget of India 2015–16.* http://indiabudget.nic.in/budget.asp.

GOI, NSSO, Ministry of Statistics and Program Implementation. 2010. *Employment and Unemployment Situation in India, NSS 64th Round.* New Delhi: GOI.

GOI, NSSO, Ministry of Statistics and Program Implementation. 2011. *Employment and Unemployment Situation in India: NSS 66th Round.* New Delhi: GOI.

GOI, NSSO, Ministry of Statistics and Program Implementation. 2015. *Employment and Unemployment Situation among Social Groups in India: NSS 68th Round.* New Delhi: GOI.

GOI, Planning Commission. 2013. *Twelfth Five Year Plan (2012–2017): Social Sectors Vol. III.* New Delhi: Sage Publications.

HelpAge India. 2015. *2014 State of Elderly in India Report.* New Delhi: HelpAge India.

Hill, E. 2010. *Worker Identity, Agency and Economic Development: Women's Empowerment in the Indian Informal Economy.* London and New York: Routledge.

Hill, E. 2013. "Extreme Jobs and the Household: Work and Care in the New India." In *The Global Political Economy of the Household in Asia,* edited by J. Elias and S. Gunawardana, 194–210. Basingstoke: Palgrave Macmillan.

Hochschild, A. 2000. "Global Care Chains and Emotional Surplus Value." In *On the Edge: Living with Global Capitalism*, edited by W. Hutton and A. Giddens, 130–146. London: Jonathan Cape.

Langer, A., F. Knaul, R. Atun, M. Aran, H. Arreola-Ornelas, Z. Bhutta, A. Binagwaho, R. Bonita, J. Caglia, M. Claeson, J. Davies, F. Donnay, J. Gausman, C. Glickman, A. Kearns, T. Kendall, R. Lozano, N. Seboni, G. Sen, S. Sindhu, M. Temin, and J. Frenk. 2015. *Women and Health: The Key for Sustainable Development.* http://dx.doi.org/10.1016/S0140-6736(15)60497-4.

Mazumdar, I. and N. Neetha. 2011. "Gender Dimensions: Employment Trends in India 1993–4 to 2009–10." *Economic and Political Weekly* 46 (43): 118–126.

NASSCOM (2009) *Gender Inclusivity in India: Building Empowered Organisations.* New Delhi: NASSCOM, Mercer.

Neetha N. and R. Palriwala. 2011. "The Absence of State Law: Domestic Workers in India." *Canadian Journal of Women and the Law* 23: 97–119.

NUEPA. 2016. *Elementary Education in India: A Graphic Representation. Based on U-DISE Data 2014–15.* New Delhi: NUEPA.

Palit, A. 2008. *Evolution of Global Production Systems and their Impact on Employment in India.* New Delhi: ILO.

Palit, A. and P. Singh. 2011. "Suicides in India: The Economics at Work", *ISAS Insights* No. 131 – 25 August 2011.

Palriwala, R. and N. Neetha. 2009. *Paid Care Workers in India: Domestic Workers and Anganwadi Workers.* Geneva: UNRISD.

Palriwala, R. and N. Neetha. 2011. "Stratified Familialism: The Care Regime in India through the Lens of Childcare." *Development and Change* 42 (4): 1049–1078.

Planning Commission (Government of India). 2013. *Twelfth Five Year Plan (2012–2017): Social Sectors, Vol.III.* http://planningcommission.gov.in/plans/planrel/12thplan/welcome.html.

PTI. 2015. *Bihar Increases Maternity Leave Period, to Give Childcare Leave.* http://zeenews.india.com/news/bihar/bihar-increases-maternity-leave-period-to-give-child-care-leave_1525964.html.

Tripathi, T. 2014. "Unhealthy, Insecure, and Dependent Elders." *Economic and Political Weekly* 49 (29): 217–223.

TNN. 2012. "Childcare Leave for Working Mothers." *Times of India.* http://timesofindia.indiatimes.com/city/kolkata/Child-care-leave-for-working-mothers/articleshow/11546075.cms.

United Nations, Department of Economic and Social Affairs, Population Division. 2013. *World Population Ageing 2013.* http://www.un.org/en/development/desa/population/publications/pdf/ageing/WorldPopulationAgeing2013.pdf.

World Bank. 2015. *Health Nutrition and Population Statistics: Population Estimates and Projections.* http://databank.worldbank.org/Data/Views/VariableSelection/SelectVariables.aspx?source=Health%20Nutrition%20and%20Population%20Statistics:%20Population%20estimates%20and%20projections.

10 Sri Lanka

Working realities and gendered fictions

Matt Withers

Sri Lankan women have traditionally been marginalised from waged work in non-agricultural sectors, but many have experienced a pronounced reconfiguration of their working lives in the period since the dramatic economic liberalisation of 1977. A concentration of economic activity in urban areas prompted the internal migration of young Sinhala women into a nascent garment industry situated within newly created export processing zones, while others made incomes as migrant domestic workers following a concurrent lifting of restrictions on foreign employment. Alongside traditional labouring in the plantation sector, these avenues of employment have since underpinned the bulk of Sri Lanka's foreign exchange earnings and steadily supplanted notions of the male breadwinner. Yet cultural expectations of women's care roles have not undergone a corresponding transformation, engendering a number of tensions at the intersection of women's productive and reproductive labour.

Background and demographics

Sri Lanka is a country of approximately 20 million people, of whom 51.6 per cent are women. The population is both religiously and ethnically diverse, with significant Sri Lankan Tamil (11.2 per cent), Sri Lankan Moor (9.2 per cent) and Indian Tamil (4.2 per cent) minorities existing alongside a dominant Sinhalese majority of 74.9 per cent (DCS 2012a). Religious beliefs are hewn roughly along ethnic lines, with 70.2 per cent of the population adhering to Buddhism, 12.6 per cent to Hinduism, 9.7 per cent to Islam and 7.2 to Christianity (DCS 2012a). Ethnic and religious cleavages form most notably in the Northern and Eastern provinces, where the majority-Tamil population has struggled for a sovereign state of Tamil Eelam since the outbreak of ethnic violence and civil war following Sri Lanka's independence in 1948. The war-affected North and East is less developed than the rest of the country and has, until recently, been excluded from the bulk of national surveys and statistics.[1]

While key economic activity is concentrated in urban areas – particularly Colombo and its surrounding regions – Sri Lanka remains a distinctly rural country, with just 18.3 per cent of the population residing within urban dwellings (DCS 2012a). A lack of decent work in the rural economy exacerbates Sri Lanka's demographic challenge of an ageing population (Figure 10.1), as a mismatch between educationally acquired skills and actual employment prospects has meant youth unemployment remains high (IPS 2013). This has prompted concern regarding the continuing provision of care for the country's elderly, particularly as young people's pursuit of employment increasingly involves internal or international migration and thus makes the physical act of care an impossibility (IPS 2013). Increasing recourse to migration may also account for shrinking household sizes, which declined from 4.9 occupants per dwelling in 1981 to just 3.9 in 2013 (DCS 2015).

Women's work and care

In the decades since the sweeping economic liberalisation of 1977, Sri Lankan women have increasingly been driven to work in poorly remunerated positions underpinning the export economy. Nevertheless, attempts to accurately gauge the extent to which women participate in paid employment are complicated by a variety of factors, ranging from inconsistent data to the statistical omission of migrant employment and the broader ambiguities of disentangling 'work' from 'care' in a highly informalised economy. Comparison of labour force participation rates published by various government bodies and the ILO exposes significant discrepancies in the recording of national-level data. A combination of methodological differences, varying definitions of 'working age' and limited access to data from the Northern and Eastern provinces have produced different estimates of female labour force participation. For example, in the Annual Labour Force Survey for 2011 (DCS 2011), 34.4 per cent of Sri Lankan women were recorded as economically active, compared with the 30 per cent recorded in the most recent census (DCS 2012a) and the 39 per cent recorded by the ILO (2013a). The extent of women's participation in paid employment is further obscured by the prevalence of foreign employment under short-term contract.

In addition, temporary labour migration to the Middle East has risen exponentially since the mid-1970s to become a defining feature of the Sri Lankan economy, yet it is not captured as labour force participation by census data or labour force surveys. The Sri Lanka Bureau of Foreign Employment (SLBFE) estimates that there were 1,932,245 Sri Lankans working abroad as of 2010 – equivalent to 25 per cent of the total labour force (SLBFE 2012). Conservative estimates of the number of women employed abroad increase the female labour force participation rate in the most recent labour force survey from 34.4 per cent to 41 per cent. For Sri Lankan women, who have historically made up the majority of Sri Lanka's labour migrants (Figure 10.2), the volume of foreign employment complicates the work/care nexus by commodifying care as a valuable foreign exchange earner, while creating a commensurate local care deficit in the wake of women's physical absence.

Meanwhile, the provision of care – be it for the young or the elderly – remains an overwhelmingly informal activity, performed almost exclusively by women. Women's participation in paid employment occurs within gendered labour market

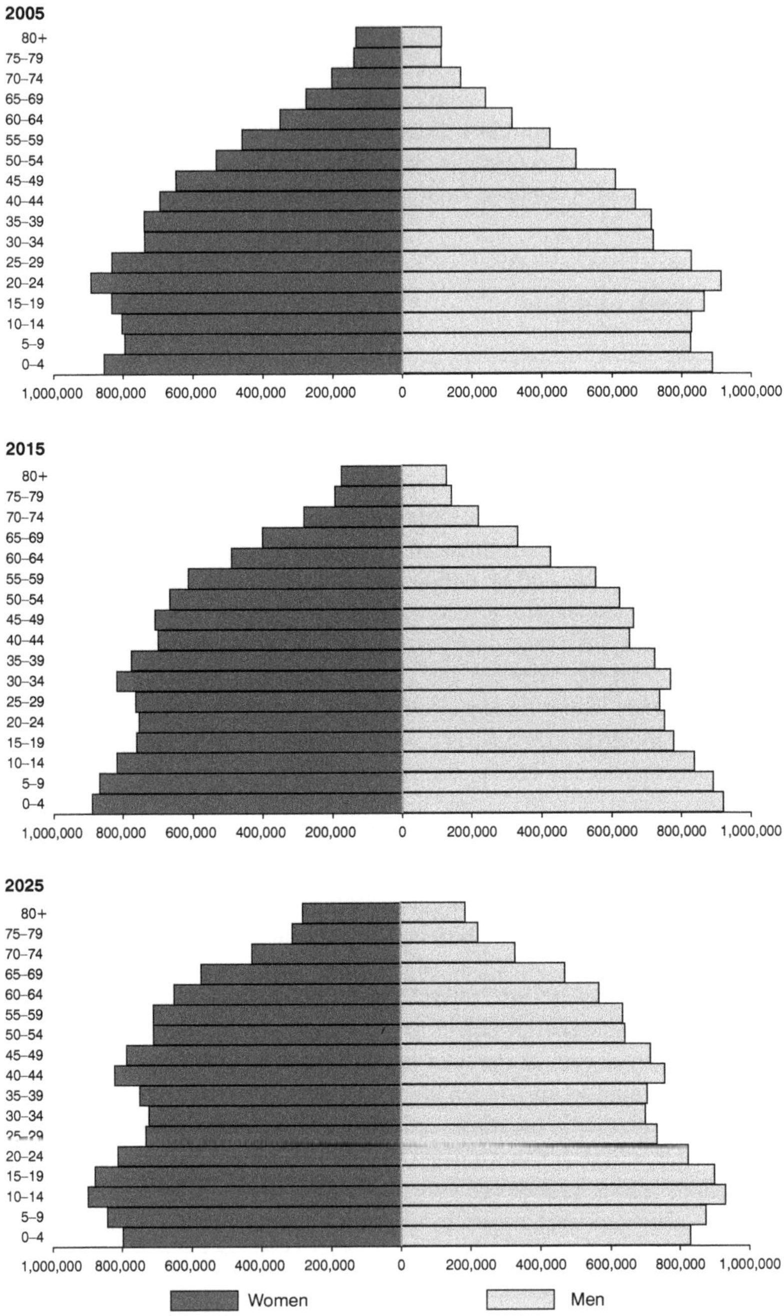

Figure 10.1 Population 2005, 2015, and 2025

Source: World Bank (2015).

Figure 10.2 Departures for foreign employment by gender 1986–2013

Source: SLBFE (2016).

institutions that exploit, rather than acknowledge or compensate for, women's burdens in the reproductive economy (Elson 1999). There is no evidence that women's participation in paid employment produces a decline in unpaid care work. A study of time use between married couples in Colombo found that when women entered paid employment their average working day increased by three hours to 16 hours per day, while the length of the average man's working day was largely unaffected (Satharasinghe 1999). Furthermore, with informal employment accounting for 61.1 per cent of all economic activity in Sri Lanka, productive and reproductive life is frequently interwoven. Many women categorised as 'economically active' are equally involved in the demands of reproductive labour; many women categorised as 'economically inactive' also perform informal productive labour. Neatly delineating between 'active' and 'inactive' does not accommodate the woman who works retail shifts by day and spends several hours cooking and cleaning by night, nor the woman who nurses a child while running a corner store, or the woman producing lunch packets from home while tending to housework and children. The assumption of mutual exclusivity between work and care roles renders much of the work performed by Sri Lankan women – paid or unpaid, productive or reproductive – largely invisible.

Despite being methodologically inconsistent and insufficiently representative, mainstream surveys report female labour force participation rising from around 19.8 per cent in 1973, during the closed-economy period, to 26 per cent amid ongoing neoliberal restructuring in 1978 (CBSL 2004). Despite dipping to lower levels in 1982, the female labour participation rate has sat consistently at about 25 per cent since then (CBSL 2004). The increase is due to women's employment in the export-processing zones that were central to the government's efforts to integrate the Sri

Lankan economy into global production networks. Many young Sinhalese women, from both urban and rural backgrounds, found work in the garment manufacturing sector established in export-processing zones (Arunatilake 2012). Sri Lanka's handloom industry – which once employed 40,000 women throughout the island – simultaneously declined, as government subsidies were retracted in favour of importing textile inputs for garment production (Kottegoda 2004). These job losses saw the centralisation of women's employment in urban export-processing zones. The decline of productive livelihoods in the rural economy similarly contributed to the development of women's temporary labour migration as a key livelihood strategy.

Today women constitute approximately 85 per cent of all employees in Sri Lanka's export-processing zones (DOLUS 2010), while also comprising the majority of estate workers on tea and rubber plantations (Kotikula and Solotaroff 2006) and, until very recently, the clear majority of temporary labour migrants (DCS 2012b). National employment data by industry shows a concentration of women's work in agriculture and manufacturing (Table 10.1). This is not a coincidence, but the result of a heavily gender segmented labour market where – excepting educational and healthcare industries to some extent – high-paid technical, bureaucratic and service positions are by and large the domain of male employment (Table 10.2), irrespective of qualifications and educational attainment (Kotikula and Solotaroff 2006). Patriarchal social structures confine the nature of 'appropriate' work for women, frustrating employment opportunities in many of Sri Lanka's high-growth industries such as trade and construction, while legislation prohibits part-time and evening work in socially acceptable service jobs, to the detriment of skilled women workers juggling the competing demands of care work (Gunatilaka 2013).

Women are, however, over-represented in the most labour-intensive, poorly remunerated occupations that together comprise the backbone of Sri Lanka's export economy (Kotikula and Solotaroff 2006). Tea and garments alone account for over half of all Sri Lanka's trade earnings (CBSL 2012), while migration brings in remittances equivalent to over 50 per cent of exports (IPS 2012). A patriarchal mode of production, formed under colonialism and restructured through neoliberalism, has curtailed women's economic life to the performance of menial labour: indentured to plantations, exploited in factories or without rights in the private homes of foreign employers (Withers and Biyanwila 2014). While the extent of women's participation in these avenues of employment is tempered by religious background, with notably less participation in the domestic workforce by Muslim and Christian women (Gunatilaka 2013), long hours, low-wages and lack of labour rights are pervasive. Several studies report a gender wage gap of around 20 per cent (Ajwad and Kurukulasuriya 2002) and while garment workers won trade union rights and improved working conditions in the late 1990s, women's unionisation remains nascent (Withers and Biyanwila 2014).

State, non-state, private and household responses

The Sri Lankan government has long implemented a comprehensive welfare system, including free universal education and healthcare, which has contributed

Table 10.1 Working population 15 years of age and over by industry and sex, 2013

Economic activity	*Male (%)*	*Female (%)*
Agriculture, forestry and fishing	29.50	35.32
Mining and quarrying	1.88	0.69
Manufacturing	14.16	23.93
Electricity, gas, steam and air conditioning supply	10.66	0.53
Wholesale and retail trade; repair of motor vehicles and motorcycles	15.19	11.55
Transportation and storage	8.88	1.14
Accommodation and food service activities	2.46	2.36
Information and communication	0.82	0.63
Financial and insurance activities	1.67	1.96
Real estate activities	0.00	0.00
Professional, scientific and technical activities	0.84	0.93
Administrative and support service activities	1.19	0.90
Public administration and defence; compulsory social security	6.01	6.90
Education	1.40	7.35
Human health and social work activities	1.11	2.52
Arts, entertainment and recreation	0.00	0.00
Other service activities	1.76	1.17
Activities of households as employers; undifferentiated goods- and services-producing activities of households for own use	1.62	1.75
Total	100.00	100.00

Source: ILO (2013a).

to Sri Lanka's regionally high human development indicators (UNDP 2013). Despite this, public health expenditures are presently very modest, accounting for only 2 per cent of GDP, the vast majority of which is targeted at in-patient facilities rather than community care services (Abeykoon 2002). Sri Lanka's ageing population and increasing birth-rate is set to intensify the need for both eldercare and childcare in the immediate future, placing additional strain on an already underfunded public healthcare infrastructure.

There is a dearth of institutional support for the care of young children and the elderly (Gunatilaka 2013). While the Ministry of Social Services operates a district-level community-based rehabilitation programme offering basic care to disabled individuals, no equivalent system exists for the care of children or the elderly (Abeykoon 2002). The Protection of the Rights of Elders Act, passed in 2000 and amended in 2011, is limited to protecting and promoting the rights of elders without provisioning scope for the reallocation of healthcare resources. With the exception of basic antenatal and postnatal home visits, state care services

Table 10.2 Gender distribution within industries, 2013

Economic activity	*Male %*	*Female %*
Agriculture, forestry and fishing	61.80	38.20
Mining and quarrying	84.15	15.85
Manufacturing	53.40	46.60
Electricity, gas, steam and air conditioning supply	97.50	2.50
Wholesale and retail trade; repair of motor vehicles and motorcycles	71.80	28.20
Transportation and storage	93.77	6.23
Accommodation and food service activities	66.89	33.11
Information and communication	71.67	28.33
Financial and insurance activities	62.17	37.83
Real estate activities	0.00	0.00
Professional, scientific and technical activities	63.65	36.35
Administrative and support service activities	72.03	27.97
Public administration and defence; compulsory social security	62.81	37.19
Education	26.91	73.09
Human health and social work activities	45.99	54.01
Arts, entertainment and recreation	0.00	0.00
Other service activities	74.53	25.47
Activities of households as employers; undifferentiated goods- and services-producing activities of households for own use	64.20	35.80
Total	65.95	34.05

Source: ILO (2013a).

are extremely limited outside of public hospitals and clinics, creating a care gap that is filled by non-state actors, alongside informal care arrangements and private healthcare. NGO services are particularly prevalent within aged care services; there are over 150 charitably run homes for the elderly in Sri Lanka (Abeykoon 2002), while HelpAge Sri Lanka runs a number of programmes providing elderly citizens with direct financial support, medical care, social facilities and day care centres. It also runs educational programmes to teach school children about aged care (HelpAge Sri Lanka 2015).

A lack of state support for eldercare extends into the realm of paid employment. Retirement systems are in place for just 25 per cent of the working population (Gaminiratne 2007) and in the absence of adequate social protection for the majority of workers, particularly women and informal workers, the burgeoning demand for eldercare is likely to strain existing work/care tensions even further. Progressively smaller household sizes and increasing old age dependency ratios (Gaminiratne 2007) are likely to deepen the negative impact of unpaid care work on women's paid work and economic security. Meanwhile, the Sri Lankan government continues to promote foreign employment and incentivise garment production in pursuit of foreign exchange earnings, placing countervailing pressure on women to increase their participation in paid employment. The 1932 Maternity Benefit Ordinance obliging employers to pay 12 weeks of non-subsidised paid maternity leave (or 6 weeks in the case of a third or subsequent child) provides an additional disincentive to the employment of women on formal terms (IPS 2013). Garment sector employers avoid having to pay benefits through the adoption of discriminatory hiring practices favouring young, unmarried women to circumvent the payment of maternity benefits (Prasanna and Kuruppuge 2013).

Private healthcare and education systems, which function in parallel to state services, are poised to meet demand for eldercare and childcare needs, but they are only accessible to a small minority of households. Only high-income earners, defined as households spending between (PPP (Purchasing Power Parity)) USD 10 and USD 100 per day, make significant outlays on private hospitals, nursing homes, specialist services, medical and pharmaceutical products, private schooling facilities, tuition fees, and boarding fees (IPS 2012). There are a number of private nursing homes and in-home nursing services, but these are costly; the most established, Ceylinco Home Nursing Services, charges USD 250 a month for their home-based care (Abeykoon 2002). Similarly, day-care centres are opening in Colombo, but they only cater to the childcare needs of wealthier Sri Lankan families (Gunatilaka 2013).

This asymmetrical division of access to private care along class lines is further reinforced by the enduring employment of domestic workers in middle- and upper-class households. Domestic work in Sri Lanka is located at the most informal end of market relations, entailing very poor pay and little respectability, and almost always involving a live-in working arrangement (Gamburd 2000). Although there is typically some reluctance to entrust childcare duties to domestic workers (Madurawala 2009), such workers undertake the full extent of household labour and thus alleviate the reproductive burden of adult females of the household, some of whom – particularly unmarried upper-class daughters – are themselves the *recipients* of care (Malhotra and de Graff 1997). In this sense, the marketised demand for care both perpetuates the employment of lower-class (and often ethnically marginalised) women in 'unskilled' and socially demeaning job roles, enabling upper-class women to pursue employment in lieu of their own performance of reproductive labour.

The reality for the majority of Sri Lanka's households, however, is that the provision of care – be it for children or the elderly – remains the responsibility of family, specifically carried out by women. Interpreted through the analytical framework of Razavi's (2007) care diamond, Sri Lanka skews heavily towards negotiating the demands of care through the private (and starkly gendered) domain of the household, with little involvement from the public institutions comprising the remaining quadrants of the diamond: the state, 'the market' and civil society. The gendered division of labour in Sri Lanka casts care work as a distinctly feminine undertaking. Men exhibit an extreme reluctance to undertake such work, even in instances where they themselves are unemployed and their wives have become breadwinners (Gamburd 2000).

With high male under- and unemployment in the rural economy, contrasted with steady demand for 'docile' female labour in Sri Lanka's export-processing zones and Middle Eastern households, this inversion of breadwinner duties has provoked a crisis of masculinity. Rather than engendering a transformation of masculine domestic roles, the deficit of care arising from women's migration in pursuit of work has tended to encourage the deferral of care work to female relatives (Gamburd 2000). Delegating care work – particularly childcare – to female relatives is a long-established and socially acceptable practice in Sri Lanka (Dias 1990), yet the proliferation of female migration amid dominant conceptions of masculinity has also resulted in intended care recipients – young girls and elderly women – being drawn into domestic roles at the expense of their own needs (Gamburd 2000). Women who do not migrate for work also develop strategies to negotiate the competing demands of work and care at the household level, specifically by way of kinship and neighbourhood networks. Childcare is often pooled among family or neighbours, affording flexibility to pursue the demands of work, particularly under informal or part-time conditions (Kottegoda 2004). Similarly, in cases of hardship or family crisis it is not uncommon for children to be 'given away' to be cared for by neighbours or relatives as a survival strategy (Kottegoda 2004).

Politics of the work/care nexus

In Sri Lanka, as elsewhere on the sub-continent, the politics of women's work and care are deeply embedded in the concept of nationhood. Women have traditionally been portrayed as nurturers and caregivers to the nation. However, the reality of women's increasing participation in key areas of the productive economy confronts and undermines this narrative, prompting a moral crisis over women's identity alongside an antagonistic material reliance on women's labour.

At the intersection of women's work and care roles is the enduring conceptualisation of women as upholders of Sri Lanka's moral identity in the face of a Westernising market economy, resulting in a pervasive stigmatisation of the working woman (Lynch 2007) and patriarchal-nationalistic veneration of the mother and caregiver (Rajapaksa 2005). This attitude is captured in *Mahinda Chintana,* a series of development manifestos published as electoral promises by the Mahinda Rajapaksa government. In both the 2005 and 2010 versions of 'Mahinda's Vision', heteronormative family relations are superimposed on processes of economic development, delimiting the role of Sri Lankan women as mother and nurturer of the nation in contrast to the productive labour carried out in the masculine domain (Firozvi 2015). The 2010 publication declares:

> The very existence of the world depends on the affection and love of the mother. It is through this affection and love that children acquire a healthy mind and a balanced personality. It is my belief that whatever may be our

> achievements, our focus should be on the family, consisting of the mother, father and the children.
>
> (Rajapaksa 2010, 22)

Rajapaksa's frequent allusion to *the Motherland* and the central role of *the Mother* in nurturing the family-cum-nation reproduces a tradition of patriarchal ethno-nationalist rhetoric first articulated by middle-class Sinhala Buddhist men seeking to define and relegate women's lives to the domestic sphere in the wake of receding colonialism (de Alwis 1996). It perpetuates what Malathi de Alwis describes as 'the idealisation of womanhood signified through the construction of the "respectable lady", the repository of tradition and domesticity, based on a valorisation of motherhood: as the creator and protector of the home, as the chaste and industrious wife and as the iconic representation of the nation' (1996, 139).

In practical terms, the rhetoric of *the Motherland* and *the Mother* is used to bolster the ideological construction of a sexual division of labour that locates Sri Lankan masculinity in the performance of productive labour and femininity in the performance of care and domestic work (Gamburd 2000). The very construction of this division, however, is made increasingly fragile by the stark social and economic reality of women's productive labour. As poverty and failing rural economies catalyse women's entry into garment manufacturing and temporary labour migration, so too do the tensions between women's work and care roles become increasingly politicised. Young women working in garment factories are pejoratively branded *Juki girls* or *Juki pieces* (in reference to a common brand of sewing machine), connoting disposability and sexual promiscuity with the inference that work and urban life has compromised the chastity and respectability that women are expected to embody as symbols of the nation (Lynch 2007). Meanwhile, migrant domestic workers hold a slightly more ambivalent position, maintaining some notion of respectability by extending the practice of care work into foreign employment, while also facing shame for disrupting the family unit and, in some cases, for falling victim to sexual abuse while abroad (Gamburd 2000).

The antagonisms between women's work and socially ascribed care duties hold a central role in public debate. The welfare of migrant domestic workers, in particular, is a hot topic in Sri Lankan tabloid journalism. Stories reporting physical, sexual and emotional violence against Sri Lankan 'maids' are frequent and serve not only to reflect the very real abuse that can and does occur in foreign employment, but also to serialise what Gamburd (2000, 229) dubs the 'migration horror story genre' within which representations of women's work are mediated and given meaning. A prominent variation of such narratives involves sensationalised stories concerning sexual promiscuity among migrant domestic workers in the Middle East, all revolving around themes of unwanted pregnancies and secret abortions, often stylised to resonate with popularly held assumptions of migrant adultery and prostitution (Gamburd 2000). Such themes reinforce the notion that women's participation in paid work is tantamount to forfeiting culturally imbued expectations of modesty and chastity considered synonymous with domesticity. The female body itself becomes a site of contestation and national pride, articulated through expressions of sexual ownership of Sri Lankan women by Sri Lankan men, and has fuelled public demands for restrictions on women's mobility (Gamburd 2000).

Legislative responses to popular concerns about migrant domestic workers have, until recently, been absent, not least because of the huge inflow of foreign exchange earnings received from women migrant workers' remittances. However, the high-profile 2013 execution of Rizana Nafeek – an under-aged Sri Lankan migrant worker sentenced to death in Saudi Arabia when a child died in her care (Weerasooriya 2013) – sparked a revitalisation of media coverage around the physical abuse of Sri Lankan women working abroad and concomitant concerns over the domestic fallout of women's migration. *Ceylon Today*, a popular English-language daily, published an opinion piece entitled 'Enough is Enough', in which the author captures the essence of the national politics surrounding private female bodies:

> Why do we continue to expose our girls to such ignominious situations? Do we not have any other avenues for foreign exchange other than selling our women? Sri Lanka, the country we are proud to be born into, is now known as the country of housemaids.
>
> (Yahampath 2013)

The Sri Lankan government responded shortly after Nafeek's beheading by increasing the minimum age of prospective migrant domestic workers to 25 (Mudugamuwa 2013), then – in response to further public concern over the 'heavy social cost on the children they leave behind' (Weeraratne 2014) – proceeded to place bans on prospective migrant women with children under the age of five (*Adaderana* 2014).

The centrality of work and care antagonisms in this debate is clear, with an opinion piece in the *Daily Mirror* asking: 'What is more important – a mother's right to choose her job or a child's need to be raised by her mother?' (Weeraratne 2014). There is a palpable sense from the government, too, that family problems arising from migration are the onus of women migrants. The chairperson of the SLBFE was quoted as saying, 'We have witnessed several broken homes since mothers have been working abroad' (*Daily Mirror* 2013a), while the Sri Lankan Ambassador to Kuwait stated, 'We are paying the price – the social impact is huge, families are breaking up' (*Daily Mirror* 2014). Further illustrating this gendered imbalance, the Sri Lankan Embassy in Oman issued a statement reporting that prospective female migrants would only be approved to work in the country 'if they get a no-objection certificate from their husbands or their relatives' (*Daily Mirror* 2013c). Pressure groups continue to receive widespread media coverage in their push for a total ban on female migration (*Daily Mirror* 2013b), while discussions over the domestic responsibilities of migrants' husbands and the gendered asymmetry of care work in Sri Lanka remain confined to dedicated women's advocacy groups, such as the Women and Media Collective and the Centre for Women's Research.

The broader paradox of women's work and care roles is illuminated by the government's competing objectives of placating public outrage over the treatment of 'their' women in the Middle East and increasing annual remittance inflows.

The government has been superficially restricting female migration in the name of protecting workers and their families, while surreptitiously taking steps to encourage continued and more profitable migration by female domestic workers who still account for 42 per cent of all departures, according to the latest available statistics (SLBFE 2012). The Sri Lanka Bureau of Foreign Employment has recently enforced mandatory National Vocational Qualification courses in order to 'rebrand' migrant domestic workers as 'domestic housekeeping assistants' capable of commanding higher wages (IPS 2014). This 'upskilling' is effectively symbolic, as the National Vocational Qualification course content differs in no discernible way from existing two-week pre-departure training conducted by the Bureau of Foreign Employment (GIC 2015), and underscores the government's intention of profiting further from 'exporting' Sri Lankan labour for the Middle Eastern 'market'.

Similar disregard for women workers is found in the garment industry, where the increasing unpopularity of textile manufacturing among Sinhala Buddhist women due to social stigma, low-wages and poor living conditions (Arunatilake 2012) has created job shortages (Fernando 2013). The industry's umbrella body, the Joint Apparel Association Forum (JAAF), had until recently planned on recruiting 35,000 foreign workers from cheap labour markets in India, Bangladesh and Myanmar, but it aborted the plan in favour of greater use of domestic labour (Chandrasena 2013). Accompanying this change in tack has been the steady integration into the garment industry of Tamil women, a majority of whom are Internally Displaced Persons seeking employment in the South after fleeing post-conflict poverty in the North (Fernando 2013). Tamil women working in the Katunayake export-processing zone have experienced discrimination in employment and working conditions, while their segregation from Sinhalese women is used to stoke ethnic tensions and undermine attempts at collective bargaining (Fernando 2013). The integration of internally displaced Tamil women into export manufacturing not only exploits ethnic divisions in the productive sphere, but also – on account of boarding single employees in factory accommodation – creates a care deficit among war-affected families, for whom the demand for able-bodied caregivers is often already acute (Bandarage 2010).

Both the Sri Lankan state and private capital manipulate the popular politics of women's work and care roles in terms of their own vested interests. Women's work takes place in a framework of patriarchal ethno-nationalism that produces a spectrum of differentiated entitlements for women across class and ethnic lines, even as they are collectively constrained by the motif of the 'respectable woman' and the need to preserve national morality through the performance of domestic care labour. For a majority of Sri Lankan women the right to work can only be exercised within particular pathways: informal local employment, garment manufacturing, or temporary labour migration. Countervailing social pressure to fulfil the gendered obligation of inhabiting the domestic sphere at the same time as performing care work makes all of these options fraught with repercussions, be it the juggling of mutually intensive work and care duties at home, the subjection to social stigma and assumed 'impurity' as a *Juki girl*, or the moral culpability of shirking motherly care and fracturing the household unit through migration.

Work and care in crisis

Women are both exploited in the realm of productive labour and culturally subordinated in the carrying out of reproductive duties for the household and nation. Differentiated by class and ethnicity, these tensions currently constrain participation in economic activity through prescribed domesticity, prompt moral backlash for shirking domestic roles in the pursuit of work through migration, or engender excessive working hours from the uneasy navigation of competing work and care demands. A paradox emerges whereby the 'nimble fingers' and the 'natural hospitality' of Sri Lankan women are recruited to nurture both the economy and the nation: as the backbone of export production and dutiful remitters of foreign earnings, while simultaneously the 'respectable lady' and patriarchy's proxy for tradition (de Alwis 1996, 139). Caught between iconic and iconoclastic representations, women are invariably unable to simultaneously embody both tropes, resulting in a politicised spectrum of constrained work and care roles that have proven largely ineffective in meeting the needs of women, of households, of communities, or the economy itself.

The inadequacies of Sri Lanka's work/care regime pose challenges for the state's governance of local communities and the economy at large. The feminisation of low-wage employment abroad and in urban centres has left many households, and in some cases entire communities, dependent on women's salaries. While often construed as avenues of upward mobility, women's work remains characterised by precarity and poor wages and for the most part is more a survival strategy than a dependable economic foundation (Kottegoda 2004). Yet, with the rise of the female breadwinner amid the declining viability of traditionally male livelihoods, large swathes of the rural economy have come to subsist on income from these poorly remunerated forms of employment. Labour migration, in particular, has long been seen as an escape valve for the declining rural economy and a crucial form of foreign exchange earnings. Yet growing household dependence on remittances in turn fosters a path dependency that can entail repeat or alternating migrations to preserve streams of foreign income, while returnees' attempts at sustainable economic reintegration are often frustrated by a continuing lack of local job opportunities (ILO 2013b).

For private capital, Sri Lanka's work/care regime has facilitated continued access to a steady supply of cheap labour that can be maintained under precarious conditions in order to remain globally competitive (Arunatilake 2012). Sri Lankan women have been described by garment industry employers as more 'manageable', 'flexible' and 'patient' than male workers, in addition to being less likely to undertake industrial action (Madurawala 2009). However, with Sri Lanka's garment industry being progressively undercut by cheap labour elsewhere in Asia, a work and care regime that ensnares women between proscriptive employment opportunities and the demands of reproductive labour also stymies potential opportunities for private sector growth in nascent areas of the economy. A combination of prejudicial gender norms, discriminatory maternity laws, insufficient care alternatives, skill mismatching and practical impediments to women's work – including a lack of safe transportation and flexible working hours – has constrained women's participation in suitable technical and professional roles (IPS 2013; Gunatilaka 2013).

Failing to address these barriers to employment only deepens Sri Lanka's inability to make use of skilled labour, as those with skills – both men and women – tend to seek better working conditions abroad (IPS 2013). Moreover, the social expectation that childcare and eldercare will be performed by women, largely irrespective of conflicting work commitments, can be seen to have prevented both the public and private provision of care alternatives for working women outside of upper-class backgrounds (Gunatilaka 2013). Existing work and care relations, therefore, contribute to Sri Lanka's struggle to bridge a concentration of labour-intensive, low value-added production into the more diverse array of value-added businesses identified as key to continued economic growth (IPS 2013).

Crises of work and care are perhaps most acute where they are directly experienced: in the household itself. Here the ineffectiveness of the existing work/care regime is attested to by the care deficit created by the internal and international migration of working women being chiefly absorbed, not by unemployed men or state services, but by the auxiliary care of other women in the family and broader community (Kottegoda 2004; Gunatilaka 2013). With the resolution of work and care tensions left largely to the private domain of the household, the dual burden of women's productive and reproductive labour tends to precondition dysfunctional familial relationships. Research reveals that the decisions of young women to pursue work in the garment industry are not so much the result of considerations of household income, but rather a claim for autonomy, a breaking free from the gendered constraints of familial and village life in order to earn independently (Hewage, Kumara and Rigg 2011). Particularly for poor women, whose families are unable to amass a significant dowry, private savings were seen as a catalyst for individual upward mobility. The gradual feminisation of the rural breadwinner and deepening male under/un-employment have engendered a crisis of masculinity, wherein compensatory increases in alcohol consumption and gratuitous idleness have also prompted women's migration abroad (Gamburd 2000; Kottegoda 2004; Gunatilaka 2013). Such instances reflect a co-mingling of repressive gendered norms with unbalanced sexual divisions of productive and reproductive labour.

A number of attitudinal, legislative and structural-economic challenges stand between the existing state of affairs and a more equitable reconfiguration of Sri Lanka's work and care regime. Attitudinal resistance to women's participation in various forms of paid employment, and to men's participation in the performance of care and reproductive work, constitutes a critical asymmetry in the sexual division of labour. Redressing male absenteeism from domestic duties and confronting the very notion of masculinity as it is defined in relation to breadwinner roles and the productive economy would both alleviate the care burden women currently shoulder and open up less exploitative and socially demeaning pathways into paid employment. Legislative overhauls are also needed in order to counteract existing work and care imbalances. Maternity laws need to be rewritten to provide state subsidies for parental leave, while compensating working mothers with an allowance for childcare costs has also been recommended as a means of alleviating the care burden and improving conditions of women's employment (IPS 2013).

Lastly, there is a very real need for a structural redistribution of economic entitlements, across ethnic divisions and from urban to rural milieus. One of the growing burdens of women's employment is the need to financially offset a lack of household income stemming from men's under/un-employment, while a lack of decent work for both men and women serves as a structural 'push factor' for rampant foreign employment. In recent years the government has invested heavily in tourism and the urban service sector, without requisite job creation for the rural economy that continues to suffer from a diminishing number of sustainable livelihoods (World Bank 2012). Without addressing the structural processes of uneven development characteristic of neoliberal economic policy it will prove difficult, if not impossible, to extricate women from their subordinate status within Sri Lanka's patriarchal mode of production.

Note

1 The reconfiguration of traditional gender roles during wartime has produced violent changes for Tamil women, including conflict-necessitated work roles, care work for the disabled and displaced, militarisation, victimisation with the explicit use of sexual violence as warfare and precarious work in the post-war economy (Bandarage 2010). This chapter is unable to address these complex issues.

References

Abeykoon, P. 2002. "Case Study: Sri Lanka." In *Long-Term Care in Developing Countries: Ten Case Studies*, 332–358. Geneva: WHO.

Adaderana 2014."Sri Lanka Expects Drop in Maid Deployment This Year." 2 November. http://www.adaderana.lk/news.php?nid=25715.

Ajwad, M.I., and P. Kurukulasuriya, 2002. *Ethnic and Gender Wage Disparities in Sri Lanka.* Working Paper No. 2859. Policy Research Working Paper. Washington DC: World Bank.

Arunatilake, N. 2012. "Precarious Work in Sri Lanka." *American Behavioral Scientist* 57 (4): 488–506.

Bandarage, A. 2010. "Women, Armed Conflict, and Peacemaking in Sri Lanka: Toward a Political Economy Perspective." *Asian Politics and Policy* 2 (3): 653–667.

CBSL. 2004. *Consumer Finances and Socio-Economic Survey 2003/04.* Colombo: Central Bank of Sri Lanka.

CBSL. 2012. *Economic and Social Statistics of Sri Lanka 2012*. Colombo: Central Bank of Sri Lanka.

Chandrasena, C. 2013. "JAAF Aborts Plans to Import Foreign Labour for Apparels." *Ceylon Today,* 17 March. http://www.ceylontoday.lk/22-29975-news-detail-jaaf-aborts-plans-to-import-foreign-labour-for-apparels.html.

Daily Mirror 2013a. "SL to Cut Down on Maid Exports." 3 January. http://www.dailymirror.lk/24712/sl-to-cut-down-on-maid-exports.

Daily Mirror 2013b. "Sri Lanka Sends Extra 10,000 Housemaids in 2012." 11 April. http://www.dailymirror.lk/28020/sri-lanka-sends-over-10000-housemaids-in-2012.

Daily Mirror 2013c. "New Rules to Protect SL Maids." 23 September. http://www.dailymirror.lk/35880/new-rules-to-protect-sl-maids.

Daily Mirror 2014. "SL Mulls Ban on Sending Maids Abroad." 11 February. http://www.dailymirror.lk/news/42928-sl-mulls-ban-on-sending-maids-abroad.

DCS. 2011. *Sri Lanka Labour Force Survey: Annual Report – 2011*. Colombo: Department of Census and Statistics.

DCS. 2012a. *Census of Population and Housing 2012: Provisional Information Based on 5% Sample.* Colombo: Department of Census and Statistics.

DCS. 2012b. *Sri Lanka Labour Force Survey: Annual Report – 2012*. Colombo: Department of Census and Statistics.

DCS. 2015. *Household Income and Expenditure Survey – 2012/2013*. Colombo: Department of Census and Statistics.

de Alwis, M. 1996. "Gender, Politics and the 'Respectable Lady.'" In *Unmaking the Nation: The Politics of Identity and History in Modern Sri Lanka*, edited by P. Jeganathan and Q. Ismail, 137–157. Colombo: Social Scientists' Association.

Dias, M. 1990. "Marriage, Motherhood and Employment." In *Women at the Crossroads: A Sri Lankan Perspective*, edited by S. Kiribamune and V. Samarasinghe, 216–227. Colombo: International Centre for Ethnic Studies.

DOLUS. 2010. *Promoting Fundamental Principles and Rights at Work in Sri Lanka (2009–2011).* Colombo: Department of Labour.

Elson, D. 1999. "Labour Markets as Gendered Institutions: Equality, Efficiency and Empowerment Issues." *World Development* 27 (3): 611–627.

Fernando, M. 2013. *Ethnic Discrimination: The Post Armed Conflict Economic Challenges of Tamil Women.* Colombo: Women's Centre Sri Lanka.

Firozvi, A. 2015. *Mahinda's Vision for the Future: The Nation as a Heteronormative Family.* Colombo: Centre for Poverty Analysis.

Gamburd, M. 2000. *The Kitchen Spoon's Handle: Transnationalism and Sri Lanka's Migrant Housemaids.* Ithaca: Cornell University Press.

Gaminiratne, N. 2007. *Population Ageing, Policy Responses and Options to Extend Retirement Coverage: Case Study of Sri Lanka.* Colombo: Institute of Policy Studies.

GIC. 2015. *Training for Migrant Workers.* http://www.gic.gov.lk/gic/index.php?option=com_info&task=info&id=17&lang=en.

Gunatilaka, R. 2013. *Women's Participation in Sri Lanka's Labour Force: Trends, Drivers and Constraints.* Colombo: ILO.

HelpAge Sri Lanka. 2015. "Our Programmes." *HelpAge Sri Lanka.* http://www.helpagesl.org/our_programmes/our_programmes.php.

Hewage, P., C. Kumara, and J. Rigg. 2011. "Connecting and Disconnecting People and Places: Migrants, Migration, and the Household in Sri Lanka." *Annals of the Association of American Geographers* 101 (1): 202–219.

ILO. 2013a. ILOSTAT Database, Annual Indicators. https://www.ilo.org/ilostat.

ILO. 2013b. *Reintegration with Home Community: Perspectives of Returnee Migrant Workers in Sri Lanka.* Geneva: ILO.

IPS. 2012. *Sri Lanka: State of the Economy 2012*. Colombo, Sri Lanka: Institute of Policy Studies of Sri Lanka.

IPS. 2013. *Sri Lanka: State of the Economy 2013*. Colombo: Institute of Policy Studies of Sri Lanka.

IPS. 2014. *Summary Report: International Conference on Policies for Mainstreaming Migration into Development in Sri Lanka, 14 August 2014.* Colombo: Institute of Policy Studies of Sri Lanka.

Kotikula, A., and J. Solotaroff. 2006. *Gender Analysis of Labor in Sri Lanka's Estate Sector*. Washington: World Bank.

Kottegoda, S. 2004. *Negotiating Household Politics: Women's Strategies in Urban Sri Lanka.* Colombo: Social Scientists' Association.

Lynch, C. 2007. *Juki Girls, Good Girls: Gender and Cultural Politics in Sri Lanka's Global Garment Industry.* Ithaca: ILR Press.

Madurawala, D. 2009. "Labour Force Participation of Women in Child-Bearing Ages." *Sri Lanka Journal of Population Studies* 11: 1–38.

Malhotra, A., and D. de Graff. 1997. "Entry Verses Success in the Labour Force: Young Women's Employment in Sri Lanka." *World Development* 25: 379–394.

Mudugamuwa, M. 2013. "Sharp Drop in Lankan Women Going as Housemaids." *The Island.* 3 October. http://www.island.lk/index.php?page_cat=article-details&page=article-details&code_title=89411.

Prasanna, R. and R. Kuruppuge, 2013. *General Wage Situation of Apparel Workers in Sri Lanka.* http://asia.floorwage.org/resources/wage-reports/general-wage-situation-of-apparel-industry-workers-in-sri-lanka.

Rajapaksa, M. 2005. *Mahinda Chintana: Victory for Sri Lanka.* Colombo: Presidential Secretariat of Sri Lanka.

Rajapaksa, M. 2010. *Mahinda Chintana: A Brighter Future.* Colombo: Presidential Secretariat of Sri Lanka.

Razavi, S. 2007. *The Political and Social Economy of Care in a Development Context: Conceptual Issues, Research Questions and Policy Options.* Geneva: UNRISD.

Satharasinghe, A. 1999. "Time-Use Analysis of Husbands and Wives." *Sri Lanka Journal of Population Studies* 2: 11–24.

SLBFE. 2012. *Annual Statistical Report of Foreign Employment 2011.* Colombo: Sri Lanka Bureau of Foreign Employment.

Sri Lanka Bureau of Foreign Employment (SLBFE). 2016. *Different Perspectives of Departure Details*. Colombo: Sri Lanka Bureau of Foreign Employment.

UNDP. 2013. *Human Development Report 2013: Sri Lanka*. United Nations Development Program.

Weeraratne, B. 2014. "Restrictions on Female Migrant Workers Discriminatory or Improving Family Wellbeing?" *Daily Mirror*, 18 December. http://www.dailymirror.lk/59215/restrictions-on-female-migrant-workers-discriminatory-or-improving-family-wellbeing.

Weerasooriya, N. 2013. "A Requiem for Rizana…" *Daily Mirror,* 10 January. http://www.dailymirror.lk/24908/a-requiem-for-rizana.

Withers, M. and J. Biyanwila. 2014. "Patriarchy, Labour Markets and Development: Contesting the Sexual Division of Labour in Sri Lanka." *IIM Kozhikode Society & Management Review* 3 (1): 33–43.

World Bank. 2012. *Turning Sri Lanka's Urban Vision into Policy and Action.* Colombo: World Bank Colombo Office.

World Bank. 2015. Health Nutrition and Population Statistics: Population Estimates and Projections. http://databank.worldbank.org/Data/Views/VariableSelection/SelectVariables.aspx?source=Health%20Nutrition%20and%20Population%20Statistics:%20Population%20estimates%20and612 %20projections.

Yahampath, S. 2013. "Enough is Enough." *Ceylon Today,* 22 December. http://sandbox.ceylontodaylk/52-112994-news-detail-enough-is-enough.html.

Part II
Familial/formal care regimes

11 Australia

The care challenge

Alexandra Heron, Rae Cooper and Gabrielle Meagher

In 2002, the then Australian Prime Minister, John Howard, noted that the conflict between work and family was the '… biggest ongoing social debate of our time. I call it a barbecue stopper' (Hudson 2002). While this now famous statement was uttered as part of the reasoning for *not* introducing a paid parental leave scheme, it nonetheless signalled that the disjuncture between women's work and care responsibilities had gained political potency, even under Howard's conservative government. At each of four successive federal election campaigns, the major parties attempted to position themselves as the party of 'working families', wooing voters with various policy initiatives designed to facilitate better workplace flexibility, improve leave arrangements for new parents and offset the cost of childcare. In this context, our chapter analyses women's work and care in Australia, attempting to understand the experiences of women in work, the link to care in the home, and the ways in which policy-makers have attempted to respond to the challenges that have emerged for business, families and women themselves.

We argue that as women have engaged in paid employment at higher rates, their participation has been overlaid by an architecture of labour market discrimination in which women's predominant role in caring responsibilities is intertwined with their workplace disadvantage. Women are corralled by glass walls (where they work in highly feminised and often undervalued occupations), glass ceilings (where men dominate in senior organisational roles and women are absent), and sticky floors (where women are concentrated in lower level occupations without prospects for advancement or development). Put simply, relative to men, women are in a disadvantaged labour market position.

In an attempt to offset this, as we outline below, there has been a significant government policy response in the last ten years aiming to assist women with work and care (for example in relation to childcare provision and paid parental leave). Yet this has not led to a fundamental rethink in practice or policy in relation to care in the home, where women perform the majority of domestic labour, nor the reshaping of work to care needs. As has long been recognised, the regulation of both work and care in Australia has been underpinned by a 'strong male breadwinner ideology' (Baxter and Hewitt 2013), with women relegated to a subsidiary earning capacity in the family and assigned the major responsibility for care. This ideology has permeated the regulatory institutions, mechanisms and processes which are critical to consider in the work and care terrain. While recent reforms acknowledge parents' (effectively mothers') needs for workplace support, the laws creating such 'rights' are framed to ensure the business 'burden' arising from them is minimal. Despite numerous public inquires investigating aspects of women's work and caring responsibilities, the approach of government has been to largely eschew the creation of substantive workplace rights for women. The emphasis is on families finding their own care solutions, aided by government payments rather than employer-funded benefits, and for employees to negotiate individual measures such as flexible working arrangements with their employers. Without rights to good part-time career options, many women's employment choices are structured toward lower-end flexible jobs. For many women this means precarious employment and few opportunities for workplace progression.

Thus in Australia, the family is the pre-eminent 'caring' institution, underpinned by significant financial assistance from the state. The state also regulates service quality in relation to the private, for-profit and not-for-profit sectors that deliver most of the formal services. Parents (notably mothers) provide the bulk of childcare with the assistance of relatives, especially grandparents. Informal carers (often mature-aged daughters still engaged in the workforce) who are acknowledged as critical 'for the functioning of the aged care system overall' (PC 2011, 325) provide the bulk of eldercare.

The context

Australia has a population of nearly 24 million and a population sex ratio of 100 women to 99 men at 34 (ABS 2014a). The total fertility rate is 1.9 (2013 rate, Australian Government 2015a, 9). Approximately 12.4 million Australians aged 15 and over, of whom 46 per cent are women, participate in the labour force (ABS 2015). Figure 11.1 shows the past, current and predicted configurations of the population by age. Currently, the largest age groups are those in the range 25–44. As those in the younger cohorts age and the larger numbers in these prime age cohorts retire, the 'dependency ratio' of those over the traditional retirement age of 65 to the working age population of 15–64 will increase, an issue that will be of concern for government (Australian Government 2015a).

Australian women's labour force participation rates have risen significantly in the past two decades, currently standing at 65 per cent (ABS 2014b). The patterns of participation have also changed. Whereas once women exited the labour force in large numbers upon having children, after which participation rates increased but did not recover to pre-children rates, it is now typical for women to continue working through their years of childbearing and infant care. In 1966, less than two-fifths of women aged 25–44 participated in the labour market; in 2013, the proportion had risen to three-quarters. From this aggregate perspective, it seems that change has been profound. Motherhood, however, has a strong impact on working time, with most mothers returning to work part-time after childbirth. Among mothers whose youngest child is 5 years of age or younger, less than a fifth work full-time, rising only to a third among those whose youngest child is aged between 6 and 14 (Meagher

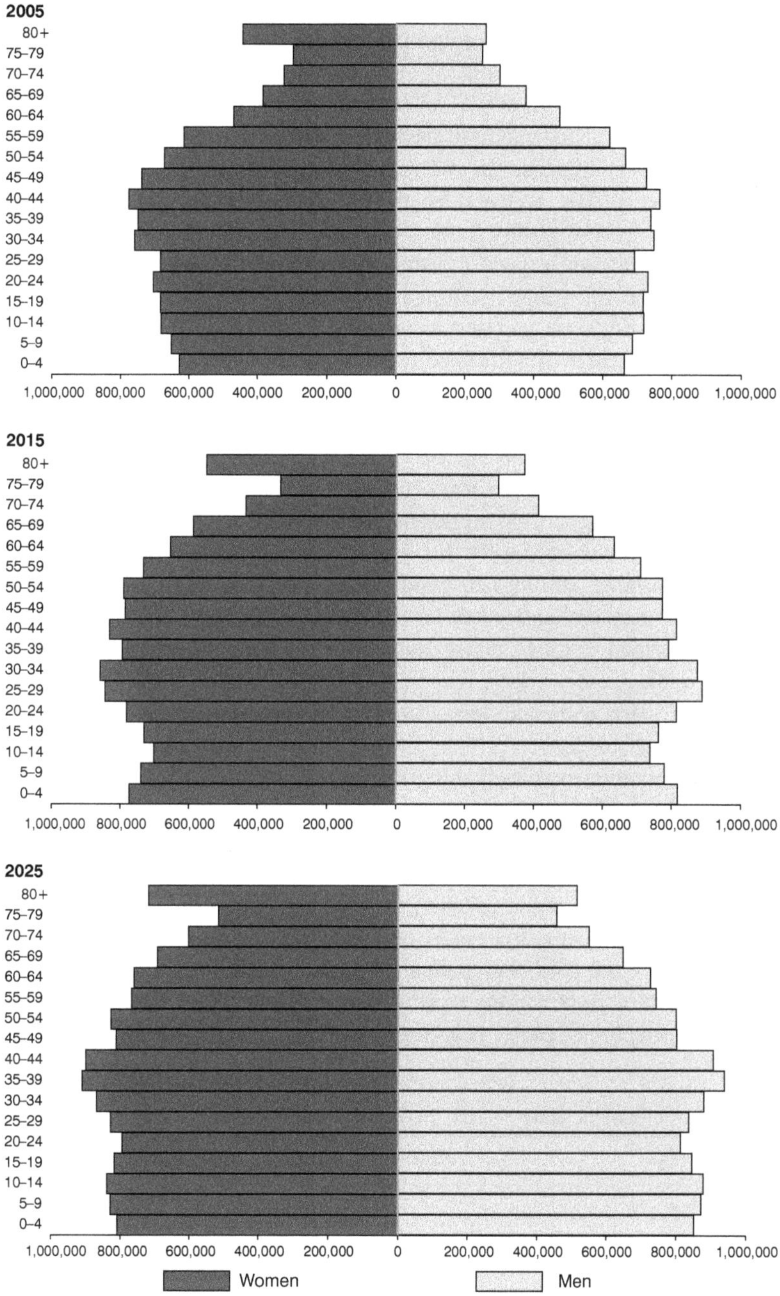

Figure 11.1 Population 2005, 2015, and 2025

Source: World Bank (2015).

2014). Lone mothers are particularly vulnerable to joblessness, with more than two-fifths of female sole parents not in employment (ABS 2011a). Thus, only a minority of mothers of children of school age or younger are economically independent. By contrast, more than four-fifths of all fathers work full-time, regardless of the age of their youngest child, as was broadly the situation in 1966 (Meagher 2014), illustrating the entrenched nature of the male breadwinner model.

The significant increase in women's participation in paid employment, albeit less than it first appears, is closely connected to women's continued disproportionate responsibility for domestic and caring work compared with their male partners. Data on the gender distribution of unpaid work shows that women spend, on average, more than five hours a day on unpaid work, compared with less than three hours for men, and that women were four times more likely than men to be the primary carer of a disabled child or parent (Meagher 2014). Australian families rarely have paid, 'live-in' domestic help. Other forms of outsourcing are also relatively rare. Survey data from 2005–2011 suggest that outsourcing of some domestic chores may be associated with a more equal sharing between partners of time spent on other tasks (Craig et al. 2016). Use of formal childcare services is widespread but by no means predominant, with family care playing a very large role. Associated with this is a strong maternal culture, with research examining changing attitudes to gender roles between 1985 and 2006 finding 'stay at home' mothers were perceived as 'better' (van Egmond et al. 2010, 160). This care overload is a key driver for labour market disadvantage, as it forces women to reduce paid working time and accept the negative effects of this move on pay, progression and conditions. 'Good' jobs in these respects are usually full-time (Baird et al. 2011).

Australian women are disadvantaged relative to men on all gauges of access to labour income and related benefits. As Table 11.1 illustrates, they are less likely to be employers and own-account workers. Women also participate less in paid work, are more likely to be underemployed (unemployed or wishing to work more hours) and, when they are employed, to work part-time (ABS 2014b). A greater proportion of female employees (23 per cent) than males (18 per cent) work as 'casuals' without the paid personal/carers and annual leave entitlements that are of particular value in managing work and care (Table 11.2). For prime age (and earning) cohorts, the disparity is greater: between 35 and 44 years of age, 19 per

Table 11.1 Employment status by sex, 2013

	Male (%)	*Female (%)*
Employees	87.92	92.04
Employers	2.62	1.57
Own-account workers	9.27	6.14
Contributing family workers	0.20	0.25
Total	100.00	100.00

Source: ILO (2013).

cent of women and 11 per cent of men are casuals (ABS 2014c). 'Casual' jobs are of poor quality as they are more insecure than permanent jobs and lack the same pay and progression prospects (Campbell, Whitehouse and Baxter 2009).

The Australian labour market is heavily sex-segregated. As Table 11.3 shows, Australian women are concentrated in a few occupations and industries that have been socially constructed as 'women's work'. Almost half of all employed women work in health, education, the wholesale or retail trade, compared with approximately 20 per cent of men, a distribution that has been stable for decades (Meagher 2014). Australian women are nearly twice as likely as men to be employed in the public sector (22 versus 13 per cent) (ABS 2014d) and many more work in publicly-funded, privately-provided social services, such as childcare and aged care.

Linked to their segregated position in the labour market, Australian women earn considerably less on average than men. The gender pay gap in average weekly full-time earnings is 18.8 per cent (WGEA 2015). Women are also disproportionately represented in low-paid employment dependent on minimum wages (Wright and Buchanan 2013) so a good minimum wage is of particular importance to them. Nevertheless, although Australia's minimum wage (established in the industrial relations system) sets a high standard (for international comparison, see OECD 2015) and operates to constrain the growth of the gender pay gap, the gap has been remarkably stable over more than 30 years.

Combining work and care can be particularly difficult for Aboriginal and Torres Strait Islander women who, on average, have more children and at an earlier age than other Australian women and are more likely to be sole parents. Aboriginal and Torres Strait Islander women also have wider 'extended family and kinship responsibilities' (Doyle and Hill 2012, 37 citing White 2007, 61), and thus face additional challenges in balancing work and care. Consequently, their labour force participation rate is lower than that for Aboriginal men and non-Aboriginal women (Biddle and Yap 2009). Research suggests that participation would be assisted by better access to affordable childcare services that are culturally appropriate for and respectful of Aboriginal and Torres Strait Islander families (Doyle and Hill 2012, 10 citing White 2007, 57; Brennan 2013). Culturally appropriate flexible work arrangements that recognise Aboriginal and Torres Strait Islander workers' community responsibilities, as well as cultural change within organisations, would also help promote greater participation, particularly

Table 11.2 Key data on sex (20–74 years) and employment, 2013

	Female (%)	Male (%)
Labour force participation rate	65	78
Employed persons, proportion employed part-time	43	14
Labour force underutilisation rate	14	10
Employees, proportion without paid leave entitlements	23	18

Source: ABS (2014b).

Table 11.3 Working population 15 years of age and over by industry and sex, 2013

	Male (%)	*Female (%)*
Agriculture, forestry and fishing	3.43	1.67
Mining and quarrying	3.66	0.76
Manufacturing	11.92	4.87
Electricity, gas, steam and air conditioning supply	1.03	0.32
Water supply; sewerage, waste management and remediation activities	0.42	0.11
Construction	14.37	2.27
Wholesale and retail trade; repair of motor vehicles and motorcycles	13.41	15.18
Transportation and storage	6.04	1.72
Accommodation and food service activities	5.60	8.22
Information and communication	4.07	2.12
Financial and insurance activities	3.13	3.98
Real estate activities	0.33	0.35
Professional, scientific and technical activities	5.74	6.07
Administrative and support service activities	3.11	3.47
Public administration and defence; compulsory social security	6.37	6.63
Education	2.57	9.04
Human health and social work activities	4.72	20.70
Arts, entertainment and recreation	1.87	2.02
Other service activities	1.24	3.21
Activities of households as employers; undifferentiated goods- and services-producing activities of households for own use	0.00	0.07
Activities of extraterritorial organisations and bodies	0.00	0.00
Not elsewhere classified	6.96	7.22
Total	100.00	100.00

Source: ILO (2013).

of women (Baird et al. 2011 citing Constable 2009). Government policy aims to halve the employment gap between Aboriginal and non-Aboriginal populations by 2018 (compared with 2008), but this target is not likely to be reached with the Government reporting 'a decline in employment outcomes since the 2008 baseline' (Australian Government 2015b, 5).[1]

Overall, Australian organisations conform to the pyramid model seen in most advanced economies, where the higher the organisational level the less likely it is that women will be represented. This holds for private, public and not-for-profit organisations. There is both a 'glass ceiling' and a 'sticky floor' phenomenon at work here. Women predominate in lower level, lower-paid jobs which are precarious and lacking in career paths, and they also are under-represented in senior and strategic roles at the upper echelons of organisational structures. At the same time there is an under-supply of career-track flexible jobs in the Australian labour market and, without mechanisms and capacity to support care (within the home or supplied by the state), Australian women are often forced to choose flexibility over a career path in order to make care ends meet.

Care of children and older people

Family care is predominant in the care of both children and older people, with mothers and daughters providing more informal care than fathers and sons, as part of the gendered division of work in the family domain. Care for children is provided by a combination of all four institutions of the family, state, market and not-for-profit sectors. There is a formal, publicly subsidised childcare system, which includes early childhood education and care for young children up to school entry, typically at 5–6 years of age, and before- and after-school care for primary school-aged children. However, the family is the main provider of care. More than two-fifths of all children aged 0–12 years are cared for by their parents only (PC 2014),[2] with mothers providing the majority of care (Baxter 2013a). A further two-fifths receive some additional informal care, mostly by other family members, especially grandparents. Of all children, less than a third receive any formal care (PC 2014). Pre-school age children receive more, with 30 per cent of 0–2 year olds receiving some formal care; this increases to 60 per cent for 3–5 year olds (Baxter 2013b).

The private, for-profit and not-for-profit sectors deliver the majority of non-family care, with 50 per cent of all formal care services provided by for-profit businesses, 35 per cent provided by not-for-profit organisations, and the remaining 15 per cent provided in the public sector (PC 2014). However, the state's role in funding formal care services for young children is much larger, with public funding accounting for approximately two-thirds of the cost of early childhood education and care. Parental fees make up the difference (PC 2014). Thus, the 'care diamond' (Razavi 2007) for *provision* of care to Australian children is weighted towards the family and the market, while the *funding* of formal provision is weighted towards the state and the family. State oversight, along with parental choice in the childcare market, is expected to regulate the quality of care.

The social organisation of eldercare is quite similar to that of care for children; family and market are important in its provision, while there is extensive public funding of the formal eldercare services received by some of those in need. Just over two-fifths of Australians aged 65 and over need assistance in their daily lives (ABS 2013a). Many of those over 65 rely partly or entirely on informal support alone, mostly from partners and daughters (ABS 2013b). Around 17 per cent receive residential care or some publicly-funded home care services to replace or complement family care (Meagher, Szebehely and Mears 2016). Just 7 per cent of older Australians live with their children (ABS 2013c). The not-for-profit sector provides 58 per cent of residential and 81 per cent of home-based eldercare (CEPAR 2014). A range of means-tested government payments are made to parents and carers of adults to assist with costs and forgone market income.

Workplaces and care: the limits of regulation

The Australian labour market is regulated by a complex set of institutions, legislation and policies that appear robust but are increasingly difficult to police. Ten statutory minimum employment conditions are set by the National Employment Standards in the Fair Work Act 2009. Several are particularly important for combining work and care but, as shown above, many of these are not available, or only partially available, to casual employees. Maximum weekly working time is broadly set at 38 hours, and 'unreasonable' overtime may be refused on the grounds of family responsibilities. Twenty days paid annual leave is available as well as 10 days paid personal sick leave, which may be taken as carer's leave. A right to request flexible working arrangements has been created for carers of children and adults and those experiencing family violence. However, employer refusal (on reasonable business grounds) cannot be challenged in the courts, unlike other National Employment Standards entitlements. Twelve months job-protected, unpaid parental leave is available per parent, with different legislation providing 18 weeks paid parental leave (and two weeks Dad and Partner Pay) at the national minimum wage.

For the majority of employees, further terms and conditions, including pay rates, are set in industry and occupation instruments known as awards. In general, where individual or collective bargaining occurs, men and male-dominated occupations win better pay and conditions than women and female-dominated ones (Cooper 2012). Contributing to this imbalance is the collapse in union membership and density in Australia. The gap between men's and women's unionisation rate has closed considerably in the past 20 years, but this is because Australian women's unionisation rates have fallen more slowly than men's (Cooper 2012). Between 1990 and 2013 female unionisation halved (from 35 to 18 per cent), but it fell by two-thirds among men during the same period (from 45 to 16 per cent). In 2013, half of all female union members were public sector employees, compared with a third of male union members (ABS 2014d).

There have been numerous and high-profile debates in Australia about women, gender equality and work; the gender pay gap is often in the news, as are problems with the cost and availability of childcare and the lack of women in leadership roles. Flexible work is advocated and pregnancy discrimination deplored. The pervasiveness of these debates engenders a sense of gap between rhetoric and reality, contributing to the impression of slow progress in eliminating barriers to women's progress at work. For example, the persistence of the gender pay gap is often condemned (WGEA 2015). Yet ideas for improvement in policy are lacking, with Australian laws providing for gender pay equity only in limited ways. Pay equity principles introduced in the 1970s did not directly address the problem of the gendered undervaluation of work in general, and of care work in particular; instead, wages and career structures in typically male and female occupations were compared, with the goal of establishing 'comparable worth' according to putatively gender neutral criteria (Cortis 2000). Since the late 1990s, some Australian jurisdictions have explicitly addressed gendered undervaluation, and a small but significant number of successful test cases have led to increased wages in specific, female-dominated industries such as social and community care (Meagher and Cortis 2010). However, the capacity of current legislative arrangements to remedy pervasive and growing pay inequality, with its multiple causes, seems limited, with institutional arrangements not being particularly strong (Charlesworth and Macdonald 2014).

This institutional deficit is mirrored in the largely ineffective system created in Australia in the 1980s to combat discrimination and promote workplace equality. Discrimination on the basis of sex and related characteristics such as pregnancy is prohibited under the Sex Discrimination Act, with added protections contained in the Fair Work Act 2009. However these laws largely rely on individuals who have faced discrimination being willing and able to undertake costly and lengthy legal proceedings, something that rarely happens (AHRC 2014). A more systemic approach to promoting gender equality is taken by the Workplace Gender Equality Act 2012, which has also existed in one form or another since the 1980s. This Act requires non-public sector employers of 100 or more employees to report annually to a statutory monitoring agency on specified data and actions viewed as promoting gender equality, but the minimum standards it sets are weak (Smith and Hayes 2015). A 2014 Australian Human Rights Commission report into pregnancy and maternity discrimination suggests that an avalanche of carer discrimination still exists at work, with up to half those employed during their pregnancy reporting they faced poor treatment on the basis of their pregnancy, maternity or leave taking (AHRC 2014). Thus, while anti-discrimination laws have had great 'practical and symbolic' impact (Gaze 2010, 108), these laws have not provided a catalyst for change (see for example, French and Strachan 2009). Employers are effectively free to choose whether and how to comply, while governments ignore recommendations for stronger laws and sufficient resources to make their provisions a reality (HREOC 2007; AHRC 2014).

The politics of policy

Against the backdrop of women's increasing labour force participation, which has gone hand-in-hand with growing employer demand for part-time and flexible workers, a striking feature of policy analysis and policy development in Australia in relation to women, work and care during the past decade, has been the tendency to deal with these issues through national inquiries. Six key inquiries, initiated by both Labor and Conservative governments, were held between 2008 and 2014. Each was tasked with consulting and recommending action in relation to key aspects of the labour force participation of women, and particularly mothers, including the terms and conditions of women's employment, the intersections of paid employment with care responsibilities, and the role that government should play in regulating action and reporting on gender equality.

In the context of an ageing population and major national debates about whether to further deregulate the labour market, the approach of employer associations in submissions to these national inquiries has been to strongly resist any increase in the compliance burden. Employers have argued that they already appreciate the business benefits of gender equality and should be trusted to enact sector-appropriate strategies to address key issues, such as flexible working conditions, leave to accommodate family responsibilities and the advancement of women. A key concern running through all the major submissions from employer associations has been to avoid increasing the burden shouldered by small and medium enterprises. Government has been encouraged instead to employ 'light touch' regulation, such as education and awareness-raising; where major associations have supported policy action, employers have preferred government to support the costs associated with innovation. By contrast, unions and major women's groups have advocated strongly for increased regulation, including the construction of a stronger minimum standards regime, higher standards for parental and other types of care-related leave, the establishment of substantive rights to flexible working arrangements, and government action to improve parents' access to quality childcare. Both unions and women's groups argue strongly for increased compliance obligations on employers in relation to matters such as pay equity and advocate a greater financial commitment to work and care provisions.

Of these six major inquiries, arguably the one providing the clearest gain for women has been that on paid parental leave (Martin et al. 2013). The scheme introduced following this inquiry places no direct financial demands on employers. However, the fact that it is set at the national minimum wage means that men, who are still usually the better-paid partner in couple relationships, cannot afford to take the payment (Martin et al. 2013). Conservative Prime Minister Tony Abbott attempted to introduce a radically improved scheme that would pay women their full replacement wage for six months, funded by a levy on big business. However this intention collapsed in the wake of opposition from employers and many of Abbott's own conservative government, despite Abbott's stated policy aim of improving women's workforce engagement. The failure of this policy proposal highlighted the profound ambivalence towards prioritising assistance to working women where any costs to business may arise. Children are cast as a private good, for whom national and collective responsibility is limited. The Productivity Commission's inquiry into childcare (PC 2014) articulated this view, recommending the apparently cost-free option of 'promoting' the value of flexible working conditions as a means of enabling more women to combine work and care.

Another strand of the work–care debate has been the high-profile and energetic discussion of the dearth of women in top leadership roles in private, non-governmental and public sector organisations. Since the landmark reports of 2002 (Equal Opportunity for Women in the Workplace Agency (EOWA) 2002a, 2002b) provided the first solid private sector data on the female share of board directors (8.2 per cent) and senior executives (8.4 per cent), proposals for government-mandated gender quotas have been met with some industry self-regulation. The Australian Securities Exchange (ASX) now requires its over 2000 listed entities to comply with its gender diversity recommendations and guidelines. These include setting, monitoring and publishing gender balance objectives. As a consequence, by early 2015 the proportion of ASX 200 board directors who are women had increased to 19.4 per cent (AICD 2015). However, these guidelines are easily ignored, with poor compliance outside big businesses (KPMG 2014). This 'voluntary' approach has not yet resulted in sufficient business action to prevent what one gender equality advocate has described as women's 'self-selection [out of leadership roles] due to the incompatibility of family life with workplace cultures demanding long hours' (Conway 2014). Here, too, flexible conditions of work for men as well as women (WGEA 2013a) is promoted as a 'cure all', though again there is a reliance on 'business case' arguments for change rather than regulation (WGEA 2013b). Individual women aspiring to senior workplace positions are largely left to manage as best they can the biases and obstacles to their advancement.

Pressure points

In addition to their benefits for children and older people, affordable and high quality childcare and eldercare support services enable women to participate in the labour market. Such services are available in Australia, in a mixed economy that involves substantial government funding and government-imposed quality standards through largely private provision by not-for-profit and for-profit organisations (Meagher and Goodwin 2015). However, there are few absolute entitlements to services; out-of-pocket costs are often high, and unmet need for services is significant. Women continue to provide most care within the family, inhibiting their capacity to engage in paid work.

Many of the gains for women in the work–care arena in recent years have been hard-won against the strong anti-regulation stance of employers, with governments to varying degrees sympathetic to business arguments. The positive changes that have occurred have generally cost business little or nothing, as is the case with paid parental leave. Where more has been required of business in order to improve gender equality – such as administering the government-funded paid parental leave payment to employees, making modest improvements in social and community workers' wages or meeting increased reporting requirements to provide gender employment data – policy has been hotly contested. At the same time, these changes are markers of increasing expectations that government should act to facilitate families' attempts to combine work and care.

This is particularly striking in relation to childcare, where, despite government claims of budgetary constraints, calls to increase its availability and affordability are unremitting. It is possible that informal elder carers who are attempting to maintain (often second) careers will also begin to call for enhanced government intervention. One way in which government may respond to these calls is to increase the currently very restricted immigration of care workers to work in private households. The Productivity Commission's childcare inquiry recommended that working holiday-makers, of whom there were a quarter of a million in 2013–14

(Howe 2014), be allowed to work for 12 months with the same employer, and that the visa age limit of 31 be removed. The aim is to facilitate the employment of in-home unskilled domestic labour as a cheaper childcare alternative for Australian families (PC 2014). In mid-2015, the federal government announced a pilot scheme to trial the feasibility of providing government childcare subsidies for shift workers, to help them pay for in-home child carers. Unlike other childcare workers, in-home child carers would not need any qualifications. This both devalues care skills and potentially encourages demand for 'au pair' migration.

In this context, work–care debates have extended beyond calls on the state to increase its role in funding formal care to demands for changes by business, in order to provide more good quality and carer-friendly flexible employment. Indeed, flexible working conditions are advocated by government, business and gender equality advocates alike as the principal solution to care dilemmas and to women's poor representation throughout the workplace hierarchy. Employer advocates continue to argue that regulation of change is not needed, because the introduction of flexible conditions of work is of benefit to employers as well as employees. However, many gender advocates remain unconvinced. Like the unions, they regard the business case for change with scepticism, and look to governments to provide the impetus for carer-friendly flexible working conditions. This may become a major pressure point for change, particularly as the Australian Council of Trade Unions is seeking a clear entitlement for parents newly returning to work after having children to carer friendly part-time work (Workplace Express 2015).

These debates point to a 'lopsided' work/care regime with 'paid work … increasingly shared, while unpaid care remains more the responsibility of women' (Pocock 2005, 43). The policy emphasis is on state financing of paid parental leave, childcare and eldercare, imposing no obligation on employers to contribute to these provisions, or to provide quality flexible working conditions to adapt work to caring. The debates on women, work and care rarely touch on gender equality in care and the role of the workplace in supporting a fairer gender distribution of unpaid family care and labour. Instead, business continues to take advantage of the increased availability of female labour provided by individual/state collaboration, with the value of caring to society – and men's potential as caregivers receiving little more than lip service.

Notes

1 This policy target is not gender disaggregated but it appears Indigenous women's employment rates grew strongly in 1994–2002, fell after 2006, and have shown some increase since, to about 40% (ABS 2011b; Gray, Hunter and Lohoar 2012).

2 This does not include school attendance. Most children aged 5 and all those aged 6 and over attend compulsory school education.

References

ABS. 2011a. *Labour Force, Australia: Labour Force Status and Other Characteristics of Families, June 2011.* Canberra: Australian Bureau of Statistics.

ABS. 2011b. *Labour Force Characteristics of Aboriginal and Torres Strait Islander Australians, Estimates from the Labour Force Survey.* Canberra: Australian Bureau of Statistics.

ABS. 2013a. "Older People – Characteristics." *Disability, Ageing and Carers 2012.* Canberra: Australian Bureau of Statistics.

ABS. 2013b. *Survey of Disability, Ageing and Carers, Australia 2012.* Canberra: Australian Bureau of Statistics.

ABS. 2013c. *Where and How do Australia's Older People Live? Reflecting a Nation.* Canberra: Australian Bureau of Statistics.

ABS. 2014a. *Australian Demographic Statistics June 2015.* Canberra: Australian Bureau of Statistics.

ABS. 2014b. "Working Population." *Gender Indicators, Australia, August 2014.* Canberra: Australian Bureau of Statistics.

ABS. 2014c. *Forms of Employment, Australia, November 2013.* Canberra: Australian Bureau of Statistics.

ABS. 2014d. *Employee Earnings, Benefits and Trade Union Membership, Australia, August 2013.* Canberra: Australian Bureau of Statistics.

ABS. 2015. *Labour Force, Australia, January 2015.* Canberra: Australian Bureau of Statistics.

AHRC. 2014. *Supporting Working Parents: Pregnancy and Return to Work National Review – Report.* Sydney: Australian Human Rights Commission.

AICD. 2015. *Statistics.* http://www.companydirectors.com.au/Director-Resource-Centre/Governance-and-Director-Issues/Board-Diversity/Statistics.

Australian Government. 2015a. *Intergenerational Report 2015*, Canberra: Commonwealth of Australia.

Australian Government. 2015b. *Closing the Gap: Prime Minister's Report 2015.* Canberra: Commonwealth of Australia.

Baird, M., S. Baldwin, S. Wright, S. Yu, T. Fattore and A. Heron. 2011. *Profile of Women's Employment in NSW: Trends and Issues*, Sydney: NSW Department of Premier and Cabinet.

Baxter, J. 2013a. *Families Working Together: Getting the Balance Right.* Australian Family Trends Fact Sheet No. 2. Melbourne: Australian Institute of Family Studies.

Baxter, J. 2013b. *Childcare Participation and Maternal Employment Trends in Australia.* Melbourne: Australian Institute of Family Studies.

Baxter, J, and B. Hewitt. 2013. "Negotiating Domestic Labor: Women's Earnings and Housework Time in Australia." *Feminist Economics* 19 (1): 29–53.

Biddle, N. and M. Yap. 2009. *Towards a Gender-Related Index for Indigenous Australians.* Centre for Aboriginal Economic Policy Research Working Paper No. 52/2009. Canberra: Australian National University.

Brennan, J. 2013. *Joining the Dots: Program and Funding Options for Integrated Aboriginal and Torres Strait Islander Children's Services.* Sydney: Secretariat of National Aboriginal and Islander Childcare.

Campbell, I., G. Whitehouse and J. Baxter. 2009. "Casual Employment, Part-time Employment and the Resilience of the Male-breadwinner Model." In *Gender and the Contours of Precarious Employment*, edited by L.F. Vosko, M. MacDonald and I. Campbell, 60–75. London: Routledge.

CEPAR. 2014. *Aged Care in Australia: Part II – Industry and Practice.* http://www.cepar.edu.au/media/127442/aged_care_in_australia_-_part_i_-_web_version_fin.pdf.

Charlesworth, S. and F. Macdonald. 2014. "Australia's Gender Pay Equity Legislation: How New, How Different, What Prospects?" *Cambridge Journal of Economics*, doi: 10.1093/cje/beu044.

Constable, J. 2009. *Engaging Aboriginal Australians in the Private Sector: A Consultative Report into Aboriginal Employment Strategies and Initiatives.* Sydney: Diversity Council Australia.

Conway, H. 2014. "Time for Targets, Not Quotas." *The Australian Financial Review* 28 November. http://www.afr.com/news/policy/industrial-relations/time-for-targets-not-quotas-20121127-jii0o.

Cooper, R. 2012. "The Gender Gap in Union Leadership in Australia: A Qualitative Study." *The Journal of Industrial Relations* 54 (2): 131–146.

Cortis, N. 2000. "Gender, Pay Equity and Human Service Work: A New South Wales Case Study." *Australian Journal of Political Science* 35 (1): 49–62.

Craig, L., F. Perales, S. Vidal and J. Baxter. 2016. "Domestic Outsourcing, Housework and Subjective Time Pressure: New Insights from Longitudinal Data". *Journal of Marriage and Family* 78 (5): 1224–1236.

Doyle, L. and R. Hill. 2012. *The Best of Every Woman: An Overview of Approaches for Philanthropic Investment in Aboriginal Women and Girls.* Sydney: AMP Foundation.

EOWA. 2002a. *Australian Census of Women Board Directors.* Sydney: EOWA.

EOWA. 2002b. *Australian Census of Women Executive Managers.* Sydney: EOWA.

French, E., and G. Strachan. 2009. "Evaluating Equal Employment Opportunity and its Impact on the Increased Participation of Men and Women in the Transport Industry." *Transportation Research Part A: Policy and Practice* 43 (1): 78–89.

Gaze, B. 2010. "The Sex Discrimination Act at 25: Reflections on the Past, Present and Future." In *Sex Discrimination in Uncertain Times,* edited by M. Thornton. Canberra: ANU E Press, 107–125.

Gray, M., Hunter, B., and Lohoar, S. 2012. *Increasing Indigenous Employment Rates.* Canberra: Australian Institute of Family Studies.

Howe, J. 2014. "Does Australia Need an Expert Commission to Assist with Managing its Labour Migration Program?" *Australian Journal of Labour Law* 27 (3): 233–257.

HREOC. 2007. *It's About Time: Women, Men, Work and Family.* Sydney: Human Rights and Equal Opportunities Commission.

Hudson, P. 2002. "Howard May Extend Family Tax Breaks." *The Age* 19 July. http://www.theage.com.au/articles/2002/07/18/1026898888567.html.

International Labour Office (ILO). 2013. *ILOSTAT Database, Annual Indicators.* https://www.ilo.org/ilostat.

KPMG. 2014. *ASX Corporate Governments Council Principles and Recommendations on Diversity: Analysis of Disclosures for Financial Years Ended between 31 December 2012 and 30 December 2013.* Sydney: KPMG.

Martin, B., M. Yerkes, B. Hewitt, M. Baird, A. Jones, E. Rose, J. Rose, K. Davis, L. Coles, A. Heron and N. Xiang. 2013. *Paid Parental Leave Phase 2 Report, Department of Families, Housing, Community Services and Indigenous Affairs*. Canberra: Australian Government.

Meagher, G. 2014. "Persistent Inequalities: The Distribution of Money, Time and Care." In *Challenging the Orthodoxy: Reflections on Frank Stilwell's Contribution to Political Economy*. edited by S.K. Schroeder and L. Chester, 79–100. New York: Springer.

Meagher, G. and Cortis, N. 2010. *The Social and Community Services Sector in NSW: Structure, Workforce and Pay Equity Issues.* Paper prepared for the Women's Equity Bureau of the NSW Department of Industrial Relations.

Meagher, G. and S. Goodwin. 2015. "Introduction: Capturing Marketisation in Australian Social Policy." in *Markets, Rights and Power in Australian Social Policy,* edited by G. Meagher and S. Goodwin, 1–27. Sydney: Sydney University Press.

Meagher, G., M. Szebehely and J. Mears. 2016. "How Institutions Matter for Job Characteristics, Quality and Experiences: A Comparison of Home Care Work for Older People in Australia and Sweden." *Work, Employment & Society* 0950017015625601. Published online 29 Feb 2016.

OECD. 2015. "Real Minimum Wages in 2013 Constant Prices at 2013 USD Purchasing Power Parities." *OECD.StatExtract* (database). DOI: http://stats.oecd.org/Index.aspx?DataSetCode=RMW.

PC. 2011. *Caring for Older Australians*, Report No. 53. Canberra: Productivity Commission.

PC. 2014. *Childcare and Early Childhood Learning*, Report No. 73. Canberra: Productivity Commission.

Pocock, B. 2005. "Work/care Regimes: Institutions, Culture and Behaviour and the Australian Case." *Gender, Work & Organization* 12 (1): 32–49.

Razavi, S. 2007. *The Political and Social Economy of Care in a Development Context.* Geneva: UNRISD.

Smith, B. and M. Hayes. 2015. "Using Data to Drive Gender Equality in Employment: More Power to the People?" *Australian Journal of Labour Law* 28 (3): 191–213.

Van Egmond, M., J. Baxter, S. Buchler and M. Western. 2010. "A Stalled Revolution? Gender Role Attitudes in Australia, 1986–2005." *Journal of Population Research* 27 (3): 147–168.

WGEA. 2013a. *Gender Strategy Toolkit.* https://www.wgea.gov.au/sites/default/files/Gender_Strategy_Toolkit.pdf.

WGEA. 2013b. *Engaging Men in Flexible Working: A Perspective Paper.* Sydney: Workplace Gender Equality Agency.

WGEA. 2015. *Gender Pay Gap Statistics.* https://www.wgea.gov.au/sites/default/files/Gender_Pay_Gap_Factsheet.pdf.

White. N. 2007. *Indigenous Women's Career Development: Voices that Challenge Cup Educational Leadership.* Ballarat: Australian Catholic University.

Workplace Express. 2015. *ACTU Seeking Increased Rights for Returning Workers*, 16 February. https://www.workplaceexpress.com.au/nl06_news_selected.php?act=2&stream=1&selkey=53105&hlc=2&hlw=ACTU++2015&s_keyword=ACTU++2015&s_searchfrom_date=631112400&s_searchto_date=1463630934&s_pagesize=20&s_word_match=2&s_articles=1.

World Bank. 2015. *Health Nutrition and Population Statistics: Population Estimates and Projections.* http://databank.worldbank.org/Data/Views/VariableSelection/SelectVariables.aspx?source=Health%20Nutrition%20and%20Population%20Statistics:%20Population%20estimates%20and%20projections.

Wright, S. and J. Buchanan. 2013. *Award Reliance.* Research Report 6/2013. Canberra: Fair Work Commission.

12 New Zealand

Caring for women or women caring?

Katherine Ravenswood and Belinda Smith

New Zealand is a developed country that in many ways has followed a trajectory on work and care not unusual for western nations; the single-breadwinner couple family is being replaced with a dual earner model, while a significant percentage of children are living in single-parent families; the use of paid childcare is increasing; and eldercare is a significant issue. Recent policy interventions around care have focused on paid parental leave and flexible work arrangements, family tax credits, cash payments for sole parents, and substantial subsidies that have increased the availability and affordability of early childhood education and care services. However, the policy framework is extremely complex, reflecting multiple, sometimes conflicting goals. Indeed, it could be argued that gender equality has not been a primary goal, and that the gender-neutral language of policy obscures the gender implications of care–work related policy (Masselot 2011).

New Zealand has a reputation for a number of 'firsts' in relation to gender and diversity (Ryan, Ravenswood and Pringle 2014), most notably the enfranchisement of women in 1893. However, its reputation for social progressiveness has masked a lack of progress for women in work (Ryan, Ravenswood and Pringle 2014). There has been slow progress towards paid parental leave (Ravenswood and Kennedy 2012) and a persistent – although internationally low – gender pay gap of approximately 11.8 per cent (Ministry for Women 2016). Over time, social goals such as women's right to work have competed with the prevailing economic concerns of government, and also continuing conservative views of women's primary role as carers (Ravenswood and Kennedy 2012). A key negative aspect of the complexity is the high transaction costs on individual women and families of multiple policy interventions, administered by different government departments and involving public and private care arrangements (Kesting and Fargher 2008).

As Razavi (2007) points out, the relative values and treatment of work and care are often hard to determine, and shift over time. In New Zealand in the 2000s, the approach to the work/care nexus was a mix of emphasis on women's entry into paid work for economic necessity and an investment approach towards early childhood education. During this period of skills and labour shortages, many new policy initiatives focused on maximising women's participation in paid work, including paid parental leave and family tax credits. Paid parental leave was said to provide time for care of babies, for mothers to recuperate, and to help families in exciting but difficult periods. Early childhood education was strongly supported from a social investment perspective, based on ideals of increasing human capital and life-long learning (Razavi 2007). Changes to employment regulation and welfare state provision for sole parents since 2008 (and a change in government) have focused on active participation in the workforce as a primary goal, and a more individual and privatised approach to care work in general. This is in part due to a decrease in women's labour participation rates during the Global Financial Crisis (2008–11), when the New Zealand economy slowed and unemployment rates rose. Eldercare, meanwhile, has been relatively neglected; publicly funded care is far from universal, is means tested, and is targeted at those most in need.

The work/care regime in context

New Zealand was colonised by Europeans in the late eighteenth and early nineteenth centuries. Its welfare system reflects institutional and cultural traits inherited from Great Britain, but with a growing sense of Māori and Pacific identity. These traits are evident in the existence of government-funded benefits and financial assistance, targeted primarily to low-income groups (Esping-Andersen 1990a, 1990b). Since colonisation, it has been assumed that couple families would consist of a breadwinner, usually the man, and a stay-at-home mother performing the household work, including childcare. The labour force participation rates for women and particularly mothers of young children were traditionally low. Some modest 'family benefits' were provided to families to offset the cost of children, but it was generally accepted that children were a private responsibility to be funded by the male breadwinner through his labour market participation. Policy frameworks around work and care adversely impact on Māori (indigenous) and Pacific people, in part because these populations are more highly concentrated in precarious and low-paid work, and also because a greater proportion of these populations receive social benefits (Reilly 2013). Women in these populations also shoulder a higher level of unpaid care work than women of other ethnicities.

Although the population is ageing, with some predictions of labour shortages in the future (Bascand 2012), this is counteracted to some extent by a fertility rate of 1.9 (Statistics NZ 2014b) and high levels of immigration, as one out of every four people in New Zealand is foreign born (Figure 12.1). Despite high ethnic diversity and immigration, the largest self-identified ethnic group in New Zealand are Europeans, who comprise 74 per cent of the population. Close to 15 per cent identify as Māori, 7.5 per cent as Pacific Peoples and 11.8 per cent as being of Asian background (Statistics NZ 2014b, 2015a). Population projections indicate that the Māori, Pacific and Asian populations will grow faster than the European population and therefore increase their proportion of the general population over the next few decades (Statistics NZ 2015c). Since 2006, the Asian ethnic group has shown the most growth (Chen 2015).

Family structure in New Zealand also changed over the latter part of the twentieth century. In 1991, 48 per cent of families – defined as two or more

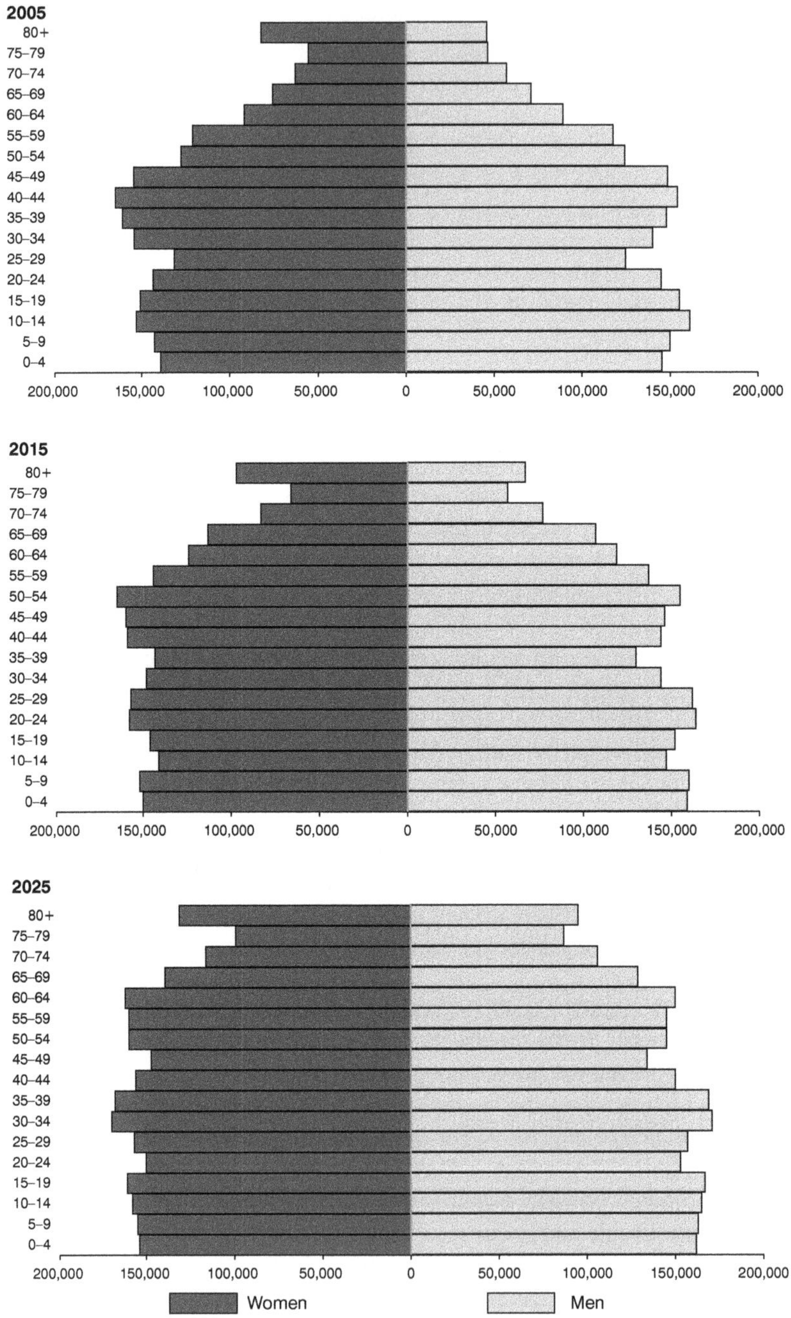

Figure 12.1 Population 2005, 2015, and 2025

Source: World Bank (2015).

people living in the same house, comprising a couple with or without children, or a parent with children – were couples with children. In 2013, the proportion of families that were couples with children was down to 41.3 per cent, with the second most common family type being couples without children (40.9 per cent). The proportion of one-parent families with children continues to increase, but most children are in 'couple with children' families (Statistics NZ 2014a). The number of extended families has increased by 54.9 per cent since 2001, from 64,929 to 100,605. More than half of these extended families included three or more generations (Statistics NZ 2014a).

Employment of women

Although women who do not have children participate in full-time work at almost the same rate as men, women in general have significantly lower rates of labour force participation. There are also strongly gendered patterns in parental and employment status, with men far more likely to work full time than women, regardless of whether they are in a couple or are single parents. However, women's labour participation rate has risen steadily from 39 per cent in 1972 to 62.9 per cent in 2014 (see Table 12.1). From 1994 to 2014, the participation rate for women aged 25–49 with no dependent children increased by 1.9 per cent to 87.3 per cent; for partnered mothers the rate increased by 7.8 per cent to 73 per cent, and for sole mothers by 23.0 per cent to 69.4 per cent (Flynn and Harris 2015). It is important to note here that women comprise the majority of single parents, at 84.2 per cent (Centre for Social Research and Evaluation 2010).

In relation to employment type, women and men follow similar trends, although men are more likely to be employers than women (see Table 12.2). This may be due to men still being predominant in executive positions in New Zealand and on Boards of Directors, leading to more opportunities to own and start businesses.

Women are most likely to be employed in professional and clerical categories (86.86 per cent), and outweigh the proportion of men in those categories (54.85 per cent) (see Table 12.3).

In terms of sectoral distribution, men work primarily in wholesale and retail trade, manufacturing and construction, while women are primarily employed in wholesale and retail trade, human health and social work activities and education

Table 12.1 Labour force participation rates, 2014

	Labour force participation rate (%)	*Employment rate (%)*	*Unemployment rate (%)*	*Part-time (of total employed %)*	*Full-time (of total employed %)*
Male	74.1	69.9	5.6	11.75	88.25
Female	62.9	58.6	6.9	34.47	65.53
Total	68.4	64.1	6.2	22.39	77.61

Source: Statistics NZ (2014c).

Table 12.2 Employment status by sex, 2013

Status in employment	*Male (%)*	*Female (%)*
Employees	81.43	88.45
Employers	6.03	2.99
Own-account workers	11.56	7.00
Members of producers' cooperatives	0.00	0.00
Contributing family workers	0.85	1.45
Workers not classifiable by status	0.14	0.00
Total	100.00	100.00

Source: ILO (2013).

Table 12.3 Working population by occupational category and sex, 2008

Occupation	*Male (%)*	*Female (%)*
Managers, professionals, and technicians	39.88	46.38
Clerical, service and sales workers	14.97	40.48
Skilled agricultural and trades workers	25.52	5.23
Plant and machine operators, and assemblers	12.81	2.79
Elementary occupations	6.36	4.71
Armed forces	0.47	0.41
Total	100.00	100.00

Source: ILO (2013).

(ILO 2013). These gendered occupational patterns are carried through to women's representation in leadership and governance: in New Zealand's top 100 listed companies, only 14.75 per cent of directors were women (Human Rights Commission 2012). In addition, women are 'still less than 30% of judges, less than 25% of senior academic staff, and less than 20% of top legal partnerships' (Human Rights Commission 2012, 4). It is also significant that the total number of people employed in the occupational group 'community and personal service' increased by 9.3 per cent from 2006 to 2013. The biggest increases were in the sub-groups of 'carers and aides', including childcarers (8.9 per cent increase) and 'health and welfare support workers', which increased by 28.1 per cent (Statistics NZ 2015b).

Women are taking a greater role in paid care work, but they also continue to dominate in the provision of unpaid care. In the 2013 New Zealand Census of Populations and Dwellings, several questions asked for information on unpaid caring activities.

As clearly indicated in Table 12.4, women in general shoulder the burden of unpaid care. Mothers' time spent caring for children exceeds fathers' time in every category; sole fathers spend three hours less than sole mothers and partnered

Table 12.4 Percentage of people undertaking unpaid care activities by age, sex, and ethnicity, 2013

Age	Sex	Ethnicity			
		European	Māori	Pacific Peoples	Asian
15–24	Male	21.0	32.5	32.1	12.4
	Female	35.1	51.3	47.5	18.5
25–34	Male	42.5	53.6	49.8	26.4
	Female	60.2	74.9	64.7	40.2
35–44	Male	64.8	60.8	52.8	49.1
	Female	77.3	76.0	62.7	59.2
45–54	Male	46.5	47.2	41.6	34.7
	Female	56.7	61.9	51.8	39.2
55–64	Male	28.4	33.7	34.8	23.4
	Female	45.6	50.1	47.6	31.8
65–74	Male	23.9	24.9	30.2	27.5
	Female	36.4	33.9	40.1	32.0
75 +	Male	14.2	15.2	20.1	18.1
	Female	13.8	17.3	19.5	17.1

Source: Statistics NZ (2013c).

fathers spend 59 per cent of the time spent by partnered mothers, although the gaps between partners is less on weekends and in families where parents have the same employment status (Statistics NZ 2013a).

Unsurprisingly, it is women in the main childbearing years (25 to 44 years of age) who are most likely to undertake unpaid care work. Māori and Pacific Peoples have significantly more unpaid care responsibilities than other ethnic groups, and Māori women generally have more unpaid care responsibilities than other ethnic groups across the age range of 25 to 54 years. The implicit converse of this is that it is far more likely that people of European and Asian ethnicities will use market-provided care.

Childcare

In relation to childcare specifically, the twin drivers of social investment in children are quality early childhood education and care and increasing the workforce participation rates of women, particularly mothers.[1] New Zealand has a relatively long history of promoting early childhood education, with kindergarten associations established in the late nineteenth century and play centres in the 1940s. During the latter half of the twentieth century, the women's movement brought renewed attention to women's right to work, and to choose their occupations. This consequently focused attention on the need for parental leave and the provision of early childhood education. However, the move to provide paid parental leave was stalled repeatedly because businesses did not support it, governments did not consider it financially viable, and many people considered that women's role was primarily to care for their children rather than be in paid work (Ravenswood and Kennedy 2012).

Investment in education and incentives for women to enter the paid workforce drove policy changes and action by the state in the 2000s that led to the introduction of paid parental leave and increased funding for early childhood education. The government does not provide early childhood education services directly, but it does provide some funding. Services are provided on a for-profit basis by private corporations or not-for-profit by community organisations (Kesting and Fargher 2008), including kindergartens and Kohanga Reo (centres that offer Māori language and culture immersion). There has been an increase in the uptake of these market-based forms of formal care, particularly by families of European ethnicity and those with higher parental incomes. However, children in formal care are not necessarily in care for many hours per week. The median number of hours of formal care is 18; 29 per cent of children in care attend for 10 hours or less, 37 per cent attend for 10–20 hours and only 33 per cent for more than 20 hours (Statistics NZ 2012).

The cost of formal early childhood education services is borne in part by families, but substantial government expenditure has supported the development of more, accessible and high quality services. Subsidies are paid directly to the licensed early childhood education service providers (Kesting and Fargher 2008). One of the most significant initiatives in funding and encouraging the use of early childhood education services in New Zealand was the introduction in 2007 of 20 hours per week of free early childhood education services for all 3- and 4-year-old children. This applies to all children enrolled in early childhood education regardless of parental income or work status. By tying the funding to licensing requirements, the scheme is designed to support quality in care and education with an emphasis on qualified early childhood education teachers. For children younger than three, and for extra hours, an additional means-tested childcare subsidy is also available for parents. These subsidies contribute significantly to minimising the cost of formal care for families, sometimes covering 100 per cent of the cost depending on enrolment hours (Statistics NZ 2010).

Family tax credits and paid parental leave provisions, meanwhile, focus on supporting parents who are in paid work. A parental leave payment was introduced in 2002, more than 20 years after the introduction of unpaid maternity leave, when New Zealand was beginning to experience skills and labour shortages.[2] Prior to this time, governments continually rejected the notion of paid parental leave, citing 'affordability' as an issue (Ravenswood and Kennedy 2012). Eligibility is tied to minimum work requirements, including length of service with the current employer and working on average a minimum of 10 hours per week during the service period of 26 weeks. It is also available to the self-employed. Payments do not reach the level of the nationally legislated minimum wage if averaged out over a 40-hour week (Ravenswood 2008), even though it is quite well accepted that the national minimum wage is less than what a family needs to survive reasonably (Living Wage Aotearoa 2015). The policy is based on the assumption that the mother will be the primary carer, although mothers can transfer their entitlements to their partners, as long as the partner satisfies the work and care tests. In 2015, eligible parents were entitled to 52 weeks unpaid parental leave between them, minus any paid leave taken. The paid parental leave entitlement is 16 weeks, which increased to 18 weeks in 2016.

Paid parental leave was supplemented in the 2000s by a combination of initiatives called Working for Families, which encompassed tax credits, childcare subsidies and accommodation assistance. Primarily aimed at families working at least 20 hours per week, the benefits are income tested in relation to the number of children and are designed to support parents wanting to stay in work. In combination, the tax credits operate to redistribute income to poorer and middle-income families with children by using income thresholds, abatement rates and entitlements per child. They represent a move away from government support only for the poor in receipt of government pensions and benefits – a long-standing feature of the New Zealand welfare state – to the working poor and middle-income earners, reflecting the focus of the National Party-led government on individual responsibility for care, and also on paid work. Sole parents who are not in work may also be entitled to the sole parent pension. This has recently been changed, and is now subject to work requirements according to the child's age, with the pension being reduced if the recipient does not meet the work requirements, for example, attending a job interview.

Attempts to extend paid parental leave entitlements have, however, been less successful. In 2013, the conservative government in power since 2008 announced it would veto a Bill to introduce 26 weeks of paid parental leave, on the basis of the cost involved. This was despite its having majority support in the parliament. The government had already promised an extension of the current scheme from 14 to 16 weeks in 2015 and to 18 weeks in 2016, and legislated for this. The veto of a further extension reflects a preoccupation within government with the privatisation of care – individuals, not the state, are responsible for themselves and their family. Business was also unsupportive of the change, with a major business peak organisation warning that increased paid parental leave would cause discrimination against women in hiring, and would also create difficulties for businesses by forcing them to find temporary cover for employees on paid parental leave (Fuatai 2012). And although trade unions have played a role in pushing for changes that improve all parents' capacity to manage work and care, it has been shown that generally they are more active in this area in female-dominated industries and female-dominated unions (Gregory and Milner 2009; Ravenswood and Markey 2011; Rigby and O'Brien-Smith 2010). Some collective agreements allow for greater parental leave (and pay) provision than is provided by legislation, but these agreements only covered approximately 6.5 per cent of employees in 2014. They are found predominantly in the public sector, and in particular education, which is traditionally more female-dominated than other industries (Blumenfeld, Ryall and Kiely 2014).

Eldercare

New Zealand's ageing population is driving policy concern for a projected increase in the future demand for aged care (Badkar, Callister and Didham 2009; Grant Thornton 2010). At the same time, however, there is also concern about labour shortages in general and in aged care in particular. Currently, paid care for the elderly is largely funded by the state, although the government does not have a direct role in eldercare. This service is delegated from the central government to local health administrative areas, which then contract out the service provision to private providers that are a mix of profit-based (some internationally-owned) and not-for-profit organisations (Kaine and Ravenswood 2014; Ravenswood and Kaine 2015).

There are three broad categories of paid aged care: community/home care; residential (including hospital, but not critical care); and supported living retirement villages. Good data on who is providing unpaid care for elderly family members in the home is unavailable, but it can be assumed that the majority of unpaid carers are female. There is also insufficient knowledge about who is undertaking informal eldercare and on what basis, for example, providing full-time care or helping out an elderly relative with housework. What is clear is that the paid workforce in both markets and not-for-profit organisations is overwhelmingly female, at approximately 92 per cent. Overseas-born caregivers still make up the minority of the labour force, but their number increased from 20 per cent of the workforce in 1991 to 31 per cent in 2014. Paid residential aged care workers are also an ageing workforce, with the majority aged 45 years or older (Callister, Didham and Badkar 2014). A number of women working in community aged care in particular choose this work because it allows them the flexibility to combine paid work with care for their own family members (Ravenswood, Douglas and Teo 2015).

In terms of policy support for family carers, there is potential for partial leave from employment in the form of a temporary reduction in working hours. Leave of this type may be requested under the right to flexible work arrangements legislated in the Employment Relations Act 2000, and which since 2014 has been available to anyone, regardless of caring responsibilities. Under this provision, a person in paid work may request a variation in their hours (or place, or times) in order to undertake care work. However, some argue that a reduction in paid work hours, with a consequential reduction in pay, equates to a care penalty; in other words carers are penalised financially for carrying out care work (Barron and West 2013). New Zealand also has a universal pension for those aged 65 and above, with some residency and citizenship requirements, which is not income- or asset-tested. The pension is based on living circumstances such as shared accommodation and marital or partner status (including civil union, de-facto and same-sex relationships). An individual may choose to have the payments incorporate their partner (even if the partner is not eligible for a pension), a provision which could be used to enable people to care for ill or disabled partners. However, neither of these policy interventions provides guaranteed or widespread financial support, either through subsidies or allowances for those providing unpaid care in the family home.

In residential aged care, approximately one-third of providers are not-for-profit. This proportion has decreased over time as national chains have bought out smaller, not-for-profit providers (Kaine and Ravenswood 2014). There has been a shift in care provision such that there is now a greater range of retirement villages, with some marketed on the basis of luxury/niche eldercare, which provide – and charge for – services that are over and above that subsidised by the government. Formal eldercare (in residential care or home support) is subsidised by the state and is asset-tested. However, the model of payment is based on the individual paying for their care, rather than supporting those who care for them. Generally, the subsidy, which provides a standard level of care, covers the full cost of care for those within the asset/income assessment. Those in receipt of the pension receive only a small personal allowance, with the bulk of their pension payments going directly to the aged care provider. Community/home care has largely been provided by not-for-profit organisations, but there is also some evidence of a trend for some larger providers, some of them international, to gain a greater market share.

The marketisation of aged care has led to some debate over quality of care, the working conditions of paid carers (Ravenswood and Kaine 2015) and how much profit private providers make. There is also debate about the level of government funding for community/healthcare and questions about whether not-for-profit organisations are subsidising the cost of care not adequately supported through state funding. Debate also surrounds the work conditions and low wages of paid carers in aged care. The providers who are widely known to make reasonable profits are the larger providers such as Ryman Healthcare Limited (Gibson 2014), and especially those that also run supported living villages. The rhetoric from these providers is that their supported apartment living in effect subsidises residential aged care, which is inadequately funded by the government. However, it could be argued that the paid carers are themselves subsidising the cost of aged care through the 'care penalty' of low wages and work conditions (Kaine and Ravenswood 2014; Ravenswood and Kaine 2015), as even those working for profit-based providers receive wages not much above the minimum wage (Kaine and Ravenswood 2014). In community care, meanwhile, workers are often not paid for travel time between clients and usually use their own private cars for work. These conditions have seen successful legal action taken under the Equal Pay Act 1972, arguing gender discrimination in pay (*Terranova Homes & Care Ltd v Service and Food Workers Union Nga Ringa Tota Inc* [2014]) and the legal obligation for workers to be paid for their travel time. Furthermore, workers' remuneration often does not accurately reflect their qualifications or skills and experience, something also perceived by the workers themselves (Ravenswood, Douglas and Teo 2015).

Politics and challenges

New Zealand's policy and support for the work/care nexus reflects changing ideologies over several decades. A strong tradition of supporting education and human capital investment has influenced the support for, and development of, early childhood education. However, this approach has not been carried through to paid parental leave which, it could be argued, was born largely out of the economic necessity to get more women into the workforce during periods of labour and skills shortages (Ravenswood 2008; Ravenswood and Kennedy 2012). The ageing population and the work/care nexus have been largely overlooked. However, one common feature of the policy interventions in both childcare and eldercare is the central, persistent idea that responsibility for both childcare and eldercare lies primarily with the individual or family. Furthermore, there are underlying assumptions that mothers will be the primary carers.

Overall, this shows no shift from traditional views of care being a domestic, women's (and unpaid) domain (Palmer and Eveline 2012; Folbre and Nelson 2000). The major shift, therefore, is not in how care work is perceived or valued (as illustrated in poor conditions for aged care workers), but in the move towards encouraging the use of formal care in market providers (and not-for-profit organisations) in order to facilitate participation in paid work. The picture is not all grim, with a series of developments from 1980 through to the 2000s showing the state's support for individuals seeking to make use of formal care. This support has taken the form of childcare subsidies and measures designed to allow paid and unpaid leave from the workforce for childcare. Indeed, the introduction of paid parental leave and early childhood education subsidies in the 2000s indicates some, perhaps reluctant, willingness on the part of government to envision more state responsibility for care.

The increasing marketisation and individualisation of care has nevertheless created a tension for women. Limited support for childcare, and in particular for eldercare – which has not benefited from the investment approach taken towards childcare in the mid-2000s – may restrict women's opportunities to be in paid work. This is evidenced in significantly lower labour participation rates for women with young children compared with women without children and men. Women may be penalised through choosing part-time work and therefore reducing their income in order to be able to provide care. These patterns may also have contributed to the lack of progress women have made over the last several decades in entering senior management, professions and governance roles in New Zealand (Human Rights Commission 2012).

As the population ages, and women's life expectancy increases, these same tensions may result in less than optimal care options for older women whose own families may have trouble balancing work and eldercare. There is a huge gap in knowledge and provision of eldercare by families. The current focus on individual, not state, responsibility for care work will not ease that strain, and a lack of interest in eldercare in general is a stumbling block to improvements in the work/care regime. A recent report from the Equal Employment Opportunities Trust identified the ageing workforce as one of the top three most pressing diversity issues. Despite this, less than 40 per cent of the Trust's member organisations taking part in the survey had any policy relating to age (McLeod, Bentley and Pio 2014).

Care work, even in the market, remains grossly undervalued, and unpaid care in the home is perceived as less important than paid work. Consequently, the work/care regime is still a major issue for working families with children and/or eldercare responsibilities. Policy needs to start by addressing the inherent gender norms that devalue care work. The provision of care – for children, the elderly and others – needs to be valued both in the market and in the home, through better work conditions for those carrying out paid care work and state support for those providing unpaid care. The importance of caring for people in the community, and the difficulty in balancing this with paid work, could be recognised through much higher paid parental leave entitlements and other forms of income support for those who have reduced their paid work hours in order to care for others. Entitlements to flexible work arrangements need to be strengthened in association with this income support, thus better enabling people in work to fulfil their care responsibilities. This is crucial in the context of an ageing population, which will see more people in paid work attempting to provide unpaid care for their older relatives. Finally, policies need to be sufficiently nuanced to be able to recognise and accommodate the different family roles of Māori and Pacific women, so as to address rather than reinforce systemic disadvantage.

Notes

1 The focus here is on the care of young, pre-school children, although it is important to note also that the system of free public schools for children aged 5–16 years in New Zealand is a significant part of the nation's childhood education and care regime.

2 A precursor to paid parental leave was the parental tax credit, introduced in 1999. An earlier benefit, introduced in 1974, provided cash payments to single mothers (and later fathers) as a substitute for the missing (male) breadwinner and in recognition that mothers were not expected to undertake paid work.

References

Badkar, J., P. Callister, and R. Didham. 2009. *Ageing New Zealand: The Growing Reliance on Migrant Caregivers.* IPS Working Paper 09/08. Wellington: Institute of Policy Studies.

Barron, D., and E. West. 2013. "The Financial Costs of Caring in the British Labour Market: Is There a Wage Penalty for Workers in Caring Occupations?' *British Journal of Industrial Relations* 51 (1): 104–123.

Bascand, G. 2012. *Planning for the Future: Structural Change in New Zealand's Population, Labour Force, and Productivity.* Paper presented at the Affording our Future Conference, Wellington, 10–11 December. http://www. statistics.govt.nz.

Blumenfeld, S., S. Ryall, and P. Kiely. 2014. *Employment Agreements: Bargaining Trends and Employment Law Update 2012/2013.* Wellington: Industrial Relations Centre, Victoria University of Wellington.

Callister, P., R. Didham, and J. Badkar. 2014. *Aging New Zealand: The Growing Reliance on Migrant Caregivers, a 2104 Update.* Wellington: Callister & Associates.

Centre for Social Research and Evaluation. 2010. *Sole Parenting in New Zealand: An Update on Key Trends and What Helps Reduce Disadvantage.* Wellington: Ministry of Social Development.

Chen, M. 2015. *Superdiversity Stocktake: Implications for Business, Government & New Zealand.* Auckland: Superdiversity Centre for Law, Policy and Business.

Esping-Andersen, G. 1990a. *Three Worlds of Welfare Capitalism*. Cambridge: Polity Press.

Esping-Andersen, G. 1990b. "The Three Political Economies of the Welfare State." *International Journal of Sociology* 20 (3): 92–112.

Flynn, S., and M. Harris. 2015. *Mothers in the New Zealand Workforce.* Wellington: Statistics New Zealand.

Folbre, N. and J. Nelson. 2000. "For Love or Money – or Both?" *Journal of Economic Perspectives* 14 (4): 123–140.

Fuatai, T. 2012. "Parental Leave Issue Debated." *Rotorua Daily Post*, 6 October. http://www.nzherald.co.nz/rotorua-daily-post/news/article.cfm?c_id=1503438&objectid=11079576.

Gibson, A. 2014. "Ryman Posts Record Half-year Result." *The New Zealand Herald*, 21 November. http://www. nzherald.co.nz/ryman-healthcare-ltd/news/article. cfm?o_id=182&objectid=11362216.

Grant Thornton. 2010. *Aged Residential Care Service Review*. Wellington: Grant Thornton.

Gregory, A., and S. Milner. 2009. "Trade Unions and Work–life Balance: Changing Times in France and the UK?" *British Journal of Industrial Relations* 47 (1): 122–146.

Human Rights Commission. 2012. *New Zealand Census of Women 2012.* Wellington: Human Rights Commission.

ILO. 2013. *Employment by Sex and Status in Employment (Thousands) – New Zealand.* ILOSTAT Database, Annual Indicators. https://www.ilo.org/ilostat.

Kaine, S., and K. Ravenswood. 2014. "Working in Residential Aged Care: A Trans-Tasman Comparison." *New Zealand Journal of Employment Relations* 38 (2): 33–46.

Kesting, S., and S. Fargher. 2008. "The Effect of Early Childhood Education and Care (ECE) Costs on the Labour Force Participation of Parents in New Zealand." *New Zealand Journal of Employment Relations* 33 (3): 16–33.

Living Wage Aotearoa. 2015. *Living Wage Movement Aotearoa NZ 2015 Update.* http://www.livingwage.org.nz/.

Masselot, A. 2011. "The Rights and Realities of Balancing Work and Family Life in New Zealand". In *Families, Care-giving and Paid Work: Challenging Labour Law in the 21st Century*, edited by N. Busby and G. James, 69–85. Cheltenham: Edward Elgar.

McLeod, L., T. Bentley, and E. Pio. 2014. *The New Zealand Diversity Survey: Findings from the First Four Quarters*. Auckland: New Zealand Work Research Institute.

Ministry for Women. 2016. *Gender Pay Gap.* http://women.govt.nz/our-work/utilising-womens-skills/income/gender-pay-gap.

Palmer, E., and J. Eveline. 2012. "Sustaining Low Pay in Aged Care Work." *Gender, Work and Organization* 19 (3): 254–275.

Ravenswood, K. 2008. "The Role of the State in Family-Friendly Policy: An Analysis of Labour-led Government Policy." *New Zealand Journal of Employment Relations* 33 (3): 34–44.

Ravenswood, K., and S. Kaine, 2015. "The Role of Government in Influencing Labour Conditions through the Procurement of Services: Some Political Challenges." *Journal of Industrial Relations* 57 (4): 544–562.

Ravenswood, K., and A. Kennedy. 2012. "From Unpaid Maternity Leave to Paid Parental Leave in New Zealand: Changing Approaches in Legislation." *Labour History* 102: 197–213.

Ravenswood, K., and R. Markey. 2011. "The Role of Unions in Achieving a Family-Friendly Workplace." *Journal of Industrial Relations* 53 (4): 486–503.

Ravenswood, K., J. Douglas, and S. Teo. 2015. *The New Zealand Aged Care Workforce Survey 2014* Auckland: New Zealand Work Research Institute.

Razavi, S. 2007. *The Political and Social Economy of Care in a Development Context.* Geneva: UNRISD.

Reilly, A. 2013. "Intersections and Equality at the Work Family Nexus: How Law Fails Some Mothers More Than Others." Paper presented at the Inaugural Labour Law Research Network Conference. Barcelona, Spain, 13–15 June.

Rigby, M., and F. O'Brien-Smith. 2010. "Trade Union Interventions in Work–Life Balance." *Work Employment and Society* 24 (2): 203–222.

Ryan, I., K. Ravenswood, and J.K. Pringle. 2014. "Equality and Diversity in Aotearoa (New Zealand)." In *International Handbook on Equality and Diversity Management at Work: Country Perspectives on Diversity and Equal Treatment* edited by A. Klarsfeld, L.A. Booysen, E. Ng, I. Roper, and A. Tatli, 175–194. 2nd edn. London: Edward Elgar.

Statistics NZ. 2010. *New Zealand Childcare Survey 2009.* Wellington: Statistics New Zealand.

Statistics NZ. 2012. *Childcare Use and Work Arrangements in 1998 and 2009.* Wellington: Statistics New Zealand.

Statistics NZ. 2013a. *Caring for Children: Findings from the 2009/10 Time Use Survey.* Wellington: Statistics New Zealand.

Statistics NZ. 2013b. *Demographic Trends: 2012.* Wellington: Statistics New Zealand.

Statistics NZ. 2013c. *New Zealand Census of Populations and Dwellings* Wellington: Statistics New Zealand.

Statistics NZ. 2014a. *Census QuickStats about Families and Households.* Wellington: Statistics New Zealand.

Statistics NZ. 2014b. *Population Indicators.* Wellington: Statistics New Zealand.

Statistics NZ. 2014c. *Earnings and Employment Survey, 2014 Q3.* Wellington: Statistics New Zealand.

Statistics NZ. 2015a. *New Zealand in Profile 2015: An Overview of New Zealand's People, Economy, and Environment.* Wellington: Statistics New Zealand.

Statistics NZ. 2015b. *Occupation of Employed People in New Zealand Treemap.* Wellington: Statistics New Zealand. http://www.stats.govt.

Statistics NZ. 2015c. *National Ethnic Population Projections: 2013 (Base) – 2038.* Wellington: Statistics New Zealand.

Terranova Homes & Care Ltd v Service and Food Workers Union Nga Ringa Tota Inc. [2014.] NZSC 196.

World Bank. 2015. *Health Nutrition and Population Statistics: Population Estimates and Projections.* http://databank.worldbank.org/Data/Views/VariableSelection/SelectVariables.aspx?source=Health%20Nutrition%20and%20Population%20Statistics:%20Population%20estimates%20and%20projections.

Part III
Familial care regimes

13 Japan

From social reproduction to gender equality

Reiko Ogawa

The work/care regime in Japan has gone through multiple transformations, the result of shaping and reshaping by structural change in the political economy and state policies affecting the gender order. Although the importance of the family for social reproduction has always been a concern of the state, the issue of women's work and care was long regarded as a trivial matter and the responsibility of individuals, not a matter requiring government policy and oversight. It was only in the 1990s, when the demographic pressures resulting from Japan's low fertility rate and ageing population became a social issue, that women's work and care entered the political agenda.

Since the 1990s and the rise of the post-industrial economy, the 'male breadwinner model' has proven inadequate, but a shift towards gender equality in both workplace and family has not yet taken place. In recent years, however, increasing demand for economic growth, coupled with the shrinking working population and the influence of the international discourse on gender equality, has profoundly challenged the existing gender order, and led to calls for a better balance in work and care for both women and men.

Contextualising work and care

When the modernisation of Japan began in the late nineteenth century, the process of creating a modern family was implemented in line with the creation of the modern nation state. The term 'good wife and wise mother' was coined and popularised through the public education system, defining women's primary role as child rearing and domestic work. Filial piety and devotion to the parents was identified with loyalty to the state and patriotism, and the family was metaphorically connected to the state apparatus through patriarchal symbolism, with the emperor at the top of the social hierarchy as 'father'. Since women were not fully entitled to citizenship – women's suffrage was not achieved until 1945 – their role was solely to reproduce the nation's citizens. The state actively constructed the link between 'womanhood' and 'nationhood', situating the central role of women as carer for the family and for the nation.

After the end of the Second World War in 1945, the Supreme Commander for the Allied Powers recognised the institutional and ideological link between the state and the family and major democratic reforms took place. While the institutional reform made the Japanese family more egalitarian by ensuring gender equality under the new constitution, the rapid economic development after the mid-1950s consolidated the idea and ideal of the 'modern family'.[1] The 'modern family', as it was conceived in Japan at this time, was a heteronormative nuclear family consisting of a male breadwinner, full-time housewife and two children living in a cosy home and enjoying an affluent urban lifestyle. This reflected the yearning towards the American lifestyle as it was repeatedly featured in popular media. Care for the family was not only a responsibility of women, it became the defining feature of women's identity.

Rapid economic development between 1955 and the mid-1970s brought a degree of affluence to Japanese families, but it also entrenched the male breadwinner employment system based on lifelong employment and seniority-based salary scales. Once the male breadwinner joined the company, job security and the family wage were guaranteed. Japanese businessmen were considered to be 'corporate warriors' embodying strong loyalty to the company and long working hours, leaving them no space to care for their families. For women, the ideal lifestyle became that of the 'housewife', strengthening the clear gendered division of labour. The women's labour force participation rate dropped from 54.5 per cent in 1960 to 45.7 per cent in 1975, and 'housewifeisation' became a way of life for women in the industrial economy (Ochiai 1994).

However, the shift towards the post-industrial economy that began in the 1990s had a significant impact on the labour market, increasing competition and flexibility and resulting in the deregulation of labour laws. The lifelong employment system quickly gave way to more precarious working conditions, making the male breadwinner model no longer viable. The downturn took its toll on working men. From the late 1990s, the suicide rate jumped to 30,000 persons per year. Of this total, 70 per cent were middle-aged men dealing with precarious employment conditions (Osawa 2002). Under the deteriorating economic and social conditions, women found that they could no longer expect to remain full-time housewives. It was necessary for them to participate in the labour market to sustain their families' livelihoods, albeit in a marginal way. As early as 1992, the number of households with a sole male breadwinner and a full-time 'housewife' was fewer than the number of double-income families.

Women's attitudes towards work and care also shifted from expectations that they would 'become a housewife' to expectations that they would 'continue to work'. In a national survey that asked single women about their ideal life courses after marriage, the option 'becoming a housewife', the most popular choice in 1987, dropped by more than 10 per cent in 1997. Over this same period, the number of women who said they expected to 'continue to work' increased by more than 10 per cent. In 2010, one-fifth of women expected to 'become a housewife' (19.7 per cent), while a further third expected 'to stop working once married, have children and return to work after the children grow up'. However, almost a third expected to 'continue to work' (30.6 per cent). A further 5 per cent expected not to marry at all, while 3 per cent expected to be in a 'double income with no children' relationship (National Institute of Population and Social Security Research 2010b).

Construction and institutionalisation of the gendered labour market

In 2014, Japan's total population was 127 million, 51 per cent of whom were women (Statistics Japan 2014). After 1945, the total fertility rate continued to drop, reaching its lowest level of 1.29 in 2003; in 2014 it increased to the current rate of 1.41. From 2008, Japan's total population started to decrease. Outside urban areas, most areas are now experiencing population decline. Japan is also an ageing society. At 86.61 years, Japanese women enjoy the world's longest life expectancy, while Japanese men rank fourth, at 80.21 years (MHLW 2013a).

While long life expectancy reflects great achievements in terms of nutrition, sanitation and medical care, when combined with a low total fertility rate and almost negligible immigration flows, it has created a huge imbalance in Japan's demographic structure. In 1950, just 5 per cent of the population was older than 65. By 2013, the population above 65 was 25.1 per cent, or one in four of the total population (Cabinet Office 2014). As the population pyramids for 2005, 2015 and 2025 show, Japan's productive population is continuing to decline and its ageing population is set to increase (Figure 13.1). It is estimated that the ageing ratio will be 33.4 per cent by 2035 and in 2060 it will reach the unprecedented level of 39.9 per cent.

The ageing of Japan's population has serious implications for the capacity of its productive workforce to sustain the nation. In 2012, the country's total workforce was just 65 million, composed of 37 million men and 27 million women (Gender Equality Bureau Cabinet Office, 2013). More women are employed in areas of the service industry such as hotels, restaurants, healthcare and social welfare, while men are concentrated in manufacturing, construction and transportation. A smaller proportion of the women who do work hold managerial or professional positions than men (Table 13.1).

In line with international norms on gender equality, measures were taken in past decades to address the gendered nature of the labour market. In 1986, in response to the United Nations Decade for Women (1975–85) and the Convention on the

Table 13.1 Working population by occupational category and sex, 2013

Occupation	*Male (%)*	*Female (%)*
Managers, professionals, and technicians	27.20	20.47
Clerical, service and sales workers	29.03	57.90
Skilled agricultural and trades workers	4.02	3.11
Plant and machine operators, and assemblers	32.02	9.96
Elementary occupations	6.48	7.15
Not elsewhere classified	1.27	1.37
Total	100.00	100.00

Source: ILO (2013).

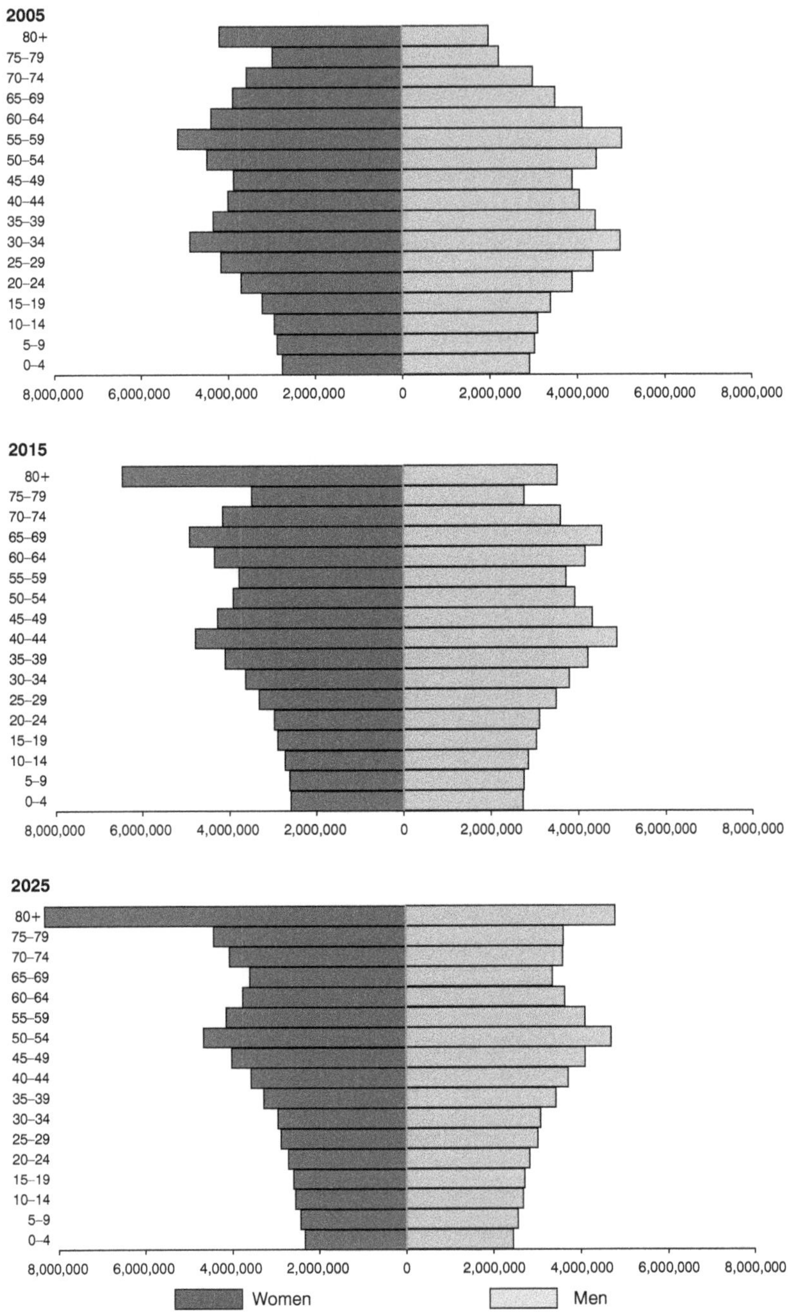

Figure 13.1 Population 2005, 2015, and 2025

Source: World Bank (2015).

Elimination of All Forms of Discrimination against Women (CEDAW), the Act for Equal Employment Opportunity of Men and Women was introduced, with the aim of eliminating gender-based discrimination in the workplace at a time when increasing numbers of women were obtaining higher education qualifications but were frustrated by the corporate sector, which openly discriminates against women.[2] This law, which was the first of its kind, states that employers have to make an effort to prevent gender-based discrimination in recruitment, placement, promotion, training, dismissal and the provision of welfare for their staff. Prior to the passing of this law, and despite some successful legal challenges to discrimination, there were virtually no legal instruments to prevent gender-based discrimination.

However, once the law was enacted, the business sector responded quickly by creating a two-tier system of recruitment based on different employment pathways. The two different employment tracks were a 'comprehensive track' (*sōgō shoku*) for workers who were considered to be future managers and who were be given more responsibilities and opportunities and transferred to other locations or divisions according to the company's needs, and a 'general track' (*ippan shoku*) for workers who were to assist the *sōgō shoku*, would not be transferred to other locations, and who would have limited responsibilities and training opportunities. Workers on the *sōgō shoku* track are expected to work long hours and be loyal and obedient towards the company in return for various benefits including higher pay and increased status. *Ippan shoku* workers, by contrast, can be easily replaced, and have few promotion opportunities. As the state continues to endorse indirect discrimination, *sōgō shoku* workers are mostly men. By contrast, more than 95 per cent of women are employed in *ippan shoku* positions.

As this discussion suggests, the 1986 law impacted on the labour market in a contradictory manner. In line with the CEDAW, it was intended to prohibit gender-based discrimination in the workplace; however, it resulted in a division between 'core' and 'marginal' workers based on gender differences, thus legitimising indirect gender-based discrimination and institutionalising it through the two-tier employment system. Strikingly, this indirect discrimination did not change radically in the 30 years that followed. In a 2011 survey of 129 companies, women held just 5.6 per cent of *sōgō shoku* positions. Among the 235 women who took up employment as *sōgō shoku* in those companies 10 years ago, 65.1 per cent had resigned, 22.1 per cent were not promoted and only 12.4 per cent were in managerial positions. This was significantly lower than the comparable figures for men. Of the 1,313 men who were employed in the same year, almost 70 per cent had achieved promotion and 39.2 per cent were in managerial positions (MHLW 2011b).

In addition, when age groups are examined more closely, Japanese women's patterns of work reflect their motherhood role. The participation of women in the workforce follows an 'M' shape, dropping when women are in their 20s and early 30s due to childcare responsibilities, before gradually increasing as they return to work in their late 30s, mostly as part-time workers. This pattern reflects the fact that more females are employed as non-regular workers compared with males and less than 50 per cent of women are employed as regular workers. Just one-third of women whose youngest child is under two years of age are in employment, while as many as 72 per cent of women with children aged nine or above are active in the labour market (National Institute of Population and Social Security Research 2010a).

This ‘M shape’ work regime is also encouraged by the state’s gender ideology, as reflected in its social policy. The Japanese system offers tax incentives to married women who undertake part-time work, thus discouraging women from choosing to fully enter the labour market. Research shows that 38.6 per cent of women restrict their working hours in order to be eligible for this tax benefit (MHLW 2001). Under this incentive, many married women make a rational choice to work part-time, which allows them to balance work and care without sacrificing their roles as mothers and wives. In this way, the state valorises the ‘model household’ of full-time husband and part-time ‘housewife’ through its social policies. For the business sector, married women are a major source of cheap labour whose part-time employment relieves business of its obligation to invest in employees’ social security; a 2001 survey found that two-thirds of part-time workers did not have social insurance (MHLW 2001).

The segregated labour market based on gender also makes it difficult for a woman to return to or be appointed to a managerial position once she exits from the labour market in order to undertake care – a fact reflected in the extremely low ratio of women in management, only 11.1 per cent (Prime Minister’s Office n.d.). Some argue that under such circumstances, the opportunity cost of having a baby is just too great for highly educated women. Calculations made in 2001 showed the losses a female junior college graduate would accrue if she started working at the age of 20, married and resigned from work to raise a child at 27, and returned to work at 33. If she were fortunate enough to be able to return to her previous position as a full-time employee, her lost income due to her six years absence, compared with those who did not take a ‘break’, would be 72,000,000 yen (USD 604,368). If she returned as a part-time worker, her losses would rise to 186,000,000 yen (USD 1,561,284) (Cabinet Office 2001). Moreover, the rigid Japanese employment system works against women who take a career break to meet the care needs of children; after an absence of between 5 and 10 years even highly educated women find it extremely difficult to return to work in the same position.

The vast majority of Japanese men and women are employees (Table 13.2). However, unequal employment conditions are reflected in a wage gap between men and women of close to 29 per cent, the second highest among OECD countries. Yamaguchi and Higuchi (2008) argue that this is due to Japan’s two-tier employment system. The fact that regular/non-regular and full-time/part-time positions are allocated primarily along gender lines rather than merit is compounded by the kinds of positions women hold and their total working years, which add to the wage gap between women and men. This occupational segregation predominantly along gender lines affects all women, but particularly those in female-headed households. In 2011, the annual income of lone mothers was 1.8 million yen, or about half of that of lone fathers and one-third of average household income (MHLW 2011a; 2013c).

Another implication of the two-tier system and the broader imbalance in the way women and men engage in paid work is the pressure that the extreme

Table 13.2 Employment status by sex, 2013

Status in employment	*Male (%)*	*Female (%)*
Employees	87.17	89.08
Employers	3.21	0.89
Own-account workers	8.28	4.26
Members of producers' cooperatives	0.00	0.00
Contributing family workers	0.89	5.26
Workers not classifiable by status	0.44	0.52
Total	100.00	100.00

Source: ILO (2013).

emphasis on the male breadwinner puts on Japanese men. Such is the pressure on Japanese men to devote themselves to work that a law was passed in 2014 to prevent *karoshi*, a term that describes sudden death as a consequence of a heart attack or stroke due to overwork and stress. In 2012, 338 *karoshi* cases were registered due to heart attack and stroke. Of these, 123 cases led to the death of the worker concerned. In addition, 475 cases of work-related mental illness were recorded, among which 93 cases resulted in suicide (MHLW 2013b). Although the gender of those involved in *karoshi* cases is not disclosed, based on the lawsuits involved, and considering that half of the claims are from those working in transportation and construction (MHLW 2013b), it is safe to conclude that more men suffer from *karoshi* than women.

The underlying problem is the long working hours. There is no legal limit on maximum working hours, which leaves workers vulnerable to excessive overtime. Although the Basic Labour Standard Law defines working hours as 8 hours per day, 40 hours per week, Article 36 allows the employer to extend the working hours if they have an agreement with the trade union. Average working hours in Japan dropped significantly from 2,126 hours per year in 1979 to 1,735 hours in 2013, less than the OECD average (OECD 2014a). However, regular workers continue to work more than 2,000 hours per year (Oishi and Shimazu 2015), with 17.6 per cent of male workers in their 30s working more than 60 hours per week (MHLW 2014a). The prevalence of long working hours for men makes it difficult for them to participate in care work. Compared with the average time that men spend on care work and domestic work in OECD countries (139 minutes per day), Japanese men spend just 62 minutes, the second least among all OECD countries (OECD, 2014b). This low level of male participation in care work and domestic work persists regardless of the employment conditions of their partners (Oishi and Moriizumi 2011).

In the face of increasing demographic pressures, it is unsustainable to force women to choose between paid work and care; it is necessary to target both women's and men's working conditions so that the work–care burden can be more equally shared. However, encouraging women to continue to work while maintaining a gender-biased social security system that penalises working women works against this outcome and does not address tensions between work and family (Cabinet Office 2001).

Demographic pressures and the crisis of care

In 1989, Japan's total fertility rate dropped to just 1.57 and the need to increase the birth rate became part of the policy agenda. In 1991, parental care leave was introduced to allow mothers and fathers to take leave for one year.[3] Of women who gave birth in 2010, 78.8 per cent had been working for at least one year before that time. Among those who were employed on a permanent basis, 93.5 per cent took parental care leave (MHLW 2012a). Strikingly, 54.1 per cent of working women resigned after giving birth. Their reasons for doing so were that they 'wanted to concentrate on childcare' (40.7 per cent), 'wanted to continue working but found it difficult to balance work and care' (35.3 per cent) and 'due to health problems related to pregnancy' (25.6 per cent). The proportion of men who took parental leave was just 2 per cent. About half of all men stated that their workplace environment was not conducive to the taking of parental leave (MHLW 2012a). This indicates that the work–care balance is extremely difficult to achieve and that the introduction of parental care leave does not in itself solve the problem.

Since 1994, the government has introduced measures to deal with the low fertility rate. These measures have focused largely on increasing the number of public and private childcare centres, expanding child benefits for parents and supporting mothers who want to return to work. However, as childcare is still considered as the responsibility of women, the total fertility rate has continued to drop. Some conservative commentators claim that the reason for the continued decline is the fact that women are working, but research suggests otherwise. Since the beginning of the twenty-first century, OECD countries with higher women's labour force participation ratios show higher fertility rates (Gender Equality Bureau Cabinet Office 2005). In other words, an effective response to low fertility rates requires government support for not only the care regime but also the work regime of women.

An even more pressing issue in the Japanese context is eldercare, given the extent and speed of population ageing. Eldercare residential facilities are always full, with long waiting lists, and home care is limited to certain services and hours. As a consequence, the primary responsibility for eldercare remains with the family, with over half of all elderly people who require care living with their spouse or children. This places a great deal of pressure on family members, both women and men. However, it is women who provide the bulk of familial aged care, with women constituting almost 70 per cent of primary carers (MHLW 2013c).

Eldercare leave was introduced as early as 1991 to allow workers to take leave for a maximum of three months at any one time to undertake caring duties. However, compared with childcare, eldercare is more unpredictable in terms of length of time and the degree of care needed. In the rigid employment system and working culture of the Japanese workplace, this makes it difficult for the family caregivers to remain in the job market. In 2006–07, 144,800 people left work due to eldercare responsibilities. More than 80 per cent of this total were women (MHLW 2012b). More than half of these women were of middle age, which also makes it extremely difficult for them to return to work of a similar level.

A scheme called Long Term Care Insurance was introduced in 2000 in response to the increasing number of aged people and the decreasing capacity of families to undertake eldercare.[4] The scheme contributes to socialising care in terms of funding and human resources, as well as helping to eliminate the stigma of being welfare-dependent and removing the psychological barriers towards institutional care. Among those households with elderly members in need of care, 78.9 per cent have used the service, mostly for day and home care (MHLW 2013c). But the high level of uptake meant that the system quickly reached its limits. The number of elderly people using the care service increased from 2.8 million in 2001 to 4.6 million in 2009. Pay-outs on insurance also skyrocketed, increasing from 3.6 trillion yen in 2000 to 8.9 trillion yen in 2012 (MHLW 2014b). The rapid increase in this form of social expenditure put pressure on the national budget and the insurance payment was cut back several times. This resulted in fewer services and accelerated labour shortages in the care sector.

It is in this context that since 2008 migrant nurses and caregivers have begun to work in Japanese hospitals and long-term care facilities.[5] This scheme was introduced not as an aspect of immigration policy or labour policy but as an 'exception' under the Economic Partnership Agreements between Japan and Southeast Asian countries (MHLW n.d.). This measure disguises the fact that there is a significant shortage in the care workforce, and was used to postpone political debate on immigration policy. Japan's population of resident foreigners is extremely low, at just 1.7 per cent of the total population, and the state is reluctant to accept migrant workers because of its concerns about protecting the domestic labour market and the imagined 'homogeneity' of the nation.

If it had been discussed in the context of immigration policy, the entry of migrant nurses and caregivers may not have taken place at all, but bilateral agreements with the Philippines, Indonesia and Vietnam opened up a small window of opportunity to accept migrant nurses and caregivers for the first time. During the negotiations, the Japan Nursing Association strongly opposed the proposal, fearing that an influx of foreign nurses would have a deleterious effect on their working conditions and jeopardise safety in medical care if the migrant nurses were not equipped with adequate medical knowledge and communication skills (JNA 2006). The Association proposed that migrant nurses be employed under the same conditions as their Japanese co-workers, that they be equipped with sufficient language proficiency to provide safe medical care, that they be required to pass the national nursing examination in Japanese, and rejected the mutual recognition of qualifications (JNA 2006). Migrant caregivers were subjected to the same conditions.

Migrant caregivers can only work in registered institutions and not in private homes, and are paid at the same level as Japanese care workers, so the migrants are well protected and have had a positive impact on hospitals and care facilities (Ogawa 2012). However, the number of migrant caregivers is fewer than 2,500 in a 1.3 million-strong care workforce, and as such it is too small to mitigate the care burden on the families or even fill the labour shortages in the sector (JICWELS 2015, MHLW 2014c). Also, the cost of training in the Japanese language to enable migrants to pass the national examination is prohibitive. To support migrant workers' study for four years – the period needed to become eligible to take the exam – it is estimated that on average it costs 2.1 million yen (Tsubota et al. 2015). This is almost equivalent to the annual salary of a Japanese part-time caregiver. In short, the admission of migrant caregivers under the Economic Partnership Agreements cannot be expected to mitigate the work–care tensions, as these agreements are first and foremost free trade agreements designed to benefit the business sector. However, if the state's attempt was to 'test the water' in anticipation of a future labour shortage in the care sector, the experiment can be said to have been successful, as the small number of care workers admitted under the Economic Partnership Agreements have been effectively integrated into the workplace and the community (Ogawa 2015).

At present, discussions on this issue are moving towards a proposal to introduce migrant caregivers under the infamous Technical Intern Training Programme, which has been widely criticised as a disguise for the import of cheap labour.[6] Also, in anticipation of the Tokyo Olympics in 2020, the government is eager to increase the acceptance of migrants under the Technical Intern Training Programme by expanding the occupational categories to construction and caregiving. In 2025, the post-war baby boomer generation will reach 75 years of age, when age-related frailty increases. There is a chronic shortage of labour in the care sector and it is likely that in contrast to the care workers who entered under the Economic Partnership Agreements – who are guaranteed their human rights, regulated under the labour law and are well integrated – this new wave of migrant caregivers will be introduced as cheap labour, thus creating a dual labour market in care work. In addition, the government is planning to pursue policies to deregulate the laws in designated 'National Strategic Special Zones' where migrant domestic workers will be introduced so that domestic/care work for double-income families can be outsourced.[7]

Gender equality and work–life balance

Since the mid-1990s, major changes have taken place in discussions on the work/care regime. In various international forums, these discussions have begun to be framed by two main discourses: gender equality and work–life balance. The 1995 Beijing Conference provided an opportunity for groups and individuals representing civil society to discuss gender issues in an international arena; at the same time, there was a growing awareness of issues related to gender equality at the grassroots level. The international environment also pressured governments to introduce gender equality policies.

In Japan, this led to the passing of the Basic Act for a Gender Equal Society in 1999. This law reiterated Japan's respect for human rights, prohibiting gender discrimination and ensuring opportunities for women and men to jointly participate as equal members of society in planning and decision-making. It also stated that social systems that impede the formation of a gender equal society should be freed from gender bias. In the preamble to the Act, the 'realisation of a gender equal society' is identified as 'the most important issue in determining the framework of 21st-century Japan'; however, many feminists have argued that the term 'gender equality' was 'lost in translation' and its use conceals the reality of discrimination against women in Japan (Ueno et al. 2001; Osawa 2000; Takemura 2003). While the English translation of the Act uses the words 'gender equal', the original Japanese translates literally as 'men and women partnership participation' (*Danjo Kyoudo Sankaku*), reflecting the government's position that gender equality had already been achieved in law, and pressures from its conservative faction, which argued that it is not possible to treat women and men in exactly the same manner (Osawa, 2002; Ito 2009). Despite this inconsistency, upon enactment of the law, local governments started to draft ordinances and the women's movement as well as public women's centres actively took part in this process. Also, positive action was introduced targeting the business sector, with the aim of increasing the ratio of women in management to 30 per cent by 2020 through the implementation of gender-equal practices.

The concept of 'work–life balance' was introduced to Japan in the early 2000s and soon became part of the government's policy initiatives.[8] It came to be seen as a framework for resolving the tension between the need to address the low fertility rate and the pressures towards gender equality, because it suggested that both women and men could enjoy 'work' and 'care' in a balanced distribution of work–life responsibilities. In the Basic Plan for Gender Equality, several targets were set for 2020: to achieve a 50 per cent decrease in working hours over 60 hours per week, to increase husbands' share in domestic and care work to 2.5 hours per day, and to increase the percentage of fathers taking parental care leave to 13 per cent (Gender Equality Bureau Cabinet Office, 2010). In 2007, the government drew up the Work–life Balance Charter with the involvement of the business sector. The charter and its associated action plan encourage diverse and flexible forms of work as a way of ensuring decent working conditions, an increase in men's parental leave, and job opportunities for women and the elderly (Cabinet Office, 2010; Gender Equality Bureau Cabinet Office, 2010).

These advances did not come without cost. In order to keep the business sector on board, policies designed to improve women's working conditions and promote work–life balance set aside, or at least decentred, the concept of 'gender equality', instead emphasising the utility of the measures proposed in addressing low fertility and facilitating economic growth. This is further evidence of the absence of political will and commitment on the part of government to eliminate gender-based discrimination in order to achieve a balanced work/care regime for both women and men.

Gender backlash and pressure points

The 1990s was the high point in the women's movement's efforts to promote gender equality in Japan. Early in that decade, former 'comfort women' from

Korea made the first testimonies about their experiences; they were followed by numerous women from other countries. In response, the Japanese women's movement organised various acts of support including lawsuits, public hearings and an international tribunal calling for compensation and an apology from the government. Women politicians also drafted a proposal to revise the civil law to allow married couples to have separate family names and gender equality in education was widely discussed. After the enactment of the Basic Act for a Gender Equal Society, public women's centres planned numerous activities in support of gender equality and many local governments drafted ordinances to promote gender equality. In one of the booklets published by the Tokyo Women's Centre, the term 'gender free'[9] was used, as part of a call for the elimination of gender stereotypes.

This last move prompted a backlash, which took the form of a coordinated campaign by a conservative group of politicians, media representatives, university professors and religious organisations, both men and women. The conservatives argued that 'gender free' education denies 'masculinity' and 'femininity' and would lead to the break-up of families and the nation-state. These arguments were reminiscent of the pre-war discourse that established the family as the foundation of the state. The conservatives first started to spread distorted claims through right-wing media that 'gender free' education would compel boys and girls to use the same changing rooms for physical education and abolish separate male/female toilets. These claims gained further publicity when politicians raised questions about 'gender free' education at schools in parliament, news of which was featured by the media. As a result, government officials started to become hesitant about working on gender issues.

The gender backlash converged with other contested issues, such as denying redress to former 'comfort women', historical revisionism denying the atrocities of the Japanese military during the Second World War, changing the Pacifist Constitution so that Japan could assume the status of full ally of the USA, educational reform to teach children patriotism, and visits to the Yasukuni Shrine where the war criminals are enshrined. Many influential politicians in the ruling party are active participants in this conservative political campaign, which makes efforts to improve gender equality and address the issue of work–life balance ever more difficult.

The conservative ideology, combined with neo-liberal economics, functions in an ambivalent fashion. On the one hand, it is taking an extremely nationalistic and revisionist form in its efforts to reassert 'pride' in being Japanese, treating the family as the moral foundation of the nation. For the conservatives, gender equality is the 'enemy' or a 'threat' to the nation-state, as it destabilises the imagined gender order, despite the fact that the male breadwinner's wage can no longer be relied upon to support a family in the post-industrial economy.

On the other hand, the state has been removing the 'barriers' to free market economics through deregulation, which makes it more likely that workers will be evaluated on the basis of merit rather than gender. With the decreasing size of the working-age population, labour shortages cannot be addressed by male workers alone, thus creating a demand for women and older people to be incorporated into the labour market. As a consequence, the rigid employment system that was established during the period of rapid economic development in the post-war period is bound to change into a more flexible and diverse system – or at least there are mounting pressures on it to change. The entry of migrants to undertake care work also seems to be inevitable, a change in policy which would make Japan's care regime not only gendered but also deeply divided according to class and ethnicity. These changes in the nature of the work/care regime will pose a challenge to the conservative ideology that continues to promote the illusion of a homogeneous nation-state that has never existed. Care work thus continues to be a contested domain, not only in terms of the social reproduction of the nation but, more importantly, in the struggle for human dignity, gender equality and democracy.

Notes

1 For further discussion on the modern family in Japan, see Ochiai (1989, 1994), Ueno (1994) and Senda (2011).
2 The law has since been revised four times to strengthen the prohibition of gender discrimination in the workplace.
3 Paid parental leave was first introduced in 1976 with limited coverage targeting public school teachers, nursery teachers and nurses.
4 The Long Term Care Insurance scheme is financed through a combination of 50 per cent tax and 50 per cent insurance. Half of the tax is contributed by the national government and half by the local government. The insurance income is derived from premiums paid by those above 40 years old.
5 For the background to the negotiations leading to this development, see Asato (2007).
6 See for example, US Department of State (2014).
7 Under the Immigration Control Law, migrant domestic workers were only allowed to work for foreign nationals. In August 2015, new guidelines for migrant domestic workers to be employed in National Strategic Special Zones were issued (Cabinet Office 2015).
8 For discussion of work–life balance in the Japanese context, see Higuchi and Fukawa (2011), Yamaguchi and Higuchi (2008) and Yamaguchi (2009).
9 For analysis on the use of the term and its implications, see Yamaguchi et al. (2006).

References

Asato, W. 2007. *The Economic Partnership Agreement and Acceptance of Foreign Nurses and Care Workers.* [In Japanese] In *International Mobility of Care and Domestic Workers.* edited by Y. Kuba, 27–50. Tokyo: Nihon Hyōron Sha.

Cabinet Office. 2001. *Report on a Study of Family and Lifestyle.* [In Japanese] http://www.caa.go.jp/seikatsu/kazoku-lifestyle-menu.html.

Cabinet Office. 2010. *Work–life Balance Charter.* [In Japanese] http://wwwa.cao.go.jp/wlb/government/20barrier_html/20html/charter.html.

Cabinet Office. 2014. *White Paper on the Ageing Society.* [In Japanese] http://www8.cao.go.jp/kourei/whitepaper/w-2014/zenbun/s1_1_1.html.

Cabinet Office. 2015. *Office on Promotion of Rural Revitalisation. Related Laws.* [In Japanese] http://www.kantei.go.jp/jp/singi/tiiki/kokusentoc/hourei.html.

Gender Equality Bureau Cabinet Office. 2005. *Report on International Comparison on Low Fertility rate and Gender Equality.* [In Japanese] http://www.gender.go.jp/kaigi/senmon/syosika/houkoku/index-kokusai.html.

Gender Equality Bureau Cabinet Office. 2010. *Third Plan for Gender Equality.* [In Japanese] http://www.gender.go.jp/about_danjo/basic_plans/3rd/index.html.

Gender Equality Bureau Cabinet Office. 2013. *White Paper on Gender Equality.* [In Japanese] http://www.gender.go.jp/about_danjo/whitepaper/h25/zentai/html/honpen/b1_s02_01.html.

Higuchi, Y., and T. Fukawa. 2011. *Work–life Balance and Family Formation.* [In Japanese] Tokyo: Tokyo University Press.

ILO. 2013. ILOSTAT Database, Annual Indicators. https://www.ilo.org/ilostat.

Ito, K. 2009. *What 'Gender Equal' Means.* [In Japanese] Tokyo: Impact Shuppan Kai.

JICWELS. 2015. *The Current Situation of Foreign Nurses and Care Worker Candidates under the Economic Partnership Agreement.* [In Japanese] Unpublished material.

JNA. 2006. *The Japanese Nursing Association's Position on Acceptance of Filipino Nurses under the Japanese-Philippines EPA.* [In Japanese] http//www.nurse.or.jp/home/opinion/wesrelease/2006pdf/20060912.pdf.

MHLW. 2001. *Comprehensive Research on Part-Time Workers.* [In Japanese] http://www.caa.go.jp/seikatsu/2001/0622kazoku-lifestyle/zuhyou.pdf.

MHLW. 2011a. *Research on Single-Headed Households in 2011.* [In Japanese] http://www.mhlw.go.jp/seisakunitsuite/bunya/kodomo/kodomo_kosodate/boshi-katei/boshi-setai_h23/.

MHLW. 2011b. *Implementation and Instruction on Employment Management based on the Tier System.* [In Japanese] http://www.mhlw.go.jp/general/seido/koyou/danjokintou/dl/cource_joukyou.pdf.

MHLW. 2012a. *The First Longitudinal Research on Babies Born in 2010.* [In Japanese] http://www.mhlw.go.jp/toukei/saikin/hw/shusshoujib/01/dl/gaikyo01.pdf.

MHLW. 2012b. *White Paper on the Ageing Society.* [In Japanese] http://www8.cao.go.jp/kourei/whitepaper/w-2012/zenbun/pdf/1s2s_3_2.pdf.

MHLW. 2013a. *Overview of Life Table.* [In Japanese] http://www.mhlw.go.jp/toukei/saikin/hw/life/life13/.

MHLW. 2013b. *Workers' Compensation Status of Heart Disease and Mental Disorders.* [In Japanese] http://www.mhlw.go.jp/stf/houdou/2r98520000034xn0.html.

MHLW. 2013c. *Basic National Life Survey.* [In Japanese] http://www.mhlw.go.jp/toukei/saikin/hw/k-tyosa/k-tyosa13/.

MHLW. 2014a. *White Paper on Health, Labour and Welfare.* [In Japanese] http://www.mhlw.go.jp/wp/hakusyo/kousei/13/.

MHLW. 2014b. *The Financing of Long Term Care Insurance.* [In Japanese] http://www.mhlw.go.jp/stf/seisakunitsuite/bunya/hukushi_kaigo/kaigo_koureisha/zaisei/index.html.

MHLW. 2014c. *Securing the Care Workforce.* [In Japanese] http://www.mhlw.go.jp/file/05-Shingikai-12601000-Seisakutoukatsukan-Sanjikanshitsu_Shakaihoshoutantou/0000062879.pdf.

MHLW. n.d. *Acceptance of Foreign Nurses and Care Worker Candidates from Indonesia, The Philippines and Vietnam.* [In Japanese] http://www.mhlw.go.jp/stf/seisakunitsuite/bunya/koyou_roudou/koyou/gaikokujin/other22/index.html.

National Institute of Population and Social Security Research. 2010a. *Fourteenth Survey on Birth Trends.* [In Japanese] http://www.ipss.go.jp/syoushika/bunken/DATA/pdf/207616.pdf.

National Institute of Population and Social Security Research. 2010b. *Fourteenth National Survey on Marriage and Birth for Single Persons.* [In Japanese] http://www.ipss.go.jp/ps-doukou/j/doukou14_s/doukou14_s.pdf.

Ochiai, E. 1989. *The Modern Family and Feminism.* [In Japanese] Tokyo: Keisō Shobō.

Ochiai, E. 1994. *Towards the 21st Century Family.* [In Japanese] Tokyo: Yūhikaku Sensho.

OECD. 2014a. *Employment Outlook.* http://www.oecd.org/els/oecd-employment-outlook-19991266.htm.
OECD. 2014b. *Balancing Paid Work, Unpaid Work and Leisure*. http://www.oecd.org/gender/data/balancingpaidworkunpaidworkandleisure.htm.
Ogawa, R. 2012. "Globalization of Care and the Context of Reception of Southeast Asian Care Workers in Japan." *Southeast Asian Studies* 49 (4): 570–593.
Ogawa. R. 2015. "Globalization of Care Work and Migrants." [In Japanese] In *The Emergence of Peace at the Community and Grassroots Levels*, edited by The Peace Studies Association of Japan. 59–77 Tokyo: Waseda University Press.
Oishi, A., and R. Moriizumi. 2011. "Work in a Low Fertility Society." In *Work Life Balance and Family Formation* [In Japanese], edited by Y. Higuchi and T. Fukawa, 149–171. Tokyo: Tokyo University Press.
Oishi, A. and A. Shimazu. 2015. "Work Live Balance and Work." [In Japanese]. In *Society and Heath: An Integrated Approach to Close the Health Gap*, edited by N. Kawakami, H. Hashimoto and N. Kondo. Tokyo: Tokyo University Press.
Osawa, M. 2000. *Women's Policy in the 21st Century and the Basic Act for a Gender Equal Society.* [In Japanese] Tokyo: Gyōsei.
Osawa, M. 2002. *Creating a Gender Equal Society*. [In Japanese] Tokyo: NHK Books.
Prime Minister's Office. n.d. *Towards a Society where Women Shine*. [In Japanese] http://www.kantei.go.jp/jp/singi/keizaisaisei/bunka/koyou/dai7/siryou3-2.pdf.
Senda, Y. 2011. *The Japanese Style Modern Family*. [In Japanese] Tokyo: Keisō Shobō.
Statistics Japan. 2014. http://www.stat.go.jp/data/jinsui/2.htm#monthly.
Takemura, Kazuko, ed. 2003. *'Post' Feminism*. Tokyo: Sakuhin sha.
Tsubota, K., R. Ogawa, S. Ohno, and O.-H. Yuko. 2015. "A Study on the Cost and Willingness to Recruit EPA Foreign Nurses and Care Workers in Japan: From the Angle of Hospitals and Care Facilities." *Health Science Research* 27: 45–53.
Ueno, C. 1994. *Establishment and Demise of the Modern Family.* [In Japanese.] Tokyo: Iwanami Shoten.
Ueno, C., M. Osawa, K. Kawano, K. Takemura, and M. Adachi. 2001. *Radically Speaking...* [In Japanese] Tokyo: Heibonsha.
US Department of State. 2014. *Trafficking in Persons.* http://www.state.gov/j/tip/rls/tiprpt/2014/?utm_source=NEW+RESOURCE:+Trafficking+in+Persons+R.
World Bank. 2015. Health Nutrition and Population Statistics: Population Estimates and Projections. http://databank.worldbank.org/Data/Views/VariableSelection/SelectVariables.aspx?source=Health%20Nutrition%20and%20Population%20Statistics:%20Population%20estimates%20and612 %20projections.
Yamaguchi, K. 2009. *Work–life Balance: Empirical Study and Policy Proposal.* [In Japanese] Tokyo: Nihon Keizai Shimbun Sha.
Yamaguchi, T., 2006, "Lost Decade of Gender-free Debate and Feminist Movement." [In Japanese] Ueno, C., S., Miyadai, T., Saito, M., Kotani, K., Suzuki, W., Goto, T., Yamamoto, H., Yoshikawa, T., Shibuya, J., Martin, B., Houston, T., Yamaguchi, E., Koyama, N., Seguchi, Y., Hasegawa, C., Ogiue. *Backlash! Why Gender Free was Bashed?* Tokyo: Soufū Sha.
Yamaguchi, K., and Y. Higuchi, eds. 2008. *Debate on the Work Life Balance in Japan* [In Japanese] Tokyo: Nihon Keizai Shimbun Sha.

14 South Korea

Work, care and the Wollstonecraft dilemma

Joohee Lee

South Korean women have gradually increased their participation in the labour market since the industrialisation drive of the 1960s. However, a traditional gender pattern is still dominant in the work/care regime. Rapid industrialisation and the drastic improvement of women's human capital have not changed the strong male breadwinner ideology in both work and the family. Approximately half of all women stay at home as full-time housewives, providing much-needed care for children and the elderly because of the poor care regime. The other half of all women do participate in the labour market, but as second-class citizens. A majority of women workers are employed under nonstandard arrangements with a significant gender gap in earnings. This was exacerbated by the Asian Financial Crisis of 1997 and subsequent neoliberal labour market reforms.

The current work/care regime in South Korea is a reflection of the country's prevailing gender order, but government policies have also contributed to the way it operates. South Korea's export-oriented economic growth model, heavily dependent on large-scale conglomerates called *chaebols,* has failed to produce sufficient employment for the population. At the same time, the low level of social spending by government has exacerbated the burden on households, given the rapidly ageing population and extremely low fertility rates. Almost all governments since democratisation in 1987 have implemented employment policies for women and increased the budget for childcare and eldercare in their competition for women's votes. The impact of these policies, however, has been minimal, and in some cases even negative, due to the fact that they were based on the patriarchal assumption that women are different from men. Thus it can be argued that the policies actually deepened and exacerbated the 'Wollstonecraft dilemma'[1] in South Korea (Lee 2012a).

The Wollstonecraft dilemma is a core dilemma in feminism. The liberal feminist agenda for a gender neutral society, where men and women are actually equal and thus should be treated equally, is in conflict with a gender-differentiated citizenship, because women have special 'care-related' capacities and duties that differentiate them from men (Hassim 1999). The Wollstonecraft dilemma, therefore, refers to the contradictions inherent in women's strategies to achieve equality in a patriarchal system. Even if a woman seeks to attain full citizenship by becoming a worker, she is treated unequally in the workplace due to the disproportionate burden of the extensive care work she carries. However, emphasising a woman's differentiated citizenship does not solve the dilemma because then she would never overcome the status of second-class citizenship. As South Korean gender policies have always been formed under the strong patriarchal assumption of women's difference, they have exacerbated the dilemma.

This chapter investigates the major characteristics of the work/care regime in South Korea with special emphasis on the role of the state. Due to the limited role of trade unions, employers' associations and not-for-profit organisations, the state has consistently increased its presence and influence in the work/care regime. Yet despite this expanding role, the involvement of families in the provision of care has not lessened, and gender equality in the labour market has also not improved. This is because the South Korean state has structured care provision in such a way that families, especially women, cannot escape their designated role as providers of both care and workplace labour.

The work and care regime in context

South Korea is a small country geographically, with a population of 5.15 million (Ministry of Government Administration and Home Affairs 2015). When the Republic of Korea was established in 1948 it was one the poorest countries in the world, but export-led industrialisation under the leadership of the authoritarian Park government (1961–79) transformed the country from a traditional agricultural economy into an industrial powerhouse. Rapid industrialisation produced a large number of blue-collar and white-collar workers and the feminisation of white-collar occupations (Koo 1990). As a result of these changes in the macro-economic structure, most of the labour force is now employed in the service and manufacturing sectors.

South Korea is relatively highly ranked in the OECD's Human Development Index (HDI) for women, due to its rapid economic growth, but its level of gender equality lags behind other measures of the HDI at the national level. Korean women's labour market participation rate is low, although it has increased from 34.3 from in 1963 to 48.8 per cent in 2013 (National Statistics Office 2015).[2] In South Korea, the labour market participation of women continues to follow a distinctive M-shape, where career disruption among women above 30 years of age lowers participation.

Table 14.1 shows that the female labour force comprises 43 per cent of total employees, but only 23 per cent of employers. Own-account workers are not necessarily better off than employees, but they are in a much better position than family workers who work in a family-owned business without payment. The proportion of family workers is small and has been shrinking. Only 30 per cent of women are own-account workers, while almost all family workers are women.

The gender composition in some South Korean industries is skewed, as Table 14.2 shows. The manufacturing sector is a case in point. The heavy manufacturing and chemical industries were the engine of rapid economic growth and export

Table 14.1 Employment status by sex, 2013

	Males (%)	*Females (%)*	*% of all males*	*% of all females*	*Total ('000s)*
Employees	56.9	43.1	71.0	74.7	18,194
Employers	76.6	23.4	7.9	3.4	1,510
Own-account workers	70.1	29.9	19.9	11.8	4,141
Family workers	13.4	86.6	1.1	10.1	1,221
Total	58.1	41.9	100.0	100.0	25,067

Source: Statistics Korea (2013).

expansion in the 1970s, and the South Korean manufacturing sector has consistently generated relatively well-paying jobs. Seventy per cent of the labour force in the manufacturing sector is male, while women workers are concentrated in low-wage service sectors, such as accommodation and food services, and health and social work.

Occupational sex segregation is also prevalent in Korea. Table 14.3 shows that women are under-represented in managerial, professional and technical positions, but over-represented in elementary occupations. Glass walls and glass ceilings, the invisible barriers and inherent discrimination in the structures and processes of organisations, are indeed very thick in South Korea, segregating women into non-managerial and menial positions (Lee and Rowley 2009). The Korea Labour Institute's 2002 National Establishment Survey, based on firms employing more than 100 workers, reported that 64 per cent of firms had no female managers at all, and only 4 per cent of firms in this category had two or more female managers. The situation has not improved in recent years. In 2013, female directors in South Korean organisations held just 1.9 per cent of board seats, while the averages were 11.8 per cent in developed countries and 7.4 per cent in emerging markets (GMI Ratings 2013). Among Asian countries, the influence of family commitments on women's decisions to leave jobs has been found to be strongest in South Korea (Sussmuth-Dyckerhoff et al. 2012), which may account for the gender gap in participation rates and leadership positions.

For a country with strong family commitments, South Korea's fertility rate is exceptionally and paradoxically low. At 1.19 in 2013, it was below the replacement fertility rate, which is approximately 2.1. It took only 23 years for the total fertility rate to fall from 6.0 in 1960 to 2.1 in 1983 (Kim 2004). During these 23 years, the rapid drop in South Korea's fertility rate was driven by the family planning policies of successive authoritarian governments, which popularised contraceptive appliances and operations (Kim and Yang 2009). However, the decline in the fertility rate has continued, even after the country reached the replacement fertility rate level. South Korea's very low fertility is partially explained by a rise in the childbearing age due to higher education levels among women (Choi 2004), but recent studies have found that its major cause is

Table 14.2 Working population by industry and sex, 2013

Industry	*Males (%)*	*Females (%)*	*% of all males*	*% of all females*	*Total ('000s)*
Agriculture, forestry and fishing	57.2	42.8	6.0	6.2	1,520
Mining and quarrying	87.5	12.5	0.1	0.0	16
Manufacturing	70.0	30.0	20.1	12.0	4,184
Electricity, gas and etc.	83.5	16.5	0.5	0.1	91
Water supply and waste management	80.8	19.2	0.4	0.1	73
Construction	92.1	7.9	11.1	1.3	1,753
Wholesale, retail trade.	54.6	45.4	13.7	15.8	3,660
Transportation and storage	90.7	9.3	8.8	1.3	1,414
Accommodation and food service	35.3	64.7	4.8	12.2	1,970
Information and communication	73.3	26.7	3.5	1.8	692
Finance and insurance	48.7	51.3	2.9	4.2	864
Real estate	64.1	35.9	2.1	1.7	485
Professional, scientific and technical activities	70.7	29.3	5.0	2.9	1,022
Administrative and support service activities	55.7	44.3	4.5	5.0	1,174
Public administration and defence	63.5	36.5	4.2	3.4	966
Education	33.2	66.8	4.0	11.1	1,748
Health and social work	18.9	81.1	2.0	12.0	1,554
Arts, entertainment and recreation	61.7	38.3	1.7	1.4	392
Other service activities	51.8	48.1	4.7	6.0	1,312
Activities of households as employers	2.3	97.7	0.0	1.6	172
Activities of extraterritorial organisations	71.4	28.6	0.0	0.0	7
Total	58.1	41.9	100.0	100.0	25,067

Source: Statistics Korea (2013).

Table 14.3 Working population by occupational category and sex, 2013

Occupation	*Males (%)*	*Females (%)*	*% of all males*	*% of all females*	*Total ('000s)*
Managers, professionals, and technicians	56.3	43.7	20.7	22.4	5,370
Clerical, service and sales workers	47.4	52.6	32.0	49.2	9,825
Skilled agricultural and trades workers	59.0	41.0	5.8	5.5	1,427
Machine operators and assemblers	86.7	13.3	31.0	6.6	5,219
Elementary occupations	47.2	52.8	10.4	16.3	3,227
Total	58.1	41.9	100.0	100.0	25,067

Source: Statistics Korea (2013).

low rates of marriage (Chung 2015). Throughout the 2000s, the fertility rate has remained at around 1.2 (National Statistics Office 2015).

The acceleration in the fall in fertility rates following the financial crisis of the late 1990s indicates the negative impact of economic recession on people's propensity for marriage. Nowadays in South Korea young people without jobs or with unstable jobs lack the financial means to marry or avoid marriage because of the rising cost of raising children. Married couples are also reluctant to have more than one child for the same reason. The cost of both private and public education is simply too high. More specifically, South Korean women avoid marriage or having children to reduce the dual burden of work and care. Few childcare facilities, sex discrimination in the workplace, and a culture of extremely long working hours all contribute to deepening their experience of the Wollstonecraft dilemma. In sum, it is fairly accurate to describe South Korea's extremely low fertility as the outcome of the very inadequate and patriarchal work/care regime.

Figure 14.1 displays the population pyramid diagrams for 2005, 2015, and 2025, which reflect the prevailing low fertility rates. In 2011, the OECD (2011) predicted that of all OECD members, South Korea would experience the largest increase in the number of very elderly people, from about 2 per cent in 2010 to about 15 per cent in 2050. These predictions suggest that South Korea is trapped in a vicious circle. Low fertility is producing a vast array of problems in the country, including a productivity decline due to the shrinking workforce, increasing costs of support for the elderly, and the fiscal crisis of social security. To solve these problems, South Korea must utilise more of the female population in its workforce; however, the current work/care regime prevents women from participating in the labour market, and at the same time, from having more children (Park 2006).

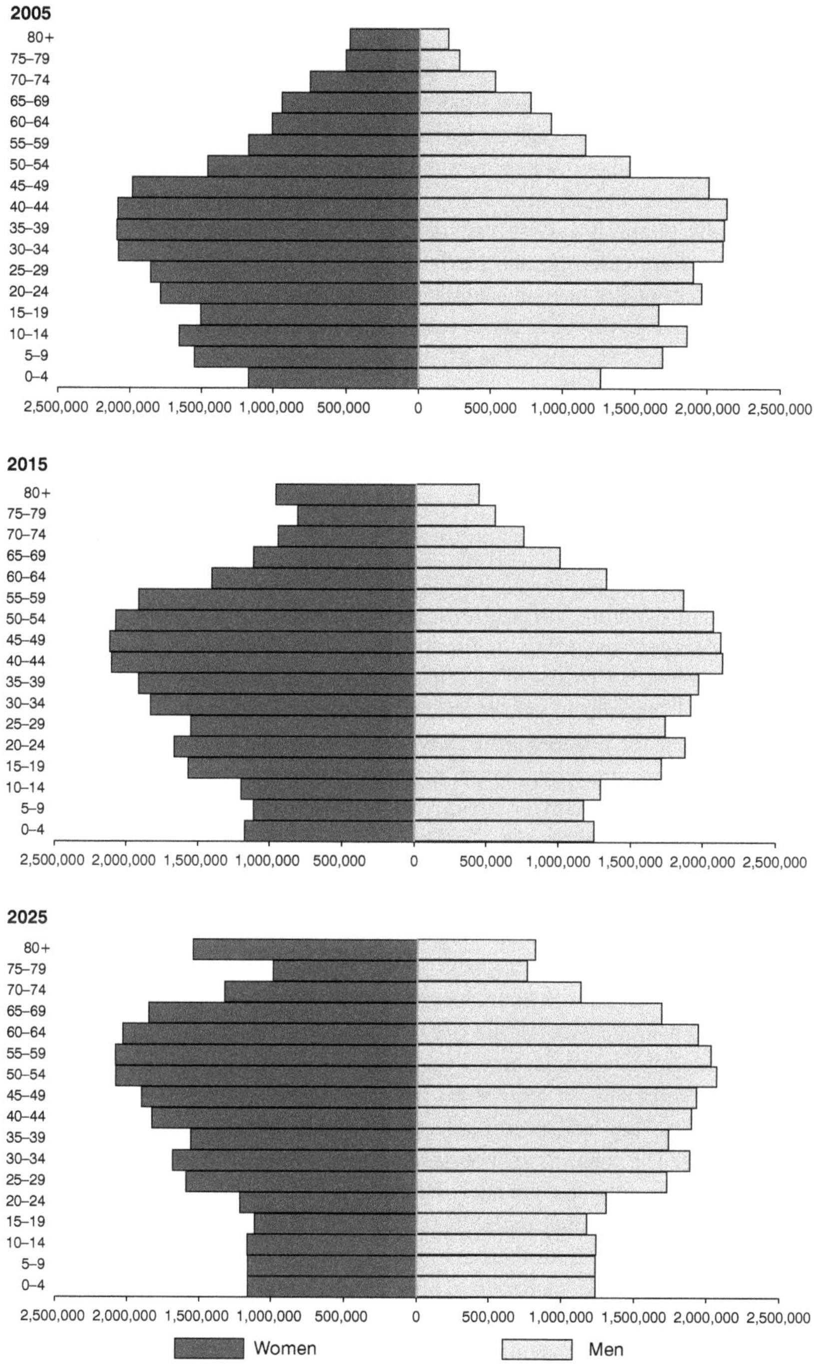

Figure 14.1 Population 2005, 2015, and 2025

Source: World Bank (2015).

The care regime

There are two pivotal family policies that shape the characteristics of a country's care regime: family leave policies that allow parents to take care of their children without career breaks or wage penalties, and public provisions for childcare that promote women's labour market participation by freeing women from caregiving burdens (Gornick and Meyers 2004). As population ageing continues in most countries, the public provision of eldercare is also gaining more importance in discussions of the care regime. South Korea recently updated and extended the coverage and contents of many family policies, but it is not clear whether these policies will have positive effects on women. In addition, paid care work by foreign or migrant labour is too limited to fill the gaps created by the poor care regime in South Korea. Interestingly, and perhaps indicative of the government's approach to the care problem, it was only after 2009 that foreign or migrant workers were included in official government surveys, and there is virtually no literature on the role of these workers in care work.

Childcare

The length and availability of paid leave has increased in almost all OECD countries in recent decades, including in South Korea. In 1990 South Korea provided mothers with just 8.5 weeks of paid leave, but since 2014, Korean mothers have had access to 15 months of paid maternity and parental leave. The development of father-specific leave is noteworthy as well. While only a few developed countries provide father-specific leave, South Korean fathers are eligible to take one year of paid parental leave (OECD 2014a). South Korea also increased the age of the children for whom parents are eligible to take parental leave. Since 2014, any individual can take 12 months leave to take care of children up to eight years old.

However, the existence of these statutory arrangements does not necessarily mean that South Korean parents are making use of them. Uptake of paid leave relies on reasonable rates of income replacement. Public expenditure on maternity and parental leave per child is very low in South Korea, at an average of USD 1,264 – only a tenth of the OECD average expenditure (OECD 2014b). In South Korea, one has to be insured under employment insurance in order to be entitled to maternity and parental leave. Since employers in large firms are responsible for two-thirds of maternity leave payments, they are more likely to discriminate against women during the hiring process. The majority of nonstandard, own-account, unpaid family workers are not insured, so only 46.6 per cent of the labour force was covered by employment insurance in 2014.[3] Income replacement rates are also low, because payments for parental leave are 40 per cent of a worker's normal wages, with a ceiling. More importantly, the number of fathers taking parental leave is still extremely low in Korea. In 2013, while 67,323 mothers used their entitlement to parental leave, the number of fathers taking parental leave was only 2,293 (3.3 per cent) (Chu 2014).

Public childcare is an important policy tool for providing women with the opportunity to participate in the labour market. South Korea has expanded childcare facilities dramatically over the last couple of decades. In 1990, only 1.2 per cent of under-five-year-old children were in childcare facilities, but this increased to 53.6 per cent in 2013 (Chu 2014). Accordingly, public spending on services for families with children, such as public childcare support, and direct financing and subsidising of providers of childcare and early childhood education facilities, amounted to 0.89 per cent of GDP in 2009, close to the OECD average of 0.95 per cent (OECD 2014c). Since Korea spends very little on child-related cash transfers to families with children,[4] early childhood education and support comprises the largest portion of public spending on family benefits. Still, total public spending on family benefits of 1.16 per cent of GDP was considerably below the OECD average of 2.55 per cent (OECD 2014c).

The proportion of children in public childcare has always been low in South Korea. In 2011, public care facilities accounted for only 5.2 per cent of all childcare facilities, catering to 10.8 per cent of children; more than 90 per cent of childcare services were provided by the private sector (Seo and Song 2011). By 2012, about 52 per cent of children were in private childcare facilities supported by government funding (Seo and Lee 2013). Meanwhile, in 2009, the conservative Lee administration introduced a parental allowance as a replacement for public childcare. Initially, these allowances were provided to low-income families only, but in 2013 coverage was extended to all households with children not in private childcare (Seo and Lee 2013). Yun (2014) argues that this policy does not encourage an expansion of women's labour market participation, as it provides a strong incentive for one parent, usually the mother, to stay at home to care for pre-school aged children.

Eldercare

Despite the fact that South Korea is classified as a country of Confucian capitalism, where adult children are supposed to take care of their parents (Yun 2010), the actual co-habitation rate of parents and adult children is low. According to a press release by the National Statistics Office in 2014, elderly couple households accounted for 20.1 per cent of all South Korean households. Only 1.8 per cent were co-habitation households of elderly parents and adult children, while elderly single-person households accounted for 7.1 per cent of all households in the country. The number of elderly single-person households is expected to increase rapidly, up to more than 15 per cent of all households in the year 2035. There have been significant changes in attitudes towards caring for elders. In 1990, about 90 per cent of adult children agreed that they should take care of their parents, but in 2010, only 36 per cent of adult children agreed with this sentiment. More than 47 per cent agreed that government, society, and family are all responsible for eldercare (Song and Jung 2013).

Facing a rapidly changing family structure and demographic pressures, the South Korean government introduced a Long Term Care Insurance scheme in 2008. At first the government estimated it would benefit 3 per cent of the elderly, but 6.1 per cent of the elderly benefited from the scheme in 2013 (National Health

Insurance Service 2014). The scheme provides residential and/or nursing home care for elderly persons with severe age-related illnesses, with state subsidies covering 18–20 per cent of insurance payments (M.-J. Lee 2014). For those elderly persons without severe illnesses but who still need assistance in their daily lives a variety of home-based eldercare services is available, on the condition that their household income is below 150 per cent of the national average. These services are mostly subsidised by local governments (S.-H. Lee 2014).

It is true that South Korea has managed to establish eldercare institutions very quickly, but there are many debates regarding who should provide services for the elderly in the long run. As in the case of childcare, the government is heavily dependent on private sector nursing homes for eldercare. Public sector nursing homes for the elderly represented only 2.9 per cent of all long-term care facilities in 2011. Among these private sector facilities, not-for-profit facilities are minimal (M.-J. Lee 2014).

This sector is also characterised by a feminised workforce. Middle-aged or older females, whose wages and working conditions are among the lowest in the country, account for an absolute majority of the workforce in the eldercare industry. Informal eldercare in the family is also predominantly provided by women, mostly wives and daughters-in-law.[5] The involvement of migrant workers in this area of care work is minimal. Considering that it is also usually mothers who take parental leave to care for children, such intensive care activities may not be compatible with participation in the labour market. In 2005, over 60 per cent of informal carers in South Korea provided more than 20 hours a week of care (Colombo et al., 2011).

The work regime

Gornick and Meyers (2004) argue that working time regulations, along with family policies, are very important for the achievement of a gender egalitarian redistribution of domestic labour. Women workers usually suffer more when labour markets remain unregulated and social policy institutions are weak (Bugra 2014). In South Korea, both long working hours and a flexible labour market without proper social protection have had consistently negative effects on women's labour market participation and their equality with men in households and the labour market. Meanwhile, the role of trade unions in redressing these labour market issues has been fairly limited, due to their patriarchal orientations and a decentralised collective bargaining structure.

Long working hours

Equality in paid work is critically dependent on equality in the provision of domestic labour. As illustrated in the Wollstonecraft dilemma, women cannot achieve equality as long as they are burdened with a disproportionately high amount of care work. Longer working hours rob male workers of their time to contribute to domestic labour, and either discourage female workers from participating in the labour market or force them to engage in part-time rather than full-time work. In South Korea, statutory working hours were reduced to 40 hours per week in 2004 but actual working hours have not declined accordingly. Average annual hours actually worked was 2,163 per worker in 2012, as against the OECD average of 1,773 hours. As these figures indicate, regular male workers tend to work very long hours.

In most countries women spend about twice as much time as men on unpaid work and care work.[6] In South Korea, however, women spend almost four times longer on care work than men (OECD 2014d). This highly skewed distribution of unpaid work and care work between women and men can lead to statistical discrimination against women in the workplace, since the burden of unpaid and care work may lower the perceived productivity of women workers in general.

Statistical discrimination against women workers is prevalent in South Korea, despite the fact that the country has adopted several pieces of legislation prohibiting sexual discrimination in the workplace, such as the Equal Employment Act in 1987. The concept of 'disparate impact' (or indirect discrimination) was introduced in the third revision of the Act in 1999, disallowing human resource management policies that seem neutral on the surface but in fact have disproportionate effects upon a group or class, namely female workers. In order to increase the enforcement power of the Act, the South Korean government introduced affirmative action measures in 2006. All public corporations and firms employing more than 500 workers became subject to affirmative action requirements. If a firm does not meet the guideline on women's employment set by the Ministry of Employment and Labour, it must submit an action plan to remedy the gender inequality (Lee and Rowley 2009). Nevertheless, there have been no visible changes in women's employment rates or the number of women managers since the introduction of affirmative action.

Why are these legislative efforts not effective? In the case of affirmative action measures, the institutional design was defective. Firms need to report only the number of women workers and managers, and the total number of workers and managers, without reporting separately the ratio of women workers in nonstandard employment arrangements. Therefore, firms can increase their female workforce simply by hiring more women nonstandard workers. Nonstandard work in South Korea is defined as temporary employment, part-time or daily work, temporary work agency employment, contract company employment and quasi self-employment.[7] Nonstandard workers' wages and working conditions are much lower than those of regular workers. In addition, since there are virtually no penalty clauses, firms do not consider these measures seriously and thus do not make sincere efforts to improve gender equality. Neither have trade unions tried to monitor and enforce these measures in the workplace. Such a lack of effectiveness implies that the profoundly gendered work regime in South Korea cannot be improved by simply introducing legislation. The male breadwinner ideology, backed by the extremely long working hours of male workers and strong care responsibilities of female workers/carers, has not been challenged in South Korea.

Nonstandard work

The Asian Financial Crisis of 1997 significantly changed the structure of the labour market. The crisis made previously stable jobs very precarious, and the number of workers in nonstandard employment arrangements grew rapidly (Lee and Lee 2004). The introduction of labour market flexibility was not gender neutral (Lee 2004). Women workers were more frequently laid off and rehired as nonstandard workers in sex-segregated industries (Cho 1999; Kum 2001).

In South Korea, the government conservatively estimates that nonstandard workers comprise about 35 per cent of all wage earners in the 2000s. Independent labour institutes, however, claim otherwise, estimating that more than half of the whole workforce are employed as nonstandard workers (Lee 2011). The gender pay gap for non-standard workers is higher than for regular workers, and while almost all regular workers are covered by social insurance, company-provided severance pay and leave policies, two-thirds to half of all nonstandard workers are without these benefits.

The rise in female part-time work was deliberately promoted under the two consecutive terms of conservative government from 2008. After the 2008 economic crisis, the Lee government restructured women's employment policies to focus on job creation and employment services for women who experienced career disruption. The newly created jobs, however, were mostly part-time, short-term and unstable, and were called 'purple jobs', strongly implying that they were intended for women workers. Eventually these gender-specific policies transformed previously full-time nonstandard jobs into part-time nonstandard jobs with only a minor reduction of working hours, further reducing women's work status and pay.

The Park government continued the previous Lee administration's policies with even more vigour after 2013. The government claimed that part-time jobs for women with career disruption would be created to achieve a 70 per cent employment rate for the country. It also maintained that it would create 'decent' part-time jobs to counter the strong opposition from women's movement groups. However, it was a case of mission impossible. Creating 'decent' part-time employment was against business interests. Large firms in South Korea preferred to utilise diverse forms of unprotected full-time nonstandard workers with great numerical flexibility (Yunhap News Agency, 2014).

The implications of the work regime for women can be better understood when examined alongside the care regime. Since the care regime does not cater fully to working women's needs and fails to free them from care work, the only logical path in the work regime is to create part-time jobs that allow women to balance work and life responsibilities, further reinforcing the Wollstonecraft dilemma. Thus some women workers embraced the governments' decision to provide women with part-time jobs, while low-income women with career disruption had no choice but to accept such jobs. These women usually work in nonstandard arrangements with shorter hours, while men hold regular or slightly higher paid nonstandard forms of employment.

At the same time, a care regime that depends heavily on the market as well as families requires a gendered labour market where women workers provide care services for minimum wages (Kim 2009). In 2010, the paid workforce in care services was overwhelmingly female, with women accounting for 92 per cent of jobs (Oh 2011). The government does not have policies that facilitate the immigration of care workers and although the number of immigrant caregivers is slowly increasing, especially in the domestic service sector, it is still too small to affect the care service sector as a whole. In summary, the South Korean work regime of highly sex-segregated labour markets and wage penalty for women subsidises the care regime's lack of public provision and proper regulation.

Gender politics in trade unions

It is not likely that trade unions or employers' associations will supplement the role of government in addressing gender imbalances. Employers' associations have always voiced their objections to any form of state intervention, advocating a reliance on market principles instead. Trade unions are male-oriented institutions with a limited capacity to act. Most unions are organised at the enterprise level, and just 5.5 per cent of women workers were organised in 2012, compared with 13.5 per cent of men (Lee 2012b). Women workers were also under-represented in the leadership of trade unions. As a result, South Korean trade unions have failed to mobilise women's support for a strong welfare state (Lee 2012b).

Trade unions in general have not been cohesive enough to fight employer demands for flexibility or to argue for wage solidarity for all workers (Lee 2010). They are also not immune from the male breadwinner ideology.[8] The two trade union confederations in South Korea, the Federation of Korean Trade Unions (FKTU) and the Korean Confederation of Trade Unions (KCTU), have provided model collective bargaining agreement clauses for maternity and parental leave provisions that are to be adopted by their affiliate unions. The union standards are usually higher than the statutory minimum, but their family-friendly policies were also targeted to benefit mainly female workers. Male workers were not encouraged to take parental leave (Lee 2014).

The only women's union, the Korean Women's Trade Union (KWTU) established in August 1999, is a significant exception. The number of KWTU members grew from 400 to 6,000 in ten years, a majority of them nonstandard workers. Because its members are isolated nonstandard workers, the KWTU's capacity to bargain with employers is limited. Instead, the KWTU's major activities are narrowly focused on legal and institutional reforms, such as improving the minimum wage (Lee 2012c).

Pressure points

The South Korean state's conservative views on women's difference penetrate almost all its family and employment policies. As a result, the work/care regime has not been an effective means of encouraging women's labour market participation.

Women still assume the lion's share of care responsibilities in both the market and the household. The labour market is heavily gendered, with women segregated into nonstandard employment arrangements and non-managerial positions. Despite conservative beliefs about women's roles, remaining as full-time housewives is no longer possible for most women, especially those from lower income families, because they need to earn wages to maintain basic living standards. Such economic necessity leads these women into low-wage, nonstandard forms of work.

South Korea is experiencing drastic demographic transformations that will certainly increase demand for long-term care of the ageing population. A declining co-residence rate and rising childlessness will exacerbate this care deficit in the near future. In addition, due to the rapid shrinkage of the working-age population as a share of total population, only 5.8 people were supporting each person over 65 years old in 2014 (National Statistics Office, 2014). All these changes require higher rates of women's labour market participation and expanded public support for childcare and eldercare.

The recent two conservative administrations' responses to these challenges have been more than disappointing. Instead of strengthening the public provision of care services, they privatised these services even further. Instead of eliminating discriminatory practices in the labour market, the government actively promoted short-term, part-time and low-paid jobs for women. As a result, South Korea is far from developing a citizen worker/carer, or dual earner/carer model that can provide women workers with equal opportunities at work, and equal division of paid and unpaid work between men and women.

It is still not clear whether the preference for a dual-income family and/or the pressures coming from low fertility rates and resultant demographic change will bring about changes in the work/care regime in South Korea. However, as long as public policies are affected by the male breadwinner model, the current stalemate is likely to remain entrenched. Women's experience of the Wollstonecraft dilemma in South Korea demonstrates that the economic necessity for women's labour market participation does not guarantee their participation in itself, let alone their equality with men. As long as the state maintains the slightly modified traditional male breadwinner model, women will continue to be treated as second-class citizens in the workplace and principal caregivers in the household.

Notes

1 Mary Wollstonecraft was a liberal feminist in the 18th century. Pateman (1989) argues that Wollstonecraft's desire for women's equal rights is contradictory, because women cannot become like men and full citizens while care work has no value for citizenship.
2 The South Korean labour market participation rate is based on the total population 15 years of age and over, while the OECD's labour participation rate is based on the total population 15–65 years of age. Therefore, the labour market participation rate as estimated by the South Korean government is slightly lower than the OECD rate.
3 Author's own calculation based on KLI (2015) statistics.
4 South Korea is one of few developed countries without a direct child allowance.
5 In 2004, about 80 per cent of primary carers for the elderly were women (Kang 2009).

6 Unpaid work includes domestic activities except for childcare or care for another person (OECD 2014d).
7 Some contract company work in Korea is a disguised form of temporary work agency employment. Temporary work agency workers and contract company workers share a similar triangular employment relationship, in which the legal employer and the client organisation that actually supervises the employee are different. Quasi self-employment combines characteristics of self-employment and wage labour. Daily work in Korea is easily found in construction industries, and it includes on-call workers in service industries as well.
8 Structural adjustments in the Hyundai Motor Company are a case in point. In May 1998, management announced that it had to lay off over 8,000 regular workers, but trade unions protested against this decision and reached a compromise in August. Eventually, 277 women workers in the HMC cafeteria were laid off (Lee and Lee 2004).

References

Bugra, A. 2014. "Revisiting the Wollstonecraft Dilemma in the Context of Conservative Liberalism: The Case of Female Employment in Turkey." *Social Politics* 21 (1): 148–166.

Cho, S.-K. 1999. "Gender Inequality in Structural Adjustment." [In Korean] *Korean Journal of Labor Studies* 5 (2): 123–147.

Choi, K. 2004. "Causes of the Recent Fertility Drop in Korea." [In Korean] *Korean Journal of Demography*. 27 (2): 35–59.

Chu, J.S. 2014. *Gender Statistics in Korea*. [In Korean] Seoul: Korean Women's Development Institute.

Chung, S. 2015. "Policy Responses to Low Fertility and Its Problems." [In Korean] *Korean Journal of Demography* 38 (2): 113–134.

Colombo, F., A. Llena-Nozal, J. Mercier, and F. Tjadens. 2011. *Help Wanted? Providing and Paying for Long Term Care*. OECD Health Policy Studies, OECD Publishing.

GMI Ratings. 2013. *GMI Ratings' 2013 Women on Board Survey*. GMI. http://www.gmiratings.com.

Gornick, J.C., and M.K. Meyers. 2004. "Welfare Regimes in Relation to Paid Work and Care." In *Changing Life Patterns in Western Industrial Societies*, edited by J. Giele and E. Holst, 45–67. Amsterdam: Elsevier.

Hassim, Shireen, 1999. "From Presence to Power: Women's Citizenship in a New Democracy," *Agenda: Empowering Women for Gender Equity* 40: 6–17.

Kang, W.-M. 2009. "Eldercare Policy Suggestions for the Aging Society." [In Korean] *The Kyungnam Development* 103: 36–47.

Kim, J. and S.-A. Yang. 2009. "Causes and Policy Implications for the Low Fertility in South Korea." [In Korean] *Women's Health* 10 (2): 113–133.

Kim, K. 2009. "A Study on the Reproducing Process of Gendered and Low-Waged Care Work: Focused on Care Work in the Informal Sector". [In Korean] *Asian Women's Studies* 48 (20): 147–184.

Kim, S.-K. 2004. "Change in Fertility Rates in Korea: Causes and Future Prospects." [In Korean] *Korean Journal of Demography* 27 (2): 1–34.

KLI. 2015. *KLI Labour Statistics*. [In Korean] Seoul: Korea Labour Institute.

Koo, H. 1990. "From Farm to Factory: Proletarianization in Korea." *American Sociological Review* 55: 669–681.

Kum, J.-H. 2001. *Women's Labour Market in Korea: Policy Analyses*. [In Korean] Seoul: Korea Labour Institute.

Lee, J. 2004. "Taking Gender Seriously: Feminization of Nonstandard Work in Korea and Japan." *Asian Journal of Women's Studies* 10 (1): 25–48.

Lee, J. 2010. "Union Politics for Nonstandard Employees: A Cross-Sectoral Comparative Analysis." [In Korean] *Korean Journal of Sociology*. 44(1):. 60–97.

Lee, J. 2011. "Between Fragmentation and Centralization: South Korean Industrial Relations in Transition." *British Journal of Industrial Relations* 49 (4): 767–791.

Lee, J. 2012a. "Policy Alternatives for Improving Labour Rights of Women: A Holistic Response to the Wollstonecraft Dilemma." [In Korean] *Journal of Korean Women's Studies* 28 (3): 35–62.

Lee, J. 2012b. "Women's Attitudes towards Trade Unions and Its Determinants." [In Korean] *Damron 201* 15 (2): 81–108.

Lee, J. 2012c. "Renewal of Solidarity or Continued Decline?: The Korean Retail Workers Struggles against Neoliberalism." In *Cross-National Comparisons of Social Movement Unionism* 18, edited by A. Suzuki, 91–145. Oxford: Peter Lang.

Lee, J. 2014. "Female Labor and the Future of Women's Labor Movements". [In Korean] *Labor Management Government Forum* 30 (2): 189–224.

Lee, J. and C. Rowley. 2009. "The Changing Face of Women Managers in South Korea" in *The Changing Face of Women Managers in Asia*, edited by C. Rowley and V. Yukongdi, 148–170. London and New York: Routledge.

Lee, M.-J. 2014. "Long-term Care Insurance and Policy Suggestions." [In Korean] *Welfare Situation*. July.

Lee, S.-H. 2014. "Policy Suggestions for Improving Care Services for Older Koreans" [In Korean] *Health and Welfare Forum*. August.

Lee, W. and J. Lee. 2004. "Will the Model of Uncoordinated Decentralization Persist?" In *The New Structure of Labor Relations: Tripartism and Decentralization*, edited by H. Katz, W. Lee and J. Lee, 43–65. Ithaca: Cornell University Press.

Ministry of Government Administration and Home Affairs. 2015. *Resident Registration Statistics*. [In Korean] http://rcps.egov.go.kr:8081/jsp/stat/ppl_stat_jf.jsp.

National Health Insurance Service, 2014. *2013 Long Term Care Insurance Statistical Yearbook*. [In Korean]. Seoul: National Health Insurance Service.

National Statistics Office, 2014. "2014 Old-age Statistics" [In Korean] Press Release, September 29, 2014.

National Statistics Office, 2015. *KOSIS*. http://kosis.kr.

OECD. 2014a. *PF2.5. Trends in Parental Leave Policies since 1970*. http://www.oecd.org/social/family/database.htm.

OECD. 2014b. PF2.1. *Key Characteristics of Parental Leave Systems*. http://www.oecd.org/social/family/database.htm.

OECD. 2014c. PF1.1. *Public Spending on Family Benefits*. http://www.oecd.org/social/family/database.htm.

OECD. 2014d. *LMF2.5: Time Use for Work, Care and Other Day-to-Day Activities*. http://www.oecd.org/social/family/database.htm1.

Oh, E.-J. 2011. *Policy Suggestions for Women's Job Creation in Social Service Sector V: Social Enterprise Business Model for Women Care Workers*. [In Korean] Seoul: Korea Women's Development Institute.

Park, B.-Y. 2006. "Family Policy in an Ageing and Low Fertile Society: Work-Family Life Balance Policies." [In Korean] *Critical Social Policy*. 22: 119–153.

Pateman, C. 1989. *The Disorder of Women*. Cambridge: Polity Press.

Seo, M.-H. and H.-M. Lee. 2013. *Evaluation of Childcare Policies in 2013 and Policy Suggestions*. [In Korean] Seoul: Korea Institute of Childcare and Education.

Seo, M.-H., and S.-Y. Song. 2011. *The Korean Childcare System in Comparative Perspective.* [In Korean] Seoul: Ministry of Strategy and Finance/Korea Institute of Childcare and Education.

Song, D.-Y. and S.-Y. Jung. 2013. "Paradigm Shift toward Comprehensive Family Policy." [In Korean] *Critical Social Policy* 39: 145–188.

Statistics Korea. 2013. *Economically Active Population Survey.* http://kostat.go.kr/portal/eng/surveyOutline/4/1/index.static.

Sussmuth-Dyckerhoff, C., J. Wang, and J. Chen, 2012. *Women Matter: An Asian Perspective.* http://www.leadershipforwomen.com.au/images/docs/2012-McKInsey-Women-Matter-An-Asian-Perspective.pdf.

World Bank. 2015. *Health Nutrition and Population Statistics: Population Estimates and Projections.* http://databank.worldbank.org/Data/Views/VariableSelection/SelectVariables.aspx?source=Health%20Nutrition%20and%20Population%20Statistics:%20Population%20estimates%20and%20projections.

Yun, H.-S. 2014. "Family Policy in the Park Geun-Hey Administration: the Expansion of Inequality in Gender and Classes." [In Korean] *Economy and Society* 101: 87–116.

Yun, J.-W. 2010. "The Myth of Confucian Capitalism in South Korea: Overworked Elderly and Underworked Youth." *Pacific Affairs* 83 (2): 237–259.

Yunhap News Agency. 2014. "One in Five Workers on Conglomerate Payrolls Indirectly Hired." July 1. http://minor@yna.co.kr.

15 Timor-Leste

Mixed messages on work and care

Michele Ford

Despite significant international pressure on Timor-Leste to comply with international gender norms during its very short time as an independent nation, gender inequality and its impact on the everyday lives of Timorese women is very much seen as being less important than more pressing matters of state-building and economic growth.[1] Despite strong policy messages from successive governments, international donors and local non-government organisations (NGOs), community acceptance of the principle of gender equality is low and the value of increased participation of women in the public sphere deeply contested. Timor-Leste also lacks the basic social infrastructure required to support such participation. As a consequence, women are left to find their own solutions to managing the competing demands of productive economic activity and reproductive care labour in a context where urbanisation and the increasing engagement of educated women in the paid workforce are testing familial models of care.

Drawing on fieldwork conducted in July 2013 and July 2015, this chapter examines the strained relationship between paid work and care in Timor-Leste.[2] It argues that the topic of work and care has failed to gain traction as a policy issue for two reasons. First, the vast majority of Timorese women engaged in income generation are located in informal sector occupations that allow them to combine work with household and care duties. Second, the agendas of government, international donors and the women's movement are dominated by debates about domestic violence and women's place in public life. The chapter concludes that although the issue of women's work and care is likely to continue to struggle for space on the policy agenda, the provision of viable alternatives to familial models of care – at the very least in urban areas – is vital if women are to play a greater role in the public sphere.

Work and care in context

Straddling Southeast Asia and the Pacific, Timor-Leste is a small, resource-rich yet poor country that has struggled to emerge from a long period of colonisation, first by Portugal and then Indonesia. Little more than a year after the fall of Indonesia's authoritarian New Order regime (1966–98), a referendum was held in which 78.5 per cent of Timorese voted for independence. After four and a half years under the United Nations Transitional Administration in East Timor (UNTAET), Timor-Leste officially became a nation-state in May 2002. It was not until two years later that the Timorese authorities nominally assumed full responsibility for operational matters (Molnar 2010). The United Nations remained deeply involved through a second peacekeeping operation, which remained in place until 2005 when a smaller political mission was established to provide further support for institution-building. Its presence was again extended after a resurgence of communal conflict in 2006–07, this time through the United Nations Integrated Mission in East Timor (UNMIT), which remained in place until December 2012.

Timor-Leste's troubled journey to statehood had serious implications for its economy. As a result of violence leading up to and after the 1999 referendum, more than 70 per cent of the territory's infrastructure and buildings was destroyed and some three-quarters of its population displaced (Leach and Kingsbury 2013). Estimates suggest that the economy lost 40 per cent of its value as modern commerce ground to a halt (Hill and Saldanha 2001). The UN presence and the aid flows that accompanied it brought significant resources to Timor-Leste. However, they also led to the development of a dual economy, resulting in growing economic inequality. Exacerbated by demographic pressures, including rural to urban migration and high levels of unemployment, this inequality contributed to the renewed outbreak of conflict in 2006, which led to further destruction and the displacement of hundreds of thousands of people (Dibley 2014). The economic situation has since improved as funds have flowed from its petroleum reserves, leading to more than a tripling of government spending between 2007 and 2011 (Sugden 2012). However, fundamental imbalances in the structure of the economy remain.

In general terms, Timor-Leste faces many of the challenges experienced by Pacific island nations such as Papua New Guinea (see Parker et al., this volume). These include geographic isolation; a narrow export and production base; high levels of imports; the high cost of service provision; and a predominantly rural population (Asian Development Bank 2014a). The government has attempted to address these challenges through successive Development Plans. The National Development Plan, released in 2002, undertook to '[t]ransform the subsistence economy and achieve a rapid economic growth that is stable and sustainable, utilising to the full the country's resources; [and] create equitable business opportunities and increase rural incomes', a task that, it was recognised, involved creating 'equal opportunities to obtain work' (RDTL 2002, 123). Elaborating on this vision, the Strategic Development Plan, released in 2011, identified as a priority the diversification of the base of the economy, with a focus on tourism and other service industries, complemented by expanded opportunities in agribusiness and light industry (RDTL 2011). This expansion was to be underpinned by growth in the private sector in both rural and urban settings, driven by local and foreign investment, and the development of an increasingly educated and skilled workforce (RDTL 2011).

Women have been very much a part of this vision. One of the guiding principles of the National Development Plan was the promotion of '[g]ender equality between women (girls) and men (boys) in access to opportunities, services, goods and privileges' (RDTL 2002, 22). The plan went on to elaborate at length the implications of this approach, including addressing discrimination against women and girls and high unemployment among women, as well as women's low wages and lack of professional skills. Among measures designed to address these problems was affirmative action through law and policy for professional and other working women – including a 'program of childcare (day care) centres for working women with children' (RDTL 2002, 134). Having identified the establishment of a 'gender-fair society' as an ongoing objective (RDTL 2011, 47), the Strategic Development Plan of 2011 points to the 'serious efforts' that have been made since independence to address gender inequality, including the passing of the Law against Domestic Violence, measures to increase the number of women candidates running for parliament, and the designation of Gender Focal Points in all ministries and local administrations (RDTL 2011, 47).[3]

The Strategic Development Plan also set out a number of strategies for achieving gender equality, including economic empowerment of women and the development of programmes to increase women's participation in the public service and in decision-making roles in the private sector, by 2030 (RDTL 2011). The latter aim was subsequently strengthened by the release of a National Strategy and Action Plan for Gender and the Private Sector (SEAPRI 2013). Yet while the 2013 plan acknowledges the challenge of providing services for young children and the burden imposed on families by chronic illness and disability among the aged, no mention is made of the impact of increased labour force participation on women's capacity to manage their responsibility for the care of children or the elderly, or indeed of the earlier commitment to develop institutional childcare as a means of providing women with equal opportunity to obtain work. Similarly, while the Appraisal Report on Timor-Leste's performance in relation to the Beijing Platform for Action (SEPI 2014) identifies women's low labour force participation rates as a serious challenge, there is no mention of any attempt to facilitate greater participation through the provision of institutional or other forms of childcare.[4]

Women and work

When thinking about women and work in Timor-Leste, it is necessary to distinguish between the public and private sector, and in the latter between formal and informal sector occupations. As of 2013, Timor-Leste had a total population of approximately 1.18 million, of whom 696,200 were classified as being of working age (LFS 2015). Just 213,200 of these working-age Timorese were in the labour force. Of the 124,500 men and 65,300 women considered to be in employment, 45.1 per cent were located in services, 40.5 per cent in agriculture and 12.7 per cent in industry. As can be seen from Table 15.1, agriculture, community, social and personal services and hospitality and trade dominate female employment, together accounting for 83.5 per cent of working females.

It is important to note also that most Timorese are not employed in the formal sector, or even in waged positions. Some 166,600 were engaged exclusively in

Table 15.1 Working population 15 years of age and over by industry and sex, 2013

Sector (excludes subsistence agriculture)	*Male ('000s)*	*% Males working*	*Female ('000s)*	*% Females working*
Agriculture, forestry, hunting and fisheries	46.9	37.67	30.0	45.94
Community, social and personal services	32.9	26.43	15.0	22.97
Transportation, storage, and communications	13.4	10.76	2.3	3.52
Construction	11.3	9.08	0.4	0.61
Wholesale and retail trade, restaurants, hotels	7.7	6.18	9.5	14.55
Manufacturing	6	4.82	4.4	6.74
Finance, insurance, real estate, business services	2	1.61	1.7	2.60
Mining and quarrying	1.2	0.96	0.0	0.00
Electricity, gas and water	0.8	0.64	0.0	0.00
Other	2.3	1.85	2	3.06
Total	124.5	100.00	65.3	100.00

Source: Adapted from LFS (2015, 113).

subsistence agriculture (LFS 2015), and therefore not considered to be in the labour force. As Table 15.2 indicates, many of those who are in the labour force are own-account workers or contributing family workers. As the public sector provides employment for 54.6 per cent of all workers in waged employment, it is evident that the proportion of private sector waged workers outside the formal economy is extremely high, with more than half of all employers and as many as 34,300 employees located in the informal sector (LFS 2015).

Table 15.2 Status in employment by sex, 2013

Status (excludes subsistence agriculture)	*Male ('000s)*	*% Males working*	*Female ('000s)*	*% Females working*
Employee	60.6	48.67	29.5	45.18
Own-account worker	40.1	32.21	18.4	28.18
Contributing family worker	19.6	15.74	16.1	24.66
Employer	4.1	3.29	1.1	1.68
Other	0.1	0.08	0.2	0.31
Total	124.5	100.00	65.3	100.00

Source: Adapted from LFS (2015, 111).

Although opportunities for waged work are increasing for both men and women, this growth has had a differential effect. Wage-earning jobs tripled between 2001 and 2010 (Asian Development Bank 2014b). During this period, the proportion of economically active men in waged work increased from 14 per cent to 31 per cent. The proportion of economically active women in waged employment increased more modestly, rising from 9 per cent to 19 per cent. By 2013, just under 49 per cent of men and just under 30 per cent of women were waged employees (Table 15.2).

Many of the best formal sector jobs were in the public sector, where women are not particularly well represented even though 51 per cent of public sector jobs are in health and education (LFS 2015). Although women account for 33 per cent of waged workers, they hold just 29 per cent of public sector positions, spread unevenly across different domains (Asian Development Bank 2014b). Their presence in senior public service roles, at 35 per cent, has grown significantly since 2004, when women accounted for just 13 per cent of those positions. However, women remain under-represented at the highest level, where they hold just 16 per cent of positions.

In terms of occupational status more broadly, women and men are relatively evenly represented in the majority of occupational categories (Table 15.3). This may be in part because many high-level private sector jobs are occupied by foreign workers, who are not included in Labour Force Survey data. It is a requirement that lower level positions must be filled by Timorese, but labour market mismatches mean that Timor-Leste relies on foreigners to fill a significant proportion of managerial and technical positions (Interview with Director-General of SEPFOPE, July 2015).

Despite the relative flat employment structure for local workers, there are significant differences in income even among those in employment. In 2012, an official minimum wage was set for the first time at USD 115 per month. As of 2013, the mean monthly income among waged workers was USD 553 for men and USD 461 for women, though more than one-quarter of employees earned less than USD 181 per month (LFS 2015). Women's average earnings were lower in every occupational category except that of technicians and associate professionals, where they earn more than twice the amount earned by men (LFS 2015). However, women are under-represented in the low-income category, which accounts for 32 per cent of men and 15 per cent of women (LFS 2015). This is most likely explained by the fact that women are under-represented in the labour force and over-represented in subsistence agriculture. A significant proportion of these women and their families live in extreme poverty, which affects 37 per cent of rural households (Asian Development Bank 2014b).

Women, work and care

The low labour force participation rate for women in both urban and rural settings reflects the fact that men continue to be seen as the main income providers, with women primarily responsible for producing food for the household, childcare, and other unpaid domestic work (Asian Development Bank 2014b). The care burden is heavy. Timor-Leste has a very young population (Figure 15.1). Moreover,

Table 15.3 Working population by occupational category and sex, 2013

Category (excludes subsistence agriculture)	*Male ('000s)*	*% Males working*	*Female ('000s)*	*% Females working*
Managers	7.6	6.10	3.7	5.67
Professionals	12.3	9.87	6.3	9.65
Technicians and associate professionals	6.7	5.38	2.0	3.06
Clerical support workers	3.6	2.89	2.6	3.98
Service and sales workers	20.9	16.79	12.8	19.60
Skilled agricultural, forestry and fishery workers	44.4	35.66	29.7	45.48
Craft and related trades workers	14.9	11.97	3.4	5.21
Machine operators and assemblers	9.3	7.47	1.2	1.84
Elementary occupations	3.3	2.65	2.8	4.29
Other	1.3	1.04	0.8	1.23
Total	124.5	100.00	65.3	100.00

Source: Adapted from LFS (2015, 114).

according to the 2010 census, its dependency rate is one of the highest in the world, with 78 children and nine elderly people for every 100 people of working age (Asian Development Bank 2014b).

As women marry early – a significant proportion before the age of twenty – their reproductive years constitute a significant proportion of their adult life. The overall labour force participation rate for married women aged 25–54 years is just 27 per cent. The rate is significantly higher among divorced, widowed and single women at between 37 and 41 per cent (LFS 2015). By comparison, men's labour force participation rate peaks at 64.8 per cent between the ages of 30 and 34 (LFS 2015).

Women's low levels of labour force participation during their reproductive years are explained in large part by their care work responsibilities. When asked in 2013 why they were not in the labour market, over half of the 78.7 per cent of females aged 15 years and above who were not economically active cited family duties as the primary reason for their inactivity (LFS 2015). This situation reflects the fact that there is very little in the way of institutional support for the provision of care in Timor-Leste, which has virtually no infrastructure for childcare or early childhood education. Only 11 per cent of those between the ages of three and six attend one of the 180 preschools in the country (RDTL 2011). There is even less support for the elderly, the majority of whom live in isolated rural areas where they have difficulty accessing primary healthcare as a consequence of poor infrastructure, poverty or physical disability (RDTL 2011).

In terms of financial support, Timor-Leste spends 15 per cent of its non-oil GDP on social security; however, 60 per cent of this budget is allocated to

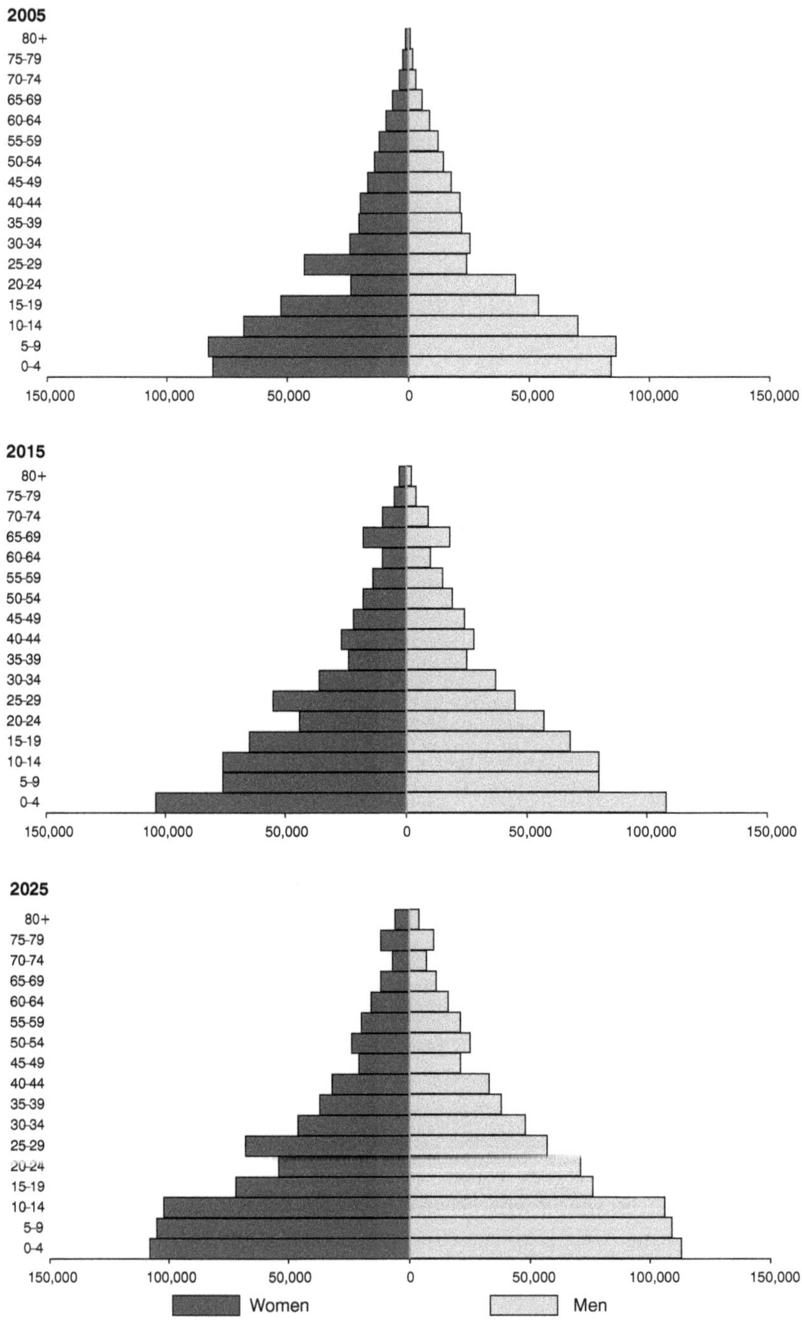

Figure 15.1 Population 2005, 2015, and 2025

Source: World Bank (2015).

veterans' pensions (World Bank 2013).[5] Although the work-related social security system is currently limited to civil servants and their families, there are plans to develop a contributory social security scheme that covers both public and private sector workers and their families (RDTL 2011). A universal basic pension scheme has been in place since 2008 for the elderly and people with severe disabilities, providing benefits of USD 30 per month (RDTL 2011). As of 2012, 84,569 people were in receipt of the elderly benefit and 5,558 people were in receipt of the disabled benefit (World Bank 2013). The scheme for the elderly has been relatively successful, with only 13 per cent of the eligible population claiming not to be in receipt of the pension despite significant challenges in terms of distribution, with nearly one-third of elderly respondents travelling over 90 minutes to collect a lump sum twice yearly (World Bank 2013).[6] The pension scheme has been far less effective for people with disabilities, with as many as 86 per cent of eligible people not in receipt of the pension (World Bank 2013).

The other major welfare programme with implications for women with care responsibilities is a scheme called Bolsa da Mãe (Mother's Purse), which was established primarily to support female-headed households where a male breadwinner had died or been incapacitated during the Indonesian occupation or subsequent conflicts. As of 2012, 15,150 children were in receipt of the first iteration of Bolsa da Mãe, which provided benefits of USD 40 per annum for primary students, USD 80 per annum for secondary students and USD 160 per annum for university students. The scheme was subsequently adapted in 2012, when transfer criteria shifted from individual vulnerable children to vulnerable families identified through a household vulnerability score and paid to a value determined by the number of children (to a maximum of five aged 17 or under) who meet the programme criteria (World Bank 2013). However, the programme has limited coverage and the level of benefits is too low to significantly improve households' financial situation (World Bank 2013), which in turn limits its capacity to facilitate the greater involvement of these women in economic activity beyond subsistence agriculture.

While the physical and financial burden of care is greatest for poor women, it also affects the likelihood of highly educated women engaging in paid work. The 2012 Labour Law recognises the 'eminent social value' of maternity and paternity. It guarantees maternal rights including 12 weeks paid maternity leave and four weeks paid leave in cases of miscarriage, time off for medical appointments during pregnancy, pre-natal leave in cases of medical risk, breastfeeding breaks for the first six months of a child's life, a guaranteed return to the same or an equivalent position at the same rate of pay, adjustment of duties on return to work, and protection against dismissal because of pregnancy, breast- or bottle feeding (RDTL 2012). Provisions are also made for five days of paid paternity leave and up to five days unpaid parental leave for childcare responsibilities pertaining to children under 10 years of age. In practice, however, these benefits are not always accessible, even in large formal sector workplaces. Many women are accorded maternity leave but not paid for it, or are paid a proportion of their salary only. There is also evidence that some large companies, including major banks, require women to undertake not to marry within the first year of employment or to fall pregnant for the first five years (Interviews, July 2015).

Perhaps even more concerning in the long term is the impact of a lack of quality institutional care on highly skilled women's decisions to remain in the paid workforce. In its absence, domestic workers – or perhaps nannies – are most likely to fill that gap. Domestic work is not recorded in the census, but according to the Working Women's Centre Timor-Leste, there are at least 159 domestic workers from the districts employed in live-in positions in Dili, in addition to local women who work each day for a family but live with their own families rather than living with their employers. However many Dili-based professional couples are concerned at the prospect of leaving their children with a non-family member who may not share their child-rearing values, particularly as they pertain to physical discipline. As a consequence, upon starting a family, many reluctantly conclude that they have no choice but for one partner – generally the woman – to give up paid work (Interviews, July 2015). Yet despite increasing demands on the urban middle class to find satisfactory alternatives to familial care, these concerns have been largely eclipsed by broader debates about women's status in Timorese society, their representation within government and efforts to reduce domestic violence.

Gender politics in a post-conflict context

As evidenced in the broader literature, contestation around the role of women is very common in post-conflict societies because conflict disturbs established gender norms. As Niner (2011) observes, Timorese gender norms were disrupted in two discrete ways during the Indonesian occupation. On the one hand, some elite and middle-class women were drawn into the public sphere through employment in the public service and their involvement in state-sponsored women's organisations and NGOs. On the other hand, women of varying socio-economic status played an important role in the resistance movement and in communities where men had been killed or were absent. Both of these elements to a greater or lesser extent disrupted 'traditional' expectations of women, who could possess symbolic or ritual power but did not participate in public or political decision-making. In the transition to a post-conflict society, concerns around women's failure to return to earlier social norms played out in public debate. Indeed, as Niner (2012, 243) writes, 'a portion of the senior male political leadership has patriotically promoted a "traditional" indigenous culture while denigrating international "gender equity" policies as foreign impositions'.

References to gender equality in the Constitution and successive development plans reflect a concerted effort by government, its international advisors and Timorese feminists to increase women's participation in the public sphere.[7] Yet despite legislative and policy measures designed to improve women's participation in many areas of social, political and economic life in Timor-Leste, deep tensions exist between the messages conveyed through foreign-funded development and civic education programmes about women's rights and perceptions of the appropriateness of what many see as foreign values. As Hall (2009, 317) has argued, 'new norms of gender equality and women's rights were not readily accepted by the political elite nor the large majority of East Timorese'; indeed '[m]any East Timorese saw a clear dichotomy between women's rights – equated with Western modernity – and tradition [and] NGOs promoting women's rights were seen as destroyers of East Timorese traditional culture'.[8] There were also concerns about the politics of norm diffusion, as expressed by Xanana Gusmão in his 2000 New Year's Eve message. Addressing his countrymen and women during the transition to independence, Gusmão warned of the dangers of 'obsessive acculturation to the standards that hundreds of international experts try to convey to the East Timorese', standards that have not been realised in those experts' home countries, among them standards related to gender (Gusmão 2000). While these concerns are undoubtedly valid, the premise that efforts to increase women's participation in public life are somehow an anathema to Timorese cultural values is deeply contested by Timorese feminists (Charlesworth and Wood 2002).

The deep contradictions borne of these competing impulses is nowhere more evident than in the political arena, which has been an important focus for women activists and international organisations concerned with increasing women's participation in public life. A quota was introduced under Law No.6/2006 on the Election of the National Parliament that required one in four candidates for the national parliament to be female. It also imposed special conditions to ensure that if a female member of parliament vacates her position, she is replaced by another woman (RDTL 2006). The law was amended in 2011 to increase the requirement for female candidates to one in three. Women won 25 of the 65 parliamentary seats in the 2012 national elections, giving Timor-Leste one of the highest proportions of women parliamentarians in the world. It has been blatantly obvious, however, that presence does not necessarily translate into power. Although women members of parliament report that they are less likely to be seen as ineffective than was the case in the early years of independence (Wigglesworth 2013), senior figures acknowledge that there remains much to be done to ensure that women can take on a 'full role' in parliament (Gusmão 2014).

A quota also exists for female participation in village (*suco*) councils. Under Decree Law No.5/2004 on Community Authorities, Timor-Leste's 442 *suco* councils must include two women and two people under 30 years of age, one of whom is female (RDTL 2004). These provisions were maintained in Decree Law No. 3/2009 on Community Leadership and their Election, which is also known as the Village (*Suco*) Law. In the 2009 elections, a total of 1,300 women occupied reserved seats in the country's 442 *suco* councils; 11 of these held the position of *suco* chief (Cummins 2011). However, as one foreign advisor observed, '[t]he village law says that women must be represented, and they are, but they are making coffee. They're not allowed to engage in decision-making' (Interview, July 2015). Cummins (2011, 89), who reports similar observations, concludes that 'local politics [is] a difficult space [for women] to navigate because of rigid notions of gender and class', which are exacerbated by the 'burdens of caring for their family' including responsibility for domestic and agricultural work.[9]

As with women's representation in politics, Timorese feminists achieved legislative change ahead of changes in attitudes to domestic violence, which is widely recognised as a 'pressing social problem' (UNDP 2013, 1).[10] When female respondents in the 2009–10 Demographic and Health Survey were asked if they had been pushed, shaken or had something thrown at them; slapped, had their arm twisted or hair pulled; been punched or hit; kicked; choked or burned; threatened or attacked with a knife, gun or other weapon; forced to have had sexual intercourse or to perform unwanted sexual acts, 38 per cent reported that they had been subjected to one or more of these forms of violence since the age of 15. This number included the more than 30 per cent of married women who had been subjected to one or more of these behaviours by their current partner (DHS 2010, 226–230).

At the same time, domestic violence is a relatively new concern even among activists. Hall (2009, 315) cites a former director of a long-standing women's NGO called Forum Komunikasi Untuk Perempuan Loro Sae (FOKUPERS) as saying that before 2000 'even she had thought domestic violence was "normal"'. Having decided to shift their focus from violence perpetrated upon women during the Indonesian occupation and the transition period to women's experiences of domestic violence, FOKUPERS staff were shocked to be told during community consultations in 2003 that economic and other issues, not domestic violence, were of primary concern to women (FOKUPERS, cited in Hunt 2017). In an attempt to drive change from above, the National Movement against Domestic Violence engaged in lobbying efforts that led to the passing of Law No.7/2010 on Domestic Violence (RDTL 2010). Attitudinal change has, however, been less forthcoming; in 2009–10, when respondents were asked by the Demographic and Health Survey team whether wife beating is ever acceptable, 80 per cent of men and 86 per cent of women indicated that there were indeed circumstances in which it was (DHS 2010).

The importance of economic empowerment was recognised in the plan of action released by the 2008 National East Timor Women's Congress, which provided a detailed analysis of priority issues and recommendations relating to culture, education, health, the economy, media, politics and justice (Rede Feto 2008). Yet while the plan focuses on issues such as literacy, access to education, healthcare, employment and micro-credit – in addition to domestic violence and cultural practices such as polygamy and *barlake* (payment of a dowry) that activists believe disadvantage women – there is no mention whatsoever of work and care. As this suggests, the relatively strong focus on women, work and care in the 2002 National Development Plan had fallen off the agenda, not only of the government but also of the women's movement, in favour of these more pressing concerns. In short, while consideration of the work/care nexus are clearly a vital element of a long-term agenda, its insertion into broader debates would require a more sophisticated account of its role in supporting women's economic empowerment, and the public goods generated by greater participation of women in economic activities outside subsistence agriculture, than is currently evident in the Timorese context.

Pressure points

At a time when Timor-Leste's economic and political structures remain relatively fluid, the women's movement has a critical part to play in developing an argument around the relationship between women's economic empowerment and the construction of adequate care infrastructure that meets the needs of Timorese women and their households, and in prosecuting that argument within the political sphere and at other levels of Timorese society. In the absence of such efforts, the emergence of focused policy discussion on work and care is likely to depend on the capacity of professional women to access quality non-familial care if they wish to continue in their careers after starting a family. And, given the paucity of institutional care facilities for children – or indeed the elderly – home-based non-familial care is likely to emerge as a more viable alternative for middle-class families than institutional care in the short to medium term.

Considered to be an important issue internationally, the status of the domestic workers most likely to provide home-based non-familial care is already attracting attention, most notably through the efforts of the Working Women's Centre Timor-Leste. Activists advocate the recognition of domestic work as work under the 2012 Labour Law, which would require limiting domestic workers' normal hours of work to 44 hours per week and a maximum of 12 hours per day, as well as payment of the minimum wage.[11] Activists acknowledge that if domestic workers were to be paid at this level – which is significantly above current market rates – vocational training would be required to improve the skills of domestic workers (Interview with WWCTL Coordinator, July 2015). They are already engaged in high-level policy discussions with government about the domestic work agenda, but it remains to be seen if they have the capacity to achieve either of these aims.

It is significant that a women's NGO, not the trade union movement, has focused on paid domestic work and thus engaged at least peripherally with the broader issue of work and care. The Working Women's Centre Timor-Leste has strong links to female trade union activists in Australia through the Australian union movement's Solidarity Support Organisation, Union Aid Abroad – APHEDA, as well as connections with domestic worker organisations internationally, among them some domestic worker unions (Interviews with WWCTL Coordinator and APHEDA Country Coordinator, July 2015). Yet although the Timorese trade union movement also has a close relationship with APHEDA, work and care is not on its agenda (Interviews with trade union leaders, July 2015). In a context where trade unions are relatively new, their bargaining position is fragile. Moreover, the fact that legislative requirements regarding maternity leave and return to work conditions are already relatively strong means that this lack of attention to work and care is not surprising. It also means, however, that more serious consideration of the impact of continuing reliance on familial care is likely to fall almost entirely to the women's movement – if, indeed, it decides that the balance between paid work and care work is an issue worthy of pursuit.

Notes

1 As used in this chapter, the term 'Timorese' refers exclusively to residents of Timor-Leste, and not to people living in Indonesian West Timor or elsewhere.
2 The study on which this chapter is based was conducted as part of an Australian Research Council Future Fellowship project entitled *'Trade Unionism and Trade Union Aid in Indonesia, Malaysia and Timor-Leste'* (FT120100778).
3 For a discussion of gender politics and governance under UNTAET, see Charlesworth and Wood (2002).
4 The 'Platform for Action for the Advancement of Women of Timor Lorosae', formulated at the first national East Timor Women's Congress, identified a number of areas of concern, including law and order, justice, violence, institution-building and poverty. Hunt (2017) notes that this document was used by UNTAET's Gender Affairs Unit as a basis for policy development.
5 About 26 per cent of recipients of the veterans' pension are women.
6 In July 2013, I witnessed pension day in Maubisse, a hill town 70 kilometres southwest of Dili. Hundreds of elderly recipients arrived on foot and on horseback and waited several hours for the distribution of funds by the district head.
7 For a critical discussion of aid organisations' co-option of the concept of culture, see Silva and Simião (2017).
8 See examples of this cited in de Araujo (2005). See also Molnar (2010, 67–68) for a particularly striking example of potential pitfalls associated with well-meaning attempts to change attitudes towards gender roles. Molnar describes how village women undertaking a civic education course interpreted messages about women's right to vote as meaning that they could call the 'gender police' if their husbands did not follow their lead at the ballot box.
9 For examples of more positive experiences among female *suco* chiefs, see Wigglesworth (2013).
10 There is a significant literature, mostly consisting of reports, on domestic violence in Timor-Leste. For an account examining the male perspective, see Myrtinnen (2012).
11 For a broader discussion of the Labour Law and industrial relations institutions and actors, see Ford (2016).

References

Araujo, M. de. 2005. Oxfam and Partners in East Timor: Creating a Voice for Women and Carving a Space for that Voice. In *Challenges and Possibilities: International Organizations and Women in Timor-Leste,* edited by D. Grenfell and A. Trembath, 14–16. Melbourne: Globalism Institute, RMIT University.

Asian Development Bank. 2014a. *Pacific Private Sector Development Initiative: Progress Report 2013–2014.* Manila: Asian Development Bank.

Asian Development Bank. 2014b. *Timor-Leste: Country Gender Assessment.* Manila: Asian Development Bank.

Charlesworth, H. and M. Wood. 2002. "Women and Human Rights in the Rebuilding of East Timor." *Nordic Journal of International Law* 71: 325–348.

Cummins, D. 2011. "The Problem of Gender Quotas: Women's Representatives on Timor-Leste's *Suku* Councils." *Development in Practice* 21 (1): 85–95.

DHS. 2010. *Timor-Leste Demographic and Health Survey 2009–2010.* Dili: National Statistics Directorate and the Ministry of Finance.

Dibley, T. 2014. *Partnerships, Power and Peacebuilding: NGOs as Agents of Peace in Aceh and Timor-Leste*, London: Palgrave Macmillan.

Ford, M. 2016. "The Making of Timorese Industrial Relations." *Journal of Industrial Relations* 58 (2): 243–257.

Gusmão, X. 2000. New Year's Message. http://www.etan.org/et2001a/january/01-06/01xanan.htm.

Gusmão, X. 2014. Address by His Excellency the Prime Minister of the Democratic Republic of Timor-Leste Kay Rala Xanana Gusmão to the Gender in Parliament International Conference Hosted by the National Parliament of Timor-Leste. Dili, 23 October. http://timor-leste.gov.tl/wp-content/uploads/2014/10/Gender-in-Parliament-23.10.14.pdf.

Hall, N. 2009. "East Timorese Women Challenge Domestic Violence." *Australian Journal of Political Science* 44 (2): 309–325.

Hill, H. and J. Saldanha. 2001. "The Key Issues". In *East Timor: Development Challenges for the World's Newest Nation*, edited by H. Hill and J. Saldanha, 3–38. Singapore: Institute of Southeast Asian Studies.

Hunt, J. 2017. "FOKUPERS – The East Timorese Women's Communication Forum: The Development of Timor's First Women's NGO". In *Women and the Politics of Gender in Post-Conflict Timor-Leste: Between Heaven and Earth*, 65–82, edited by S. Niner. Abingdon: Routledge.

Leach, M. and D. Kingsbury. eds. 2013. *The Politics of Timor-Leste: Democratic Consolidation after Intervention*. Ithaca, NY: Cornell University Press.

LFS. 2015. *Timor-Leste Labour Force Survey 2013*. Dili: Ministry of Finance and SEPFOPE.

Molnar, A. 2010. *Timor-Leste: Politics, History, and Culture*. Abingdon: Routledge.

Myrtinnen, H. 2012. "Violence, Masculinities and Patriarchy in Post-conflict Timor-Leste." In *Men and Masculinities in Southeast Asia*, edited by M. Ford and L. Lyons, 103–120. Abingdon: Routledge.

Niner, S. 2011. "Hakat Klot, Narrow Steps." *International Feminist Journal of Politics* 13 (3): 413–435.

Niner, S. 2012. "Between Earth and Heaven: The Politics of Gender." In *The Politics of Timor-Leste: Democratic Consolidation after Intervention*, edited by M. Leach and D. Kingsbury, 239–258. Ithaca: Cornell Southeast Asia Program Publications.

RDTL. 2002. *East Timor National Development Plan*. Dili: Planning Commission.

RDTL. 2004. *Decree Law No.5/2004 on Community Authorities*. Dili: RDTL.

RDTL. 2006. *Law No.6/2006 on the Election of the National Parliament*. Dili: RDTL.

RDTL. 2010. *Law No.7/2010 on Domestic Violence*. Dili: RDTL.

RDTL. 2011. *Timor-Leste Strategic Development Plan, 2011–2030*. Dili: RDTL.

RDTL. 2012. *Law No.4/2012 on the Labour Code*. Dili: RDTL.

Rede Feto. 2008. *Plan of Actions East Timor Women 2008–2012*. Dili: Rede Feto.

SEAPRI. 2013. *National Strategy and Action Plan for Gender and the Private Sector, 2014–2017*. Dili: SEAPRI.

SEPI. 2014. *Timor-Leste Beijing Platform for Action National Review and Appraisal Report*. Dili: SEPI.

Silva, K. and D. Simião. 2017. "Negotiating Culture and Gender Expectations in Timor-Leste: Ambiguities in Post-colonial Governance Strategies." In *Women and the Politics of Gender in Post-Conflict Timor-Leste: Between Heaven and Earth*, 187–206, edited by S. Niner. Abingdon: Routledge.

Sugden, C. 2012. *Is Timor-Leste's Growth Inclusive?* Manila: Asian Development Bank.

UNDP. 2013. *Breaking the Cycle of Domestic Violence in Timor-Leste: Access to Justice Options, Barriers, and Decision Making Processes in the Context of Legal Pluralism*. Dili: UNDP.

Wigglesworth, A. 2013. "Community Leadership and Gender Equality: Experiences of Representation in Local Governance in Timor-Leste." *Asian Politics & Policy* 5(4): 567–584.

World Bank. 2013. *Timor-Leste Social Assistance Public Expenditure and Program Performance Report.* Washington DC: World Bank.

World Bank. 2015. *Health Nutrition and Population Statistics: Population Estimates and Projections.* http://databank.worldbank.org/Data/Views/VariableSelection/SelectVariables.aspx?source=Health%20Nutrition%20and%20Population%20Statistics:%20Population%20estimates%20and%20projections.

16 Papua New Guinea

Work and care in a subsistence economy

Jane Parker, James Arrowsmith and Anne Boyd

Papua New Guinea is by far the largest island country in the South Pacific and the most diverse in terms of geography and population. It was formed from Papua, a British colony that came under Australian administration in 1884, and New Guinea, a German colony ceded to Australia at the end of the First World War. Governance institutions were reformed by the Papua and New Guinea Act of 1949, which provided for a Legislative Council, judicial system, civil service and local government, and a House of Assembly was established in 1964. The country gained independence from Australia in 1975 and remains a member of the British Commonwealth with the Queen as head of state.

The economy of Papua New Guinea reflects the country's profound and uneven development. It is dominated by the informal sector, and subsistence agriculture is the main source of living for 85 per cent of the population. Most people live in remote settlements, in which over 850 languages are spoken. The pidgin language Tok Pisin is widely used alongside English, which is taught in schools (Cunningham, Ingram and Sumbuk 2006). The small formal private-sector economy is dominated by large multi-national companies involved in the export of natural resources, especially copper, gold and oil. Demand for commodities has driven strong economic growth, with GDP rising from USD 3 billion in 2003 to USD 16.7 billion in 2011. This has also boosted government expenditure; in 2006 mining and petroleum taxes alone accounted for 36 per cent of all state revenues. This trend is expected to continue as a major liquefied natural gas (LNG) project, the ExxonMobil venture, begins to come on stream. ExxonMobil has invested USD 4.42 billion in Papua New Guinea, with 9,000 Papua New Guineans (and a further 12,000 expatriates) working on the project at peak employment in 2012. Production commenced in 2014 and it is expected that over nine trillion cubic feet of gas will be sold (PNG LNG 2015).

Nonetheless, Papua New Guinea remains one of the world's poorest countries and is a major recipient of foreign aid. Australia is Papua New Guinea's largest aid donor, contributing almost 70 per cent of the country's total official development assistance (CIA 2012; OECD 2014). Socio-economic and political challenges facing the country include poor infrastructure; land tenure issues; endemic health and law and order problems; inadequate public services; corruption; lack of access to capital; and the effects of rapid population growth and urbanisation (CIA 2012). All these factors compound social problems in terms of employment, housing, education, health and access to clean water, and have particular implications for the role of women in households and at work.

The work/care regime in context

In 2011, the population of Papua New Guinea was 7.1 million, distributed across some 1.4 million households (NSO 2011a). Almost nine out of ten people (87 per cent of the population) were based in rural settlements. As in many developing countries, the population is very young. More than a third are children aged under 15, and a further fifth are young people aged between 15 and 24 years. The middle and older age groups are in a minority, with only 36.2 per cent aged between 25 and 54, 5.2 per cent aged between 55 and 64 and just 3.9 per cent aged 65 or over (Figure 16.1). The population pyramid is therefore very bottom heavy due to a relatively high fertility rate (4.3 live births per woman) and low life expectancy (58.7 years for women and 56.8 years for men at birth). This means that much of the work and care burden for women is defined by child dependency rather than eldercare, as relatively few people survive into dependent old age. The elderly are still typically cared for by children and/or grandchildren on the basis of inter-generational reciprocity, within a wider collectivist village framework. This means that any burden associated with care is shared, including between the sexes (Diamond 2012). This model of village care is, however, increasingly challenged by features of modernisation such as urban drift (von Poser 2011). It will also be challenged by demographic change, with the population profile shifting from pyramid to pillar in recent decades due to improved healthcare and declining birth rates.

The status of women varies throughout the regions and provinces of Papua New Guinea, which reflects the country's high diversity of cultures (Brouwer, Harris and Tanaka 1998). The Highlands region, for example, is very patriarchal, differing from matrilineal provinces such as Milne Bay where women's customary rights over land provide a measure of authority for women. In general, however, there are three features of work and care that are common to women's experience across the country. First, women are typically engaged in work, mostly in the informal economy. Second, there are serious problems relating to ill-health and often crime and violence. Third, there is limited social support from the state.

Women and work

The collection and veracity of labour market data are severely limited in Papua New Guinea (ILO 2008). There is no Labour Force Survey and *ad hoc* surveys such as the Household Income and Expenditure Survey (HIES), most recently conducted in 2010, contain very few work-related questions (see NSO 2011b). Even the official national census contains minimal information relating to work (ILO 2013a). It does, however, suggest that, in 2011, Papua New Guinea had a working age population (15–54 years) of 3.8 million, 1.8 million of whom were

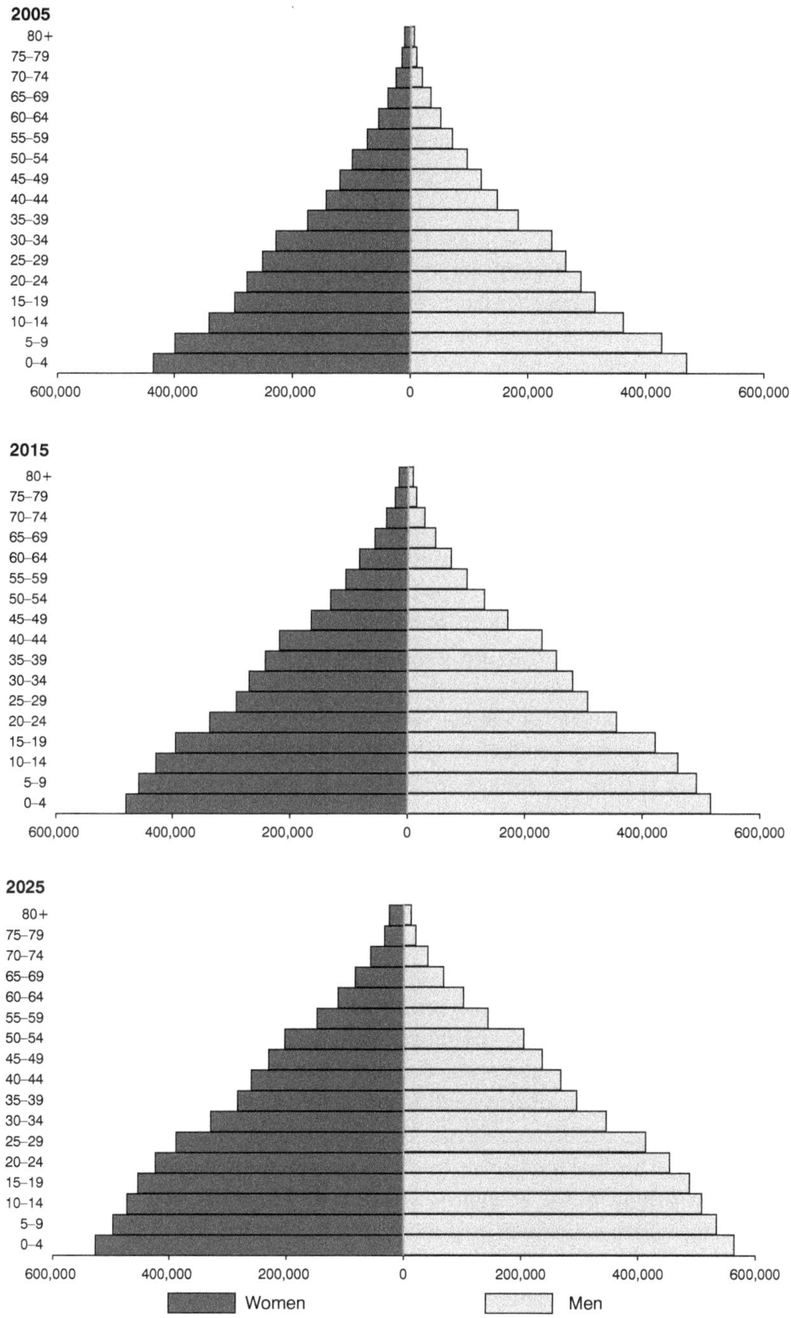

Figure 16.1 Population 2005, 2015, and 2025

Source: World Bank (2015).

women. It also estimates a higher labour force participation rate for women, at 74.2 per cent compared with 71.6 per cent for men. The distribution of males and females by industry and occupation is also not known with certainty. Piecemeal data indicates that women have virtually no opportunity to work in forestry; their informal involvement in the fishing industry accounts for 20 to 50 per cent of the annual yields; and there are not many job opportunities for women in urban areas and the formal sector (JICA 2010; ILO 1998).

There has traditionally been no concept of the male 'breadwinner' in Papua New Guinea, with women confined to the home or engaged in supplementary work. Women routinely perform important non-care, productive work in addition to home and family labour (Imbun 2006). As for men, this work is conducted overwhelmingly in the informal sector. Only 5 per cent of women and 15.2 per cent of men are in waged employment (Government of PNG and UN Development System 2007). The lower rate of female participation in the formal economy, and lower rates of pay, have been linked to discrimination and educational disadvantage (Johnson 1993). Notwithstanding this, in urban areas, more and more men are becoming family breadwinners, while women are confined to housework. Moreover, it has been reported that 'men seem to think that bringing home the money allows them to control the housewives' daily routine, and in case of non-compliance, gives them the right of physical punishment' (Gönitzer 2003, 66).

Most women and men work in household-based subsistence agriculture and on smallholdings (which may be owned by the wider family or community), where some production goes to market (ILO 2012). It is estimated that women produce over 80 per cent of Papua New Guinea's food and undertake 60 to 70 per cent of work in crop production (ILO 2013a). Most tilling, planting, weeding and harvesting is done by women, with men focusing on heavier manual labour (Bourke and Harwood 2009). According to von Poser (2011, 4), subsistence living in Papua New Guinea 'basically relies on harmony in male–female relations ... gender complementarity is significant for maintaining a sociable life within the extended web of relationships'. Women are also commonly involved in the production of clothing and crafts for cash or barter. Around half the total number of women engage in market trading, compared with one in three men (IFC 2010).

The extent of family labour also means that it is not easy or necessarily useful to differentiate in the Papua New Guinea context between the unpaid contribution of women in 'productive' labour and that directed towards the social reproduction of labour through caring (Razavi and Staab 2012). Child labour is extensive and it is estimated that children comprise around one-fifth of the active labour force (Singh 2009). This is largely due to the dominance of subsistence agriculture, forestry and fishing in the economy, although child labour is also found in the formal sector where it is driven by poverty, poor education and rapid urbanisation. Children may also support adult family employees involved in plantations or commercial trading and manufacturing work (e.g. Simon 2009). As a consequence, though much child labour is benign, there is also widespread abuse of child workers and evidence of children's engagement in risky activities such as street working and commercial sexual exploitation (ILO 2011). Child trafficking is also a problem, linked to customary practices around debt settlement, adoption and child marriage. Boys and girls alike perform labour as part of their household and family obligations, but some of the worst forms of child labour disproportionally impact on girls as they are more likely to be used as indentured labour in domestic service or trafficked to pay off debts (ILO 2013b).

Women and care

Women in Papua New Guinea generally face two sets of severe challenges in their care roles due to high levels of ill health and domestic violence, which impact directly on them and on those for whom they care. Communicable diseases, including pneumonia, malaria, tuberculosis, diarrheal diseases, meningitis and HIV/AIDS, account for around half of all deaths in Papua New Guinea (WHO 2011). According to the Household Income and Expenditure Survey, nearly one in three people suffered from a disease, and one in five reported that this disrupted their daily activities. Around half of the respondents said they did not seek treatment when unwell, with the biggest problem being distance to a health facility (World Bank Group in PNG 2013). The government has inaugurated a policy of free primary healthcare, but this has yet to have significant impact in remote areas (UNDP 2014a), and healthcare provision for most people is either non-functioning or non-existent (PNG Department of Health 2013). The current rate of 0.58 primary health professionals per 1,000 people falls well short of the WHO minimum standard of 2.5 (Australian Doctors International 2015).

A lack of professional healthcare services means that the care burden is intensified for households in general and women in particular. It especially impacts on women in pregnancy and early childcare. The maternal mortality rate is the second highest in the world (733 deaths per 100,000 live births) as fewer than half (48 per cent) of rural births are attended by skilled health personnel, compared with 88 per cent in urban areas (UNDP 2014a). The infant (under-five) mortality rate is 7.4 per 100 live births (NSO 2013), and 48 per cent of children under five are physically underdeveloped (World Bank Group in PNG 2013).

Domestic, criminal and tribal violence is also rife in many areas. An estimated three-quarters of women and children have experienced violence, which is primarily domestic (ILO 2013a; UN 2005).[1] This includes sexual abuse, with half of these having experienced forced sex (ILO 2012). Much gender violence is linked to deep-seated traditional cultural beliefs and practices, including polygamy, child marriage, 'bride price' customs, sorcery and witchcraft including 'witch hunts' based on voodoo (ILO 2012; UNICEF 2012). The level and nature of violence in Papua New Guinea, and that directed towards women, varies greatly by region. Data and research are rare, although an early important study by the Law Reform Commission (1987, 1992) found that the acceptability of wife-beating ranged from 17 per cent of men and 7 per cent of women in New Ireland to 95 per cent of men and 98 per cent of women in the Eastern Highlands. Notwithstanding this variation in cultural expectations and practice, a recent gender assessment by the World Bank (2012, 12) stated that 'the high prevalence of such violence in Papua New Guinea is a cross-cutting issue, with very serious implications for public health and social policy, economic development, and justice and law enforcement'.

At the same time, gender violence is also driven by the social dislocation associated with increased modernity. This combines urbanisation and youth unemployment in the cities together with increased poverty and rural decay in traditional communities, where inter-generational ties are eroding (Chandler 2014). There is a growing problem of substance abuse amongst young people and a continued failure by the state to provide mechanisms for the enforcement of formal legal rights and judicial redress (Jolly, Stewart and Brewer 2014). Police are woefully under-resourced and insufficiently interested in or trained to respond to issues such as domestic violence. They have very limited presence across most of the country, and communities police themselves according to customary law. Again, these violence and crime issues impact on women directly and in their role as primary carers (UNDP 2014a). In the recent Household Income and Expenditure Survey, for example, only 39 per cent of women reported that 'crime does not stop me from doing anything' compared with 63 per cent of men (World Bank Group in PNG 2013).

Women and the state

The state has a very limited role or profile outside the main urban areas, whether in terms of healthcare, policing or the judicial system, as noted above. The same applies to wider social security and even the provision of roads and other infrastructure such as utilities. The minimalist state means that notwithstanding increased government expenditure and developments in policy and law (see below), there is a profound lack of state support for women, whether at work or in the home.

One of the outstanding limitations of the state is the lack of social or welfare provision (Majid 2014). There are plans to develop social security systems using the returns from a sovereign wealth fund that was established in 2011 (ILO 2012). As yet, however, there is no system of unemployment benefit or social assistance, including state pensions, in Papua New Guinea, although there is an occupational superannuation scheme for public sector employees that was extended to firms in the private sector with 15 or more employees in 2002. These pensions may also be partly accessed in the event of unemployment, but they cover only a very small minority of workers.

Although it is mainly met by self-organised forms of social assistance, the gap in state welfare is also addressed in very small part by business initiatives. There is some provision by large businesses (particularly in the primary sector) of subsidised housing, education and healthcare as a means to maintain and retain a productive workforce (Thomason and Hancock 2011). These activities also demonstrate corporate social responsibility, given controversies around the negative impact of mining and plantations on local communities. For example, in addition to beneficial reward practices such as revenue sharing, since 2009 Ok Tedi Mining Limited has funded the North Fly Health Services Development

Programme that has brought significant improvements in maternal and child health (UNDP 2014a). It also has a zero-tolerance domestic violence policy for its staff at Tabubil.

However, given the limited scope of direct employment, most people rely on the customary system of 'wantok' for assistance. The wantok (literally 'one talk' in Tok Pisin) system describes the connection of people through family and/or place. It has strong pre-colonial origins in the tribal identities associated with language, as well as techniques of defence and conquest, whereby small village communities competed with each other over resources (Roscoe 2000). Today, wantok obligations are defined more by mutual support mechanisms and increasingly involve cash transfers whereby earnings are used to assist extended families and offer favours to others in the network (Singh and Nadarajah 2011; also Imbun 2006). These transfers are commonly extended to women, for example, to provide for children's school fees or assist in producing and selling market garden produce. At the same time, women's earnings may be used to support those migrating to urban areas in search of jobs, or to host visiting wantoks. Hence, it is not a simple matter to say whether the wantok system benefits or disadvantages women in work and care terms, as the concept is collective and less defined by gender and immediate family networks. Its application also varies according to circumstance, on an understanding of give and take.

The most positive aspect of state support for communities generally and for females in particular is support for schooling. The introduction of free (though not compulsory) basic education, which became fully effective in 2012, led to a jump in the enrolment rate from 53 per cent in 2007 to 75 per cent in 2010 (OECD 2012). This benefited girls in particular (the male rate increased only marginally, from 73 to 77 per cent), though gender disparities are wider in provinces where schools are more remote from village settlements. This is linked to increasing state investment in basic education and health. Government expenditure more than doubled in real terms between 2002 and 2012 on the back of the commodities boom. This has also had the effect of significantly enhancing employment and leadership opportunities for women (Table 16.1).

Concerns remain over the quality of provision due to inadequate facilities and teacher numbers (UNICEF 2012; World Bank Group in PNG 2013). These intensify at the post-primary level, where gender disparities in participation increase. Currently, at the secondary level, only 67 girls are enrolled for every

Table 16.1 Women in primary school and health clinic leadership and working roles (%)

	Principals		*Teachers (grade 5)*		*Health managers*		*Health workers*
	2002	*2012*	*2002*	*2012*	*2002*	*2012*	*2012*
Overall	13	27	27	55	36	41	52
Government	15	31	27	59	49	57	40
Church	10	19	26	49	29	36	73

Source: Howes et al. (2014).

100 boys and the rate drops to 63 per cent in tertiary education (NSO 2013). There is also a major legacy of disadvantage. Just 6.8 per cent of women aged 25 years or older, and 14.1 per cent of men, have had at least some secondary education (UNDP 2014a). A lack of vocational education and training provision also adversely impacts on access to the labour market generally, including for women (ILO 2013a).

Regulating work and care

One legacy of Papua New Guinea's close links with Australia is a system of labour laws informed by Australian practice and the conventions and recommendations of the International Labour Organisation, which Papua New Guinea joined the year after independence (UN 2007). The state has ratified the International Labour Organisation's eight fundamental Conventions, one priority Convention and 17 other technical Conventions, including standards relating to maternity protection, termination of employment and minimum wages. In total, Papua New Guinea has ratified 26 International Labour Organisation Conventions, of which 24 remain in force (ILO 2015). It also ratified the Convention on the Elimination of all Forms of Discrimination against Women (CEDAW) in 1995.

The key issue, however, is operationalising these labour standards. This is achieved for public service employees through a well-developed system of employment regulation and dispute resolution under the auspices of the Public Service Commission. In the public sector, the regulatory framework relating to terms and conditions of employment is primarily governed by the Public Services (Management) Act 1995 (amended 2014), the Public Services Conciliation and Arbitration Act 1969 and accompanying Public Service General Orders. The private sector is governed by the Employment Act 1978, the Industrial Organisations Act 1963, the Industrial Relations Act 1963 (as amended 1992 and 1998), the Industrial Safety Health and Welfare Act 1965, the Occupational Health Safety Act 1990 and the Workers Compensation Act 1990. Other relevant legislation includes the Informal Sector Development and Control Act of 2004, a significant achievement for Papua New Guinea and the Pacific. This Act uniquely recognises the legitimacy of the informal economy and attempts to maintain a balance between controlling and developing the informal economy, as well as regulating the development of informal businesses for the protection of public health and safety. However, its applicability has been very much limited to the National Capital District and to some extent other urban centres, with minimal or no application to the rural informal economy (Wenego 2014), which involves the bulk of Papua New Guinea's population and is overwhelmingly dominated by women. Meanwhile, the Lukautim Pikini Act 2009 is the main statute dealing with the care and protection of children, including while in employment.

As in many developing countries, particularly in the Pacific Islands region, public sector workers generally enjoy relatively favourable employment conditions, as they have stronger rights and entitlements that are actually implemented. To take maternity leave as one example, the Employment Act stipulates that women employed in the private sector are entitled to unpaid maternity leave for the period necessary for hospitalisation and six weeks following confinement, although there is little by way of job protection. By contrast, under the Public Service General Orders, female employees in the public services are entitled to up to 12 weeks maternity leave with six weeks available both before and after the birth of a child. For the period prior to confinement, the mother may be paid using sick leave credits if sufficient sick leave has been accumulated. Following the birth, she is entitled to full pay during the six weeks of leave.

This disparity is linked to high rates of union organisation in the public sector. The law provides for the right to form and join trade unions, and there are 73 registered trade unions in Papua New Guinea (ILO 2008), although the extent to which all registered unions are 'active' is unknown. About half of all wage-earners in the formal economy are union members. The Public Employees Association has some 12,000 members (one-third of the public sector workforce) and almost all of the public sector labour force is unionised through the Public Employees Association and other occupational-based unions representing teachers, police and nurses. Private sector unions are organised at enterprise level and are present in sectors such as mining, transport, waterside and communications where the workforce is larger and more stable. However, these unions are much more under-resourced, with few full-time officials (ILO 2013a). There are also formal tripartite arrangements at national government level to address both sector-specific and inter-sector labour market issues and policy. This is limited in practice, however, and not just because the social partners (and trade unions in particular) face a lack of resources (ILO 2013a). Existing arrangements relating to the composition of the National Tripartite Consultative Council, for instance, require the presence of several government ministers for the committees to be quorate, and this is seldom achieved (ILO 2012). This impacts on the development of relevant labour policy and legislative proposals. Nevertheless, tripartite constituents (the Department of Labour and Industrial Relations, Papua New Guinea Employers Federation and the Papua New Guinea Trade Union Congress) have developed a Decent Work Country Programme with the International Labour Organisation.

Hence, on the face of it, there is a well-ordered system of employment regulation and industrial relations that offers a measure of 'voice' and protection to workers, at least in the formal economy and particularly in the public sector. Of course, this covers only a very small minority of workers but it is significant for women, given that the public services provide much of their formal employment opportunities (especially in teaching and health). Outside the public sector, the key problems for women in work are a lack of effective legislation governing the informal economy. Much of the legislation that applies to the private sector is outdated, with gaps around important issues such as equal pay and harassment. There is also a lack of awareness-raising, inspection and enforcement, so compliance with existing legislation is low. This is also compounded by inadequate penalties; for example, the maximum penalty under the Employment Act for breaches of provisions prohibiting discrimination against women is K 200 (USD 75). In acknowledgement of this issue, an on-going review of Papua New Guinea's labour legislation that aims to better integrate and modernise regulatory arrangements has been in progress for a number of years (UNDP 2010). This process is informed by international best practice, and since 2011 has been provided with technical assistance from the ILO (ILO 2012).

Pressure points

The vast majority of the citizens of Papua New Guinea live completely detached from modern institutions of governance and social welfare. The 'care diamond' concept usefully reminds us that there are four actors or institutions normally involved in the provision of social care – the family, the state, the market and civil society in the form of voluntary community and not-for-profit associations (Razavi 2007). In the developing context of Papua New Guinea, however, there is no experience of provision through the market and virtually no state role in the care of dependent people such as young children, the frail elderly, the chronically ill and people with physical and mental disabilities. The care burden is borne by families and village communities, with some involvement by churches, non-governmental organisations and charities.

Rapid economic growth offers a series of opportunities and challenges. The state is investing in healthcare and education, and has plans to introduce social security transfers. It is also building roads and other infrastructure projects to integrate communities, and promises to address problems of domestic abuse, criminality and violence. However, these investments are proceeding from an extremely low base. There are also huge human capital constraints, as evidenced by difficulties in meeting the skills requirements of healthcare expansion (UNDP 2014b). Furthermore, demographic changes brought about by population growth, urbanisation and, in the longer term, ageing will place increased demands on the state at the same time as they undermine traditional mechanisms of support.

The state recognises that one important way to improve the work/care framework is to grow the informal economy. Unlike governments in most countries in the world, the Papua New Guinea government takes a positive view of the informal economy as a means to inculcate entrepreneurialism and the generation of wealth. This was recognised through legislation that accepts the legitimacy of the informal economy, subject to safeguards around public health and safety (Conroy 2011). The dominance of the subsistence way of life means that the informal cash economy is too small rather than too big. The generation of income-earning opportunities will help individuals, families and communities to save and invest, and it is likely that this will reinforce a shift to market-based forms of care. This is already beginning to happen as migrant young people remit earnings back from the city to their elderly relatives in the villages (von Poser 2011).

Another imperative facing the government is the modernisation of regulations pertaining to the formal economy. The existing legislative framework in employment, particularly with respect to the private sector, is somewhat dated and impacts on the extent to which it can be effectively enforced. An integrative Employment Policy is required to 'join up' policy development at the strategic level and ensure adequate resources are dedicated to awareness-raising and inspection in order to ensure adherence to standards around pay, hours of work, working conditions and child labour. However, this remains elusive and there seems to be insufficient political will to improve mechanisms of labour governance.

In many ways, therefore, the state needs to step up and utilise the opportunities provided by exploitation of the country's mineral wealth to build on some of the positive initiatives already undertaken. There are serious problems that need addressing in healthcare, education and training, to develop effective institutions of regulation, provide financial support for the unemployed, elderly, sick and disabled, and address problems of crime and the abuse of women and children. In terms of gender equality, Papua New Guinea is starting from a very low base. The Gender Inequality Index places it at 140 of 179 countries (UNDP 2012). As part of the process of improvement, there needs to be much better representation of women in leadership roles. In 2010 only one out of 109 seats in parliament was held by a woman and there was only one female judge in the 27 national level judicial positions (JICA 2010). From independence until the 2012 elections, only four women had been elected to the national parliament, and three of these entered in the first elections of 1977. In 2012, following a series of campaigns for female representation, there were 135 women candidates (out of around 3,500) and three women were returned.[2]

All of these initiatives would require more effective engagement with the institutions of civil society, particularly the churches, which are active in social care, and local community elders, as well as international development partners. One example where a 'gender mainstreaming' approach is showing early promise is in the operation of the Seasonal Work programme, which since 2010 has sent temporary workers to Australia, and since 2013 also to New Zealand, for horticultural work. The Seasonal Work programme has rapidly become an important part of Papua New Guinea's human capital and community development strategy. It aims to raise household and community living standards, including access to health and schooling, through direct remittances and investment from savings (McKenzie and Gibson 2010).

The government believes that workers can acquire savings, skills, and 'a more productive work ethic' through the Seasonal Work programme, thereby addressing economic and social problems associated with unemployment and under-employment in the rural districts and reducing urban drift (PNG SWCO 2011; ILO 2014). Workers interviewed as part of our research also reported gaining financial and interpersonal life skills as well as technical competencies in using new machinery and tools which were subsequently put to use in their villages (ILO 2014). Crucially, women are seen as important to sustaining the programme and leading the transfer of skills and wealth back to their communities. By 2013, the 'work-ready pool' of those with the necessary vetting and visa processing consisted of 158 people from the Southern region, 78 from the Highlands and 40 from Momase. A large proportion of these were women – 27 per cent, 69 per cent and 55 per cent respectively (ILO 2014).

To conclude, Papua New Guinea is undergoing profound and rapid transformation. Communities are not as isolated and untouched as they were until recently. Improvements are being made in education and health, with the prospect of further social investment to improve social cohesion. The pace of change presents huge challenges in shifting to a 'modern' work/care regime that involves state and market institutions while revolutionising existing informal patterns of work and care. The future holds some promise, providing that the government maintains its commitment to use its new-found wealth for the betterment of the citizenry as a whole. Change will, as Pocock (2005) observes in the Australian context, require a new mobilisation around a well-articulated and well-supported common agenda.

Notes

1 Gender-based violence is also a serious problem in Timor-Leste. See Ford (this volume).

2 The Equality and Participation Act 2011 provides for 22 reserved seats for women in the national parliament, but the required Bill to amend the Constitution failed to attract the necessary votes in 2012 (e.g. PNG Department for Community Development 2014).

References

Australian Doctors International. 2015. *PNG Health Statistics*. http://www.adi.org.au/health-in-png-2/png-health-statistic/.

Bourke, R.M. and T. Harwood, eds. 2009. *Food and Agriculture in Papua New Guinea*. Canberra: ANU E-Press.

Brouwer, E., B. Harris, and S. Tanaka, eds. 1998. *Gender Analysis in Papua New Guinea*. Washington: World Bank.

Chandler, J. 2014. *Violence Against Women in PNG: How Men are Getting Away with Murder*. Sydney: Lowy Institute.

CIA. 2012. *The World Factbook*. https://www.cia.gov/library/publications/the-world-factbook/geos/pp.html.

Conroy, J. 2011. *PNG: Policy for the Informal Economy*. http://devpolicy.org/papua-new-guinea-policy-for-the-informal-economy20110519/.

Cunningham, D., D.E. Ingram and K. Sumbuk. 2006. *Language Diversity in the Pacific*. Clevedon: UNESCO.

Diamond, J. 2012. *The World Until Yesterday: What Can We Learn from Traditional Societies?* New York: Viking.

Gönitzer, G. 2003. "In Contrast to Diversification: Androcentric Structures of Power in Papua New Guinea." In *Gender and Power in the Pacific: Women's Strategies in a World of Change*, edited by K. Ferro and M. Wolfsberger, 65–70. Münster: Lit Verlag.

Government of PNG and UN Development System. 2007. *United Nations Country Programme: Papua New Guinea 2008–2012 – A Partnership for Nation-building*. http://www.unicef.org/about/execboard/files/Papua_New_Guinea_-2012.pdf.

Howes, S., A. Mako, A. Swan, G. Walton, T. Webster and C. Wiltshire (2014). *A Lost Decade? Service Delivery and Reforms in Papua New Guinea 2002–2012*. Canberra: The National Research Institute and Development Policy Centre, ANU.

IFC. 2010. *Annual Report 2010*. http://www.ifc.org/wps/wcm/connect/corp_ext_content/ifc_external_corporate_site/annual+report/previous+annual+reports/2010+printed+report+default+content.

ILO. 1998. *Unit 2: Gender Issues in the World of Work: Labour Market Gender Issues by Country – Papua New Guinea.* South-East Asia and the Pacific Multidisciplinary Advisory Team (SEAPAT). http://www.ilo.org/public/english/region/asro/mdtmanila/training/unit2/ptssxsum.htm.

ILO. 2008. *Decent Work Country Programme: PNG, 2009–2012.* http://www.ilo.org/public/english/bureau/program/dwcp/download/papua.pdf.

ILO. 2011. *Child Labour in Papua New Guinea – Report on the Rapid Assessment in Port Moresby on Commercial Sexual Exploitation of Children and Children Working on the Streets.* Port Moresby: ILO.

ILO. 2012. *Situational Analysis of Employment Policies in PNG.* By J. Parker, J. Arrowsmith and M. Nemani. Fiji: ILO South Pacific Countries Office.

ILO. 2013a. *PNG: Decent Work Country Programme.* http://www.ilo.org/public/english/bureau/program/dwcp/download/png.pdf.

ILO. 2013b. *National Policy and Action Plan to Eliminate (the Worst Forms of) Child Labour, including Child Trafficking, in PNG.* By J. Parker and J. Arrowsmith. Fiji: ILO South Pacific Countries Office.

ILO. 2014. *Assessment of Legislation, Policy and Management Frameworks with Regard to PNG's participation in the Australian Seasonal Worker Prog*ram. By J. Arrowsmith and J. Parker. Fiji: ILO South Pacific Countries Office.

ILO. 2015. *Ratifications for PNG.* http://www.ilo.org/dyn/normlex/en/f?p=NORMLEXPUB:11200:0::NO::P11200_COUNTRY_ID:103487.

Imbun, B. 2006. "Local Laborers in Papua New Guinea: Attracted or Compelled to Work?' *The Contemporary Pacific* 18 (2): 315–333.

Japan International Cooperation Agency (JICA). 2010. *Country Gender Profile: Papua New Guinea.* http://www.jica.go.jp/english/our_work/thematic_issues/gender/background/pdf/e10png.pdf.

Johnson, P.L. 1993. "Education and the 'New' Inequality in Papua New Guinea." *Anthropology & Education Quarterly* 24 (3): 183–204.

Jolly, M., C. Stewart and C. Brewer, eds. 2014. *Engendering Violence in Papua New Guinea.* Canberra: ANU E-Press.

Law Reform Commission (LRC). 1987. *Interim Report.* Port Moresby: Papua New Guinea Law Reform Commission.

Law Reform Commission (LRC). 1992. *Final Report on Domestic Violence.* Report No. 14. Port Moresby: Papua New Guinea Law Reform Commission.

Majid, N. 2014. "Measuring Employment in Developing Countries." *World Economics* 15 (3): 1–31.

McKenzie, D. and J. Gibson. 2010. *The Development Impact of a Best Practice Seasonal Worker Policy.* Policy Research Working Paper 5488. Washington: World Bank.

NSO. 2011a. *National Census of Housing and Population – PNG.* http://spmt.files.wordpress.com/2010/09/preliminary-figures-census-2011-1.pdf.

NSO. 2011b. *2009–2010 Papua New Guinea Household Income and Expenditure Survey: Summary Tables*, Port Moresby: National Statistical Office. http://catalog.ihsn.org/index.php/catalog/3243.

NSO. 2013. *2009–10 PNG Household Income and Expenditure Survey: Summary Tables.* Port Moresby: National Statistical Office.

OECD 2012. *Closing the Gender Gap: Act Now.* Paris: OECD Publishing.

OECD. 2014. *Aid (ODA) Commitments to Countries and Regions [DAC3a].* OECD StatExtracts. http://stats.oecd.org/Index.aspx?DatasetCode=TABLE2A.

PNG Department for Community Development. 2014. *Beijing +20: Papua New Guinea National Review on the Implementation of the Beijing Declaration and the Platform for Action and the Outcomes of the 23rd Special Session of the General Assembly.* http://www.unescapsdd.org/files/documents/Beijing20_national_review_PNG.pdf.

PNG Department of Health. 2013. *National Health Plan 2010–2020, Sector Performance Annual Review 2013.* Port Moresby: Department of Health.

PNG LNG. 2015. *About PNG LNG.* http://pnglng.com/project/about.

PNG Seasonal Worker Coordination Office (PNG SWCO). 2011. "PNG Seasonal Worker Scheme." *1st Quarter PLLSMA and Annual Provincial Administrators' Consultative Conference*, Goroka, March.

Pocock, B. 2005. "Work/care Regimes: Institutions, Culture and Behavior and the Australian Case." *Gender, Work and Organisation* 12 (1): 32–49.

Razavi, S. 2007. *The Political and Social Economy of Care in a Development Context.* Geneva: UNRISD.

Razavi, S. and S. Staab. 2012. "Introduction. Global Variations in the Political and Social Economy of Care – Worlds Apart?' In *Global Variations in the Political and Social Economy of Care: Worlds Apart*, edited by S. Razavi and S. Staab, 1–28. Abingdon: Routledge.

Roscoe, P. 2000. "New Guinea Leadership as Ethnographic Analogy: A Critical Review." *Journal of Archaeological Method and Theory* 7 (2): 79–125.

Simon, A. 2009. "Child Labour in PNG." *Papua New Guinea Post – Courier*, 19 August.

Singh, S. 2009. "Poverty Breeds Child Labour and Sex Tourism in the South Pacific." *ILO Office for Pacific Island Countries Newsletter* no.1. http://www.ilo.org/public/english/region/asro/suva/pdfs/newsletter0409.pdf.

Singh, S. and Y. Nadarajah. 2011. *School Fees, Beer and 'Meri': Gender, Cash and the Mobile in the Morobe Province of Papua New Guinea.* Institute for Money, Technology and Financial Inclusion Working Paper, 2011-13.

Thomason, J. and M. Hancock. 2011. *PNG Mineral Boom: Harnessing the Extractive Sector to Deliver Better Health Outcomes.* Discussion Paper 2, January. Canberra: Development Policy Centre, Australian National University. http://papers.ssrn.com/sol3/papers.cfm?abstract_id=1919304.

UN. 2005. *World Report on Violence Against Children.* http://www.crin.org/docs/UNVAC_World_Report_on_Violence_against_Children.pdf.

UNDP. 2010. *MDG Progress Report for Papua New Guinea (2010).* http://www.pg.undp.org/content/dam/papua_new_guinea/docs/MDG/UNDP_PG_MDG%20Comprehensive%20Report%202010.pdf.

UNDP. 2012. *Gender Inequality Index and Related Indicators.* http://hdr.undp.org/en/media/HDR_2011_EN_Table4.pdf.

UNDP. 2014a. *2014 National Human Development Report: PNG.* http://hdr.undp.org/sites/default/files/final_png_nhdr.pdf.

UNDP. 2014b. *Human Development Report 2014: Sustaining Human Progress: Reducing Vulnerabilities and Increasing Resilience.* http://hdr.undp.org/sites/default/files/hdr14-report-en-1.pdf.

UNICEF. 2012. *UNICEF Annual Report 2012 for PNG.* http://www.unicef.org/about/annualreport/files/Papua_New_Guinea_COAR_2012.pdf.

von Poser, A. 2011. *Ageing and Taking Care of the Elderly in Contemporary Daiden (Northeast Papua New Guinea).* Working Paper no. 129, Max Planck Institute for Social Anthropology Working Papers. http://www.eth.mpg.de/download.php?f=mpi-eth-working-paper-0129.pdf.

Wenego, B.J. 2014. *New Law Tries to Establish Balance in PNG's Informal Economy.* http://asopa.typepad.com/asopa_people/2014/10/considerations-in-the-regulation-of-pngs-informal-economy.html.

WHO. 2011. *Country Health Information Profile: PNG*. Geneva: WHO.

World Bank. 2012. *Papua New Guinea – Country Gender Assessment for the Period 2011–2012. Country Gender Assessment, 31 December*. http://www-wds.worldbank.org/external/default/WDSContentServer/WDSP/IB/2013/03/15/000356161_20130315143634/Rendered/PDF/755800REVISED0011020120Final0Report.pdf.

World Bank. 2015. *Health Nutrition and Population Statistics: Population Estimates and Projections.* http://databank.worldbank.org/Data/Views/VariableSelection/SelectVariables.aspx?source=Health%20Nutrition%20and%20Population%20Statistics:%20Population%20estimates%20and%20projections.

World Bank Group in PNG. 2013. *PNG Economic Briefing: From the Last Days of the Boom to Lasting Improvements in Living Standards.* http://www.worldbank.org/content/dam/Worldbank/document/EAP/Papua%20New%20Guinea/PNG-Economic-Brief-2013-1.pdf.

Index

For Product Safety Concerns and Information please contact our EU
representative GPSR@taylorandfrancis.com
Taylor & Francis Verlag GmbH, Kaufingerstraße 24, 80331 München, Germany

www.ingramcontent.com/pod-product-compliance
Ingram Content Group UK Ltd.
Pitfield, Milton Keynes, MK11 3LW, UK
UKHW020014200926
475702UK00014B/1873
* 9 7 8 0 3 6 7 1 8 6 1 7 3 *